"WE WANT OUR FREEDOM"

"We Want Our Freedom"

Rhetoric of the Civil Rights Movement

W. STUART TOWNS

Westport, Connecticut
London

Library of Congress Cataloging-in-Publication Data

"We want our freedom" : rhetoric of the Civil Rights Movement / [compiled by] W. Stuart Towns.
    p. cm.
    Includes bibliographical references and index.
    ISBN 0–275–97004–3 (alk. paper)
    1. African Americans—Civil rights—History—20th century—Sources. 2. African Americans—Civil rights—History—19th century—Sources. 3. African Americans—History—1877–1964—Sources. 4. Civil rights movements—United States—History—20th century—Sources. 5. Civil rights movements—United States—History—19th century—Sources. 6. United States—Race relations—Sources. 7. Southern States—Race relations—Sources. 8. Speeches, addresses, etc., American. I. Towns, W. Stuart, 1939–
E185.61.W34 2002
973'.0496073—dc21   2001057737

British Library Cataloguing in Publication Data is available.

Library of Congress Catalog Card Number: 2001057737
ISBN: 0–275–97004–3

First published in 2002

Praeger Publishers, 88 Post Road West, Westport, CT 06881
An imprint of Greenwood Publishing Group, Inc.
www.praeger.com

Printed in the United States of America

The paper used in this book complies with the Permanent Paper Standard issued by the National Information Standards Organization (Z39.48–1984).

10 9 8 7 6 5 4 3 2 1

To Helen Ruth, Stuart, and Beth, who have all pretty well tolerated my love of libraries, books, speeches, and old papers for all these years.

CONTENTS

Photo essay follows page 122.

INTRODUCTION

The second most important historical fact in the long history of the South swept the region from 1954 to 1965: the Civil Rights Movement.[1] Only the Civil War and Reconstruction had a more dramatic impact on the region, but it can be argued that the effect of the Civil Rights Movement will be even more important and long-lasting. The changes wrought in the South and the nation as a whole by the activists across the region in the 1950s and 1960s began to truly change the patterns of relationships, the ways of thinking, and the attitudes of white southerners toward their black neighbors. The Civil War ended slavery; Reconstruction and its aftermath created a mythology of the Lost Cause and a society based on white supremacy in which black southerners were disfranchised second-class citizens intimidated with violence and threats of violence; the Civil Rights Movement fostered an atmosphere in which true change could occur and the rights enjoyed by white southerners could, finally, be enjoyed by black southerners as well. In many ways, the Civil Rights Movement in the South can be compared in importance to the collapse of the Soviet Union, the destruction of the Berlin Wall, and the fall of communism in Eastern Europe in 1989–90. Both European communism and southern segregation were considered by many to be unassailable and invulnerable. Few predicted those series of events in Eastern Europe, nor did many in the South foresee the fall of segregation and the beginnings of civil rights and true freedom for southern blacks.[2]

The speeches anthologized in this collection show some of the passion, the commitment, the dreams and aspirations of both black and white southerners who sought a new relationship between the races in the South, as well as the sentiments and perceptions of those who intended to keep black southerners second-class citizens. Before turning to them, however, we need to understand why there had to be a Civil Rights Movement; what were the conditions in the South for the black southerner?

For some time after the Civil War, northern and Republican Party interests were focused on helping the recently freed slaves. The Freedman's Bureau, northern churches, and private philanthropic organizations flooded into the South for several years and did what they could in the midst of the shattered southern economy. Segregation of the races was, however, common in the institutions created by this wave of goodwill. Churches, poor houses, hospitals, and schools quickly developed on a segregated basis and segregation spread to all forms of social intercourse: hotels, theaters, railway and trolley transportation, even cemeteries. As Reconstruction ended around the South, northern clergy, who had led the efforts to improve the Negroes' situation, "ceased to demand civil rights, admitted the Negro was not equal and discarded the cause of black Americans."[3] In short, the South had lost the Civil War, but had won the battle to deal with black southerners on their own terms, with little or no interference.

By 1878, most southern states had school segregation laws on the books and the practice was universal in the region by the 1890s. The segregated schools were nowhere near equal. The average spending per pupil across the South was abysmally out of proportion: in 1916, $10.32 per student was spent on white students' education, whereas black students were allocated an average of $2.89.

Almost total disfranchisement of the black voter in the South was the norm. The black southerner could not even exercise this most fundamental right of Americans in the hope to change his conditions. Through fraud, intimidation, violence, lengthy residency requirements, white-only voter registration officials, white primaries, poll taxes, and literacy tests, the vote was prohibited to blacks. Historian Carl Degler sums up this era when he writes, "The South after the war, like the antebellum South, was the region in which legal institutions, as well as social and political practice, were extraordinarily hostile toward black people."[4]

The *Plessy v. Ferguson* case in 1896 provided the opportunity for the U.S. Supreme Court to declare that the "separate-but-equal" doctrine was

constitutional. This concept was practically an axiom throughout the region and now, with the federal government's stamp of approval, it became embedded in rock during the early decades of the twentieth
century. Equal treatment and equal facilities was, of course, never to be
seen in public or private situations and the wall between the two races
grew stronger, wider, and higher as the years wore on.[5] As Howard
Rabinowitz sums up, "the policy of separate and *unequal* treatment of
the races had become firmly entrenched in the South by the turn of the
century."[6]

In 1913, Thomas Pearce Bailey, a southern university professor, wrote
the following "racial creed" of the South. At that time, there were few
white southerners who would disagree with him, and fewer still who
would do it in public:

1. Blood will tell.
2. The white race must dominate.
3. The Teutonic peoples stand for race purity.
4. The Negro is inferior and will remain so.
5. This is a white man's country.
6. No social equality.
7. No political equality.
8. In matters of civil rights and legal adjustments give the white
   man, as opposed to the colored man, the benefit of the doubt;
   and under no circumstances interfere with the prestige of the
   white race.
9. In educational policy let the Negro have the crumbs that fall
   from the white man's table.
10. Let there be such industrial education of the Negro as will best
    fit him to serve the white man.
11. Only Southerners understand the Negro question.
12. Let the South settle the Negro question.
13. The status of peasantry is all the Negro may hope for, if the
    races are to live together in peace.
14. Let the lowest white man count for more than the highest Ne-
    gro.
15. The above statements indicate the leadings of Providence.[7]

With the "leadings" of Providence itself, how could white southerners argue with these assumptions? They did not, for the most part, for over half a century.

By the 1920s, the racial etiquette that served to define the relationship between the two races was fully formed. Southern whites had a perspective on the black race that included several specific stereotypical qualities that served to shape the way whites acted toward and communicated with blacks. These characteristics included these and more: The black race was dependent on the white race; they were childlike, prone to stealing and violence; they were lazy, happy in the conditions of segregation, oversexed, and stupid. There were many aspects of this behavior and communication on the part of whites. Sarah Patton Boyle wrote, "It was assumed by every member of my family that a Negro's word was unreliable"; "Ignorant-Negro was practically one word. Ignorance was a 'racial trait' "; "You never, never, never sat at table with a Negro in your own dining room"; "Everywhere one is taught not to treat whites and Negroes in the same way, this rule taking precedence over all other social distinctions."[8] Whites expected and required less of their black counterparts. Blacks were rewarded by the white establishment when they acted out those stereotypes and followed the routine, always saying "sir" and "ma'am" with downcast eyes and a deferential demeanor. On the other side, the whites never shook hands with a black, always used generic terms like "boy" or "uncle" and always only first names, never "Mr." or "Mrs." In short, the southern white population created a social system that reinforced the perceived superiority of the white race and the supposed inferiority of the black race.[9]

A list of the goals of a local group known as the "Southern Association on Inter-Racial Good Will and Negro Improvement" in Columbiana, Alabama, begins by asserting that its purpose is to "teach the Negro that it is of prime importance to his well-being to earn the good will of his White Neighbor." One of its other aims, out of a lengthy list, is to "teach the Colored people that if they will always be mindful of the fact, and act upon that principle, that all service, however lowly, is true service, an important step will have been taken in proving their loyalty to the dominant race."[10]

Dissent was silenced in the South of segregation. If any daring white southerner harbored misgivings about the system, he or she had to keep it largely to themselves. Deviation from the norm of racial relationships was not tolerated. Jobs could be lost, businesses boycotted, crosses burned in front yards for the neighbors to see, homes firebombed or torched, and in general, life could be made hell for those straying from the straight and narrow. Wilbur Cash put it this way: "In a word, here, explicitly defined in every great essential, defined in feeling down to the last detail, was what one must think and say and do. And one thought it, said it, did it, exactly as it was ordained, or one stood in pressing peril of being cast out for a damned nigger-loving scoundrel in league with the enemy."[11]

Or as James Dabbs saw it, the South was too defensive—"a defense of Southern forces against outside force—insiders against outsiders—or a defense of the inner ruling group against the inner subservient group."[12] The South had been a defensive, almost paranoid region since around 1820, when the debates over the admission of Missouri brought the issue of slavery to the forefront. For the next century and a half, the South found itself often on the defensive. After fighting abolitionists for forty years, the region was crushed by the Union forces in the bloody Civil War and left economically and emotionally drained and poverty stricken. Reconstruction and all of its attendant ills and the myths of Negro domination and carpetbag rule that grew out of that unfortunate era reinforced the region's paranoia. An almost unreasonable fear of strong central government and intrusive government gripped the region. The end of slavery as the driving economic force and the means of social control of the black race created the perception in white southerners' minds that society and culture had disintegrated and there was no stability and no center to rely on. As a result, the cries of "outside agitators," "northern aggression," "Yankee domination," and "racial amalgamation," were all conditioned reflexes for many white southerners in the twentieth century. The strong Jim Crow laws gave them a sense of control, and when that control was threatened by anyone, white or black, northern or southern, the rallying cries went up and the wagons circled. The Civil Rights Movement of the 1950s and 1960s was just one more of the "outside agitations" that tried to change the South and its "way of life," as so many speakers for decades had put it. First, it was opposition to slavery, now it was opposition to segregation.

In writing about the Mississippi Delta region in the mid-1940s—a microcosm of the South's feelings about race—James Cobb describes the "dominant white planter group" living in "constant fear that some outside person or idea will threaten the status quo in respect to race relations." He goes on to illustrate the "Delta's white power structure . . . waging a determined and sometimes violent campaign against internal dissent even as it girded itself to repulse an external assault on a status quo that had served it so long and so well."[13] This campaign against dissent and external assault formed the resistance to the claims of black southerners that they deserved and demanded the rights of all Americans.

Chapter 1 includes two speeches presented in the U.S. House of Representatives, one in the U.S. Senate, and one gubernatorial inauguration address. These speeches, presented in elite, prestigious venues, are examples of how southern leadership guided their constituents to accept the concepts of segregation and white supremacy. James C. Harper, a western North Carolina, small-town political figure, urges his House colleagues to oppose two bills protecting the civil rights of blacks, laws he calls a "crowning act of oppression." He tells the House that the Negroes in his district know "nothing of that social equality which these bills propose to invest him with, and is as loath to demand as the whites will be to grant it." Benjamin Ryan Tillman, a much more famous southern politician, was a South Carolina governor and later U.S. Senator and nationally known speaker on the subject of race and white supremacy. In his 1891 inaugural address, Tillman trumpets the claim that "today there is less race prejudice and race feeling between the white men and black men of South Carolina than has existed at any time since 1868." He then reassures his listeners: "The whites have absolute control of the State Government, and intend at any and all hazards to retain it." Wade Hampton was a Civil War General, governor of South Carolina, and U.S. Senator who "redeemed" his state from Republican carpetbag rule in 1876. In this speech to the Senate, Hampton supports the idea of emigration of black southerners to Africa under the assumption that it would be good for them to reap "the rich fruits of civilization and of Christianity" and scatter "them broadcast among his yet benighted brethren." He then goes on to make and defend the claim that "every race, save the Caucasian, is and ought to be regarded as alien in the United States. . . . The declared and wise policy of the country is that of exclusion of all alien races." Hampton claims there is a "deep-seated, ineradicable race antagonism, and it is idle for us to shut our eyes to this fact and to endeavor to conceal it." The final speech of the four is from a Georgian, James M. Griggs, who served in the U.S. Congress for 14 years. His address to the House of Representatives is a model for an often-repeated genre of public speech used by the racist orators of the South; its foundation is a rape story and the theme is the protection of white southern women from the bestiality of black southern men. With speeches like these from the elite leadership of the South, it is no wonder racism, segregation, and white supremacy became the law of the land.

Chapter 2 includes speeches by four black leaders who began after

World War I to challenge the system. James Weldon Johnson, an important writer and NAACP executive, challenges his audience in New York City to begin to consider the conditions in the South regarding black voting, "which not only runs counter to the popular conception of democracy in America but which runs counter to the fundamental law upon which that democracy rests, and which, in addition, is a negation of our principles of government and a menace to our institutions." He reminds his listeners that, "The Negro in the matter of the ballot demands only that he be given his right as an American citizen." A. Philip Randolph, one of the most important early leaders for civil rights for blacks who was still active when the Civil Rights Movement arrived in the 1950s, challenged the federal government itself in the early 1940s after a long career building a major black labor union, the Brotherhood of Sleeping Car Porters. He put pressure on the Roosevelt administration in 1941, calling for a national "March on Washington" to protest working conditions and segregation in the government and military forces. After the planned march was called off, he created an organization to carry on the concept and this speech in 1942 is to that organization. It sounds like a blueprint for much of the movement that flowered a decade and a half later. In his speech to the NAACP Wartime Conference in 1944, Thurgood Marshall, one of the most important lawyers in the quest for racial justice, who argued the *Brown* case before the Supreme Court and later became a member of the Court, explained the aim of the NAACP in its court battles: "The struggle for full citizenship rights can be speeded by enforcement of existing statutory provisions protecting our civil rights. The attack on discrimination by use of legal machinery has only scratched the surface." In the fourth speech, W.E.B. Du Bois, a long-time activist and NAACP leader and editor, came into the heartland of the enemy, Columbia, South Carolina, in 1946, and addressed the closing session of the Southern Youth Legislature, a meeting sponsored by the Southern Negro Youth Congress. Here he puts the struggle into a broader context: "This is the firing line not simply for the emancipation of the American Negro but for the emancipation of the African Negro and the Negroes of the West Indies; for the emancipation of the colored races; and for the emancipation of the white slaves of modern capitalistic monopoly."

Chapter 3 gets into the heart of the movement with the speeches of the early years of the campaign. John Hope Franklin, a noted historian and writer, presented his speech over the airways on the British Broadcasting Corporation in September 1955, only four months after the *Brown* decision was announced by the Supreme Court. In it, Franklin tries to broaden the scope of the issue by urging the South to solve this problem of race and get on with the more pressing problems of the changing South: urbanization, revolution in agriculture, and poor education. These are the problems the South needs to be dealing with, but, instead, it has a "new dilemma"—how to accommodate the breakdown of segregation. The Montgomery Bus Boycott brought to regional attention Martin Luther King Jr. In this speech to the filled sanctuary at Holt Street Baptist Church in Montgomery, King focuses on forging a sense of solidarity and purpose:

> We are here this evening for serious business. We are here in a general sense because first and foremost we are American citizens, and we are determined to apply our citizenship to the fullness of its means. We are here because of our love for democracy, because of our deep-seated belief that democracy transformed from thin paper to thick action is the greatest form of government on earth. But we are here in a specific sense, because of the bus situation in Montgomery. We are here because we are determined to get the situation corrected.

Roy Wilkins, long-time executive secretary of the NAACP, A. Philip Randolph, and King spoke to a 1957 Prayer Pilgrimage to Washington on the third anniversary of the *Brown* decision. Wilkins sounded more like a preacher than an administrator, when he reminded his audience: "We are here because the rulers of the darkness of this world, the darkness of ignorance, arrogance, prejudice, and hatred, have been permitted to rise up and ravage the peace of our nation, to recruit and inflame the wicked, and to browbeat the righteous.

"We are here because spiritual wickedness in high places—in the mansions of certain Governors, in the law departments of certain states, in the legislative chambers of some state capitols, and under the dome of our nation's capitol—has caused a deaf ear to be turned to our plea for justice.

"We have been given not bread, but a stone; not peace, but a sword."

In this brief speech in Washington, DC, Randolph throws his support behind the efforts of the NAACP and of King and counsels his audience:

> Be not dismayed by the frightful wave of violence and persecution against persons of color now sweeping the South. It is written in the stars that the old order of southern feudalism, with its remnants and vestiges of lynching, peonage, vagrancy laws, mob violence,

Ku Klux Klan, anti-labor union practices expressed in right-to-work laws, widespread illiteracy, low wages, is dying; its death will come as a result of the emergence of the dynamic impulse for freedom surging in the hearts of Negroes, together with the march of industrialization, urbanization, labor union organization, extension of education and the modernization of government through the spread of the ballot. These new forces will create and build a new South, free for the white and black masses to pursue a life of dignity and decency.

Martin Luther King's remarks at the Prayer Pilgrimage did not become as famous as his "I Have a Dream" speech six years later, but they did boost his reputation as the leader of the developing movement, as he urged Congress to support registration and voting rights for southern blacks: "Give us the ballot and we will transform the salient misdeeds of bloodthirsty mobs into the calculated good deeds of orderly citizens."

Four months later, a new leader burst onto the scene, as Daisy Bates, of Little Rock, Arkansas, shepherded nine young black students into Little Rock Central High School and triggered the integration crisis at Central. Late in that school year, Bates spoke at the Detroit Branch of the NAACP and described her perceptions of those days:

September 1957, it was our only desire that the nine children selected by the school board would be able to walk to school as any other American citizen, and that the only time their names would appear in print would be in routine school news. The turn of events that followed that fatal day when the governor of Arkansas called out the National Guards [*sic*] to prevent nine children exercising their rights under the Constitution of the United States, far exceeded our wildest dreams, and started a chain of events that was felt around the world. Little did the nine children realize that their actions that morning would write a new chapter in American history.

The final speech in chapter 3 comes from a future martyr to the cause, Medgar Evers of Jackson, Mississippi, a long-time NAACP leader in his home state. In this speech to the Los Angeles NAACP Branch, Evers describes his perceptions of the

truth about the conditions under which Americans of African descent live here in this great country during the century of wonders—United Nations, sputniks, explorers, space, atom—the

twentieth century. . . . To enumerate all of the injustices against Negro Americans in Mississippi would be next to impossible, so I
shall make mention of injustices that are most prominent, along
with others less prominent.

Evers then goes on to recite a litany of injustices and violence against
his fellow Mississippians.

Chapter 4 moves into the heart of the Civil Rights Movement in the
1960s. James M. Lawson Jr.'s address to the founding conference of the
Student Nonviolent Coordinating Committee in Raleigh, North Carolina,
set the tone for the activism to follow.

In the first instance, we who are demonstrators are trying to raise
what we call the "moral issue." That is, we are pointing to the
viciousness of racial segregation and prejudice and calling it evil
or sin. The matter is not legal, sociological or racial, it is moral
and spiritual. Until America (South and North) honestly accepts the
sinful nature of racism, this cancerous disease will continue to rape
all of us. . . . In the second instance, the non-violent movement is
asserting, "get moving." The pace of change is too slow.

Martin Luther King Jr. came to Birmingham in May 1961, after a
group of Freedom Riders was attacked. At a rally in their honor, King
called on the federal government to act "forthrightly in the South to
assure every citizen his constitutional rights. . . . The Federal Government must not stand idly by while blood thirsty mobs beat non-violent
students with impunity." Despite the violence in Birmingham, King urges
his followers "to continue to follow the path of non-violence. . . . This I
am convinced is our most creative way to break loose from the paralyzing shackles of segregation." One of the major student leaders was Diane
Nash, who was a leader from the start in the Nashville sit-ins and later
played a significant role in the Student Nonviolent Coordinating Committee (SNCC). At a conference in Detroit in 1961, Nash presented her
"personal interpretation of my own experience within the region known
as 'Dixie.' " In 1963, King led his forces to a showdown in Birmingham.
In early May, his campaign was marked by some of the most brutal
scenes ever recorded on U.S. television: the fire hoses and police dogs
of Birmingham being turned loose on school children and adults as they
nonviolently marched and protested segregation. On May 3, King spoke
at the Sixteenth Street Baptist Church, later that year to be the scene of

the horrific bombing and murder of four girls. King, ever mindful of his call for nonviolence, said:

> Birmingham was a mean city today. But in spite of the meanness of Birmingham, we must confront her with our kindness and our goodness and our determination to be nonviolent. As difficult as it is, we must meet hate with love. As hard as it is, we must meet physical force with Soul Force. And let us keep going down the path of nonviolence because somebody must have sense in this world.

Less than three weeks before his murder, Medgar Evers spoke over radio and television in Jackson, Mississippi, in a rebuttal to a televised speech by the Jackson mayor that claimed that blacks in Mississippi were content and had a decent living. Evers says the Negro plantation worker in the Delta looks at Jackson and "sees a city where Negro citizens are refused admittance to the City Auditorium and the Coliseum; his children refused a ticket to a good movie in a downtown theater; his wife and children refused service at a lunch counter in a downtown store where they trade; students refused the use of the main public libraries, parks, playgrounds, and other tax-supported recreational facilities." Several weeks later, Roy Wilkins, executive director of the NAACP, spoke at Evers' funeral in Jackson. He eulogized his fallen comrade: "There have been martyrs throughout history, in every land and people, in many high causes. We are here today in tribute to a martyr in the crusade for human liberty, a man struck down in mean and cowardly fashion by a bullet in the back."

John Lewis, now a U.S. Congressman from Georgia, was a significant leader in the movement in SNCC and later in the Southern Regional Council. At the 1963 march on Washington, Lewis delivered the speech published here. In a much more provocative speech than King's "I Have a Dream" (delivered later that day), Lewis asserts,

> The revolution is at hand, and we must free ourselves of the chains of political and economic slavery. The non-violent revolution is saying, "We will not wait for the courts to act, for we have been waiting for hundreds of years. We will not wait for the President, the Justice Department, nor Congress, but we will take matters into our own hands and create a source of power, outside of any national structure that could and would assure us a victory." . . . We cannot

be patient, we do not want to be free gradually, we want our freedom, and we want it *now*.

On Sunday morning, September 15, 1963, the Sixteenth Street Baptist Church in Birmingham was blown apart and four young girls were killed in the blast. Three days later, King spoke to the 8,000 mourners and the nation at large:

> They are the martyred heroines of a holy crusade for freedom and human dignity. So they have something to say to us in their death. They have something to say to every minister of the gospel who has remained silent behind the safe security of stained-glass windows. They have something to say to every politician who has fed his constituents the stale bread of hatred and the spoiled meat of racism. They have something to say to a federal government that has compromised with the undemocratic practices of southern Dixiecrats and the blatant hypocrisy of right-wing northern Republicans. They have something to say to every Negro who passively accepts the evil system of segregation, and stands on the sidelines in the midst of a mighty struggle for justice. They say to each of us, black and white alike, that we must substitute courage for caution. They say to us that we must be concerned not merely about *who* murdered them, but about the system, the way of life and the philosophy which *produced* the murderers. Their death says to us that we must work passionately and unrelentingly to make the American dream a reality.

Over to the west in Mississippi, Fannie Lou Hamer made a name for herself as a grassroots worker for the rights of her fellow black Mississippians. Not often does a person with a sixth-grade education testify before a Congressional Committee, but on June 16, 1964, Ms. Hamer did, as she described some of her experiences in attempting to register to vote: "After I was beaten by the first Negro, the State highway patrolman ordered the other Negro to take the blackjack. The second Negro, he began to beat." A fellow Mississippian, Aaron Henry, was the leader of the Mississippi state branch of the NAACP. In the speech published here, Henry urged the 1964 state meeting of the NAACP to "call upon the Administration and the Department of Justice to become dedicated to the cause of securing the right to vote for all of America's Citizens. With the right to vote we can resolve many of the other problems that beset us here in Mississippi."

By 1967, it could be argued that the Civil Rights Movement in the South was over. King had begun his protests of the Vietnam War, which cost him much of his white support, and he would be assassinated the next year. The Voting Rights Act and Civil Rights Act had been passed, which met the major goals of the movement. Additionally, the thrust of those who were still active in the Congress of Racial Equality (CORE) and SNCC, like Stokely Carmichael, was away from nonviolence and toward what he called Black Power; the Black Panthers organization was a result of this change in direction and emphasis. In this speech at Morgan State University, Carmichael challenged his student audience: "I think it is crystal clear in our minds what we must do in this generation to move for Black Power. Our mothers scrubbed floors. Our fathers were Uncle Toms. They didn't do that so we could scrub floors and be Uncle Toms. They did it so that this generation can fight for Black Power— and that is what we are about to do and that is what you ought to understand."

Black southerners were not the only soldiers in the battle for civil rights. As Florida Governor LeRoy Collins pointed out in a 1959 speech, "There are forces at work in the South—men and women who do not have their faces turned to a bygone era—that have much to offer the world in this present-day crisis."[14] There was a small, but valiant and outspoken, band of white southerners who stood up for what they knew was right. Chapter 5 provides us a window into their beliefs as they supported the struggles of black southerners. Clark Foreman spoke to the Southern Youth Legislature in 1946 and confirmed for his listeners that

> The day of Uncle Tom is over. More and more the people of the South are realizing that complacency and subservience are not the answers to segregation and discrimination. To those who say, "the Negro must keep his place," there can be but one reply: the only possible meaning that phrase can convey is that the Negro must take his place as an equal along side his fellow white citizens under the Constitution of the United States.

In Virginia, Sarah Patton Boyle, a member of an elite white southern family, urged a group of black southerners in 1956 to realize that, "As colored Southerners you have an obligation to yourself, your group, the whole South, the nation and the world to set a standard of what an American Citizen is supposed to be. Why does this obligation fall on you? It falls on you because the colored Southerner is carrying the banner for democracy today." Perhaps the most well-known southern white liberal was Georgia writer Lillian Smith. In 1960, Smith spoke in Washington, DC, about the "spiritual crisis which the South and its people are facing." As student sit-ins began that year, Smith saw "a new quality of hope" in the fight for civil rights for black Americans. Yet another white southerner who stood up for the rights of southern blacks was Anne Braden, a journalist and activist from Kentucky. Speaking to the 1962 annual convention of the Southern Christian Leadership Conference in Birmingham, Braden, like Smith, saw hope. "I believe it is entirely possible that because of the work of groups like this one, Alabama and other Deep South states, so benighted now, may someday become a force for good that will influence the whole course of man's history by showing to the world a new kind of relationship among men."

There were, however, many white southerners who not only did not agree with Foreman, Boyle, Smith, and Braden, they fought desperately to kill their hope and preserve the status quo. In chapter 6, we hear from some of the white leadership that galvanized their constituents into a solid front against change in racial relationships in the South, starting with Senator James O. Eastland's address to the U.S. Senate in 1954, shortly after the *Brown* decision was announced. The Mississippi senator went straight to his attack on the nation's highest court:

> What the Court has done has been to legislate additional civil rights, which were admittedly not heretofore authorized by the Constitution or by Congress. The Court has overturned a great principle of law and has made illegal the acts of States which the great judges who have heretofore composed the Court had held for generations did not violate the 14th amendment to the Constitution.

Thomas Pickens Brady was another Mississippian committed to preserving segregation. A judge in his home state, Brady spoke in San Francisco in October 1957, while the Little Rock Central High crisis was still at fever pitch. In his address to the Commonwealth Club, Brady asserted:

> Segregation in the South is a way of life. It is a precious and sacred custom. It is one of our dearest and most treasured possessions. It is the means whereby we live in social peace, order, and security. It is the guarantee whereby our wives and children are afforded the common decency and protection which is essential if any harmonious relationship is to exist between two different races. Segre-

gation exists not simply because we prefer it, but because we must maintain it.

Governor Orval E. Faubus vaulted into national and even international notoriety when he called out the Arkansas National Guard to prevent integration of Little Rock Central High School in the fall of 1957. After a year of turmoil at Central, Faubus closed the Little Rock schools at the start of the next school year. On September 18, 1958, Faubus delivered this statewide radio and television address defending his decision to close the schools.

Finally, we hear from Governor J.P. Coleman of Mississippi, in a "farewell" speech presented on statewide radio and television in June 1959. Among a laundry list of achievements for his administration, what he seems the most proud about is his claim that "I have adopted the rule of stopping integration anywhere it raises it head, regardless of the town, and I have enforced that rule."

But these dinosaurs of southern politics did not prevail. The conscience of the South, and, indeed, of the nation, was finally stirred by the long string of rhetorical and dramatic events that many southerners did not fully understand: Supreme Court decisions, sit-ins, bus boycotts, marches, mostly nonviolent but passionate and determined protests, politicians saying "Never!" and standing in school house doors to prevent integration, brutal murders, bombings, cross burnings, and hundreds of small, private harassments and intimidations of black citizens finally made their impact. Leslie W. Dunbar, an executive director of the Southern Regional Council, predicted in 1961 that, "Once the Negro has secured the right to vote, has gained admittance to the public library, has fought his way into a desegregated public school, has been permitted to sup at a lunch counter, the typical white Southerner will shrug his shoulders, resume his stride, and go on."[15] That is mostly what happened. Blacks were quickly accepted into all the places where previously they had been denied access. The South accepted black voter registration and that made a major difference in the politics of the region. In 1940, 2 percent of the eligible blacks registered to vote in the South. By 1972, after the Voting Rights Act was law, 56 percent were registered and southern politics was forever changed, as eleven southern states elected Governors who ran on a moderate platform and who were able to totally avoid all references to race in their campaigns.[16]

More than a century before, Alexis de Tocqueville wrote, "In democratic societies there are scarcely any but small minorities that desire revolutions; but minorities can sometimes make them."[17] In the mid-twentieth-century U.S. South, a revolution was fought and won. The speeches published here provide substantial insight into how that happened.

NOTES

1. John Shelton Reed points out that one of the two biggest stories of the twentieth-century South was "the transformation effected by the Civil Rights movement." (The other was the shift from an agricultural to an urban society.) "Forty Defining Moments of the Twentieth-Century South," *Southern Cultures* 7 (summer 2001), 95.

2. Vincent Harding, *Hope and History: Why We Must Share the Story of the Movement* (Maryknoll, NY: Orbis Books, 1990), 3–12.

3. Paul C. Brownlow, "The Pulpit and Black America: 1865–1877," *Quarterly Journal of Speech* 58:4 (1972), 432.

4. Carl Degler, *Place over Time: The Continuity of Southern Distinctiveness* (Baton Rouge: Louisiana State University Press, 1977), 126.

5. See W. Stuart Towns, "Resolving the South's Problem: Defining the Segregated South," in *Oratory and Rhetoric in the Nineteenth-Century South: A Rhetoric of Defense* (Westport, CT: Praeger, 1998), 161–179.

6. Howard N. Rabinowitz, *The First New South, 1865–1920* (Arlington Heights, IL: Harlan Davidson, Inc., 1992), 141.

7. Quoted in C. Vann Woodward, *Origins of the New South, 1877–1913* (Baton Rouge: Louisiana State University Press, 1951), 355–56.

8. Sarah Patton Boyle, *The Desegregated Heart: A Virginian's Stand in Time of Transition* (New York: William Morrow & Company, 1962), 17, 18, 23, 24.

9. For a full discussion of the South's racial etiquette, see David R. Goldfield, *Black, White, and Southern: Race Relations and Southern Culture, 1940 to the Present* (Baton Rouge: Louisiana State University Press, 1990), 2–6.

10. Southern Association on Inter-Racial Good Will and Negro Improvement, Columbiana, Alabama. "Aims." No date. Original found in Special Collections, University of Arkansas Library, Fayetteville, AR.

11. Wilbur J. Cash, *The Mind of the South* (New York: Vintage Books, 1941), 138.

12. James McBride Dabbs, *Haunted by God* (Richmond, VA: John Knox Press, 1972), 97.

13. James C. Cobb, *The Most Southern Place on Earth: The Mississippi Delta and the Roots of Regional Identity* (New York: Oxford University Press, 1992), 203, 209.

14. LeRoy Collins, "The South and the Nation," speech to Southern Association of Colleges and Secondary Schools, Louisville, KY, December 1, 1959. (Atlanta, GA: Southern Regional Council, 1960).

15. Leslie W. Dunbar, "The Annealing of the South," *The Virginia Quarterly Review* 37 (autumn 1961), 499.

16. See W. Stuart Towns, "New Southern Leadership: An Authentic New South," in *Public Address in the Twentieth-Century South: The Evolution of a Region* (Westport, CT: Praeger, 1999), 193–223, for speeches by these new politicians.

17. Alexis de Tocqueville, *Democracy in America*, translated and edited by Harvey C. Mansfield and Delba Winthrop (Chicago: University of Chicago Press, 2000), 611.

CHAPTER 1

"THE WHITES HAVE ABSOLUTE CONTROL OF THE STATE GOVERNMENT, AND WE INTEND AT ANY AND ALL HAZARDS TO RETAIN IT": WHY THERE HAD TO BE A CIVIL RIGHTS MOVEMENT

It may seem a bit out of place to include in an anthology on the Civil Rights Movement of the 1950s and 1960s several speeches made by white southerners in the late nineteenth century and opening year of the twentieth. They are, however, indispensable to understanding why there had to be a movement. These speeches, and many hundreds like them, set the tone, created the cultural environment, and reflected the segregated South that forced the black southerner into second-class citizenship. Only by understanding the mind-set as illustrated in these speeches can one begin to truly comprehend the rigid system of racial control established by the white southern leadership by the first decade of the twentieth century. The denial of civil rights and equality and the beliefs in black inferiority that were challenged in the 1950s and 1960s were all put into place by the leadership typified by these four speeches.

The structure of racial relationships that had been maintained through two centuries of slavery was overturned by the Civil War and emancipation. Hardly had the guns cooled and the veterans returned home before white southern leadership began casting about for a new means of control of the black race, which they, almost universally, assumed was inferior, even savage, and ultimately doomed for extinction. Based on those assumptions, the region began to create a new order and structure that was essentially in place by the beginning of the twentieth century; it did not begin to deteriorate until the middle of the century. Benjamin

R. Tillman described the problem as seen from the white viewpoint: "The irrepressible conflict between liberty and slavery destroyed slavery, but it has left to the South an irrepressible conflict between intelligence and ignorance, between vice and virtue, between barbarism and civilization."[1]

The foundation of the entire process was the assumption that America and the South was a white man's country and should always remain such. A clear statement of this outlook came from Hoke Smith, a leading example of the southern demagogue of the era and a Georgia politician who served as governor and U.S. senator. On June 29, 1905, in a campaign speech at Madison, Georgia, Smith asserted: "Back also of the entire question is the broad proposition that this must be preserved as a white man's country with a white man's government."[2]

Railroads were the first major institution successfully segregated by law across the South; between 1887 and 1891 nine southern states had enacted Jim Crow laws regarding rail travel accommodations.[3] During the decade of the 1890s, laws were placed on the books and were rigidly enforced segregating every element of public life in the South. Soon, schools, hotels, barber shops, restaurants, parks, drinking fountains, theaters and other entertainment facilities, courts, hospitals, mental institutions, prisons, residential areas, cemeteries, and even sidewalks were all bound up in the restrictions of segregation.

Not only were the abilities and freedom of southern blacks to move about freely and utilize public facilities on the same basis as their white neighbors sharply constrained, basic constitutional freedoms, such as the all-important right to vote, were denied them. Beginning with Mississippi in 1890, southern state after southern state disfranchised their black citizens by requiring a poll tax receipt, property qualifications, or by an "understanding clause" that required a prospective voter to interpret a section of the federal or state constitution to the satisfaction of a white registrar. South Carolina followed its governor, Benjamin Tillman, by writing disfranchisement into its new state constitution in 1895, followed by Louisiana in 1989. The other southern states completed the disfranchising process by 1910.

The Supreme Court aided the march toward second-class citizenship in 1896 when it handed down its infamous *Plessy v. Ferguson* decision, which declared that a state's doctrine of "separate but equal" with regard to public accommodations was constitutional. Justice John Marshall Harlan wrote an eloquent dissenting opinion.

But in view of the Constitution, in the eye of the law, there is in this country no superior, dominant, ruling class of citizens. There is no caste here. Our Constitution is color-blind, and neither knows nor tolerates classes among citizens. In respect of civil rights, all citizens are equal before the law. The humblest is the peer of the most powerful. The law regards man as man, and takes no account of his surroundings or of his color when his civil rights as guaranteed by the supreme law of the land are involved.[4]

Despite Harlan's argument, it would be almost six decades before the Court would overturn the *Plessy* ruling.

Of course, "separate but equal" was a facade that could not withstand even superficial examination. It is safe to say that nowhere in the South were facilities equal. Fulton County, Georgia, is an example. New facilities were built for the poor in 1889; the brick facility for whites cost the county $8,000 whereas the housing for blacks consisted of six wooden cottages that cost $1,500. Around the South, black teachers were receiving up to 40 percent less salary than white teachers; the black schools were wooden, the white schools, brick. In Nashville, Tennessee, the student-teacher ratio in 1912 was 33:1 for the white classes, 71:1 for black classes.[5]

Lillian Smith, in her perceptive *Killers of the Dream*, sums up the era with this vivid description:

After the Civil War, when things were in chaos and misery was everywhere and people were without food and learning and shelter and medicine, our politicians picked up the symbol of White Supremacy and made it a flag and a doctrine and a passion by which to "unify" poor white and rich white (who felt they had little in common) in a natural hostility against the Negro. It was one easy way to build power.[6]

This power was built and it denied basic civil rights to an entire race of people for more than half a century.

The Negro's "place" in the new order was tightly constrained and clearly defined, and these new legal codes of white supremacy were more complex and just as rigidly enforced as the system that had existed before the Civil War.[7] Violence and the threat of violent action against any black man (or white), who dared to challenge the system kept the structure in place, and a rigid system of racial etiquette governed the social relationships between the races. By the turn of the century, the promises of freedom for black southerners were a mockery. The four speeches that follow help illustrate the worldview that enabled this misuse of power to occur.

JAMES CLARENCE HARPER

James C. Harper was one of the grassroots leaders of small-town America. These leaders receive little notice outside of their local areas, but they reflect and shape the thinking, culture, and society of their hometowns and counties. In a few cases, their community's respect and admiration might take them to the state capital or even to Washington, DC, where they may have an opportunity to have an impact on state or national issues before returning home to quietly live out their lives. James Harper was one of those unsung leaders.[8]

Little is known about him, but he was born in Cumberland County, Pennsylvania, in 1819 and moved with his family to Darke County, Ohio, in 1831. He received a common school education, and in the late 1830s he answered a call from his uncle, James Harper, a businessman in North Carolina, to move to Caldwell County where he became involved in surveying and various businesses. In 1841, he laid out the town of Lenoir, and several years later he surveyed the turnpike from Lenoir to Blowing Rock and founded the turnpike company.

Harper lived at Patterson, a few miles from Lenoir, where he established several businesses in the 1850s: a tannery, gristmill, cotton and woolen mills, a blacksmith shop, and an icehouse, among other ventures. He also farmed and logged.

Over the years, Harper held several local offices and entered the state militia in 1861, but his poor health prevented him from serving in the Civil War. He served in the North Carolina legislature in 1865 and 1866 and was elected to Congress in 1870. He played a minor role in the Forty-second Congress, and the speech anthologized here was his only oratorical effort on the floor of Congress. Poor health forced his retirement from Congress after only one term, but he continued in local public service for the rest of his life. Among other positions, Harper was on the board of directors of the Western North Carolina Hospital and was a trustee of the Davenport Female College in Lenoir. Harper died on January 8, 1890.

In this speech opposing the Civil Rights Act, Representative Harper perpetuates the age-old southern myth that, "we live together, the old masters and the old slaves, side by side, in perfect peace, in perfect civil equality before the law, in the equal enjoyment of the civil, moral, educational, and religious privileges." He goes on to express the commonly held belief by whites in both North and South regarding the "social and intellectual inferiority" of the Negro race. His major point is that this bill and others like it will create a high set of expectations about social equality that will ultimately frustrate, and not help, the southern Negro.

"SEPARATE SCHOOLS FOR WHITE AND COLORED WITH EQUAL ADVANTAGES"; MIXED SCHOOLS NEVER![9]

U.S. House of Representatives
May 4, 1872

Mr. Speaker, the bill which has been for some time pending in the morning hour, and on which the final vote has been ordered by a vote of yeas 100, nays 78, entitled "A bill supplemental to an act entitled 'An Act to protect all citizens of the United States in their civil rights, and to furnish the means for their vindication,' " provides as follows:

> That no citizen of the United States shall, by reason of race, color or previous condition of servitude, be expected or excluded from the full and equal enjoyment of any accommodation, advantage, facility, or privilege furnished by innkeepers; by common carriers, whether on land or water; by licensed owners, managers, or lessees of theaters or other places of public amusement; by trustees, commissioners, superintendents, teachers, and other officers of common schools and other public institutions of learning, the same being supported by moneys derived from general taxation, or authorized by law; by trustees and officers of cemetery associations and benevolent institutions incorporated by national or State authority.

Since the last action had on this bill another one of similar import has been introduced and referred, which provides—

> That no citizen of the United States shall, by reason of race, color, or previous condition of servitude, be excepted or excluded from the full and equal enjoyment of any accommodation, advantage, facility, or privilege furnished by trustees, commissioners, superintendents, teachers, and other officers of common schools, under any State, city, county, parish or other school system, and other public institutions of learning, the same being supported by moneys derived from general taxation, or authorized by law; by trustees and officers of cemetery associations and benevolent institutions incorporated by national or State authority; by innkeepers; by common carriers, either by land or water; or by licensed managers, owners, or lessees of theaters or other places of public amusement . . .

The vital blows aimed by these bills at the moral, religious, and educational interests of my constituents, the people of North Carolina, and of the whole South, render it impossible for me to sit longer in silence; and although I have hitherto refrained from troubling the House, and have contented myself with voting against legislation calculated to injure my section, and in favor of whatever measures the friends of the South have introduced, yet in this case I am compelled to add to my vote my spoken and earnest protest against this crowning act of oppression. That the vote and the protest will be alike unavailing, I am well advised. The southern Conservative members know, from the sad and bitter experiences of the last four years, what it is to go back to their people and tell them for their consolation that there is scarcely any ground of hope. They know what it is to ask the majority here for bread and be given a stone; to demand in the name of a despairing constituency the barest justice, and to get by way of answer legislation as insulting as that which would be vouchsafed a nation of serfs. Notwithstanding this, sir, my duty to myself and to those who sent me here forces me to utter what I am about to say. The evils which the passage of either of these bills will bring upon the present generation are apparent enough. The provisions contained in them are fraught with the most dangerous consequences to both North and South, and if enacted will entail a heritage of woe upon the future.

The want of a consistent practical policy in the dominant party, having for its object the real interest of a reunited country, has never been more manifest than it now is. The bills under consideration afford an instance of sectional legislation in which an oppressive law is to be imposed upon our people in this case against the expressed wishes of the best portion even of the Republican party in those States in which it is intended to operate most. It is a significant fact that but one State convention of the Republican party in the southern States has expressed any sympathy for this measure, and in that case the proposition met with a storm of opposition. To show the spirit of the Republican press, which no doubt reflects the sentiment of that party, I read from a late number of the *Richmond* (Virginia) *Journal*, the leading Republican paper in that State:

Mixed Schools.—The Dispatch of this morning bewails the attempts of the Republican party to make capital by endeavoring to secure social equality between white and black, and especially by that odious measure of mixed schools. To all which we answer that the Republican party, neither in this State nor in the nation, is doing so. Neither white nor colored Republicans in any manner desire mixed schools here. If the attempt is made, we shall be found, as a true friend of the colored race, not less than the white, fighting to the last against it as destructive to the best interests of both races. We know that to adopt mixed schools would be to destroy our school system altogether. We are in favor of giving all the children of the State thorough education, free to rich and poor alike. We insist upon the right of every child to be educated, and the duty of the State to provide the means and to secure the attendance of the children at the school by compulsory measures. But we insist, also, that each race shall be allowed its own schools. Healthful and friendly competition will then stimulate each to do its best, lest it fall behind in the race for knowledge. We are confident that our opinions are held by a vast majority of the Republicans of Virginia, and by none more tenaciously than the colored people themselves. We appeal to the candor and self-respect of our opponents to refrain from raising an issue so clearly fictitious as this in the approaching contest. No good can possibly come of it, and much bitterness of feeling cannot fail to be excited by the rehearsal of accusations wholly unfounded and unjust.

Other proof of the same kind could be furnished, if necessary. I have selected this because it so well expresses the truth, except that it is blind to the intention of its party in this House.

It appears almost impossible to convey to any one, not a citizen of the South, a correct idea of the condition of society there, our customs, our traditions, and especially of the relations now subsisting there between the white and colored races. To the ignorance on such matters prevailing among the Republican members from the North it is charitable to attribute something of the unsuitable and extraordinary legislation which has here been invented and carried out.

I have the honor to represent the mountaineers of western North Carolina, a hardy and intelligent people, who, like their mountain brethren of Switzerland, have always kept alive among their forests and on their hilltops the sacred fires of liberty. They are men who, born free, wish so to live and so to die. They have the instincts of their Caucasian race more strongly, if possible, than the dwellers on the plains; and what I have to say of their manner of treating the negroes, therefore, and of their relations with a class whom they will always believe to be their inferiors, can be applied in a less rather than in a greater degree to the inhabitants of my whole State.

Our slave element was never a large one, and the majority even of the wealthier among us owned but few slaves. When the war ended those who had been in servitude generally were found on the premises where they had lived for years. Many of them stayed on; hiring, at first, for a portion of the crop, afterward at daily or monthly wages. A few, impatient to prove to themselves that they had the right to run about as they chose, left their old masters and sought new homes, or betook themselves to the distant camps of the Freedmen's Bureau. In the course of a few years the more prudent among them settled, having acquired homes either by purchase or lease. The lazy and the shiftless moved to warmer sections, and our floating negro population has almost wholly disappeared. What we have with us are citizens in every sense of the term.

They accept and exercise, with not only the acquiescence but the approval of the whites, every civil right secured to them by the legislation of the period since their liberation. Their rights of property are peculiarly protected, and the exercise of these rights encouraged. The negro has the fullest and freest enjoyment of his equal rights in our courts, in our schools, and at the ballot-box. If he is injured, the courts are prompt to give him redress; his children are provided with schools on precisely the same terms as the white children; his vote is never challenged or refused. Should he wish to attend public worship, the doors of every church are open to him. Should he desire to commune, and is worthy, the elements are never denied him. Should he be destitute and unable to labor, he goes, not to the wardens of the poor, but to his old master, who, if the fortunes of war, and of misrule, worse than war, have spared him anything, never fails to help. If he is sick, he tries to get near his old mistress, and calls for the doctor who used to practice on his old plantation. If he is in trouble of any kind, he applies, as a rule, to some one who, once having owned slaves, knows best, he thinks, how to advise him. He knows nothing of that social equality which these bills propose to invest him with, and is as loath to demand as the whites will be to grant it. He sits with us in the jury box and in the halls of legislation as our equal; elsewhere he is ill at ease, uncomfortable, and under restraint. They have their code of manners as we have ours, and they are governed by that code.

And so, sir, we live together, the old masters and the old slaves, side by side, in perfect peace, in perfect civil equality before the law, in the equal enjoyment of the civil, moral, educational, and religious privileges. And so we should continue to live, each race helping the other, the whites teaching the blacks economy of time, improved methods of labor, and the cultivation of those qualities which give a man self-respect and the good will of his fellows. And the colored race, lending to the whites their strong arms and trained muscles, giving their labor for wages to support themselves and their families. Generations hence, should the negro exist that long, will see no change in the relations between the races, the whites acknowledging the civil equality of the blacks, and habituated to it; the blacks equally cognizant of and believing in their social and intellectual inferiority to the whites. To disturb this state of things will cause, not a civil war, but a strife equally distressing—a social war. These bills, if passed into laws and enforced, contain the fire-brands destined to kindle the fires of social discord and hatred.

The negro is very emotional and excitable, with a childlike fondness for what is new, and a blind and reckless haste in following whatever pleases his sight or his fancy. Place the vision of absolute social equality before his eyes; tell him that this social condition in which he finds himself is a relic of slavery, that he is good enough, wise enough, and white enough to send his children to school with our sons and daughters, to sleep in our beds, and occupy our best rooms at the hotels; that the reason he does not do all these things is not because it is unfitting and unnatural, but because we hate and despise him, and are trying to keep him down, so as to put him back into slavery, and he will not believe it at first; but keep preaching it to him from the stump, the bench, and the pulpit, add to your untiring recitations the solemn testimony of a law of the United States Congress; tell him that if he is refused any of these things it is because he is black, and he will by and by believe that is the only reason for such refusal. Tell him that there is a law to punish every offender for every refusal by a heavy fine and an imprisonment; and tell him, too, that under this law he can drag the daring believer in the social superiority of the Caucasian race three hundred miles away from his home, away from his kindred and friends, among strangers, to be tried by a strange tribunal whose very name affrights him— therefore a jury, if not packed, at least ill-selected. Tell him all this, and you make the temptation too great, the prize too dazzling for poor, simple, misguided African human nature to withstand.

And now, sir, let us suppose that after being fully instructed in this new gift of social equality, secured to him by the passage of one of these bills, some colored man in one of our country towns determines to avail himself thereof. He sends his children to the teacher of a free school for whites, or to one of our incorporated academies or colleges, and demands that they be received and educated. The teacher, looking to the provisions of our school laws which provides for the colored children precisely as for the whites in the common schools, declines to admit them because they are colored. The father then seeks some United States commissioner, or, more in accordance with the practice lately prevailing in my own district, hunts up some deputy United States marshal, who carries his pocket full of blank warrants signed by a commissioner. The teacher is forthwith arrested, carried before a commissioner, examined and bound over to a Federal court in Raleigh, from two to three hundred miles distant. If he is poor and unable to give security he will be committed to jail, where he must await the pleasure of an attorney or his assistants, and a grand jury, every one of whom has been selected with a view to his political status. The trial comes on, and the teacher, as a matter of course, is found guilty, and is fined $500 or imprisoned thirty days, supposing he gets off with the lightest punishment imposed. Then as soon as he pays his fine or is released from jail he can be again sued by the aggrieved negro for damages, and a recovery of $500 obtained in an action on the case.

Suppose the officers of the county or of the township, or the trustees of a female or other college, intrusted by law with the management and superintendence of the school in question, dare to approve or sustain the teacher's action, and the whole vindictive force and penalties of this law are turned on them, until they are compelled to abandon their pride of descent and self-respect, and perhaps escape a prison only by a sacrifice of their possessions.

In all this I am only following the strict course of the law and of that action under it which must inevitably follow its adoption. The whole machinery of our common school system will be broken up, and the schools will be discontinued, for no white man will suffer his children to attend a school taught by a colored man, or by a white man with a black conscience. Education for the whites, at the public charge, will become an impossibility. The torch of learning, just relighted since the war, will be extinguished, and our people must maintain private tutors at home, or send their children to distant and expensive private establishments, neither of which is within the means of my people.

But, sir, this is only the beginning of the evils to be entailed by this bill. The negro will soon discover that he can drive a good business by enforcing his rights to social equality; by receiving a fee of $500 and it will be proclaimed far and near in the dwellings of Ham that any black man whose sensitiveness on the score of social equality is touched by the refusal of a white man to recognize it may have his wounded feelings healed by the soothing application of that sum. Then will the barber and house servant go about seeking for some white man rich enough to lacerate their sensibilities profitably. Some smart hotel waiter discharges himself, and well aware that there is a spare bed or two in the house, goes to the landlord and demands that a private room be forthwith given him and his dusky wife. He is refused, and likely enough kicked out of the hotel. The machinery of this bill is then started, the mill proceeds to grind, and the hotel-keeper comes out, if he comes out at all, bankrupt and out of business.

The same experiment will be tried on the great lines of public conveyance, and the same results will follow. The conductors who order and the brakemen who execute the ejectment of an insolent, presuming colored man from a first-class Pullman sleeping car, the superintendent who sustains this action, and the president and directors who upheld the superintendent, will all be indicted and suffer the penalty of the law.

This all may seem like trifling; but I protest that I am only imagining what may well be the result of an attempt to enforce acquiescence on the part of the white citizens in this doctrine of social equality thinly veiled in the bill under consideration by the name of civil rights. I do not desire or intend to trifle with so serious a subject; but I do wish the gentlemen on the other side of the House to see for themselves, as we of the South are likely to see, the palpable and inevitable consequences of the passage of this or any similar law.

The bills under consideration in the House are not as complete in their provisions as the similar measure pending in the Senate, inasmuch as the latter extends the scope so as to include churches. And, looking at the history of the legislation here for the past few years, it is but fair to presume that the crusade will go on until our churches even will not be permitted to interpose even a cherished denominational restriction to prevent the accession of unworthy members. The people of my district are emphatically a religious people. A grown man or woman in our mountains who is not a regular member of some church or who does not attend church with his or her family, is as rare as one who has no visible means of support. We love our churches, sir; we cherish and stand by them as stoutly as we do anything left us by the war. We have always, in other days as well as now, allowed the colored population free access to every place of worship. They have every facility there that we can have, except that of sitting in the pews or seats intended exclusively for the whites; and now it is intended to pull down this restraint, the last barrier between the social relations of the two races, created by the Almighty with such evident marks of distinction as will render it impossible for them ever to mingle as one.

Grant that we give up our schools; that we travel and lodge, eat and drink with the colored race; that our places of amusement are closed to respectable and fashionable life; that the Masonic Lodges and other benevolent institutions are disbanded, there is yet one thing we never will give up as long as the spirit of our fathers is in us; and that is, the right to worship God in our own dear old way. Our churches may be shut up and deserted, as they will be whenever a United States marshal tries to thrust his negro *protégé* into positions where our customs forbid him to go; but we will stick to our observances in spite of that. As long as we can find in our highlands a covert from the storm, we will follow the glorious example of the Waldenses and the Covenanters, conducting the worship and celebrating the rites of our churches under the shadow of the groves and behind the shelter of the everlasting hills.

I have thus confined myself to the effects which may be expected to be produced in my own district and State. But the operations of this kind of legislation will extend throughout the entire South; and in every community where the negro element is at all prevalent we may expect to see the same dreadful spectacle of schools destroyed, churches deserted, and one race arrayed against the other.

Nor will the northern States be exempt from similar afflictions. When the negroes there see the means of plundering the whites ready made to their hands, and observe how at the South the whole power of the Federal Government is exerted to enforce the social as well as the civil equality of their kindred, they will begin to think that white men have no rights which they cannot share, and will attempt to force themselves into the schools, the colleges, the sleeping-cars, the hotels, the fashionable theaters, Masonic and other lodges, and the churches heretofore kept exclusively for their white race.

I am much mistaken if the zeal and charity shown by gentlemen on this floor from the great commercial and manufacturing centers of the North will go quite so far as to be willing to receive the objects of their good will to the enjoyment of the same privileges which they seem determined that we of the South shall afford them. White blood up there is not much different from that which runs in our veins. The Caucasian will not mix with the African any sooner in Massachusetts than in North Carolina; and although the feebleness of the latter element at the North may not compel New England to participate in all the direful consequences of the kind of legislation which I am opposing, enough will certainly transpire there to open the eyes of the people, and force them to see something of the wretchedness and affliction which the policy of their representatives is causing their brethren of the southern States.

In all my public life, hitherto, I have been the warm and earnest advocate of popular education. Whenever a measure has come before those Legislatures of North Carolina of which I have had the honor to be a member, intended to extend the inestimable benefits of free schools to any of her children, rich or poor, white or black, it has always found in me a zealous supporter. The records of those sessions which I attended will show that I never failed to vote in favor of every law by the operation of which instruction could be given to any class of society. Such has been my interest on this floor in this question of education, that on the adoption of the amendment offered by the gentleman from West Virginia [Mr. Hereford] to the act to establish an educational fund, and to apply the proceeds of the public lands to the education of the people, whereby the provisions of the act were not to be withheld from any State by reason of her refusal to establish mixed schools, I cordially cast my vote in favor of the bill, although I was well aware that the policy of the bill was opposed by a majority of the Conservative members here. I so voted purely in the interest of free education, as I would vote for any measure not vitally obnoxious, which would enable two children to be educated where only one was educated before. The free schools of my State are very dear to me, and I cannot sit here in silence and see a bill pushed to its passage which I honestly believe will cause the destruction of that noblest of our charities, which will take the means of education from our people and compel them to bring up their children in ignorance.

Education is, next to religion, the patron of every virtue and the foe of every vice. Take it away from us, and you compel us to bring our children up candidates for crime, and destitute of those safeguards which are so essentially necessary to them in their passage through life.

Besides all these objections to this bill, sir, I confess I am totally unable to see a single reason in its favor. The negroes have all they want. They do not desire such privileges as this law would give them. That they would claim them, if given, after being taught so to do by adventurers from other States who have, for political considerations, infested our borders, does not by any means prove that they wish them, or that they would be benefited by them. They are an imitative race, and follow blindly the example of any self-made leader. But they do not ask the passage of this bill, and on reflection would, I am persuaded, be unwilling that it should pass. We have given them schools to which they greatly prefer to send their children, and other accommodations which, from the practice of many years, we and they are convinced are most suitable to them and their habits.

I am convinced that the adherence of the white Republicans of my district and the State at large to their party is not caused by any belief in such a doctrine as this bill teaches. They are as far from being willing to send their children to mixed schools as the Conservatives are; and I do not know one of them with whom white men commonly associate who would not scorn the imputation that he was an advocate of the social equality of the races. If his bill passes I believe my Republican fellow citizens will make common cause with the Conservatives; their differences will be forgotten at the ballot box, and every white man will protest against this wicked attempt to compel him to acknowledge as an equal and associate any one whom his reason, his education, his habits, and every tradition of his kindred have caused him to look upon as his moral and social inferior. The bill proposes to confer on the blacks nothing which can do them good; and it will inevitably tear open old sores now healing, and widen differences now almost obliterated between them and the whites. Instead of joining the races as one, a thing which eternal wisdom and power has rendered impossible, it will counteract the effects which years of peace have had in harmonizing those races, and array the stronger against the weaker, until, perhaps, the extinction of the latter will become a question merely of time.

There are instincts in our bosoms which lie deeper than laws; feelings which elude, and passions which defy, the ministers of justice. Every such act of oppression as this will only serve to arouse these instincts, stimulate these feelings, and excite these passions, until there is developed that might and majesty of public opinion all over the land which will not only render the execution of such laws impossible, but will overwhelm in a common ruin their authors and the race for those whose pretended good they were contrived.

I have refrained from saying anything about the unconstitutionality of this bill. I am no lawyer, and could not put my opinions on that question into legal and orderly phrase; but looking at it simply as a practical man, I confess it seems to me that if the founders of our institutions had foreseen that any such legislation as this would ever have been attempted, they would have hesitated long before they would have given us, under the name and form of republican Government, that which enables a minority of the whites with the aid of the blacks to crush and torture the majority of the white men of this country. If Congress has the power to pass this bill and make it a law it has the power to enact laws to regulate the minutest social observances of domestic or fashionable life. It has the right to say to my neighbor, "You must ride in the same car, eat at the same table, and lodge in the same room with a negro." It can also say that you must not interpose an objection on account of his color to any advances he may make toward your children or family.

Finally sir, I appeal to the majority here, on behalf of my good old State, one of the original thirteen—a State known and honored for the steady habits of her people, the law-abiding character of her citizens, and for the dignity which her sons have imparted to our national councils; a State where, no matter what trumped-up stories calculated to defame her have been circulated by men careless of reputation and greedy of gain; where, I say, the laws are reverenced and held to be supreme, in whose wildest mountains a stranger would be safer at midnight than in the city of New York at noon; a State which has been stripped of wealth, whose great public works are yet incomplete by reason of her poverty, and whose public charities are barely maintained by the self-sacrifice of her citizens; a State which, prosperous and advancing ten years ago, is now destitute of everything but her soil, her schools, and her charitable institutions, and whose children have lost almost everything but their self-respect; in behalf of this State, this old North Carolina, sir, I appeal to the members here to pause and well consider before they commit themselves to measures which will deprive us of what little we have left, which will ruin our schools and colleges, perhaps shut up our churches, and leave us to the mercies of an inferior, unprogressive race.

BENJAMIN RYAN TILLMAN

After an undistinguished career as a farmer in Edgefield County, South Carolina, Benjamin Ryan Tillman embarked on a political odyssey that led him to the governorship of his state and to four terms in the U.S. Senate. One of the classic "Southern Demagogues," and an effective template for that genre of southern leadership, Tillman controlled South Carolina politics for several years and was recognized in the Senate and around the nation as an outspoken and radical white supremist racist, as well as a spokesman for the small farmer.[10]

Tillman was born on August 11, 1847, the son of a slave-owning farmer who died when the boy was two years old. Tillman left school in 1864 to join the Confederate Army but became ill and was incapacitated for two years. He lost an eye due to the illness, which exacerbated his already rough and unruly appearance. After marrying in 1868, he worked a four-hundred acre farm next to his mother's family estate. His first venture into the political arena came in 1876 as he helped to redeem South Carolina and elect Wade Hampton to the governorship by frightening potential black voters away from the polling places. In 1885–1886 he organized the Farmers' Association and strongly supported the small upland farmer against the Hampton regime. One of their causes was better agricultural education and Tillman was able to persuade the state to accept a bequest by Thomas G. Clemson for the establishment of an agricultural college. By 1890, Tillman was strong enough to capture the Democratic nomination for governor; he was easily elected over an independent Democrat, Alexander C. Haskell. Unfortunately for Tillman, the legislature he addressed in his Inaugural speech published here was not totally supportive of his plans; later he assailed it as "dead, rotten driftwood." But by 1892, the legislature was in his hands, and he was in control of state politics. Tillman was reelected in 1892 and in 1894 defeated Matthew C. Butler for U.S. senator, a post to which he was reelected in 1900, 1906, and 1912. Although he retained his Senate seat until his death, a series of strokes impaired his speaking abilities, and his political power gradually diminished. He died on July 3, 1918.

"Pitchfork Ben" earned his nickname in his 1894 Senate campaign when he pledged to stick a pitchfork into President Cleveland's ribs when he got to Washington. This epithet stuck with him and is a fine example of his mesmerizing oratory. He played on the emotions of his listeners and constituents and always delighted in putting on a show for them.

In 1895, he was successful in calling a convention that rewrote the state constitution. Among other things, the new document, at Tillman's urging, redrew Congressional districts to discriminate against South Carolina blacks. Additionally, the constitution contained a provision that set property and educational qualifications for voting. This stipulation essentially disfranchised black voters in the Palmetto State.

In his Inaugural address, Tillman clearly demonstrates his loyalty to the small farmer, the Democratic Party, his staunch belief in the evils of the Reconstruction era, and his rabid white supremacy perspective. He praises the white voter as he points out that, "In our own State, the triumph of Democracy and white supremacy over mongrelism and anarchy, of civilization over barbarism, has been most complete." His description of the standard southern viewpoint of Reconstruction is virtually word for word the view of the typical white southerner for the next half a century or more:

> The dismal experiment of universal negro suffrage, inspired by hate and a cowardly desire for revenge; the rotten government built upon it and propped with bayonets; the race antagonism which blazed up and is still alive; the robbery under the form of taxation; the riot and debauchery in our legislative halls and in our capital; the prostitution and impotence of our courts of justice while rape, arson and murder stalked abroad in open daylight; the paralysis of trade; the stagnation of agriculture; the demoralization of society; the ignorance, the apathy, the despair which followed and brooded over the land—all these things have we endured and survived.

Words like these from the white leadership of the late–nineteenth century South forced the region into the mold of white supremacy, segregation, racial, and sectional antagonisms, and created the climate in which the Civil Rights Movement of the 1950s and 1960s was the only solution, short of outright revolution.

INAUGURAL AS SOUTH CAROLINA GOVERNOR[11]

Columbia, South Carolina
December 4, 1890

Gentlemen of the General Assembly: It is seldom in the history of politics that a man is so honored as I am. It is customary to perform the ceremony of inauguration in public, but only once before, that I am aware, has it been necessary in South Carolina to hold it in the open air in order to let the people see. To the large number of my fellow citizens who have done me the honor to come as witnesses of this impressive ceremonial, I can only say in simple words, I thank you. To the people I owe my election, after a most memorable canvass. To the people only I owe allegiance, and to the people I pledge loyal service. This is no mere holiday occasion. The citizens of this great commonwealth have, for the first time in its history, demanded and obtained for themselves the right to choose their Governor, and I, as the exponent and leader of the revolution which brought about the change, am here to take the solemn oath of office, and enter upon the discharge of its onerous duties. Before doing this, it is proper, and usage makes it obligatory on me, to make known my views and opinions on the important questions agitating the public mind, and to show where and how reforms are needed and can be wrought.

With such an audience as this, sympathetic and enthusiastic, I might, if I were an orator, attempt to play upon your feelings, and win applause by flights of what some call eloquence; but which sensible people consider as "glittering generalities"—the tinsel and brass buttons of a dress parade meaning nothing and worth nothing. The responsibilities of my position, the reliance of the people upon my leadership, the shortness of our Legislative session (one-fourth of which is already gone), alike demand the display of practical statesmanship and business methods. We are met to do the business of the people—not to evolve beautiful theories, or discuss ideal government. We come as reformers, claiming that many things in the Government are wrong, and that there is room for retrenchment and reduction of taxes. Our task is to give the people better government, and more efficient government, as cheaply as is possible. We must, however, never lose sight of the fact that niggardliness is not always economy. The people will pay even more taxes than at present if they know those taxes are wisely expended, and for their benefit.

Before I proceed to discuss, in plain, straightforward fashion, the legislation I shall ask you to consider, I desire to congratulate you upon the signal victory achieved by the people at the recent election. Democracy, the rule of the people, has won a victory unparalleled in its magnitude and importance, and those whose hearts were troubled as they watched the trend of national legislation in its unblushing usurpation of authority, its centralizing grasp upon the throats of the States, its abject surrender to the power of corporate money and class interests— all such must lift up joyful hearts of praise to the All-Ruler, and feel their faith in the stability of our republican institutions strengthened. In our own State, the triumph of Democracy and white supremacy over mongrelism and anarchy, of civilization over barbarism, has been most complete. And it is gratifying to note the fact, that this was attended by a political phenomenon which was a surprise to all of us. Our colored fellow citizens absolutely refused to be led to the polls by their bosses. The opportunity of having their votes freely cast and honestly counted, which has been claimed is denied the negroes, caused scarcely a ripple of excitement among them. They quietly pursued their avocations, and left the conduct of the election to the whites. Many who voted, cast their ballots for the regular Democratic ticket, and the consequence is, that today there is less race prejudice and race feeling between the white men and black men of South Carolina than has existed at any time since 1868.

The dismal experiment of universal negro suffrage, inspired by hate and a cowardly desire for revenge; the rotten government built upon it and propped with bayonets; the race antagonism which blazed up and is still alive; the robbery under the form of taxation; the riot and debauchery in our legislative halls and in our capital; the prostitution and impotence of our courts of justice while rape, arson and murder stalked abroad in open daylight; the paralysis of trade; the stagnation of agriculture; the demoralization of society; the ignorance, the apathy, the despair which followed and brooded over the land—all these things have we endured and survived. Nearly a quarter of a century has passed since the two peoples who occupy our territory were taught to hate each other. The carpet-bag vampires and baser native traitors who brought it about and have kept it alive for their own sinister purposes are nearly all gone. There never was any just reason why the white men and black men of Carolina should not live together in peace and harmony. Our interests are the same, and our future, whether for weal or woe, cannot be divorced. The negro was a staunch friend and faithful servant during the war, when there was every opportunity to glut upon our wives and children any hatred or desire for revenge. He had none. There is not a single instance on record of any disloyalty to his master's family during that trying and bloody period. The recollection of this fact should make us charitable towards him for the excesses to which he was excited by the opportunity, example, and instigation of his white leaders during the dark days I have just depicted. His conduct in the recent political campaign shows that he has begun to think for himself and realizes at last that his best friends and safest advisers are the white men who own the land and give him employment. When it is clearly shown that a majority of our colored voters are no longer imbued with the Republican idea, the vexed negro problem will be solved, and the nightmare of a return of negro domination will haunt us no more. Cannot I appeal to the magnanimity of the dominant race? Cannot I pledge in your behalf that we white men of South Carolina stand ready and willing to listen kindly to all reasonable complaints? To grant all just rights and safe privileges to these colored people? That they shall have equal protection under the law and a guarantee of fair treatment at our hands?

That the colored people have grievances, it is idle to deny. That the memory of the wrongs and insults heaped upon the whites by the blacks during their eight years' rule has provoked retaliation and often injustice, is true. It was natural and inevitable. But we owe it to ourselves as a Christian people; we owe it to the good name of our State which has been blackened thereby, and its prosperity retarded, that these things should be stopped. The whites have absolute control of the State Government, and we intend at any and all hazards to retain it. The intelligent exercise of the right of suffrage, at once the highest privilege and most sacred duty of the citizen, is as yet beyond the capacity of the vast majority of colored men. We deny, without regard to color, that "all men are created equal"; it is not true now and was not true when Jefferson wrote it, but we cannot deny, and it is our duty as the governing power in South Carolina to insure, to every individual, black and white, the "right to life, liberty, and the pursuit of happiness."

With all the machinery of law in our hands, with every department of the Government—Executive, Legislative, and Judicial—held by white men: with white juries, white Solicitors, white Sheriffs, it is simply infamous that resort should be had to lynch law, and that prisoners should be murdered because the people have grown weary of the law's delay and of its inefficient administration. Negroes have nearly always been the victims; and the confession is a blot on our civilization. Let us see to it that the finger of scorn no longer be pointed at our State because of this deplorable condition of affairs. Let us hunt out the defects in our laws; let us make plain and simple the rules of court which have outraged justice by granting continuances and new trials upon technicalities. Let us insist that only intelligent, sober, virtuous citizens sit on our juries. Let punishment for crime, by whomsoever committed, be prompt and sure, and with the removal of the cause the effect will disappear. And as a last desperate remedy, to be used only when others fail, grant the Executive the power of absolute removal of any Sheriff who fails to prevent any such act of violence in his County after the law has taken control of the prisoner.

I have thought it wise to speak in emphatic terms on this subject, because every Carolinian worthy the name must long to see the time when law shall reassert its sway, and when our people will not be divided into hostile political camps, and all classes and colors shall vie with each other in friendly rivalry to make the State prosperous and happy.

Having never aspired to or held any political office before, my place in South Carolina has simply been that of a voter and tax payer. Hence I am not as conversant with the details of the different departments of the State Governments as I could wish. With such knowledge as I possess, I will now, as briefly as possible, direct your attention to such matters of public interest as seem of most importance.

The improvement of the free school system, and the wise adjustment of means to ends in the management of our institutions of higher education so as to obtain the best results, demand your best care and prompt action. The patriotism, intelligence, and virtue of the individual citizen is the foundation upon which rests free representative government. The education and proper training of the voters who must choose the public officers to carry on the State's affairs, is, therefore, a sacred duty which cannot be neglected without injury to the State and to society. No one will dispute this. But, how much is South Carolina doing in this behalf?

Is our present system a good one? Are we doing all we can to train our youth and fit them for the duties of life? I answer unhesitatingly: No! In our towns and villages, by reason of supplementary taxes and voluntary contributions, the schools are fairly good. Among the farmers in the country, the good school is the exception, while inferior schools, which run three or four months, are the rule. There is just enough effort by the state to paralyze private schools, and there is absolute retrogression in education with corresponding increase of illiteracy. We spend in round numbers for free common schools per annum about five hundred thousand dollars, and for higher education about one hundred thousand. This is fifty-two cents per capita of population, and allows less than two dollars to each child of school age. It must not be forgotten that the whites pay nearly all of this, except what is obtained from the poll tax. Without giving reasons, which will readily occur to every thinking mind, I suggest the following scheme to improve the free school system as a basis of permanent and lasting schools: The respective Counties should be divided by a reliable surveyor into school districts as nearly square as their contour and the larger streams and swamps will permit. These should be of an area not greater than thirty-six, nor less than sixteen, square miles, in proportion as population is dense, and with one white and one colored school in each, all the public school funds should be concentrated to run these alone. The trustees should be elected by the residents of said districts, only free holders being eligible to that office. The poll tax should be three dollars, instead of one dollar, as now, and this will require a Constitution amendment. Empower the trustees to erect suitable buildings as near the centre of districts as practicable, with money borrowed for that purpose, and set apart for each year so much of the school fund as may be necessary to liquidate the debt in ten years, principal and interest. Then allow the voters of each district to levy at their option, and without further legislative action, a supplementary tax for its sole use and benefit up to five mills, if they so desire, with the privilege to each tax payer of designating the school to which this additional tax shall be applied. Finally let the State arrange, alone, if need be, but in company with other Southern States, if possible, to have suitable school books compiled or published on royalty, or bought at wholesale, as may be cheapest, and furnish the same to scholars a cost, allowing no others to be used in public schools. The school book trust robs our people of anonymous amount of money every year. It is possible to buy an edition of the Waverly Novels, twenty volumes, for one dollar, while a Child's Primer costs twenty-five cents, and all other books in proportion. Then we find in our school histories Confederate soldiers designated as "rebels," and Southern statesmen called traitors. The State alone can remedy these evils, and the State should do it. It need not cost anything except to enact the law and put its execution in competent and loyal hands. And in regard to the proposed changes in the management of our free schools, there is a popular demand that the State shall do more—make the system effective, or do nothing, and abolish the two mill tax, leaving education altogether to the people themselves.

The condition of our higher institutions of learning is equally unsatisfactory and the State has been making some costly experiments. For five years there has been active and persistent agitation on the subject of what the State can afford to do in this line and what is best for it to do. One side contended for literary and scientific training and the university system, which necessarily costs the student more, and the State more per student educated. The other demanded cheap, practical education, in which the application of knowledge and science to the business of bread winning and the up-building of our agriculture and the mechanic arts should be the main objects. Both sides were right from their standpoints, but no agreement or compromise has been possible heretofore. The State has lost three valuable years, has wasted some eighty or ninety thousand dollars, and now the whole system must be overhauled and readjusted in accordance with the will of the people as shown at the recent election. Let us now exert our energies in trying to start right at last, and endeavor to harmonize conflicting interests and opinions. The people have decided that there is no use for a grand university at Columbia, but they are equally determined that the South Carolina College as a school of liberal education in the classics, in the theoretical sciences, and in literature, "shall be liberally supported."

After consultation with the President and some of the Professors and Trustees, I recommend that the University system be abolished, the Experiment Farm at Columbia sold and the proceeds covered into the treasury, the mechanical department with all its belongings transferred to Clemson College, and that a complete reorganization be ordered. A "liberal" appropriation and one which will suffice to give the institution stability and character ought to be made. Thirty thousand dollars for all purposes and tuition fees can be profitably used, in my opinion, and I hope it will receive that amount by perpetual annual grant so as to remove the College altogether from political influences and antagonisms . . .

Of the Citadel Academy, I shall have little to say. It is unfortunate, in my opinion, that it was ever re-opened as a beneficiary military school. The money, $60,000, which has been recently spent in rebuilding the burned wing, and in repairing and equipping the whole building, could, in my judgment, have been far more profitably used in erecting an Industrial and Normal School for girls, and the $20,000 annual appropriation which it takes to run the Citadel, would have gone far towards supporting such a valuable and necessary addition to our educational system.

But the money has been spent. The buildings are in splendid order, the school is in a flourishing condition, and it holds a warm place in the hearts of many of our people as a landmark of the old regime. A conservative regard for the rights and wishes of even a small minority ought to have weight with those who have themselves so long been denied what they wish. There are too few lights in South Carolina for us to wantonly put out any of them, and for the present I recommend that the usual appropriation be granted. Under the terms of the Land Grant Act, military science and tactics must be taught at the Clemson College. At that college a boy can learn everything now imparted at the Military Academy, and much besides. Its industrial feature will help poor boys to educate themselves without discrimination, while the Citadel furnishes free education, board, clothing, etc., to a limited number, under conditions which savor often of favoritism. Whether, after the Clemson College is started and there will be duplication of teaching force and identity of curriculum with the Citadel, the State can afford to maintain three schools for her sons, and not one for her daughters, will be for the people to decide. At present the Citadel is doing better work in proportion to cost than the University. When, however, the latter shall be reorganized as proposed, and when the Clemson College shall furnish the military training and practical scientific education which can now be obtained only at the Military Academy, that school will have to show cause for its existence as a charity school for military training.

But, whatever is done in that regard, there is imperative need for an industrial school for girls in the State. Our system of education for women looks to training their minds and giving them accomplishments for the adornment of society. But reverses of fortune or death often bring the necessity of bread winning, and the tender mother left a widow, or daughter left an orphan, finds how little worth in dollars and cents is the music, drawing, and painting, etc., upon which money and time had been lavished in her so-called education. The State has never done anything for its women except appropriating a small amount of the Winthrop Training School for Teachers. It would be wrong to enter in competition with our private female colleges by establishing an ordinary school, but one in which the industrial arts and sciences, telegraphy, designing, stenography, bookkeeping, the chemistry and practice of cookery, housekeeping, etc., are taught, will, I am sure, supply a long-felt and pressing want. The State may not be prepared to undertake this work right at this time, but justice and enlightened statesmanship will not allow it to be long delayed. . . .

After a thorough examination of the methods and work of the Winthrop Training School, I am positive in saying no money spent by the State for education promises a richer return than that given this institution. The cry comes from all over the State for better teachers and trained teachers. There are in our white public schools 1,102 male and 1,586 female teachers, showing that women are most in demand. What effort is made to supply it? The State gives $150 per annum to one woman beneficiary from each County who attends the Winthrop School, and none are admitted except those who are avowedly preparing themselves as teachers. The course is one year. Now mark the contrast. Three hundred dollars are spent annually on each beneficiary at the Citadel; two are allowed from each County; the course is four years, and the graduates are virtually released from the obligation to teach in the public schools, while many of them have left the State as soon as they graduated. Truly, it would appear that

"Man to man so oft unjust,
Is always so to woman";

And here we have not only injustice, but a woeful lack of common sense and no regard for that adjustment of means to ends which alone can justify taxation for education. I will close these extended remarks on education by repeating the words of a deep thinker: "If we educate our men, their children MAY be educated; but when we educate our women, we know their children WILL be educated." Carolina's daughters are her brightest jewels. Love, patriotism, justice, all demand that they be no longer neglected, or treated like poor relations.

I have made one brief visit to the Lunatic Asylum, and have made such inquiry and investigation as I could in regard to its system of management. The institution is very full; and the appropriation for this year has been $110,000, with an income in addition of about $10,000 from pay patients. The outlay on this charity, after deducting the interest on the State debt, is about one-fifth of our entire State expenditure. The Report of the Superintendent shows 445 white and 333 colored patients in the institution and a per capita expenditure of 37 cents a day. But the comparison with institutions whose patients are all white is unfair and misleading. A glance at the accommodation, clothing, etc., of the colored patients shows that they do not cost anything like this amount; and, therefore, the white patients are costing much more per capita than is shown in the report. I am not prepared to say whether there is room for retrenchment or not in the management; but I am very positive on two points:

(1) There are people in the Asylum who ought not to be there because they can be more economically supported elsewhere; and

(2) A change should be made in the law so as to require each County to support its own insane.

There are many reasons for this change which I will enumerate. The Asylum has three classes of patients:

(1) Those who are supported by the State.

(2) Those who are partly supported by the State.

(3) Those who pay for their own support.

Again, its patients are divided into:

(1) Patients who are insane, but curable.

(2) Patients who are insane, and incurable.

(3) Patients who are idiots.

(4) Patients who are epileptics.

(5) Patients who are imbeciles.

Lastly into two general classes: Patients who are dangerous, and patients who are harmless.

Society, for its own protection and for the sake of humanity, must provide for its unfortunates. There can be no dispute about this. Pay patients, whose friends can watch after their welfare and provide for it, can be left out of the account. Pauper patients should, under restraint when needed, receive kind treatment, plain substantial food, skilled medical attendance, and comfortable clothing. Every taxpayer wants this much done. But poor taxpayers, of whom we have plenty, ought not to be expected to support pauper lunatics in better style than they themselves are able to afford . . .

Next in magnitude and importance to the Asylum of our public institutions is the Penitentiary. The number of convicts in the latter is nearly the same as the patients in the former, and I am of opinion that the Penitentiary ought at least to support the Asylum. The results obtained at the institution have not been satisfactory to the people, and the bane of its management is *politics*. The General Assembly, when called on to fill positions of honor or profit, finds itself besieged by a class of men who are hunting a "soft place" and who have or make claims on individual members for votes as a reward for political support in the past, or promise of such support in the future. Offices requiring high order of business talent are given to men who can speak well or who have rendered political services, while they are wholly lacking in administrative ability. This being the case, it is small wonder that we so often find mismanagement in government business and incompetent men in high offices. This is a vice that is inherent in republican government, and in proportion as its influence is great or small in legislative bodies, is that government good or bad. The antidote is an opposition party to watch those in office and show to the people any short-comings. We have been denied this blessing in South Carolina by reason of the necessity of the whites remaining united . . .

But I must hurry on, for there are so many important questions with which we have to deal, that I shall tire your patience, and still leave much unsaid.

It is twenty-two years since the Constitution under which we live was forced upon an unwilling people by aliens. While many of its provisions are wise and cannot be improved, there is much in it unsuited to our condition and wants. All attempts to remedy its most glaring defects have failed. Some provisions in it cannot be obeyed, others we have never tried to obey, while others still have been trampled under foot, to the great injury of certain Counties and sections. I cannot consume time in pointing out all these things, but I am unalterably fixed in the belief that a convention of the people should be called to make the change if needed, and incorporate such additional features as will adapt it to our people and their surroundings. The cost of such a convention should not weigh in the least against such action, for the benefits to be expected will so far exceed the cost that money cannot enter as a factor. The people, I am sure, want a new organic law, and are willing to pay for it . . .

Thus far, matters which require outlay and increased expenditure, or from which no income is derived, have been discussed. I will next touch on the means of saving the people money, reducing and equalizing taxes, and increasing the state's income from the phosphate royalty. There is nothing which will save the people more money than a good railroad law, administered by an honest, impartial, fearless Commission. The people have demanded relief from the imposition and injustice of these powerful corporations. Hitherto all efforts to legislate in their behalf have failed because the railroads have wielded an undue influence with our General Assembly. With the present body I am sure the only question is as to what is best to be done, and, after such investigation as I have been able to give the subject, I unhesitatingly advise that a law similar to that of Georgia be enacted. The people of that State are perfectly satisfied with it and the railroads must be, because our sister State leads in the miles of new road constructed. Whether the choice of commissioners shall devolve upon the people, the General Assembly, or the Executive, is for you to determine. Our platform demands that it be given to the people, but an immediate reorganization of the Commission is desirable, while our next election is two years off, and, if proper men are selected, I am sure that the State will receive instant and great benefit. Of one thing I am certain, the division of the State into sections from which the Commissioners must be drawn is wrong in principle and in policy. We need the best men for the place, let them come from where they may, and let us hope that as there was absolute obliteration of the lines between "low country and up-country" in the last political campaign and the reform wave swept from the mountains to the sea, so may the Democrats who won, and those who lost, bear and forbear with each other, and, locking shields again, as becomes brethren and Carolinians, forget and forgive the bitterness which has been engendered. Let us in future know no sectional line in the State, and, in selecting men for positions of honor or trust, ask not whether a candidate is a "Reformer" or not, but whether he is the best man for the place. Democracy and fitness alone should determine the matter. A law may be ever so good and wise, but, if it is not properly administered, it will fail to give satisfaction. The General Assembly may enact the Georgia law, but if it fails to obtain the right men, there will be no relief to the people. We must get men like the Georgia Commissioners, able, honest, and fearless, or we had better abolish the Commission and make no attempts at controlling the railroads at all. In this connection it may be well to say that in seeking to control railroads and other corporations strict regard should be had for their rights and interests. Corporations are not public enemies, although they are, if unbridled, apt to be oppressive. Much of the material development and progress of the age is the fruit of corporate efforts, and many men acting under one head and guided by one will have done for our country what no individual could have possibly accomplished. Therefore we should carefully watch to see that nothing is done to injure our railroad or manufacturing companies. Let us protect the people against their greed, but let us be just and fair in our dealings with them . . .

Gentlemen of the Senate and House of Representatives, I must apologize for the time I have consumed in discussing these important matters, and with a few remarks as to the relations which ought to exist between the Executive and the representatives of the people, I will close. During the recent campaign the lines were sharply drawn, and I was elected on a platform which, among other things, demands "rigid economy in public expenditures; the abolition of useless offices; reduction of salary and fees of all offices, State and County, to conform to the increased purchasing power of money and the decreased ability of the people to pay taxes; that public officers be paid in proportion to their labor and responsibility." An overwhelming majority of both your honorable bodies was elected on the single issue as to whether you endorsed this platform and its exponent. We are here to redeem these pledges, and it is yours to make the laws, and mine to execute. The responsibility is squarely on us, and we cannot shirk it. There are some minor matters to which I will direct your attention in special messages from time to time. The observations I have made, and the recommendations I have offered, are for your consideration. Your duty is not discharged unless you sift, amend, alter, and add to these suggestions anything which, in your judgment, will perfect them, and subserve the object which alone should actuate us all—the public welfare. I have given you the best light I have, but I am not infallible, and have no pride of opinion. There is a fearful responsibility resting on me, by reason of the reliance upon my leadership. But you cannot avoid the responsibility resting on your own shoulders, and you will do wrong to cast a single vote against your judgment, no matter whence comes the recommendation. In the matter of appointments, I must rely almost wholly on your advice and suggestion, where the people have left us any choice. The most important appointive officer in each County is the Jury Commissioner. The pressure brought to bear on this officer by friends and attorneys of men indicted for murder, is very strong; and unless he is incorruptible, the jury gets "fixed," and justice is cheated. The office of Trial Justice is one of large power and importance, and no man who ever drinks to intoxication should hold it.

Only three weeks remain of the usual legislative session, which has been limited to Christmas by unwritten law. You have to deal with many matters of great importance, and whether you can perform these duties properly in so short a time, must depend on your diligence and an absolute refusal to waste time on silly, wildcat schemes and local and special legislation, which are the curses of our time. Pledging you my best efforts and hearty co-operation in your arduous labors, and invoking the guidance and blessing of the Father upon our labors in behalf of our beloved State and its people, I am now ready to call Heaven to witness and enter upon the duties of my office.

WADE HAMPTON

Wade Hampton was one of the leading citizens of South Carolina. Son of one of the wealthiest families in the state, he was a planter, the highest ranking Confederate cavalry officer in the Civil War, governor of the state, and finally, U.S. senator.[12]

Hampton was born on March 28, 1818, in Charleston, and after receiving private tutoring, attended and graduated from South Carolina College (now the University of South Carolina) in 1836. He studied law, but did not enter the bar, and never practiced. He continued his family's tradition as a prosperous planter, living on and operating one of the family's plantations in Mississippi. He returned to South Carolina and was elected to the state legislature in 1852, where he served until 1856 when he was elected to the state senate. When the Civil War erupted, Hampton raised and commanded "Hampton's Legion," an infantry, cavalry, and artillery unit that was highly honored during the war. Hampton was wounded three times and was perceived as a true southern war hero by many fellow southerners. He was promoted to brigadier general in 1862 and closed out the war as one of only two Confederate lieutenant generals of cavalry.

In 1876, Hampton led the Red Shirt campaign and was elected the "Redeemer Governor" of South Carolina, defeating Daniel Chamberlain by only 1,134 votes in a bitterly contested election in which fraud was rampant. Chamberlain protested the results and was sworn into office, but the State Supreme Court ruled in favor of Hampton. After being barred from the capital by federal troops, the Democratic Party governor took office on April 10, 1877, thus ending Reconstruction in South Carolina. Hampton was re-elected in 1878 but soon resigned to become U.S. senator. He served two terms in the Senate but was defeated for re-election in 1890. After leaving the Senate, President Grover Cleveland appointed him U.S. railroad commissioner. Hampton died in Columbia, South Carolina, on April 11, 1902.

Hampton tried to improve the lot of the black man in South Carolina, but from a strongly paternalistic and white supremacy point of view. Called by one historian "the impeccable paternalist," Hampton addressed to black audiences his campaign slogan of "free men, free schools and free ballots."[13] He did include several Negroes in his administration in minor appointments and did for some time truly advocate a better situation for the black South Carolinian. In 1876, he asserted, "Not one single right enjoyed by the colored peoples today shall be taken from them. They shall be the equals, under the law, of any man in South

Carolina."[14] He claimed that he was "the first man in America—certainly the first in the South—who advocated the granting of the right to vote to the colored man."[15] But by 1879, the climate had changed enough in his state that when he advocated the recognition of the rights of Negroes in a speech at Abbeville, he was booed by his white audience.[16]

In this Senate speech from 1890, Hampton is seen supporting the voluntary emigration of blacks to Africa, where they could establish a land for themselves and "carry as missionaries to the dark continent the blessed light of the gospel, together with the arts, the sciences, the civilization, and the government which have made this country the wonder of the world." He goes on to claim that he is not hostile to the Negro, but that there is on both sides "a deep-seated, ineradicable race antagonism," between the white and black races and that segregation would be the best for both races.

NEGRO EMIGRATION[17]

U.S. Senate
January 30, 1890

Mr. President, I have detained the Senate much longer than I desired in dealing with this matter personal to myself; and now dismissing it, I trust forever, I turn willingly to discussion of subjects of far greater interest and importance to the public.

The opinions expressed by myself in regard to the emigration of negroes have been misconstrued in some quarters as advocating the forcible expulsion of these people from the United States. Never for one moment has such a solution of this question occurred to me as desirable or practicable. I recognize as fully as anyone the political rights of colored fellow-citizens, and amongst those rights is that supreme one allowing every citizen of the Union to choose his home. The forcible expulsion of negroes would not only be unlawful, but impolitic, unjust, and cruel. No thoughtful, patriotic man can contemplate such action. I certainly have never contemplated any measure of this character, and none such would meet my approval. But whilst patriotism, wisdom, and an enlarged philanthropy would condemn any proposition looking to that end, it may still be a question whether some feasible plan might not be adopted by which the generous and fostering aid of this great and rich Government could not be extended to such of the colored race as desired to seek a new home where under their own rule they could work out their own destiny free from contact with the white races and from the many obstacles which here check their aspirations for equality and independence. Something Mr. President, is due to these people, if only on the grounds of kindness and benevolence; and whether our obligation to aid them is placed on that score, or on that higher one of gratitude for services rendered. I for one, recognize the full weight of the obligation under which we rest and I would cheerfully do all in my power to secure the enduring welfare of all of them who seek to build up a nationality for their race. I believe that some measure of this character is perfectly feasible, and that it could be carried into effect without endangering any of the industries of the country, without unsettling, in any serious degree, the labor systems, and with infinite and permanent benefit to the best interests of both races concerned.

In discussing the means by which some practical and satisfactory solution of this grave question may be reached, I shall avail myself largely of much valuable information which has recently been laid before the public in several works of striking originality and of profound reflection. The very fact that so many publications touching this subject have recently emanated shows how earnestly public opinion has been attracted to it and with what grave consideration it has been treated by thoughtful and patriotic men of both races. It deserves such consideration from all men of such character, and, as my colleague has well said, this question rises far above all party issues, all angry discussion, all sectional bitterness. It is too great a subject for the display of invective or vituperation, however clothed in rhetorical phrases, and it should be considered on the elevated and broad plane of a catholic patriotism which has for its sole end the prosperity of the whole country and the welfare of all of its citizens. Such, at least, is the spirit in which it shall be approached by myself.

Mr. President, is it desirable that there should be a separation of the races? Let us suppose that there were now in the United States no negroes and that a proposition should be made to import seven millions of them as citizens, clothed with all the rights, the duties, and the responsibilities of citizenship, would there be one white man or woman in this country who would advocate such a measure? The question carries with it its own conclusive answer, and, if this be so, why would it not be equally beneficial to both races if the negro would, of his own free will, leave this land, in which for two centuries he was a slave, to found a nation in some congenial clime, where, under sunny skies, on fertile soil, he could transplant the civilization he has acquired here, teach the truths of Christianity which here alone his race has learned, and prove to the world his capacity for self-government. Then, indeed, would the hard trials to which centuries of slavery have subjected him be amply compensated by his reaping the rich fruits of civilization and of Christianity and by scattering them broadcast among his yet benighted brethren.

I can conceive of no higher destiny for our colored citizens, no motive more alluring than those which would prompt them to carry as missionaries to the dark continent the blessed light of the gospel, together with the arts, the sciences, the civilization, and the government which have made this country the wonder of the world. The negro has patriotism and ambition, and I doubt not that many of the best and ablest of the race would be fired by the desire to carry to the land of their forefathers the blessings of which they have here been the recipients. Many of them have already expressed this desire, and it needs but the aid of our Government to enable them to fulfill it. Thinking, then, as I do, that there is a wide-spread and growing wish among these people to migrate, and believing, as I conscientiously do, that the segregation of the black race would be of ultimate and lasting benefit to both races, I shall lend my aid to any practical and humane measure looking to that end . . .

Every race, save the Caucasian, is and ought to be regarded as alien in the United States, and the Indians, the aborigines, the former owners of this broad land of ours, are now so looked upon and treated. The declared and wise policy of the country is that of exclusion of all alien races, and President Harrison enunciated this policy when he said that "We are clearly under a duty to defend our civilization by excluding alien races whose ultimate assimilation with our people is neither possible nor desirable." This utterance may have been leveled at the Chinese—those unfortunate and misguided victims of confidence in the binding force of a solemn treaty—but it is none the less applicable to the negro, for no one will deny that his "ultimate assimilation with our people is neither possible nor desirable." This being an indisputable fact, should we not consider now, wisely and dispassionately, how we may best find a solution of the grave problem confronting us, the gravest ever presented to a people for solution?

His presence amongst us has been the sole disturbing cause, preventing the realization of the labors and the hopes of our fathers, when they sought to establish "a more perfect union" between the States; and so long as he remains here, occupying, as he always must do, his present amorphous condition, we can never hope to see that perfect union. He has cost this country billions of precious treasure and hundreds of thousands of lives, far more precious than all "the wealth of Ormus and of Inde." Mr. President, it is not hostility to the negro which prompts the desire for his removal from amongst us; it is a deep-seated, ineradicable race antagonism, and it is idle for us to shut our eyes to this fact and to endeavor to conceal it. This feeling exists among the blacks in even a greater degree than it does among the whites. The native African, who knew the white man in his country only by his deeds of cruelty, paints his devils white; and wherever the negro holds sway he excludes jealously all white men from participation in governmental affairs. The means so often resorted to by nations to protect themselves would seem to justify us in applying it in this case, but I do not propose to dwell on this question of race antagonism, for the Senator from Alabama and my colleagues have made it so apparent that it does exist that any farther argument on that point would be superfluous. Philanthropists may deplore it and fanatics deny it, but it has existed from time immemorial, and will undoubtedly continue to do so until the millennium, or perhaps to "the last syllable of recorded time." Be that as it may, we are forced to recognize it as now existing, and it is an important factor in discussing the question under consideration. Many of the wisest statesmen and purest philanthropists of the country, from Jefferson to Lincoln, have advocated the policy of colonization of the blacks on some foreign soil, and President Grant advocated the same policy.

The utterances of these distinguished men have already been quoted in this debate, so that nothing farther than a reference to them is necessary, but I have seen other utterance from a high authority, which should have great weight, at least in one quarter. I do not vouch for its genuineness, and as I prefer to deal with facts rather than with vague newspaper paragraphs, it shall not appear in the *record* if it turns out to be a fabrication. I have seen, as coming from *The Atlanta Constitution*, a widely known paper, the following extract:

> Unless history is a false teacher, it is not possible for two distinct races, not homogenary—that is, which can not assimilate by intermarriage and the mingling of blood—to exist upon terms of political equality under the same government. *One or the other must go to the wall.*

This is signed J.J. Ingalls. Whoever may have said this, it embodies in my judgment a profound truth, expressed in the epigrammatic language so natural to the Senator from Kansas. Not only was the policy of emigration for the blacks urged by the great men whom I have mentioned, but, sir, in the earlier and perhaps better days of the Republic, when political vision was less obscured than at present by party strife, the same policy was urged. In 1825 the Hon. Rufus King, Senator from New York, introduced a resolution in this body, of which the following is an extract:

> The whole of the public land of the United States, with the net proceeds of all future sales thereof, shall constitute and form a fund, which is hereby appropriated; and the faith of the United States is hereby pledged that the said fund is inviolably applied to aid the emancipation of such slaves within any of the United States, and to aid the removal of such slaves and the removal of such free persons of color in any of the said States as by the laws of the States respectively may be allowed to be emancipated to any territory or country without the limits of the United States.

It is unfortunate that there was not sufficient wisdom in the country at that time to adopt the policy proposed by this resolution; but, taught by bitter experience, we may be wise enough now to act in the direction indicated. "Better late than never," and no time can be more opportune than the present, for every day's delay but augments the difficulties and the dangers surrounding its solution. That it will and must be solved, I have no doubt. My prayer, as is that of every patriot, is that its solution may come through peaceful agencies, on terms beneficial to both races interested, and not through a revolution, the horrors of which would shock humanity. Mr. President, the history of Hayti is fresh in our memory with all the ghastly scenes depicted on its dark pages; we want no repetition of such scenes on the free soil of the United States. A conflict of races here, while the result would be far different from that in Hayti, would be full of unspeakable horrors which no tongue could depict, no imagination conceive. God forbid that any such direful calamity should ever occur, and in my opinion the surest means of guarding against such a contingency is to separate the races, leaving the destiny of this country in the hands of the only people who know what liberty is and how to save it; that people before whom all others have gone down; the people of that race which was described by the Senator from Kansas as "the conquering and unconquerable race," and to which "all other races have been its enemies or its victims—the irresistible Caucasian; that race who discovered this land, who wrested it from barbaric savagery, who brought hither the arts and sciences, the civilization, and, above all, the blessed light of Christianity, who "conquered the wilderness and dedicated an empire to freedom." They want no alien race here to frame their laws or to contaminate their blood. Let us keep our land free of all alien races, saying to them, as did the Patriarchs of old, "Let there be no strife, I pray thee, between thee and me. Is not the whole land before thee? Separate thyself, I pray thee, from me." The great Author of creation, when He formed divers races, "determined the bounds of their habitation." Africa is the natural home of the negro, and if our African Americans will carry back to their ancestral land the experience and the civilization they have acquired here they will take with them untold blessings. Should they desire to go we should extend to them the most generous aid, wishing them God-speed on their noble and patriotic mission to found a nation and to redeem a continent from the darkness which has brooded over it for centuries. No nobler work could be accomplished by the most intelligent and best men of the colored race than that of bearing to the land of their forefathers the blessings of civilization and of Christianity, and, in my judgment, by doing this they would confer the greatest benefit, not only on their race, but on ours. Will they respond to the "Macedonian cry" which comes and has come for ages from that benighted land,

> Where Africa's sunny fountains roll down their golden sand?

Will the divine fire of patriotism—love not alone for the land of his fathers, but for this, which has been his enforced and adopted home—move him to devote himself to the service of both? The answer must depend on himself alone, and I have faith sufficient in the wisdom, the intelligence, and the patriotism of our best colored citizens to believe that it will be answered affirmatively.

If any of them wish to emigrate it is our duty to provide comfortable transportation for them, to secure for them pleasant homes, and to furnish them ample means of support for one year at least. I, for one, am willing to do this or aught else to make their venture an assured success. But to secure this success more will be necessary, I think, than is provided for in the bill introduced by my colleague, and whilst I am in full accord with the measure he proposes, I hardly think that the remedy he suggests can meet the requirements of this case, which is not one to be cured by homeopathic treatment. Stronger remedies must be resorted to if we hope to restore the health of the body politic, and we must be prepared to give not only largely of our abounding wealth, but much of earnest consideration, if we hope to bring it to a successful issue. We have not yet sufficient information on which to base intelligent action, and until we do obtain this all action on our part would be premature. Let us ascertain, in the first place, if any negroes are in favor of emigration; if there are, we can then learn what destination they prefer. We must see if a suitable location can be found for them and obtain some approximate estimate of the cost of establishing them in their new home. How these objects can best be accomplished I leave to wiser heads than mine, but until we know how to carry them out we shall be working in the dark.

There should certainly be wisdom enough in the best intellects of the whites and blacks to enable us to arrive at a satisfactory conclusion . . .

It must be remembered, Mr. President, that if the removal of the negro is ever effected it will be done only after the lapse of many years, so that his gradual withdrawal could threaten no serious danger to our labor system. In two fields of labor he would probably linger long, perhaps much longer than elsewhere—those of the cultivation of rice and of sugar—but even in these an efficient substitute may eventually be found. In the production of the great staple—cotton—which has brought such wealth to the country, the withdrawal of his labor would be beneficial to the planters, rather than injurious. By his labor, as he now gives it, the cost of producing cotton is nearly as great as the price it brings, and if the crop were smaller that price would be greatly enhanced. These are some very significant facts going to show how much less valuable is the labor of the negro as a freedman in the cotton fields than it was as a slave. The cotton crop of 1860 amounted to 4,669,770 bales, and the census of that year gave the number of slaves as 3,953,760. Had the institution of slavery existed until the present time it would be a very low estimate to say that the present crop would have reached at least 10,000,000 bales. The last crop, that not yet in the market, is estimated at 7,000,000 of bales, and statistics go to prove that three-fifths of that number have been made by white labor. In other words, though the negro population has nearly doubled in the period mentioned, they made last year only 2,800,000 bales, not much more than half of what they produced in 1860. These figures show the progress which the negro has made as a freedman, working for himself. If white labor can produce 5,000,000 of bales, or near that number, the planter would receive a much higher price for his cotton than he now does, and the general wealth of the country would be augmented in the same proportion. I can not go into detail on this occasion to verify the statistics given, for I am consuming too much of the time of the Senate, and am taxing my strength overmuch, but the subject is worthy of the serious consideration of our white laborers who are seeking the means of profitable employment.

In presenting my views to-day, Mr. President, I have endeavored to do so in a calm, frank, and dispassionate manner, with a sincere desire to show the deep interest I have in the welfare of the blacks as well as of the whites. In every relation which I have borne to the negro I have been a true friend. When he was made free by the fiat of war my voice was the first, in either the North or the South, which advocated the policy of conferring on him, under educational restrictions, the right of suffrage. In my capacity as private citizen, and as governor of South Carolina, I have striven earnestly to protect him in all of his just rights, and I shall ever be ready to do so on this floor. When Rome was threatened by the invasion of her territory by a powerful enemy one of her patriotic sons averted disaster and saved his country. Of him Rome's great poet said: *"Tu maximums ille ile es; unus qui nobis cunctando, restituis rem."* Could I, sir, restrain those evil-doers, those worst enemies of the South, who by violence and outrage bring shame on our boasted civilization, humiliation on our people, and disgrace upon themselves, I should wish no higher tribute than that given to the Roman patriot. As it is, I can only labor in my humble way to bring about a better state of things, and in all that I have said to-day I have been actuated by the earnest wish to promote the best interests of all our citizens, of both races, and to aid, as far as lies in my power, to secure to our country the blessings of prosperity and of perpetual peace under "that more perfect union" of the free States of this great Republic contemplated by our fathers.

JAMES MATHEWS GRIGGS

James M. Griggs was born in LaGrange, Georgia, on March 29, 1861. After attending the common schools in Georgia, he graduated from Peabody Normal College in Nashville, Tennessee, in 1881. For the next two years, he taught school and studied law. In 1883 he was admitted to the bar and began to practice law in Alapaha, Georgia. He moved to Dawson, where he served in various legal positions, including solicitor general and judge of the Pataula judicial circuit. In 1896 he was elected to Congress where he remained until his death in Dawson on January 5, 1910. As a member of the Congressional committee on post offices and post roads, Griggs was a strong supporter of extending the rural free mail delivery service and the parcel post system. He chaired the Democratic Party congressional campaign committee in 1902 and 1906. After his death, his constituents in Dawson raised a monument in honor of his work.[18]

Griggs' brief speech in Congress is a representative example of the white southern point of view on race at the turn of the new century. The central story he tells, of the rape of a white woman and the murder of her husband and child by a Negro, was repeated time and again in various guises throughout the South and served as one of the major foundations for the segregation mentality and the defense of lynching in the twentieth century. In an effort to take some of the pressure off of the South and his home state, Griggs also makes it clear that these problems are not just southern problems, but that they occur nationwide; again, a common rhetorical tactic of turn of the century southern orators. Griggs refers to the men who lynched and burned the Negro involved in this case, "Those men were standing for civilization—Anglo-Saxon civilization. They were fighting for the purity and the virtue and the safety of the Southern home. We propose to protect the women of the South. We propose to fight for and to maintain the supremacy of the Anglo-Saxon race. . . . The people of Georgia, the people of all the South, propose in the name of that same great civilization to stand by their traditions, to preserve the integrity of the race and to preserve its control everywhere, under all circumstances, whenever it is threatened from any source." This theme song echoed throughout the South and in the halls of Congress and state legislatures for decades. By 1908, Griggs went even further in his anti-Negro oratory in a Congressional speech, when he boldly asserted, "the utter extermination of a race of people is inexpressibly sad, yet if its existence endangers the welfare of mankind it is fitting that it should be swept away."[19]

WE PROPOSE TO MAINTAIN THE SUPREMACY OF THE ANGLO SAXON RACE IN THE SOUTH[20]

U.S. House of Representatives
February 1, 1900

Mr. Chairman: I had not intended to make any remarks during this debate, but the remarkable performance of the gentleman from North Carolina [Mr. Linney] seems to demand notice from some one of the Southern members against whose States wholesale charges of disorder, mobocracy, and lynchings have been made so recklessly.

I shall not attempt anything now except to reply to some aspersions of that gentleman against the State of Georgia, which I have the honor in part to represent upon this floor. His speech, "pregnant with little learning and much ignorance," affords a spectacle to the people of the United States that must be humiliating to the good people of the State which sends him here. I have no personal quarrel with him for his opinion. He has a right to his opinions, and I have no right to quarrel with him for those opinions. I can see no occasion for the intrusion of this question here but for political effect. If so, Mr. Chairman, when the gentleman knows so well the cause of the great majority of lynchings in the South, it is wholly unjustifiable and utterly without excuse.

I am reminded by it of an occurrence between old Col. Sam Tate, of Tennessee, and Col. Jim Robertson, of Georgia, on the one side, in the old times of railroad building in the South, and a railroad president with whom they were having a controversy in Chattanooga. After spending the entire day in discussion, the matter being finally concluded and the railroad man gone, Robertson turned to Colonel Tate and said, "Colonel, I think he is honest, don't you?" "Yes," said Colonel Tate, "I reckon he is honest, Robertson, but he has the allfiredest notions of honesty of any man I ever saw," [Laughter.] Mr. Chairman, the gentleman from North Carolina may be a good man in his way, but he has the most remarkable ideas of political decency of any gentlemen whom I ever had the pleasure of knowing.

So far as Georgia is concerned, Mr. Chairman, we have no repressive or suppressive laws regarding the ballot. We do not need them. There is manhood suffrage in Georgia. Every man, black or white, rich or poor, educated or illiterate, is entitled to vote, provided he pays $1 poll tax in the year before he offers to vote. So far as the law is concerned, therefore, Georgia stands clear. We do not have the law complained of by the gentleman; we do not need such law; and the Georgia legislature, by an almost unanimous vote, not over six weeks ago, declined to pass any law of that character.

I have no criticism upon those States which need them and have enacted them. They know their necessities and they have the right under the Constitution which our fathers gave us to enact legislation in consonance with that great

instrument to protect the civilization of their States. I have not read the North
Carolina statute complained of, but I presume it must be a good law, as I am
informed that under its provisions the gentleman from North Carolina [Mr. Lin-
ney] will probably be left at home the next election, when he will be free to
enjoy the sweets of circuit court riding among his native hills. [Applause.] He
is more to be pitied than blamed.

I can see no reason for intruding this question but, as charged by the gentleman from North Carolina [Mr. Kluttz], political necessity. The gentleman says
he was once a Democrat, and he talks as if he knows much of the alleged
devious ways of that great party in North Carolina.

Before he makes too many disclosures I want to commend to him, Mr. Chairman, a story I have heard, which was said to have occurred between a preacher
and a lawyer once in Georgia. It is said that this drunken lawyer one Sunday
morning walked into church during the services, and as he was staggering up
the aisle the minister stopped his discourse and said to him in sepulchral tones,
"Sir, I will testify against you in the day of judgment." The lawyer replied,
"That's all right, old man; I have been practicing law twenty years, and it has
been my experience at all times that the damndest rascal was always first to
turn state's evidence." [Laughter and applause.] I hope the gentleman does not
intend to turn state's evidence, Mr. Chairman.

Now, Mr. Chairman, as I said, he is not to be blamed so much as pitied. He
was once a Democrat and is now a Republican.

> God, Thou know'st
> Howe'er they smile and feign and boast,
> What happiness is theirs who fall.

Having seen better days, he loves to talk of them and perhaps enjoys his
performance in that connection. Now, Mr. Chairman, with references to lynchings in Georgia. I shall not deny that we are cursed with occasional lynchings.
I do not believe there is a State in the Union in which Judge Lynch has not at
some time presided. But let me tell you of a case that happened in Georgia last
year. A little family a few miles from the town of Newnan were at supper in
their modest dining room. The father, the young mother, and the baby were
seated at the table. Humble though it was, peace, happiness, and contentment
reigned in that modest home. A monster in human form, an employee on the
farm, crept into that happy little home and with an ax knocked out the brains
of that father, snatched the child from its mother, threw it across the room out
of his way, and then by force accomplished his foul purpose. More than that,
Mr. Chairman, he was afflicted with the most loathsome disease known to human kind. In that room—the husband and father dead and weltering in his own
blood, the infant senseless on the floor—he spent four hours alone with that
poor woman. When, more dead than alive, she at last escaped and gave the

alarm, the people were frenzied with passion, and when they captured him they lynched him. They burned him at the stake.

I do not seek to justify that, but I do say that the man who would condemn those people unqualifiedly under these circumstances has water instead of blood to supply his circulation. [Applause.] Not the limpid water that flows from the mountain streams, Mr. Chairman, but the fetid water found in the cesspools of the cities. [Applause.]

Mr. Chairman, can you blame those people for that? I appeal to you, gentlemen—you fathers, you husbands; to all men, white or black, North or South, East or West—do you blame those people for that burst of human fury? God forbid that there should be any man on this continent who would! Thank God, there is not a man in Georgia who does. Bring it home to yourselves, gentlemen, and answer me in the light of truth.

Mr. Chairman, those men were standing for civilization—Anglo-Saxon civilization. They were fighting for the purity and the virtue and the safety of the Southern home. We propose to protect the women of the South. We propose to fight for and to maintain the supremacy of the Anglo-Saxon race—that race which gentlemen have sought to justify here today in shooting brown men in the Philippines in the name of civilization; that race which is today shooting Boers in South Africa in the name of civilization. The people of Georgia, the people of all the South, propose in the name of that same great civilization to stand by their traditions, to preserve the integrity of the race and to preserve its control everywhere, under all circumstances, whenever it is threatened from any source. [Applause.]

Gentlemen who attack lynching in the South should at the same time attack the crime which most largely incites lynching. I speak only for Georgia, Mr. Chairman. Other gentlemen can and doubtless will speak for the States they represent. Fully five-sixths of the lynchings in Georgia come from this one cause. I deplore the fact, but fact it is.

But the South has no monopoly on lynchings, Mr. Chairman. I have time to call your attention to only a few in widely separated States, not for purposes of recrimination, but I assert that so long as there are lynchings in Illinois, in Indiana, Ohio, and Kansas, in New York, Pennsylvania, and Colorado, the difference between the people of those States and the people of Georgia and the people of Alabama and the people of Mississippi is simply a difference in degree and not in kind.

This editorial in the *Washington Star* seeks to "alter the bearing of the recent lynchings" in Kansas by showing that it was done as a warning to Kansas officials to enforce the law more vigorously in future.

Here is a press dispatch from Dunbar, Pa., of December 19, last year, giving an account of the lynching of a negro for murder.

Here is an account of a Sunday celebration in Carterville, Ill., where seven poor negroes were slain in cold blood for the crime of seeking work, while the gatling-gun quarantine of the governor of the great State threatened against the importation of negro miners into the State was public talk all over the country last year. I have merely to mention Pana, Virden, and Rockford to call to your mind vivid pictures of mob violence.

Three years ago a negro was roasted in Ouray, Colo., for shooting a white girl.

Even in staid old Massachusetts, Mr. Chairman, mobs have in time past defied the law, and once her great Senator [Mr. Hoar] addressed a crowd in Worcester while not a criminal but an officer of the law was making his escape through the back door of the court-house from the infuriated mob. It is useless to multiply words, Mr. Chairman; human passions are the same the world over.

The Anglo-Saxon of New England, while perhaps slower, is as sure as the Anglo-Saxon of the South. I doubt not that if the 600,000 negroes of Georgia were transported to Massachusetts tomorrow and the ravishment of their white women began by the lowest of this alien race there would be two or three solemn and dignified trials. After that the blood of the men who wrested Magna Charta from King John would assert itself and the oaks of Massachusetts' hills and dales would be desecrated with the bodies of the victims of "lynching bees."

I would not have you understand me as presenting here a wholesale indictment against the colored race of the Southern States. As a rule they are peaceful, happy, contented, and law-abiding. They have their churches and their schools and are progressing, I hope, toward a higher civilization. The brutes who suffer at the hands of infuriated mobs are hardly worth a thought from the better classes of either race. It remains, nevertheless, Mr. Chairman, that the people of the South have a hard problem before them.

A distinguished member of this House from a far Northern State—a partisan Republican—said to me on yesterday, "This is your problem, and you have nothing from me but sympathy." I appeal to every Anglo-Saxon within the sound of my voice, I appeal to every white man who believes in his race, wherever he may live, give to us, the people who must solve this problem, at least your sympathy while we labor for its solution with justice to the black man and safety for the white man. [Mr. Griggs concluded amid loud applause.]

NOTES

1. Benjamin R. Tillman, "The Race Issue and Annexation of the Philippines." U.S. Senate, January 29, 1900 (Washington. D.C.: n.p., 1900), 13.

2. Hoke Smith, "Speech at Madison, Georgia," June 29, 1905 (n.p., n.d.), 25.

3. Edward L. Ayers, *The Promise of the New South: Life after Reconstruction* (New York: Oxford University Press, 1992), 137.

4. *Plessy v. Ferguson*, 163 U.S. 537. Dissent by Justice John Marshall Harlan, May 18, 1896. In Otto H. Olsen, *The Thin Disguise: Turning Points in*

Negro History, Plessy v. Ferguson, A Documentary Presentation (New York: Humanities Press, 1967), 117.

5. Howard N. Rabinowitz, *The First New South, 1865–1920* (Arlington Heights, IL: Harlan Davidson, Inc., 1992), 139.

6. Lillian Smith, *Killers of the Dream*, rev. ed. (Garden City, NY: Anchor Books, 1963), 222.

7. C. Vann Woodward, *Origins of the New South 1877–1913* (Baton Rouge: Louisiana State University Press, 1951), 212.

8. Most of this biographical material is taken from John L. Bell, Jr., "Harper, James Clarence," in *Dictionary of North Carolina Biography*, Vol. 3, William S. Powell, ed. (Chapel Hill: University of North Carolina Press, 1988), 38–39.

9. Speech in the U.S. House of Representatives, May 4, 1872. (Washington: F. & J. Rives & Geo. A. Bailey, 1872).

10. This biographical sketch is taken mostly from Francis B. Simkins, "Tillman, Benjamin Ryan," in Dumas Malone, ed., *Dictionary of American Biography*, vol. XVII (New York: Charles Scribner's Sons, 1936), 547–49; Robert M. Burts, "Tillman, Benjamin Ryan," in David C. Roller and Robert W. Twyman, eds., *The Encyclopedia of Southern History* (Baton Rouge: Louisiana State University Press, 1979), 1235; and William J. Cooper, Jr., "Tillman, Benjamin Ryan," in John A. Garraty, ed., *Encyclopedia of American Biography* (New York: Harper & Row, 1974), 1101–02.

11. Tillman's Inaugural Address was delivered on December 4, 1890, in Columbia, SC. I have edited out of the lengthy speech many tedious details of his program and plans for implementation and funding that were relevant only to that audience and time and the issues of the day. *Inaugural Address of B.R. Tillman, Governor of South Carolina* (Columbia, SC: James H. Woodrow, State Printer, 1890).

12. The leading biography of Hampton, and the source for this sketch, is Hampton M. Jarrell, *Wade Hampton and the Negro: The Road Not Taken* (Columbia, SC: University of South Carolina Press, 1949).

13. Joel Williamson, *A Rage for Order: Black/White Relations in the American South Since Emancipation* (New York: Oxford University Press, 1986), 41.

14. Quoted in George B. Tindall, *South Carolina Negroes, 1877–1900* (Baton Rouge: Louisiana State University Press, 1966), 12.

15. Quoted in C. Vann Woodward, *Origins of the New South, 1877–1913* (Baton Rouge: Louisiana State University Press, 1951), 79.

16. Tindall, 39.

17. Wade Hampton, "Negro Emigration." Speech in the U.S. Senate, January 30, 1890 (Washington, D.C.: n.p., 1890).

18. This biographical material comes from *Biographical Directory of the American Congress, 1774–1996* (Alexandria, VA: CQ Staff Directories, Inc., 1997), 1126–27; *The National Cyclopaedia of American Biography*, Vol. XXXVI (New York: James T. White & Company, 1950), 131–32.

19. Speech in U.S. Congress, April 17, 1908; *Congressional Record*, 60th

Congress, 1st session, 4876. Quoted in I.A. Newby, *Jim Crow's Defense: Anti-Negro Thought in America, 1900–1930* (Baton Rouge: Louisiana State University Press, 1965), 189.

20. Speech in the U.S. House of Representatives, February 1, 1900 (Washington, D.C.: n.p., 1900).

FOR FURTHER READING

Cell, John W. *The Highest Stage of White Supremacy: The Origins of Segregation in South Africa and the American South.* New York: Cambridge University Press, 1982.

Hale, Grace Elizabeth. *Making Whiteness: The Culture of Segregation in the South, 1890–1940.* New York: Pantheon Books, 1998.

Johnson, Guion Griffis. "The Ideology of White Supremacy, 1876–1910." In Fletcher Melvin Green, ed., *Essays in Southern History.* Chapel Hill: University of North Carolina Press, 1949, pp. 124–56.

Meier, August. *Negro Thought in America, 1880–1915.* Ann Arbor: University of Michigan Press, 1963.

James Clarence Harper

Biographical Directory of the American Congress, 1774–1949. Washington, D.C.: U.S. Government Printing Office, 1950, p. 1269.

Benjamin Ryan Tillman

Biographical Directory of the American Congress, 1774–1949. Washington, D.C.: U.S. Government Printing Office, 1950, p. 1921.

Clark, E. Culpepper. "Pitchfork Ben Tillman and the Emergence of Southern Demagogery." *Quarterly Journal of Speech* 60 (1983), 423–33.

Dorgan, Howard. " 'Pitchfok Ben' Tillman and the 'Race Problem from a Southern Point of View.' " In Cal M. Logue and Howard Dorgan, eds., *The Oratory of Southern Demagogues.* Baton Rouge: Louisiana State University Press, 1981, pp. 47–65.

Kantrowitz, Stephen. *Ben Tillman and the Reconstruction of White Supremacy.* Chapel Hill: University of North Carolina Press, 2000.

Simkins, Francis Butler. *Pitchfork Ben Tillman: South Carolinian.* Baton Rouge: Louisiana State University Press, 1944.

Tillman, Benjamin R. "The Race Problem." In W. Stuart Towns, *Public Address in the Twentieth Century South: The Evolution of a Region.* Westport, CT: Praeger, 1999, pp. 48–54.

Wade Hampton

Wellman, Manly. *Giant in Gray: A Biography of Wade Hampton of South Carolina*. New York: Scribner's Sons, 1949.

James Mathews Griggs

Who Was Who in American Politics. New York: Hawthorn Books, 1974, p. 279.
Who Was Who in America, Vol. I. Chicago: A.N. Marquis Co., 1942, p. 489.

CHAPTER 2

THE RIVER OF CHANGE: BEGINNING TO QUESTION THE RACIST SYSTEM, 1920s TO 1940s

Despite the ranting and raving of the demagogic leadership of the white South, there began a small trickle of resistance which grew to a river of change by the decade following World War II. At the end of World War I, southern blacks returned home to face severe racial distress. Lynching increased throughout the region. The Ku Klux Klan enjoyed a resurgence of popularity. Not only were there rumors of violence and even of an impending race war, actual racial violence erupted around the nation. In East St. Louis, a July 2, 1917, riot caused the deaths of 39 blacks and 9 whites.[1] A 50-mile radius of Elaine, Arkansas, was the scene of violence on October 1, 1919, in which at least two died.[2] Rosewood, a small, largely black community in central Florida, was destroyed by a riot of rampaging whites in 1923. The worst example was in Greenwood, the prosperous black section of Tulsa, Oklahoma. On May 30–June 1, 1921, approximately three hundred Tulsans were killed in a riot by deputized whites who had been given free rein by the sheriff's department to "go out and kill you some damn niggers."[3]

Economic issues made life in the South almost unbearable for southern blacks. The great migration to northern cities in search of better conditions drained labor from southern plantations. The separate but definitely unequal facilities, especially in education, showed clearly who was on top in the cultural hierarchy of the South, and the blacks' inability to even register to vote so they could make any effort to change the system was stifling. The laws and the Constitution may have outlawed slavery, but the conditions of blacks in the South in the decades between the world wars was not far removed from it.

Additionally, even the so-called white liberals of the South were of no help, for they universally agreed with the system of segregation. They did, however, urge the region to make the facilities truly equal—but still segregated.

During this period, valiant efforts began to challenge the system. The National Association for the Advancement of Colored People (NAACP) was founded in 1910, the Commission on Interracial Cooperation (CIC) was established after World War I, and the Southern Commission for the Study of Lynching spun off from the CIC in 1930. The Fellowship of Reconciliation formed during World War I; the Southern Conference on Human Welfare (1934); the Fellowship of Southern Churchmen (1934); the Southern Conference for Human Welfare (1938); and the Southern Regional Council (1944; a descendent of CIC) were established in a biracial effort to ameliorate the desperate conditions of blacks in the South, as well as to address other issues of human dignity and freedom. Although not hugely successful against the ingrained defense of the status quo so prevalent in the South, these organizations did succeed in moving the idea of racial justice and harmony more into the forefront of white consciousness in the region.

The tactics of resistance during this era were focused largely on the courts and the ballot box. The NAACP, especially, first through the leadership of its chief counsel, Charles Houston, and then under Thurgood Marshall's guidance, took case after case to the court system in an effort to break down Jim Crow restrictions in the South. Gradually, they began to win. First came *Smith v. Allwright* in 1944, which declared the white primary unconstitutional; second was *Sweatt v. Painter*, which in 1950 required the University of Texas to admit a qualified black student to law school; and finally came the biggest victory of all, *Brown v. School Board*, in 1954.

The four speakers included in this chapter were among the giants of the early movement for change. James Weldon Johnson, who led the NAACP for years, was a participant in the Harlem Renaissance, a flowering of black art, literature, drama, and music in the 1920s. A. Philip Randolph, a major figure in the union movement, headed the Brotherhood of Sleeping Car Porters; his influence and advocacy of a March on Washington, DC, in 1941 forced President Roosevelt to take seriously the issue of discrimination in the military and the defense industry during World War II. Thurgood Marshall successfully argued many important cases before the Supreme Court before becoming an Associate Justice himself. W.E.B. Du Bois was an early instigator of collective action among black people, was one of the founders of the NAACP and its long-time editor, and was a lifelong advocate of human rights.

JAMES WELDON JOHNSON

A multitalented leader of black America in the first half of the century, James Weldon Johnson is perhaps best known for his composition "Lift Every Voice and Sing," which he wrote in 1900; by the 1930s it was considered the "Negro National Anthem." Johnson was a poet and novelist who contributed in a major way to twentieth-century African-American literature and life.[4] He was also a diplomat, an editor, a leader in the civil rights quest for black Americans, and an accomplished and renown orator who spoke frequently on civil rights issues.

Johnson was born in Jacksonville, Florida, on June 17, 1871, and received his undergraduate degree from Atlanta University in 1894. He returned to his hometown where he became principal at Stanton School, which he had attended as a young boy. While at Stanton he read law and was admitted to the Florida Bar in 1898, but in 1902, he and his brother, John Rosamond, moved to New York City where they worked as a song-writing team. After campaigning for Theodore Roosevelt in 1906 and upon Booker T. Washington's recommendation, he was rewarded with an appointment from Roosevelt as U.S. counsel to Venezuela and later Nicaragua. Johnson served in the diplomatic corps until 1913. During this time he published his only novel, *The Autobiography of an Ex-Colored Man*. In 1917, he became a field secretary for the NAACP and worked for some time in the South in a successful attempt to increase the organization's membership. From 1920 to 1930, Johnson served as the first African-American executive secretary of the NAACP and, as such, played a major role in building the organization into a strong national force for the rights of black Americans. Also during this decade he was an active supporter of and participant in the Harlem Renaissance. Johnson published an important anthology, *The Book of American Negro Poetry*, as well as two volumes of spirituals and other works of his own poetry, including *God's Trombones: Seven Sermons in Verse*. From 1930 until his death in 1938, he served as a professor of creative literature and writing at Fisk University. He died in an automobile accident in Maine on June 26, 1938.

In this speech, Johnson focuses on the issue of voting rights for blacks in the South: "I come directly to a condition which exists in that section of our country which we call 'the South,' where millions of American citizens are denied both the right to vote and the privilege of qualifying themselves to vote." Not only does he defend the right to vote for black southerners, he also shows how this process of perpetuating white supremacy results in making "the South a section not only in which Negroes are denied the right to vote, but one in which white men dare not express their honest political opinions." He goes on to assert the "actual and total result of this practice has been not only the disfranchisement of the Negro but the disfranchisement of the white man." He challenges the South and the nation with a clear and ringing statement of the demands of his race: "The Negro in the matter of the ballot demands only that he should be given the right as an American citizen to vote under the identical qualifications required of other citizens. He cares not how high those qualifications are made—whether they include the ability to read and write, or the possession of five hundred dollars, or a knowledge of the Einstein Theory—just so long as these qualifications are impartially demanded of white men and black men." Leadership of the Civil Rights Movement of the 1950s and 1960s made the same argument, but it was not until the passage of the Voting Rights Act in 1965 that their goal was achieved.

OUR DEMOCRACY AND THE BALLOT[5]

New York City
March 10, 1923

Ladies and Gentlemen:

For some time since I have had growing apprehensions about any subject—especially the subject of a speech—that contained the word "democracy." The word "democracy" carries so many awe-inspiring implications. As the key-word of the subject of an address it may be the presage of an outpour of altitudinous and platitudinous expressions regarding "the most free and glorious government of the most free and glorious people that the world has ever seen." On the other hand, it may hold up its sleeve, if you will permit such a figure, a display of abstruse and recondite theorizations or hypotheses of democracy as a system of government. In choosing between either of these evils it is difficult to decide which is the lesser.

Indeed, the wording of my subject gave me somewhat more concern than the speech. I am not sure that it contains the slightest idea of what I shall attempt to say; but if the wording of my subject is loose it only places upon me greater reason for being more specific and definite in what I shall say. This I shall endeavor to do; at the same time, however, without being so confident or so cocksure as an old preacher I used to listen to on sundry Sundays when I taught school one summer down in the backwoods of Georgia, sometimes to my edification and often to my amazement.

On one particular Sunday, after taking a rather cryptic text, he took off his spectacles and laid them on the pulpit, closed the Bible with a bang, and said,

"Brothers and sisters, this morning I intend to explain the unexplainable, to find out the indefinable, to ponder over the imponderable, and to unscrew the inscrutable."

OUR DEMOCRACY AND THE BALLOT

It is one of the commonplaces of American thought that we have a democracy based upon the free will of the governed. The popular idea of the strength of this democracy is that it is founded upon the fact that every American citizen, through the ballot, is a ruler in his own right; that every citizen of age and outside of jail or the insane asylum has the undisputed right to determine through his vote by what laws he shall be governed and by whom these laws shall be enforced.

I could be cynical or flippant and illustrate in how many ways this popular idea is a fiction, but it is not my purpose to deal in *cleverisms*. I wish to bring to your attention seriously a situation, a condition, which not only runs counter to the popular conception of democracy in America but which runs counter to the fundamental law upon which that democracy rests and which, in addition, is a negation of our principles of government and a menace to our institutions.

Without any waste of words, I come directly to a condition which exists in that section of our country which we call "the South," where millions of American citizens are denied both the right to vote and the privilege of qualifying themselves to vote. I refer to the wholesale disfranchisement of Negro citizens. There is no need at this time of going minutely into the methods employed to bring about this condition or into the reasons given as justification for those methods. Neither am I called upon to give proof of my general statement that millions of Negro citizens in the South are disfranchised. It is no secret. There are the published records of state constitutional conventions in which the whole subject is set forth with brutal frankness. The purpose of these state constitutional conventions is stated over and over again, that purpose being to exclude from the right of franchise the Negro, however literate, and to include the white man, however illiterate.

The press of the South, public men in public utterances, and representatives of those states in Congress, have not only admitted these facts but have boasted of them. And so we have it as an admitted and undisputed fact that there are upwards of four million Negroes in the South who are denied the right to vote but who in any of the great northern, mid-western or western states would be allowed to vote or would at least have the privilege of qualifying themselves to vote.

Now, nothing is further from me than the intention to discuss this question either from an anti-South point of view or from a pro-Negro point of view. It is my intention to put it before you purely as an American question, a question in which is involved the political life of the whole country.

Let us first consider this situation as a violation, not merely a violation but a defiance, of the Constitution of the United States. The Fourteenth and Fifteenth

Amendments to the Constitution taken together express so plainly that a grammar school boy can understand it that the Negro is created a citizen of the United States and that as such he is entitled to all the rights of every other citizen and that those rights, specifically among them the right to vote, shall not be denied or abridged by the United States or by any state. This is the expressed meaning of these amendments in spite of all the sophistry and fallacious pretense which have been invoked by the courts to overcome it.

There are some, perhaps even here, who feel that it is no more serious a matter to violate or defy one amendment to the constitution than another. Such persons will have in mind the Eighteenth Amendment. This is true in a strictly legal sense, but any sort of analysis will show that violation of the two Civil War Amendments strikes deeper. As important as the Eighteenth Amendment may be, it is not fundamental; it contains no grant of rights to the citizen nor any requirement of service from him. It is rather a sort of welfare regulation for his personal conduct and for his general moral uplift.

But the two Civil War Amendments are grants of citizenship rights and a guarantee of protection in those rights, and therefore their observation is fundamental and vital not only to the citizen but to the integrity of the government.

We may next consider it as a question of political franchise equality between the states. We need not here go into a list of figures. A few examples will strike the difference:

In the elections of 1920 it took 82,492 votes in Mississippi to elect two senators and eight representatives. In Kansas it took 570,220 votes to elect exactly the same representation. Another illustration from the statistics of the same election shows that one vote in Louisiana has fifteen times the political power of one vote in Kansas.

In the Congressional elections of 1918 the total vote for the ten representatives from the State of Alabama was 62,345 while the total vote for ten representatives in Congress from Minnesota was 299,127, and the total vote in Iowa, which has ten representatives, was 316,377.

In the Presidential election of 1916 the states of Alabama, Arkansas, Georgia, Louisiana, Mississippi, North Carolina, South Carolina, Tennessee, Texas and Virginia cast a total vote for the Presidential candidates of 1,870,209. In Congress these states have a total of 104 representatives and 126 votes in the electoral college.

What becomes of our democracy when such conditions of inequality as these can be brought about through chicanery, the open violation of the law and defiance of the Constitution?

But the question naturally arises, What if there is violation of certain clauses of the Constitution; what if there is an inequality of political power among the states? All this may be justified by necessity.

In fact, the justification is constantly offered. The justification goes back and makes a long story. It is grounded in memories of the Reconstruction period. Although most of those who were actors during that period have long since died, and although there is a new South and a new Negro, the argument is still made that the Negro is ignorant, the Negro is illiterate, the Negro is venal, the Negro is inferior; and, therefore, for the preservation of civilized government in the South, he must be debarred from the polls. This argument does not take into account the fact that the restrictions are not against ignorance, illiteracy and venality, because by the very practices by which intelligent, decent Negroes are debarred, ignorant and illiterate white men are included.

Is this pronounced desire on the part of the South for an enlightened franchise sincere, and what has been the result of these practices during the past forty years? What has been the effect socially, intellectually and politically, on the South? In all three of these vital phases of life the South is, of all sections of the country, at the bottom. Socially, it is that section of the country where public opinion allows it to remain the only spot in the civilized world—no, more than that, we may count in the blackest spots of Africa and the most unfrequented islands of the sea—it is a section where public opinion allows it to remain the only spot on the earth where a human being may be publicly burned at the stake.

And what about its intellectual and political life? As to intellectual life I can do nothing better than quote from Mr. H.L. Mencken, himself a Southerner. In speaking of the intellectual life of the South, Mr. Mencken says:

> It is, indeed, amazing to contemplate so vast a vacuity. One thinks of the interstellar spaces, of the colossal reaches of the now mythical ether. One could throw into the South France, Germany and Italy, and still have room for the British Isles. And yet, for all its size and all its wealth and all the "progress" it babbles of, it is almost as sterile, artistically, intellectually, culturally, as the Sahara Desert. . . . If the whole of the late Confederacy were to be engulfed by a tidal wave tomorrow, the effect on the civilized minority of men in the world would be but little greater than that of a flood on the Yang-tse-kiang. It would be impossible in all history to match so complete a drying-up of a civilization. In all that section there is not a single poet, not a serious historian, not a creditable composer, not a critic good or bad, not a dramatist dead or alive.

In a word, it may be said that this whole section where, at the cost of the defiance of the Constitution, the perversion of law, the stultification of men's consciousness, injustice and violence upon a weaker group, the "purity" of the ballot has been preserved and the right to vote restricted to only lineal survivors of Lothrop Stoddard's mystical Nordic supermen—that intellectually it is dead and politically it is rotten.

If this experiment in super-democracy had resulted in one one-hundredth of what was promised, there might be justification for it, but the result has been to make the South a section not only in which Negroes are denied the right to vote, but one in which white men dare not express their honest political opinions. Talk about political corruption through the buying of votes, here is political corruption which makes a white man fear to express a divergent political opinion. The actual and total result of this practice has been not only the disfranchisement of the Negro but the disfranchisement of the white man. The figures which I quoted a few moments ago prove that not only Negroes are denied the right to vote but that white men fail to exercise it; and the latter condition is directly dependent upon the former.

The whole condition is intolerable and should be abolished. It has failed to justify itself even upon the grounds which it is claimed made it necessary. Its results and its tendencies make it more dangerous and more damaging than anything which might result from an ignorant and illiterate electorate. How this iniquity might be abolished is, however, another story.

I said that I did not intend to present this subject either as anti-South or pro-Negro, and I repeat that I have not wished to speak with anything that approached bitterness toward the South. Indeed, I consider the condition of the South unfortunate, more than unfortunate. The South is in a state of superstition which makes it see ghosts and bogymen, ghosts which are the creation of its own mental processes.

With a free vote in the South the specter of Negro domination would vanish into thin air. There would naturally follow a breaking up of the South into two parties. There would be political light, political discussion, the right to differences of opinion, and the Negro vote would naturally divide itself. No other procedure would be probable. The idea of a solid party, a minority party at that, is inconceivable.

But perhaps the South will not see the light. Then, I believe, in the interest of the whole country, steps should be taken to compel compliance with the Constitution, and that should be done through the enforcement of the Fourteenth Amendment, which calls for a reduction in representation in proportion to the number of citizens in any state denied the right to vote.

And now I cannot sit down after all without saying one word for the group of which I am a member.

The Negro in the matter of the ballot demands only that he should be given the right as an American citizen to vote under the identical qualifications required of other citizens. He cares not how high those qualifications are made—whether they include the ability to read and write, or the possession of five hundred dollars, or a knowledge of the Einstein Theory—just so long as these qualifications are impartially demanded of white men and black men.

In this controversy over which has been waged battles of words and battles of blood, where does the Negro himself stand?

The Negro in the matter of the ballot demands only that he be given his right as an American citizen. He is justified in making this demand because of his undoubted Americanism, an Americanism which began when he first set foot on the shores of this country more than three hundred years ago, antedating even the Pilgrim Fathers; an Americanism which has woven him into the woof

and warp of the country and which has impelled him to play his part in every
war in which the country has been engaged, from the Revolution down to the
late World War.

Through his whole history in this country he has worked with patience, and
in spite of discouragement he has never turned his back on the light. Whatever
may be his shortcomings, however slow may have been his progress, however
disappointing may have been his achievements, he has never consciously sought
the backward path. He has always kept his face to the light and continued to
struggle forward and upward in spite of obstacles, making his humble contributions to the common prosperity and glory of our land. And it is his land.
With conscious pride the Negro can say:

> This land is ours by right of birth,
>   This land is ours by right of toil;
> We helped to turn its virgin earth,
>   Our sweat is in its fruitful soil.
>
> Where once the tangled forest stood,—
>   Where flourished once rank week and thorn,—
> Behold the path-traced, peaceful wood,
>   The cotton white, the yellow corn.
>
> To gain these fruits that have been earned,
>   To hold these fields that have been won,
> Our arms have strained, our backs have burned
>   Bent bare beneath a ruthless sun.
>
> That banner which is now the type
>   Of victory on field and flood—
> Remember, its first crimson stripe
>   Was dyed by Attucks' willing blood.
>
> And never yet has come the cry—
>   When that fair flag has been assailed—
> For men to do, for men to die,
>   That we have faltered or have failed.

The Negro stands as the supreme test of the civilization, the Christianity and
the common decency of the American people. It is upon the answer demanded
of America today by the Negro that there depends the fulfillment or the failure
of democracy in America. I believe that that answer will be the right and just
answer. I believe that the spirit in which American democracy was founded,
though often turned aside and often thwarted, can never be defeated or destroyed
but that ultimately it will triumph.

If American democracy cannot stand the test of giving to any citizen who
measures up to the qualifications required of others the full rights and privileges

of American citizenship, then we had just as well abandon that democracy in name as in deed. If the Constitution of the United States cannot extend the arm of protection around the weakest and humblest of American citizens as around the strongest and proudest, then it is not worth the paper it is written on.

A. PHILIP RANDOLPH

Asa Philip Randolph was one of the true giants of the quest for equality and freedom in America.[6] Born in Crescent City, Florida, on April 15, 1889, he was encouraged by his father to go into the ministry, but he was more inspired to seek a position from which he could fight for the rights of black Americans. He moved to New York as a young man and while attending City College of New York quickly became involved in labor issues. He published a magazine, *The Messenger*, which took a radical stance opposing U.S. involvement in World War I, supported rights for black Americans, and provided an outlet for various writers and poets of the Harlem Renaissance. In 1925, Randolph took over the effort to organize the sleeping-car porters on America's railroads. The Pullman Company had resisted every effort to unionize the porters, and they continued to resist Randolph's efforts for a decade, finally giving in to his demands in 1935 and allowing the Brotherhood of Sleeping Car Porters to organize the country's first black union. Randolph remained active in the labor movement, as he founded the Negro American Labor Council and served as the first black vice president of the AFL-CIO, the most powerful and largest federation of unions in the nation.

In 1940 on the verge of World War II, Randolph took on the federal government with a protest campaign against discrimination and segregation in the armed services and the nation's defense plants. He challenged President Franklin Roosevelt on the issue, but the president refused to take decisive action. Randolph continued to plan the march, first calling for 10,000 blacks to march on the city, then gradually increasing the numbers to 100,000. Roosevelt, his wife, Eleanor, and others in the president's administration tried to talk Randolph out of the march, but he continued to pursue it. Finally, on July 25, 1941, Roosevelt signed Executive Order 8802, which banned discrimination in the defense industry and established the Fair Employment Practices Committee. As a result, Randolph cancelled the march over widespread protests from other black leaders who thought he had sold out to the Roosevelt Administration.

During the Civil Rights Movement of the 1950s and 1960s, Randolph was eclipsed and bypassed by younger and more militant leadership, but he still remained a well-respected figure for other civil rights activists. He was a moving force behind the August 28, 1963, march on Washington. He and Bayard Rustin planned and organized the march, gaining the support of a large coterie of national labor, civil rights, and religious organizations to participate in the march.

Due to age and poor health, Randolph resigned as president of the Brotherhood of Sleeping Car Porters in 1968 and he died in New York City on May 16, 1979.

Randolph initiated the "March on Washington Movement" organization to carry on the work and support the ideals raised by the aborted 1941 march. On September 26, 1942, the Policy Conference of the group, meeting in Detroit, heard the speech published here.[7] "Thus our feet are set in the path toward equality," Randolph said, "economic, political and social and racial" equality. He was even more specific: "But our nearer goals include the abolition of discrimination, segregation, and Jim-Crow in the Government, the Army, Navy, Air Corps, U.S. Marines, Coast Guard, Women's Auxiliary Army Corps and the Waves, and defense industries; the elimination of discriminations in hotels, restaurants, on public transportation conveyances, in educational, recreational, cultural, and amusement and entertainment places such as theatres, beaches, and so forth." This 1942 speech clearly defined an agenda for the 1950s and 1960s Civil Rights Movement.

MARCH ON WASHINGTON ADDRESS

Detroit, Michigan
September 26, 1942

FELLOW MARCHERS AND DELEGATES TO THE POLICY CONFERENCE OF THE MARCH ON WASHINGTON MOVEMENT AND FRIENDS:

We have met at an hour when the sinister shadows of war are lengthening and becoming more threatening. As one of the sections of the oppressed darker races, and representing a part of the exploited millions of the workers of the world, we are deeply concerned that the totalitarian legions of Hitler, Hirohito, and Mussolini do not batter the last bastions of democracy. We know that our fate is tied up with the fate of the democratic way of life. And so, out of the depth of our hearts, a cry goes up for the triumph of the United Nations. But we would not be honest with ourselves were we to stop with a call for a victory of arms alone. We know this is not enough. We fight that the democratic faiths, values, heritages and ideals may prevail.

Unless this war sounds the death knell to the old Anglo-American empire systems, the hapless story of which is one of exploitation for the profit and power of a monopoly capitalist economy, it will have been fought in vain. Our aim then must not only be to defeat Nazism, fascism, and militarism on the battlefield but to win the peace, for democracy, for freedom and the Brotherhood of Man without regard to his pigmentation, land of his birth or the God of his fathers. . . .

When this war ends, the people want something more than the dispersal of equality and power among individual citizens in a liberal, political democratic system. They demand with striking comparability the dispersal of equality and power among the citizen-workers in an economic democracy that will make certain the assurance of the good life—the more abundant life—in a warless world.

But, withal, this condition of freedom, equality and democracy is not the gift of the gods. It is the task of men, yes, men, brave men, honest men, determined men. . . .

Thus our feet are set in the path toward equality—economic, political and social and racial. Equality is the heart and essence of democracy, freedom and justice. Without equality of opportunity in industry, in labor unions, schools and colleges, government, politics and before the law, without equality in social relations and in all phases of human endeavor, the Negro is certain to be consigned to an inferior status. There must be no dual standards of justice, no dual rights privileges, duties or responsibilities of citizenship. No dual forms of freedom. . . .

But our nearer goals include the abolition of discrimination, segregation, and Jim-Crow in the Government, the Army, Navy, Air Corps, U.S. Marines, Coast Guard, Women's Auxiliary Army Corps and the Waves, and defense industries; the elimination of discriminations in hotels, restaurants, on public transportation conveyances, in educational, recreational, cultural, and amusement and entertainment places such as theatres, beaches, and so forth.

We want the full works of citizenship with no reservations. We will accept nothing less.

But goals must be achieved. They are not secured because it is just and right that they be possessed by Negro or white people. Slavery was not abolished because it was bad and unjust. It was abolished because men fought, bled and died on the battlefield.

Therefore, if Negroes secure their goals, immediate and remote, they must win them and to win them they must fight, sacrifice, suffer, go to jail and, if need be, die for them. These rights will not be given. They must be taken.

Democracy was fought for and taken from political royalists—the kings. Industrial democracy, the rights of the workers to organize and designate the representatives of their own choosing to bargain collectively is being won and taken from the economic royalists—big business.

Now the realization of goals and rights by a nation, race or class requires belief in and loyalty to principles and policies. . . . Policies rest upon principles. Concretely a policy sets forth one's position on vital public questions such as political affiliations, religious alliances. The March on Washington Movement must be opposed to partisan political commitments, religious or denominational alliances. We cannot sup with the Communists, for they rule or ruin any movement. This is their policy. Our policy must be to shun them. This does not mean that Negro Communists may not join the March on Washington Movement.

As to the composition of our movement: Our policy is that it be all-Negro, and pro-Negro, but not anti-white, or anti-Semitic, or anti-labor, or anti-Catholic. The reason for this policy is that all oppressed people must assume the responsibility and take the initiative to free themselves. Jews must wage their battle to abolish anti-Semitism. Catholics must wage their battle to abolish anti-Catholicism. The workers must wage their battle to advance and protect their interests and rights.

But this does not mean that because Jews must take the responsibility and initiative to solve their own problems that they should not seek the cooperation and support of Gentiles, or that Catholics should not seek the support of Negroes, or that the workers should not attempt to enlist the backing of Jews, Catholics, and Negroes in their fight to win a strike; but the main reliance must be upon the workers themselves. By the same token because Negroes build an all-Negro movement such as the March, it does not follow that our movement should not call for the collaboration of Jews, Catholics, trade unions and white liberals to help restore the President's Fair Employment Practice Committee to its original status of independence, with responsibility to the President. That was done. William Green, President of the AF of L, and Philip Murray, President of CIO, were called upon to send telegrams to the President to restore the Committee to its independence. Both responded. Their cooperation had its effects. Workers have formed citizens committees to back them while on strike, but this does not mean that they take those citizens into their unions as members. No, not at all.

And while the March on Washington Movement may find it advisable to form a citizens committee of friendly white citizens to give moral support to a fight against the poll tax or white primaries, it does not imply that these white citizens or citizens of any racial group should be taken into the March on Washington Movement as members. The essential value of an all-Negro movement such as the March on Washington is that it helps to create faith by Negroes in Negroes. It develops a sense of self-reliance with Negroes depending on Negroes in vital matters. It helps to break down the slave psychology and inferiority complex in Negroes which comes and is nourished with Negroes relying on white people for direction and support. This inevitably happens in mixed organizations that are supposed to be in the interest of the Negro. . . .

Therefore, while the March on Washington Movement is interested in the general problems of every community and will lend its aid to help solve them, it has as its major interest and task the liberation of the Negro people, and this is sound social economy. It is in conformity with the principle of the division of labor. No organization can do everything. Every organization can do something, and each organization is charged with the social responsibility to do that which it can do, it is built to do.

I have given quite some time to the discussion of this question of organizational structure and function and composition, because the March on Washington Movement is a mass movement of Negroes which is being built to achieve a definite objective, and is a departure from the usual pattern of Negro efforts and thinking. As a rule, Negroes do not choose to be to themselves in anything, they are only to themselves as a result of compulsive segregation. Negroes are together voluntarily for the same reason worker[s] join voluntarily into a trade union. But because workers only join trade unions, does not mean that the very same workers may not join organizations composed of some non-workers, such as art museums or churches or fraternal lodges that have varying purposes. This same thing is true of Negroes. Because Negroes only can join the March on Washington Movement, does not indicate that Negroes in the MOWM may not join an interracial golf club or church or Elks Lodge or debating society or trade union.

No one would claim that a society of Filipinos is undemocratic because it does not take in Japanese members, or that Catholics are anti-Jewish because the Jesuits won't accept Jews as members or that trade unions are illiberal because they deny membership to employers. Neither is the March on Washington Movement undemocratic because it confines its members to Negroes. Now this reasoning would not apply to a public school or a Pullman Car because these agencies are public in nature and provide a service which is necessary to all of the people of a community.

Now, the question of policy which I have been discussing involves, for example, the March on Washington Movement's position on the war. We say that the Negro must fight for his democratic rights now, for after the war it may be too late. This is our policy on the Negro and the war. But this policy raises the question of method, programs, strategy, and tactics; namely, how is this to be done? It is not sufficient to say that Negroes must fight for their rights now, during the war. Some methods must be devised, programs set up, and strategy outlined.

This Policy Conference is designed to do this very thing. The first requirement to executing the policies of the March on Washington Movement is to have something to execute them with. This brings me to the consideration of organization. Organization supplies the power. The formulation of policies and the planning process furnish direction. Now there is organization and organization. Some people say, for instance, Negroes are already organized and they cite The Sisters of the Mysterious Ten, The Sons and Daughters of I Will Arise, the Holy Rollers, the social clubs, and so forth. But these organizations are concerned about the individual interest of helping the sick and funeralizing the dead or providing amusement and recreation. They deal with no social or racial problem which concerns the entire people. The Negro people as a whole is not interested in whether Miss A. plays Contract Bridge on Friday or not, or whether the deacon of the Methodist Church has a 200 or 500 dollar casket when he dies. These are personal questions. But the Negro race is concerned about Negroes being refused jobs in defense plants, or whether a Negro can purchase a lower in a Pullman Car, or whether the U.S. Treasury segregates Negro girls. Thus, while it is true Negroes are highly organized, the organizations are not built to deal with and manipulate the mechanics of power. Nobody cares how many Whist Clubs or churches or secret lodges Negroes establish because they are not compulsive or coercive. They don't seek to transform the socio-economic racial milieu. They accept and do not challenge conditions with an action program.

Hence, it is apparent that the Negro needs more than organization. He needs mass organization with an action program, aggressive, bold and challenging in spirit. Such a movement is our March on Washington.

Our first job then is actually to organize millions of Negroes, and build them into block systems with captains so that they may be summoned to action overnight and thrown into physical motion. Without this type of organization, Negroes will never develop mass power which is the most effective weapon a minority people can wield. Witness the strategy and maneuver of the people of India with mass civil disobedience and non-cooperation and the marches to the sea to make salt. It may be said that the Indian people have not won their freedom. This is so, but they will win it. The central principle of the struggle of oppressed minorities like the Negro, labor, Jews, and others is not only to develop mass demonstration maneuvers, but to repeat and continue them. The workers don't picket firms today and quit. They don't strike today and fold up. They practice the principle of repetition. . . .

We must develop huge demonstrations because the world is used to big dramatic affairs. . . . Besides, the unusual attracts. We must develop a series of marches of Negroes at a given time in a hundred or more cities throughout the country, or stage a big march of a hundred thousand Negroes on Washington to put our cause into the main stream of public opinion and focus the attention of world interests. This is why India is in the news.

Therefore, our program is in part as follows:

1. A national conference for the integration and expression of the collective mind and will of the Negro masses.

2. The mobilization and proclamation of a nationwide series of mass marches on the City Halls and City Councils to awaken the Negro masses and center public attention upon the grievances and goals of the Negro people and serve as training and discipline of the Negro masses for the more strenuous struggle of a March on Washington, if, as, and when an affirmative decision is made thereon by the Negro masses of the country through our national conference.

3. A march on Washington as an evidence to white America that black America is on the march for its rights and means business.

4. The picketing of the White House following the March on Washington and maintain the said picket line until the country and the world rec-

ognize the Negro has come of age and will sacrifice his all to be counted as men, free men.

This program is drastic and exacting. It will test our best mettle and stamina and courage. Let me warn you that in these times of storm and stress, this program will be opposed. Our Movement therefore must be well-knit together. It must have moral and spiritual vision, understanding and wisdom.

How can we achieve this?

Our Movement must be blueprinted. Our forces must be marshaled with block captains to provide immediate and constant contact. Our block captains must hold periodic meetings for their blocks to develop initiative and the capacity to make decisions and move in relation to direction from the central organization of the Division.

Our educational program must be developed around the struggle of the Negro masses.

This can be done by developing mass plans to secure mass registration of the Negro people for the primaries and elections. Through this program the Negro masses can be given a practical and pragmatic view of the mechanics and function of our government and the significance of mass political pressure.

Plans should be mapped by the various divisions to fight for Negro integration in the public utilities as motormen and conductors. During the war women may be placed on these jobs. We must make a drive now to see to it that Negro men and women receive their appropriate consideration in every important field of American industry from which Negroes are now generally barred.

Our day-to-day exercise of our civil rights is a constant challenge. In theatres, hotels, restaurants, amusement places, even in the North now there is discrimination against Negroes. This is true in every large city. Negroes have the moral obligation to demand the right to enjoy and make use of their civil and political privileges. If we don't, we will lose the will to fight for our citizenship rights, and the public will consider that we don't want them and should not have them. This fight to break down these barriers in every city should be carefully and painstakingly organized. By fighting for these civil rights the Negro masses will be disciplined in struggle. Some of us will be put in jail and court battles may ensue, but this will give the Negro masses a sense of their importance and value as citizens and as fighters in the Negro liberation movement and the cause for democracy as a whole. It will make white people in high places and the ordinary white man understand that Negroes have rights that they are bound to respect.

The giant public protest meetings must continue. They are educative and give moral strength to our movement and the Negro masses.

For this task we need men and women who will dedicate and consecrate their life, spirit, mind, and soul to the great adventure of Negro freedom and justice.

Our divisions must serve as Negro mass parliaments where the entire community may debate the day-to-day issues such as police brutality, high rents, and other questions and make judgments and take action in the interest of the community. These divisions should hold meetings at least twice a month. In them every Negro should be made to feel his importance as a factor in the Negro liberation movement. We must have every Negro realize his leadership ability, the educated and uneducated, the poor and wealthy. In the March on Washington Movement the highest is as low as the lowest and the lowest is as high as the highest. Numbers in mass formation is our key, directed, of course, by the collective intelligence of the people.

Let us put our weight behind the fight to abolish the poll tax. This will give the black and white workers of the South new hope. But the Negro people are not the only oppressed section of mankind. India is now waging a world shaking, history making fight for independence. India's fight is the Negro's fight.

Now, let us be unafraid. We are fighting for big stakes. Our stakes are liberty, justice, and democracy. Every Negro should hang his head in shame who fails to do his part now for freedom. This is the hour of the Negro. It is the hour of the common man. May we rise to the challenge to struggle for our rights. Come what will or may, let us never falter.

THURGOOD MARSHALL

Thought of by many as perhaps the "most important lawyer of the twentieth century,"[8] Thurgood Marshall led the legal attack on the bastions of segregation. The future associate justice of the U.S. Supreme Court was born in segregated Baltimore on July 2, 1908. He graduated from Lincoln University in Pennsylvania in 1930, then from Howard University Law School three years later. After practicing law in his home town for a short period, he joined the NAACP as assistant special counsel in 1936. When the NAACP Legal Defense and Educational Fund was established in 1940, Marshall was selected to be its director. From that post, he won twenty-nine of the thirty-two cases he argued before the Supreme Court, including the key landmark in the struggle: *Brown v. Board of Education*. During the late 1940s and early 1950s, Marshall's impeccable reasoning and thoroughly supported and documented arguments, which were presented in a conversational manner, won virtually all of the major decisions that were breaking down the walls of segregation. These decisions included *Smith v. Allwright* (1944), *Morgan v. Virginia* (1946), *Shelley v. Kraemer* (1948), *Sweatt v. Painter* (1950), and *McLaurin v. Oklahoma State Regents* (1950).

Marshall was involved in the Autherine Lucy attempt to enter the University of Alabama in 1955 and successfully appealed to the Supreme Court for an order to enroll her. He was with her on the campus on February 6, 1956, when she was attacked by a mob. She was suspended, but Marshall obtained a federal court order to reinstate her. The trustees later expelled her from the university, and she withdrew her case. While the counsel for the "Little Rock Nine" who desegregated Central High School in 1957, Marshall won several appeals to the Supreme Court in that celebrated case.

During the Civil Rights Movement, Marshall opposed the confrontational tactics of the marchers and protesters across the South, believing that the more lasting victories would come from the courts. He did, however, defend many of the protesters in court, including those who participated in the sit-ins and the Freedom Rides, and he aided in the suit regarding the Montgomery Bus Boycott that resulted in the Supreme Court decision that held that segregated seating in local transportation was unconstitutional.

In 1961, President Kennedy appointed Marshall a judge on the Federal Second Circuit Court of Appeals. President Johnson selected him to be U.S. solicitor-general four years later and in 1967, appointed him the first African-American associate justice of the U.S. Supreme Court, a position he held until he retired in 1991. Justice Marshall died on June 24, 1993.

THE LEGAL ATTACK TO SECURE CIVIL RIGHTS[9]

NAACP Wartime Conference
1944

On last night we heard a clear statement of some of the problems facing us today. My job tonight is to point out a part of the general program to secure full citizenship rights.

The struggle for full citizenship rights can be speeded by enforcement of existing statutory provisions protecting our civil rights. The attack on discrimination by use of legal machinery has only scratched the surface. An understanding of the existing statutes protecting our civil rights is necessary if we are to work toward enforcement of these statutes.

The titles "civil rights" and "civil liberties" have grown to include large numbers of subjects, some of which are properly included under these titles and others which should not be included. One legal treatise has defined the subject of civil rights as follows: "In its broadest sense, the term *civil rights* includes those rights which are the outgrowth of civilization, the existence and exercise of which necessarily follow from the rights that repose in the subjects of a country exercising self government."

The Fourteenth and Fifteenth Amendments to the Constitution are prohibitions against action by the states and state officers violating civil rights. In addition to these provisions of the United States Constitution and a few others, there are several statutes of the United States which also attempt to protect the rights of individual citizens against private persons as well as public officers. Whether these provisions are included under the title of "civil rights" or "civil liberties" or any other subject is more or less unimportant as long as we bear in mind the provisions themselves.

All of the statutes, both federal and state, which protect the individual rights of Americans are important to Negroes as well as other citizens. Many of these provisions, however, are of peculiar significance to Negroes because of the fact that in many instances these statutes are the only protection to which Negroes can look for redress. It should also be pointed out that many officials of both state and federal governments are reluctant to protect the rights of Negroes. It is often difficult to enforce our rights when they are perfectly clear. It is practically impossible to secure enforcement of any of our rights if there is any doubt whatsoever as to whether or not a particular statute applies to the particular state of facts.

As to law enforcement itself, the rule as to most American citizens is that if there is any way possible to prosecute individuals who have willfully interfered with the rights of other individuals such prosecution is attempted. However, when the complaining party is a Negro, the rule is usually to look for any possible grounds for *not* prosecuting. It is therefore imperative that Negroes be thoroughly familiar with the rights guaranteed them by law in order that they may be in a position to insist that all of their fundamental rights as American citizens be protected.

The Thirteenth Amendment to the Constitution, abolishing slavery, the Fourteenth Amendment, prohibiting any action of state officials denying due process or the equal protection of its laws, and the Fifteenth Amendment, prohibiting discrimination by the states in voting, are well-known to all of us. In addition to these provisions of the Constitution, there are the so-called Federal "Civil Rights Statutes" which include several Acts of Congress such as the Civil Rights Act and other statutes which have been amended from time to time and are now grouped together in several sections of the United States Code. The Original Civil Rights Act was passed in Congress in 1866, but was vetoed by President Andrew Johnson the same year. It was, however, passed over the veto. It was reintroduced and passed in 1870 because there was some doubt as to its constitutionality, having been passed before the Fourteenth Amendment was ratified. The second bill has been construed several times and has been held constitutional by the United States Supreme Court, which in one case stated that "the plain objects of these statutes, as of the Constitution which authorized them, was to place the colored race, in respect to civil rights, upon a level with the whites. They made the rights and responsibilities, civil and criminal, of the two races exactly the same" (*Virginia v. Rives*, 100 U.S. 313 [1879]).

The Thirteenth and Fourteenth and Fifteenth Amendments, along with the civil rights statutes, protect the following rights:

1. Slavery is abolished and peonage is punishable as a federal crime. (Thirteenth Amendment.)

2. All persons born or naturalized in the U.S. are citizens and no state shall make or enforce any law abridging their privileges or immunities, or deny them equal protection of the law. (Fourteenth Amendment.)

3. The right of citizens to vote cannot be abridged by the United States or by any state on account of race or color. (Fifteenth Amendment.)

4. All persons within the jurisdiction of the United States shall have the same right to enforce contracts, or sue, be parties, give evidence, and to the full and equal benefit of all laws and proceedings as is enjoyed by white citizens.

5. All persons shall be subject to like punishment, pains, penalties, taxes, licenses, and extractions of every kind, and to no other.

6. All citizens shall have the same right in every state and territory, as is enjoyed by white citizens to inherit, purchase, lease, sell, hold and convey property.

7. Every person who, under color of statutes, custom or usage, subjects any citizen of the United States or person within the jurisdiction thereof to the deprivation of any rights, privileges, or immunities secured by the Constitution and laws is liable in an action at law, suit in equity, or other proper proceedings for redress.

8. Citizens possessing all other qualifications may not be disqualified from jury service in federal or state courts on account of race or color; any officer charged with the duty of selection or summoning of jurors who shall exclude citizens for reasons of race or color shall be guilty of a misdemeanor.

9. A conspiracy of two or more persons to deprive any person or class of persons of any rights guaranteed by Constitution and laws is punishable as a crime and the conspirators are also liable in damages.

Most of these provisions only protect the citizen against wrong-doing by public officials, although the peonage statutes and one or two others protect against wrongs by private persons.

Despite the purposes of these Acts which the United States Supreme Court insisted in 1879 "made the rights and responsibilities, civil and criminal, of the two races exactly the same," the experience of all of us points to the fact that this purpose has not as yet been accomplished. There are several reasons for this. In the first place, in certain sections of this country, especially in the deep South, judges, prosecutors and members of grand and petit juries, have simply refused to follow the letter or spirit of these provisions. Very often it happens that although the judge and prosecutor are anxious to enforce the laws, members of the jury are reluctant to protect the rights of Negroes. A third reason is that many Negroes themselves for one reason or another hesitate to avail themselves of the protection afforded by the United States Constitution and statutes.

These statutes protecting our civil rights in several instances provide for both criminal and civil redress. Some are criminal only and others are for civil action only. Criminal prosecution for violation of the federal statutes can be obtained only through the United States Department of Justice.

Up through and including the administration of Attorney General Homer S. Cummings, Negroes were unable to persuade the U.S. Department of Justice to enforce any of the civil rights statutes where Negroes were the complaining parties. The NAACP and its staff made repeated requests and in many instances filed detailed statements and briefs requesting prosecution for lynch mobs, persons guilty of peonage and other apparent violations of the federal statutes. It was not until the administration of Attorney General Frank Murphy that any substantial efforts were made to enforce the civil rights statutes as they apply to Negroes. Attorney General Murphy established a Civil Rights Section in the Department of Justice.

During the present administration of Attorney General Francis Biddle there have been several instances of prosecution of members of lynch mobs for the first time in the history of the United States Department of Justice. There have also been numerous successful prosecutions of persons guilty of peonage and slavery. However, other cases involving the question of the beating and killing of Negro soldiers by local police officers, the case involving the action of Sheriff Tip Hunter, of Brownsville, Tennessee, who killed at least one Negro citizen and forced several others to leave town, the several cases of refusal to permit qualified Negroes to vote, as well as other cases, have received the attention of the Department of Justice only to the extent of "investigating." Our civil rights as guaranteed by the federal statutes will never become a reality until the U.S. Department of Justice decides that it represents the entire United States and is not required to fear offending any section of the country which believes that it has the God-given right to be above the laws of the United States and the United States Supreme Court.

One interesting example of the apparent failure to enforce the criminal statutes is that although the statute making it a crime to exclude persons from jury service because of race or color was declared unconstitutional by the U.S. Supreme Court in 1879, and is still on the statute books, there have been no prosecutions by the Department of Justice in recent years for the obvious violations of these statutes. The Department of Justice has most certainly on several occasions been put on notice as to these violations by the many cases carried to the Supreme Court by the NAACP and in which cases the Supreme Court has reversed the convictions on the ground that Negroes were systematically excluded from jury service. One wholehearted prosecution of a judge or other official for excluding Negroes from jury service because of their race would do more to make this particular law a reality than dozens of other cases merely reversing the conviction of individual defendants.

There are, however, certain bright spots in the enforcement of the federal statutes. In addition to the lynching and peonage cases handled by the Washington office of the Department of Justice, there have been a few instances of courageous United States Attorneys in such places as Georgia who have vigorously prosecuted police officers who have used the power of their office as a cloak for beating up Negro citizens.

As a result of the recent decision in the Texas Primary Case, it is possible to use an example of criminal prosecution under the civil rights statutes by taking a typical case of the refusal to permit the Negroes to vote in the Democratic Primary elections. Let us see how a prosecution is started: In Waycross, Georgia, for example, we will suppose a Negro elector on July 4, 1944 went to the polls with his tax receipt and demanded to vote in the Democratic Primary. He should, of course, have witnesses with him. Let us also assume that the election officials refused to let him vote solely because of his race or color.

As a matter of law, the election officials violated a federal criminal law and are subject to fine and imprisonment. But how should the voter or the organized Negro citizens, or the local NAACP branch go about trying to get the machinery of criminal justice in motion? Of course, the details of what happens must be put in writing and sworn to by the person who tried to vote and also by his witnesses. Then the matter must be placed before the United States Attorney. This is the *federal* district attorney.

I wonder how many of the delegates here know who is the United States Attorney for their district, or even where his office is. Every branch should know the United States Attorney for that area, even if a delegation goes in just to get acquainted and let him know that we expect him to enforce the civil rights laws with the same vigor as used in enforcing other criminal statutes.

But back to the voting case. The affidavits must be presented to the United States Attorney with a demand that he investigate and place the evidence before the Federal Grand Jury. At the same time copies of the affidavits and statements in the case should be sent to the National Office. We will see that they get to the Attorney General in Washington. I wish that I could guarantee you that the Attorney General would put pressure on local United States Attorneys who seem reluctant to prosecute. At least we can assure you that we will give the Attorney General no rest unless he gets behind these reluctant United States Attorneys throughout the South.

There is no reason why a hundred clear cases of this sort should not be placed before the United States Attorneys and the Attorney General every year until the election officials discover that it is both wiser and safer to follow the United States laws than to violate them. It is up to us to see that these officials of the Department of Justice are called upon to act again and again wherever there are violations of the civil rights statutes. Unfortunately, there are plenty of such cases. It is equally unfortunate that there are not enough individuals and groups presenting these cases and demanding action.

The responsibility for enforcement of the civil provisions of the civil rights statutes rests solely with the individual. In the past we have neglected to make full use of these statutes. Although they have been on the books since 1870, there were very few cases under these statutes until recent years. Whereas in the field of general law there are many, many precedents for all other types of action, there are very few precedents for the protection of civil liberties.

The most important of the civil rights provisions is the one which provides that "every person who, under color of any statute, ordinance, regulation, custom or usage of any state or territory subjects or causes to be subjected any citizen of the United States or person within the jurisdiction thereof to the deprivation of any rights, privileges or immunities secured by the Constitution and laws shall be liable to the party injured in an action at law, suit in equity or other proper proceeding for redress." Under this statute any officer of a state, county or municipality who while acting in an official capacity, denies to any citizen or person within the state any of the rights guaranteed by the Constitution or laws is subject to a civil action. This statute has been used to equalize teachers' salaries and to obtain bus transportation for Negro school children. It can be used to attack *every* form of discrimination against Negroes by public school systems.

The statute has also been used to enjoin municipalities from refusing to permit Negroes to take certain civil service examinations and to attack segregation ordinances of municipalities. It can likewise be used to attack all types of discrimination against Negroes by municipalities as well as by states themselves.

This statute, along with other of the civil rights statutes, can be used to enforce the right to register and vote throughout the country. The threats of many of the bigots in the South to disregard the ruling of the Supreme Court of the United States in the recent Texas Primary decision has not intimidated a single person. The United States Supreme Court remains the highest court in this land. Election officials in states affected by this decision will either let Negroes vote in the Democratic Primaries, or they will be subjected to both criminal and civil prosecution under the civil rights statutes. In every state in the deep South Negroes have this year attempted to vote in the primary elections. Affidavits concerning the refusal to permit them to vote in Alabama, Florida and Georgia have already been sent to the United States Department of Justice. We will insist that these election officials be prosecuted and will also file civil suits against the guilty officials.

It can be seen from these examples that we have just begun to scratch the surface in the fight for full enforcement of these statutes. The NAACP can move no faster than the individuals who have been discriminated against. We only take up cases where we are requested to do so by persons who have been discriminated against.

Another crucial problem is the ever-present problem of segregation. Whereas the principle has been established by cases handled by the NAACP that neither states nor municipalities can pass ordinances segregating residences by race, the growing problem today is the problem of segregation by means of restrictive covenants, whereby private owners band together to prevent Negro occupancy of particular neighborhoods. Although this problem is particularly acute in Chicago, it is at the same time growing in intensity throughout the country. It has the full support of the real estate boards in the several cities, as well as most of the banks and other leading agencies. The legal attack on this problem has met with spotty success. In several instances restrictive covenants have been declared invalid because the neighborhood has changed, or for other reasons. Other cases have been lost. However, the NAACP is in the process of preparing a detailed memorandum and will establish procedure which will lead to an all-out legal attack on restrictive covenants. Whether or not this attack will be successful cannot be determined at this time.

The National Housing Agency and the Federal Public Housing Authority have established a policy of segregation in federal public housing projects. A test case has been filed in Detroit, Michigan, and is still pending in the local federal courts. The Detroit situation is the same as in other sections of the country. Despite the fact that the Housing Authority and other agencies insist that they will maintain separate but equal facilities, it never develops that the separate facilities are equal in all respects. In Detroit separate projects were built and it developed that by the first of this year every single white family in the area eligible for public housing had been accommodated and there were still some 800 "white" units vacant with "no takers." At the same time there were some 45,000 Negroes inadequately housed and with no units open to them. This is the inevitable result of "separate but equal" treatment.

I understand that in Chicago a public housing project to be principally occupied by Negroes is being opposed by other Negroes on the ground that it will depreciate their property. It is almost unbelievable that Negroes would oppose public housing for the same reason used by real estate boards and other interests who are determined to keep Negroes in slum areas so that they may be further exploited. The NAACP is in favor of public housing and works toward that end every day. It will continue to do so despite real estate boards and other selfish interests opposing public housing whether they be white or Negro. The NAACP is, of course, opposed to segregation in public housing and will continue to fight segregation in public housing.

We should also be mindful of the several so-called civil rights statutes in the several states. There are civil rights acts in at least 18 states, all of which are in the North and Middle West. These statutes are in California, Colorado, Connecticut, Illinois, Indiana, Iowa, Kansas, Massachusetts, Michigan, Minnesota, Nebraska, New Jersey, New York, Ohio, Pennsylvania, Rhode Island, and Washington. California provides only for civil action. Illinois, Kansas, Minnesota, New York, and Ohio have both civil and criminal provisions. In New Jersey the only action is a criminal action, or an action for penalty in the name of the state, the amount of the penalty going to the state.

In those states not having civil rights statutes it is necessary that every effort be made to secure passage of one. In states having weak civil rights statutes efforts should be made to have them strengthened. In states with reasonably strong civil rights statutes, like Illinois and New York, it is necessary that every effort be made to enforce them.

The Chicago branch has the record of more successful prosecutions for violation of the local civil rights statute than any other branch of the NAACP. In New York City resort to the enforcement of the criminal provisions has greatly lessened the number of cases. Outside of New York City there are very few successful cases against the civil rights statutes because of the fact that members of the jury are usually reluctant to enforce the statutes. I understand the same is true for Illinois. The only method of counteracting this vicious practice is by means of educating the general public, from which juries are chosen, to the plight of the Negro.

It should also be pointed out that many of our friends of other races are not as loud and vociferous as the enemies of our race. In Northern and Mid-Western cities it repeatedly happens that a prejudiced Southerner on entering a hotel or restaurant, seeing Negroes present makes an immediate and loud protest to the manager. It is very seldom that any of our friends go to the managers of places where Negroes are excluded and complain to them of this fact. Quite a job can be done if our friends of other races will only realize the importance of this problem and get up from their comfortable chairs and actually go to work on the problem.

Thus it seems clear that although it is necessary and vital to all of us that we continue our program for additional legislation to guarantee and enforce certain of our rights, at the same time we must continue with ever-increasing vigor to enforce those few statutes, both federal and state, which are now on the statute books. We must not be delayed by people who say "the time is not ripe," nor should we proceed with caution for fear of destroying the "status quo." Persons who deny to us our civil rights should be brought to justice now. Many people believe the time is always "ripe" to discriminate against Negroes. All right then—the time is always "ripe" to bring them to justice. The responsibility for the enforcement of these statutes rests with every American citizen regardless of race or color. However, the real job has to be done by the Negro population with whatever friends of the other races are willing to join in.

W.E.B. DU BOIS

A giant in the history of black America, W.E.B. Du Bois's contributions to the struggle for freedom and justice span more than half a century. Active in leadership of his race in the last decade of the nineteenth century, Du Bois continued to exert influence and power well into the Civil Rights Movement of the 1960s.[10]

Du Bois was born in Great Barrington, Massachusetts, on February 23, 1868. Before graduating from high school he was a correspondent for two black newspapers. He went to Fisk University in Nashville, Tennessee, where he edited the school newspaper. He received a bachelor's degree from Fisk in 1888. While attending Fisk, Du Bois taught school in a small Tennessee town and was affected by the poor conditions suffered by southern blacks. He received another B.A. (cum laude) from Harvard in 1890, with a M.A. the following year. After studying at the University of Berlin, Du Bois returned to the United States and began his teaching career at Wilberforce University in Ohio. In 1895, he became the first black to receive a Ph.D. from Harvard. After teaching at the University of Pennsylvania, Du Bois moved South and began a career at Atlanta University where he taught from 1897 to 1910.

In 1905, Du Bois organized a group of black leaders who were strong advocates for full political and economic rights for black Americans. This group became known as the "Niagara Movement" after their first meeting place in Fort Erie, Ontario. America's racism proved to be too strong a foe at the time, and Du Bois' group disbanded in 1910. That same year, Du Bois teamed with influential white leadership and founded the NAACP. Du Bois was the director of publications and research and, as such, was the editor of the *Crisis*, the NAACP's official publication. He remained the editor for almost twenty-five years and projected the *Crisis* into a major leading role as an outlet for black concerns and issues. In 1934, after a split with the NAACP official position regarding segregation, Du Bois resigned and returned to Atlanta University as chairman of the department of sociology.

After a series of visits to the Soviet Union and China, Du Bois publicly supported their governments and urged African nations to seek their support. In 1951, due to his support of Communism, the U.S. State Department denied him and his wife travel visas. In 1958 the ban was lifted, and he once again traveled to Africa and the Soviet Union. He joined the Communist Party and moved to the West African nation of Ghana; he became a citizen of Ghana in 1963. Du Bois died in that same year on the eve of the historic March on Washington.

BEHOLD THE LAND[11]

Columbia, South Carolina
October 20, 1946

The future of American Negroes is in the South. Here 327 years ago, they began to enter what is now the United States of America; here they have made their greatest contribution to American culture; and here they have suffered the damnation of slavery, the frustration of reconstruction and the lynching of emancipation. I trust then that an organization like yours is going to regard the South as the battleground of a great crusade. Here is the magnificent climate; here is the fruitful earth under the beauty of the Southern sun; and here, if anywhere on earth, is the need of the thinker, the worker and the dreamer. This is the firing line not simply for the emancipation of the American Negro but for the emancipation of the African Negro and the Negroes of the West Indies; for the emancipation of the colored races; and for the emancipation of the white slaves of modern capitalistic monopoly.

Remember here, too, that you do not stand alone. It may seem like a failing fight when the newspapers ignore you; when every effort is made by white people in the South to count you out of citizenship and to act as though you did not exist as human beings while all the time they are profiting by your labor; gleaning wealth from your sacrifices and trying to build a nation and a civilization upon your degradation. You must remember that despite all this, you have allies and allies even in the white South. First and greatest of these possible allies are the white working classes about you. The poor whites whom you have been taught to despise and who in turn have learned to fear and hate you. This must not deter you from efforts to make them understand, because in the past in their ignorance and suffering they have been led foolishly to look upon you as the cause of most of their distress. You must remember that this attitude is hereditary from slavery and that it has been deliberately cultivated ever since emancipation.

Slowly but surely the working people of the South, white and black, must come to remember that their emancipation depends upon their mutual cooperation; upon their acquaintanceship with each other; upon their friendship; upon their social intermingling. Unless this happens each is going to be made the football to break the heads and hearts of the other.

White youth in the South is peculiarly frustrated. There is not a single great ideal which they can express or aspire to that does not bring them into flat contradiction with the Negro problem. The more they try to escape it, the more they land in hypocrisy, lying and double-dealing; the more they become what they least wish to become, the oppressors and despisers of human beings. Some of them, in larger and larger numbers, are bound to turn toward the truth and to recognize you as brothers and sisters, as fellow travelers toward the dawn.

If now you young people, instead of running away from the battle here in Carolina, Georgia, Alabama, Louisiana and Mississippi, instead of seeking freedom and opportunity in Chicago and New York—which do spell opportunity—nevertheless grit your teeth and make up your minds to fight it out right here if it takes every day of your lives and the lives of your children's children; if you do this, you must in meetings like this ask yourselves what does the fight mean? How can it be carried on? What are the best tools, arms and methods? And where does it lead?

I should be the last to insist that the uplift of mankind never calls for force and death. There are times, as both you and I know, when

T'ho' love repine and reason chafe,
There came a voice without reply,
'Tis man's perdition to be safe
When for truth he ought to die.

At the same time and even more clearly in a day like this, after the millions of mass murders that have been done in the world since 1914, we ought to be the last to believe that force is ever the final word. We cannot escape the clear fact that what is going to win in this world is reason if this ever becomes a reasonable world. The careful reasoning of the human mind backed by the facts of science is the one salvation of man. The world, if it resumes its march toward civilization, cannot ignore reason. This has been the tragedy of the South in the past; it is still its awful and unforgivable sin that it has set its face against reason and against the fact. It tried to build slavery upon freedom; it tried to build tyranny upon democracy; it tried to build mob violence on law and law on lynching.

Nevertheless, reason can and will prevail; but of course it can only prevail with publicity—pitiless, blatant publicity. You have got to make the people of the United States and of the world know what is going on in the South. You have got to use every field of publicity to force the truth into their ears, and before their eyes. You have got to make it impossible for any human being to live in the South and not realize the barbarities that prevail here. You may be condemned for flamboyant methods; for calling a congress like this; for waving your grievances under the noses and in the faces of men. That makes no difference; it is your duty to do it.

There are enormous opportunities here for a new nation, a new economy, a new culture in a South really new and not a mere renewal of an Old South of slavery, monopoly and race hate. There is a chance for a new cooperative agriculture on renewed land owned by the state with capital furnished by the state, mechanized and coordinated with city life. There is a chance for strong, virile trade unions without race discrimination. with high wages, closed shops and decent conditions of work, to beat back and hold in check the swarm of landlords, monopolists and profiteers who are today sucking the blood out of this land. There is a vast field for consumer cooperation, building business on public

service and not on private profit as the mainspring of industry. There is chance
for a broad, sunny, healthy home life, shorn of the fear of mobs and liquor, and
rescued from lying, stealing politicians, who build their deviltry on race prejudice.

Here in this South is the gateway to the colored millions of the West Indies,
Central and South America. Here is the straight path to the greater, freer, truer
world. It would be shame and cowardice to surrender this glorious land and its
opportunities for civilization and humanity to the thugs and lynchers, the mobs
and profiteers, the monopolists and gamblers who today choke its soul and steal
its resources. The oil and sulphur; the coal and iron; the cotton and corn; the
lumber and cattle belong to you the workers, black and white, and not to the
thieves who hold them and use them to enslave you. They can be rescued and
restored to the people if you have the guts to strive for the real right to vote,
the right to real education, the right to happiness and health and the total abolition of the father of these scourges of mankind—*poverty*.

"Behold the beautiful land which the Lord thy God hath given thee." Behold
the land, the rich and resourceful land, from which for 100 years its best elements have been running away, its youth and hope, black and white, scurrying
north because they are afraid of each other, and dare not face a future of equal,
independent, upstanding human beings, in a real and not a sham democracy.

To rescue this land, in this way, calls for the *Great Sacrifice*; this is the thing
you are called upon to do because it is the right thing to do. Because you are
embarked upon a great and holy crusade, the emancipation of mankind, black
and white; the upbuilding of democracy; the breaking down, particularly here
in the South, of forces of evil represented by race prejudice in South Carolina;
by lynching in Georgia; by disfranchisement in Mississippi; by ignorance in
Louisiana; and by all these and monopoly of wealth in the whole South.

There could be no more splendid vocation beckoning to the youth of the
twentieth century, after the flat failures of white civilization, after the flamboyant
establishment of an industrial system which creates poverty and the children of
poverty, which are ignorance and disease and crime; after the crazy boasting of
a white culture that finally ended in wars which ruined civilization in the whole
world; in the midst of allied people who have yelled about democracy and never
practiced it either in the British Empire or in the American Commonwealth or
in South Carolina.

Here is the chance for young men and women of devotion to lift again the
banner of humanity and to walk toward a civilization which will be free and
intelligent; which will be healthy and unafraid: and build in the world a culture
led by black folk and joined by peoples of all colors and races—without poverty,
ignorance and disease!

Once a great German poet cried: *"Selig der den Er in Sieges Glanze findet"*—
"Happy man whom Death shall find in Victory's splendor."

But I know a happier one: he who fights in despair and in defeat still fights.

Singing with Arna Bontemps the quiet, determined philosophy of undefeatable men:

> *I thought I saw an angel flying low,*
> *I thought I saw the flicker of a wing*
> *Above the mulberry trees; but not again,*
> *Bethesda sleeps. This ancient pool that heated*
> *A Host of bearded Jews does not awake.*
> *This pool that once the angels troubled does not move.*
> *No angel stirs it now, no Saviour comes*
> *With healing in His hands to raise the sick*
> *And bid the lame men leap upon the ground.*
> *The golden days are gone. Why do we wait*
> *So long upon the marble steps, blood*
> *Falling from our open wounds? and why*
> *Do our black faces search the empty sky?*
> *Is there something we have forgotten? Some precious thing*
> *We have lost, wandering in strange lands?*
>
> *There was a day, I remember now,*
> *I beat my breast and cried, "Wash me God,*
> *Wash me with a wave of wind upon*
> *The barley; O quiet one, draw near, draw near!*
> *Walk upon the hills with lovely feet*
> *And in the waterfall stand and speak!*

NOTES

1. Elliott Rudwick, *Race Riot at East St. Louis* (Carbondale: Southern Illinois University Press, 1964).

2. O.A. Rogers, Jr., "The Elaine Race Riots of 1919," *Arkansas Historical Quarterly* 19 (summer 1960), 142–50.

3. Brent Staples, "Unearthing a Riot," *The New York Times Magazine* (December 19, 1999), 64–69.

4. This biographical sketch is taken largely from Jerry Ward, "Johnson, James Weldon," in Charles D. Lowery and John F. Marszalek, eds., *Encyclopedia of African-American Civil Rights: From Emancipation to the Present* (Westport, CT: Greenwood Press, 1992), 284–85; and from Eugene Levy, "Johnson, James Weldon," in John A. Garraty and Mark C. Carnes, eds., *American National Biography*, vol. 12 (New York: Oxford University Press, 1999), 89–90.

5. Address delivered at a dinner for Congressman F.H. LaGuardia at the Hotel Pennsylvania in New York City, March 10, 1923. Text in Carter G. Wood-

son, *Negro Orators and Their Orations* (New York: Russell & Russell, 1969), 663–71.

6. Most of this biographical sketch is taken from John D'Emilio, *The Civil Rights Struggle: Leaders in Profile* (New York: Facts on File, 1979), 119–22; and from Isaac Rosen, "A. Philip Randolph," in Barbara Carlisle Bigelow, ed., *Contemporary Black Biography*, vol. 3 (Detroit, MI: Gale Research Inc., 1993), 198–201.

7. "March on Washington Address," Detroit, Michigan, September 26, 1942. See text in Daniel J. O'Neill, ed. and comp., *Speeches by Black Americans* (Encino, CA: Dickenson Publishing Co., 1971), 112–21.

8. Thomas G. Krattenmaker, quoted in Stephen A. Smith, "Thurgood Marshall," in Richard W. Leeman, ed., *African-American Orators: A Bio-Critical Sourcebook* (Westport, CT: Greenwood Press, 1996), 249. This biographical sketch is from this chapter by Smith and from Mark Kram, "Thurgood Marshall," in Michael L. LaBlanc, ed., *Contemporary Black Biography* (Detroit, MI: Gale Research, 1992), 146–149; John D'Emilio, *The Civil Rights Struggle: Leaders in Profile* (New York: Facts on File, 1979), 100–04; and Neil A. Lewis, "Thurgood Marshall: Slave's Great-Grandson Who Used the Law to Lead the Rights Revolution," *The New York Times*, June 28, 1991.

9. Marshall delivered this speech to the NAACP Wartime Conference in 1944. See text in Daniel J. O'Neill, ed. and comp., *Speeches by Black Americans* (Encino, CA: Dickenson Publishing Co., 1971), 122–31.

10. Most of this biographical sketch is from Michael E. Mueller, "W.E.B. Du Bois," in Barbara Carlisle Bigelow, ed., *Contemporary Black Biography*, vol. 3 (Detroit, MI: Gale Research, Inc., 1993), 52–57; and Stacy L. Smith and Martha Solomon Watson, "William Edward Burghardt Du Bois," in Richard W. Leeman, ed., *African-American Orators: A Bio-Critical Sourcebook* (Westport, CT: Greenwood Press, 1996), 98–109.

11. Du Bois delivered this speech in Columbia, South Carolina, on October 20, 1946, at the closing session of the Southern Youth Legislature, a meeting of about one thousand young people. The meeting was sponsored by the Southern Negro Youth Congress, a 1930s and 1940s group whose agenda and tactics were similar to the later Student Nonviolent Coordinating Committee. The closing program was held at Benedict College and Du Bois spoke to an overflow crowd, part of which listened to him over loudspeakers outside the auditorium. See text in *Southern Exposure* IX (spring 1981), 117–19.

FOR FURTHER READING

Kesselman, Louis C. *The Social Politics of FEPC: A Study in Reform Pressure Movements*. Chapel Hill: University of North Carolina Press, 1998.
Sitkoff, Harvard. *A New Deal for Blacks: The Emergence of Civil Rights as a National Issue*. New York: Oxford University Press, 1978.

Tushnet, Mark V. *The NAACP's Legal Strategy Against Segregated Education, 1925–1950*. Chapel Hill: University of North Carolina Press, 1987.

James Weldon Johnson

Johnson, James Weldon. *Along This Way: The Autobiography of James Weldon Johnson*. New York: Viking, 1933; Da Capo, 1973.
Levy, Eugene. *James Weldon Johnson: Black Leader, Black Voice*. Chicago: University of Chicago Press, 1973.
Skinner, Curtis. "Johnson, James Weldon." In Hal May and Susan M. Trosky, eds., *Contemporary Authors*, vol. 125. Detroit, MI: Gale Research, Inc., 1989.

A. Philip Randolph

Amana, Harry, "A. Philip Randolph." In Sam G. Riley, ed., *American Magazine Journalists, 1900–1960, First Series*. Detroit, MI: Gale Publishing, Inc., 1996, pp. 271–85.
Anderson, Jervis. *A. Philip Randolph: A Biographical Portrait*. New York: Harcourt Brace Jovanovich, 1972.
Davis, Daniel S. *Mr. Black Labor: The Story of A. Philip Randolph, Father of the Civil Rights Movement*. New York: Dutton, 1972.
Garfinkel, Herbert. *When Negroes March: The March on Washington Movement in the Organizational Politics for FEPC*. Glencoe, IL: The Free Press, 1959.
Panetta, Edward M. "Asa Philip Randolph." In Richard W. Leeman, ed., *African-American Orators: A Bio-Critical Sourcebook*. Westport, CT: Greenwood Press, 1976, pp. 294–301.
Pfeffer, Paula F. *A. Philip Randolph, Pioneer of the Civil Rights Movement*. Baton Rouge: Louisiana State University Press, 1990.

Thurgood Marshall

Goldman, Roger, and David Gallen. *Thurgood Marshall: Justice for All*. New York: Carroll & Graf Publishers, Inc., 1992.
Tushnet, Mark V. *Making Civil Rights Law: Thurgood Marshall and the Supreme Court, 1936–1961*. New York: Oxford University Press, 1994.
Williams, Juan. *Thurgood Marshall: American Revolutionary*. New York: Times Books, 1998.

W.E.B. Du Bois

Broderick, Francis L. *W.E.B. Du Bois: Negro Leader in a Time of Crisis*. Stanford, CA: Stanford University Press, 1959.

Clarke, John Henrik et al. *Black Titan: W.E.B. Du Bois: An Anthology by the Editors of* Freedomways. Boston: Beacon Press, 1970.

Du Bois, W.E.B. *The Autobiography of W.E.B. Du Bois: A Soliloquy on Viewing My Life from the Last Decade of Its First Century*. New York: International Publishers, 1968.

Lewis, David Levering. *W.E.B. Du Bois: Biography of a Race, 1868–1919*. New York: Henry Holt, 1993.

———. *W.E.B. Du Bois: The Fight for Equality and the American Century, 1919–1963*. New York: Henry Holt, 2000.

Marable, Manning. *W.E.B. Du Bois: Black Radical Democrat*. Boston: Twayne, 1986.

Merriam, Allen H. "William Edward Burghardt Du Bois." In Bernard K. Duffy and Halford R. Ryan, eds., *American Orators of the Twentieth Century: Critical Studies and Sources*. Westport, CT: Greenwood Press, 1987.

Sundquist, Eric J., ed. *The Oxford W.E.B. Du Bois Reader*. New York: Oxford University Press, 1996.

CHAPTER 3

BLACK SOUTHERNERS CHALLENGE THE SYSTEM, THE 1950S: THE MOVEMENT BEGINS

Much had happened in the 1940s to prepare the seed bed for the beginning of the movement in the 1950s. Beginning with the New Deal era of Franklin Roosevelt, the federal government began to touch the lives of private citizens to an unprecedented degree. The national government gradually began to support and respect the basic rights of black Americans. The federal government began to make a difference in the politics of civil rights beginning with Roosevelt's Executive Order 8802 in 1941 that established the Fair Employment Practices Committee; the series of Supreme Court decisions that struck down the white primary, found segregation on interstate bus travel, literacy tests for voting prerequisites, and railroad dining car segregation unconstitutional; and President Harry S. Truman's Executive Order 9808 in 1946 that established the Presidential Committee on Civil Rights.[1]

World War II also marked a departure in the relationships between the races. American propaganda defending the U.S. system of democracy highlighted the racist theories of Hitler and a careful reading of our pronouncements showed clearly that white southerner racism would not be able to withstand scrutiny. Black Americans had fought and died for democracy around the world and many of them came back home to the South determined to create a more democratic environment for their families. The G.I. Bill provided opportunities for former soldiers and sailors to obtain a higher education, and a series of Supreme Court decisions began to open the doors in a token fashion for blacks to enter graduate schools in at least the border states.

The Cold War helped as well as the nation entered the late 1940s and early 1950s. The Soviet Union used racial issues in its propaganda in order to embarrass the United States and to win converts in the newly emerging nations of Africa. Thinking Americans realized that each lynching, each race riot, each publicized case of Jim Crow discrimination was spread far and wide by advocates of Communism. America saw itself locked in a death struggle with the Soviets and these setbacks in the propaganda war could not easily be tolerated.

The increased involvement of the federal government and the rising expectations created by World War II, as well as the scattered successes in higher education and voting rights fueled the revolution that began in earnest in the 1950s. In 1954 came the landmark *Brown v. Board of Education* decision that declared that separate but equal was inherently unequal. Although the *Brown II* decision the next year, telling the South to proceed "with all deliberate speed," was sufficiently ambiguous to provide many opportunities for the region to drag its feet on school desegregation, the process had been set in motion.

In August 1955, Emmett Till, a young black teenager, was brutally murdered in Mississippi for supposedly flirting with a white woman; his highly publicized murder led many blacks around the nation to believe that something had to be done about racism in America. On December 1, 1955, Rosa Parks refused to move to the black section of a city bus in Montgomery, a one-day boycott was called; it lasted for more than a year and thrust a young black minister, Martin Luther King Jr., into the forefront of civil rights leadership. On December 21, 1956, King and other black Montgomery citizens re-entered the city buses and sat where they chose.

The year 1957 proved to be an important one for the Civil Rights Movement. On May 17, the third anniversary of the *Brown* decision, King, A. Philip Randolph, and Roy Wilkins organized a Prayer Pilgrimage in Washington, DC, in support of the Civil Rights Act of 1957, which Congress was deliberating. Among other things, that rally established King as the national spokesman for the movement and provided national visibility for him and his Southern Christian Leadership Conference. King's rich baritone voice urged Congress:

> Give us the ballot and we will no longer plead to the federal government for passage of an anti-lynching law; we will by the

power of our vote write the law on the statute books of the southern states and bring an end to the dastardly acts of the hooded perpetrators of violence.

Give us the ballot and we will transform the salient misdeeds of bloodthirsty mobs into the calculated good deeds of orderly citizens.

Give us the ballot and we will fill our legislative halls with men of good will, and send to the sacred halls of Congress men who will not sign a Southern Manifesto because of their devotion to the manifesto of justice.

Give us the ballot and we will place judges on the benches of the South who will "do justly and love mercy," and we will place at the head of the southern states governors who have felt not only the tang of the human, but the glow of the divine.

Give us the ballot and we will quietly and nonviolently, without rancor or bitterness, implement the Supreme Court's decision of May 17, 1954.

But without the ballot, in September of 1957, the first in a long series of battles over school desegregation erupted in Little Rock, Arkansas, when Governor Orval E. Faubus called out the Arkansas National Guard to protect the public welfare, an act that effectively suspended the integration of Little Rock Central High School. Eventually, and somewhat reluctantly, President Eisenhower intervened and sent troops from the 101st Airborne Division to enforce the school board's plan for integration. A new leader emerged from that conflict, as Daisy Bates, a longtime NAACP official and crusading black journalist from Little Rock, took the lead in mentoring and inspiring the "Little Rock Nine," who were the first black students to enter Central High.

The 1950s also saw the beginning of Massive Resistance, the calls for state interposition, the Citizen's Councils, the reinvigoration of the Ku Klux Klan, and the widespread resistance to the movement that is discussed further in chapter 6. Unfortunately, much of this white resistance to justice, equal rights, and human dignity was the result of the leadership of the southern congressmen and senators who wrote and signed the Southern Manifesto to which King referred at the Prayer Pilgrimage. This document pledged its signers to take all legal action possible to prevent the implementation of the *Brown* decision. With regional leadership like that, the ballot would still be almost a decade away.

JOHN HOPE FRANKLIN

John Hope Franklin might easily be considered one of the "deans" of the Civil Rights Movement.[2] From his early teaching career in the mid-1930s at Fisk University to his 1997 appointment by President Bill Clinton as the chairman of the advisory board for the President's Initiative on Race, Franklin has been active in black issues and one of the premier scholars in African-American history. He was born on January 2, 1915, in Rentiesville, Oklahoma, the son of a prominent black lawyer whose law office was destroyed during the Tulsa race riot of 1921. Franklin was selected to Phi Beta Kappa and graduated magna cum laude from Fisk in 1935 and received an M.A. a year later at Harvard University. In 1941 he received a Ph.D. at Harvard. His teaching career took him to tenures at St. Augustine's College, North Carolina College, Howard University, Brooklyn College, the University of Chicago, and Duke University, as well as several other universities as visiting professor. He served as president of the American Historical Association and the Organization of American Historians, among other professional associations. He has written several important books on various aspects of black life in America, including *From Slavery to Freedom: A History of Negro Americans* (Knopf), which has gone through several editions since first being published in 1947. In the early 1950s, Franklin helped with the research and writing of the brief submitted to the Supreme Court in the *Brown* school desegregation case. Over the years, Franklin has received many awards and honorary degrees in recognition of his scholarship.

In the speech presented here, Franklin urges the South to forget the "emotion-charged problem of race," and turn instead to its other, more critical, problems of the changes in agriculture, the growth of urbanization, and the poor quality of southern schools. These issues, says Franklin, "go unattended and unsolved, while the South faces its new dilemma."

DESEGREGATION—THE SOUTH'S NEWEST DILEMMA[3]

London
September 8, 1955

Within the past century the South has had to face a number of dilemmas, each related in some way to Negro–white relations and each creating tensions and dissipating greatly needed energies and resources. Before the Civil War there was the vexatious problem of slavery. When the institution was condemned by people in other parts of the country and abroad as economically unsound and morally reprehensible, the South found itself having to make a choice. It could either adhere to the principles of equality that were gradually becoming a part of the American tradition or it could repudiate those principles and launch an all-out defense of the "cornerstone" of its civilization. The principles of equality had been expressed by no one more eloquently than by the South's greatest philosopher, Thomas Jefferson. But even this fact did not sanctify them, and they were rejected as having no validity for the Southern way of life.

The South's choice, in this instance, plunged the section into a period characterized by intolerance, specious rationalizations, and violence. It began to pursue a course that logically led to secession, Civil War, and incalculable tragedy.

The decision of the battlefield in 1865 relieved the South neither of its right to make a choice nor of its apparent determination to make its choice on the basis of emotion and sentiment. After the Civil War, with the flower of its mankind killed or broken in body and spirit, with its slave property taken from it, and its countryside laid waste, the South faced another choice. The industrial revolution in America was in full swing and was rapidly transforming almost every aspect of life in the country. Soon, the South felt the full effects of these far-reaching changes; and it was called upon to make some adjustments to them. It could either accept the full implications of the new social and economic order or it could qualify it to the point of nullifying the possible benefits that it might bring. In refusing to accept the Negro into full citizenship and in excluding him from the benefits of the new industrial and agricultural order, it created a situation that, in the long run, dissipated the human and physical resources of the South and made it a colony of the North and the rest of the world.

The choice that the South made at that critical juncture in its history was clear, unmistakable, and deliberate. Whites declined to join hands with their Negro fellows to forge a dynamic and effective new order. Instead, they chose to cavil over the Negro's inadequacies and to embrace Northern and European capital to develop the section. The arrangement that followed was thoroughly disadvantageous to the South. White Southerners confused their needs with their wants. They lost sight of their needs and got what they wanted most of all: domination of the Negro. Northerners needed and wanted the same thing, and they got it: domination of the South's economic life, which has been maintained down to the present day.

At the turn of the century, when much of the nation was in the ferment of reform and was promoting the idea of greater economic and political democracy, the South again made a choice. Tempting as progressivism was, with its refreshing vitality and its many reforms, the South would not embrace it altogether. It accepted only portions of it, and whenever it did, it threw around it the sign, "For Whites Only." Meanwhile, it disfranchised the Negro, when other parts of the country were extending the suffrage. It was enacting segregation statutes, when other parts of the country were admitting the shame of racial discrimination in their first step toward doing something about it. Its politicians were campaigning for office on white supremacy platforms and its scholars were "discovering" new evidences of the inferiority of the Negro, when the rest of the nation was trying to forget its long record of shameful mistreatment of the American Negro. The South proclaimed to all the world the choice it had made by writing its new views on white supremacy into the constitutions and laws of the states and by accelerating its lynching of Negroes. It had deliberately chosen to turn the clock back to an earlier, less civilized era in the history of mankind.

The curious thing about the choices that the South has made is that they have not only been out of harmony with the dominant trend in American life but have generally been against the best interests of the South itself. These choices have led to a war in which the South suffered the most, to an economic order in which the South has been at a clear disadvantage, and to a political and social order that has not only been unprogressive but, in some respects, stagnant as well. These choices have rendered almost impossible the creation of satisfactory relations among the people of the South or between the South and other parts of the country.

Another curious thing is that invariably the South has looked upon its choice as one involving high principles of honor and morality. This has, of course, made retreat or compromise difficult, if not impossible. Choices made in such a context have propelled the South to a series of points of no return, with failure or disaster ahead of her and humiliation or embarrassment behind her.

These experiences, these consequences of making the choices that the South has made, have embittered the section, but they have hardly been sobering or instructive. They are the background, however, that the South brings to its newest and, in some respects, its most perplexing dilemma. This new problem was created by the 1954 decision of the United States Supreme Court declaring racially segregated schools unconstitutional. It was further aggravated by the Court's order in 1955 that states having segregated schools must make a "prompt and reasonable" start toward complying with the Court's decision and should proceed with "all deliberate speed."

The decision and the order came as a terrible and bitter disappointment to most of the South's leaders and to a considerable number of the rank and file of the white citizens of the South. For more than two generations they had considered segregated schools the bulwark of their way of life, a "cornerstone," as it were, to Southern civilization. Perhaps they could tolerate Negroes voting, or make some slight concessions to them in the economic sphere, or, if absolutely necessary, tolerate them in the same railroad car. But they would never, never permit Negroes to go to "their" schools. Separate schools had made possible not only the diversion of the lion's share of public funds to schools for whites but had helped to strengthen the argument for segregation. As inadequately prepared Negroes emerged from inadequately supported schools, the whites could point to them as examples of the inability of the Negro to assimilate learning. It mattered not that in some instances the educational opportunities available to white children were many times greater than those available to Negro children. Ill-prepared and ignorant Negroes were proof that they should be segregated, proof, too in the South's curious way of reasoning, that they should not have equal opportunities.

Southern whites became frightened some fifteen years ago when the first breach in the wall of segregated schools was made by the Supreme Court's decision that Negroes were entitled to the same graduate and professional education within the state that was available to whites. Southern states began immediately to establish graduate and professional schools for Negroes in order to continue to exclude them from the white institutions. But these efforts were in vain, for the Supreme Court then decreed that Negroes were entitled to attend the *same* graduate and professional schools that whites attended. Entertaining a growing fear that white elementary and secondary schools might be opened to Negroes by court order, Southern school boards began to improve Negro schools. Where unpainted, unheated, ill-equipped, one-room schools for Negroes had stood for generations, there were now erected modern, well-equipped structures. This expensive, frantic program had not been nearly completed when the Supreme Court handed down its recent momentous decision.

Small wonder that many white Southerners reacted vehemently to the decision. Forgetting, for the moment, the basic assumptions underlying their maintenance of separate schools and the many years of inequity in the use of public funds for the education of black and white children, they declared that the Supreme Court interfered with peaceful, local solutions to a difficult problem. Nothing rankled white Southerners more than the Court's mandate that legal segregation should be ended with all deliberate speed. Time, and plenty of it, was one thing that Southerners had always insisted upon in dealing with the race question. Those who suggested that speed could be employed in any manner merely revealed their ignorance of the almost immutable nature of the problem.

Turning their full wrath on the highest judicial body in the land, some of the South's most responsible and respected leaders described the work of the Supreme Court as reckless and irresponsible. One leading Southern editor referred to the Supreme Court justices as "that inept fraternity of politicians and professors" and declared that the Court "repudiated the Constitution, spit upon the tenth amendment, and rewrote the fundamental law of this land to suit their own gauzy concepts of sociology." The legislature of one state passed a resolution by unanimous vote declaring that it was not possible to educate children of both races in the same school. The governors of several states expressed unalterable opposition to the decision and said that, if necessary, they would recommend the closing of the public schools in order to prevent the "mixing of the races" in the school rooms.

Most Southern states have postponed any substantial implementation of the decision with the excuse that they are making a "study" of the situation. And in the few instances, outside the District of Columbia and Delaware, where communities have proceeded to desegregate their schools, they have been roundly denounced for being precipitate in their actions and for not "holding the line."

The real tragedy of the South, today as previously, is that it has subordinated the crucial and terribly perplexing problems that it confronts to the problem of race that has been magnified and kept alive for many generations. In the 1850's too few Southerners were concerned with the growing crisis in their economic life and clung to the erroneous notion that more slaves and better land could solve all their problems. In the post–Civil War period most Southerners seemed willing to sacrifice almost any economic advantages in return for the guarantee that Negroes would share in none of the rights and privileges usually accorded to citizens. Today, the South loses sight of some of its gravest issues in its desperate determination to keep Negroes and whites separated.

Today, Southerners are certainly giving insufficient attention to the far-reaching changes that give every indication of achieving a full-scale revolution in the region. To be sure, several revolutions are occurring simultaneously, and they are inextricably interrelated. There is the agricultural revolution, with its mechanical cotton picker, its new techniques in tobacco growing and curing, and its diversification of crop production. These developments are heralding the dawn of a new era in that sphere. There is the industrial revolution, which has attracted enormous capital and know-how from the outside, has drawn hundreds of thousands of Southerners into the orbit of industrial life, and has created new and complex problems growing out of automation and difficult labor-management relations. And there is the social revolution, involving extensive urbanization, new standards of living, new relationships of social classes, and the pressure to jettison the time-honored relationships of Negroes and whites.

Naturally the South is giving some attention to the many changes taking place. Here and there one senses an appreciation for the tremendous impact of agriculture on the South's rural population. Now and then one hears a discussion of the impact of automation on the industrial population of the South. Neither these changes nor the critical nature of current international relations are of as much concern to the average white Southerner as the possibility of one Negro child's attending a previously all-white school. On July 18, 1955, the day on which the four heads of state met at Geneva, a morning newspaper of a large Southern industrial city devoted a brief one-column article to that historic meeting. In the same issue, there were five articles on the first page dealing with unfavorable comments and reactions to the Court's order of May 31, 1955, on desegregation. During the months of June and July the same newspaper carried no discussion of the grave agricultural and industrial problems that are affecting every person in the region.

Thus, the region dissipates its energies on the emotion-charged problem of race and leaves little time or resources that may be directed toward the solution of its other pressing problems. They go unattended and unsolved, while the South faces its new dilemma.

Within the framework of a civilized community's commitment to obedience to the law, and to the idea of public education, the South's predicament hardly presents a real dilemma. As regards the law of the land the South can either comply with the decision or go beyond the pale and defy the decision by continuing to segregate its children in the schools. As far as public education is concerned, it can either integrate and strengthen its schools or it can abandon the system of free public education. As one Supreme Court justice observed, the Southern states can always exercise their right to permit their children to grow up in ignorance. These hardly constitute alternatives that a responsible citizenry can seriously consider. Yet, thousands of white Southerners are rejecting the law and are embracing the alternative choice. In some states they are proceeding to organize stand-by corporations that will operate private segregated schools, if necessary. They are enjoining Negro teachers from affiliating with organizations that advocate the enforcement of the Supreme Court decision. Tax-paid public servants are formulating ingenious ways to evade or frustrate the clear mandate of the Court. In such numerous instances the South is moving dangerously close to a collapse of community responsibility and the deterioration of law and order.

For the South has persuaded itself that a real dilemma exists. It regards itself as faced with the alternative of yielding to "a specious sociological" Supreme Court decision that presumes to interfere with its internal affairs or maintain its right "by lawful resistance" to preserve its local and racial integrity. Thus, it proceeds to wrestle with the age-old problem of race relations in the age-old context of honor and morality. With the law of the land against it, with national and world opinion apparently out of sympathy with it, and with its own larger interests clearly arrayed against it, the South firmly holds to its untenable position.

The South cannot win in the present struggle; and sober, thoughtful Southerners know it. In an editorial significantly entitled, "We Can't Win," a leading South Carolina newspaper said, "South Carolina people need to hear realism. They need to hear truth. They need to prepare themselves for a realistic future— not an impossible future constructed out of the words and blind hopes of those who have not accepted the inevitable. . . . Segregation is going—it's all but gone. South Carolina and the rest of the South can't reverse the trend." It would appear that the only thing that the South can achieve through stern resistance to compliance is time; and what it will do with the time that it gains is an important question. Whether it will be able to gain sufficient time to enable it to retreat gracefully remains to be seen. For a section without experience in the art of retreat this presents a most difficult problem. Perhaps it will have to be dragged, kicking and screaming, into a state of legal obedience and into the new dispensation that calls for the complete equality of man.

What one really hopes is that the South can extricate itself from its preoccupation with race issues soon enough and long enough to be able to devote some attention to its other problems. For if it does not face up to the realities of a new social and economic order, it is conceivable that the section will be swept up by the engulfing tide of change. And in its wake will be left untold damage and incalculable debris in the form of wrecked human and physical resources. It would be a real tragedy if the South's economy collapsed in the face of new revolutionary developments because it exhausted its energies defending the "lost cause" of segregation and discrimination. It would be equally tragic if the South failed to benefit from the many new opportunities in education, science, and technology because it was more concerned with seeing to it that Negroes were excluded. If the South fails to meet the *real* challenges of the present and if its social and economic order deteriorates as a result, the problem of reconstruction and readjustment will be immeasurably greater than any problem the South has ever faced.

MARTIN LUTHER KING JR.

Considered by most observers to have been the major catalyst in the Civil Rights Movement, Martin Luther King Jr. used his powerful ministerial rhetoric to challenge both whites and blacks to come together and dream a dream for the future of the races.[4] His vision garnered him a Nobel Peace Prize, seventeen jailings, and, ultimately, an assassin's bullet in Memphis, Tennessee.

King was born in Atlanta, Georgia, on January 15, 1929, the son of a Baptist minister, and the young King followed in his father's footsteps when he was ordained a minister in 1947. A year later, he received an A.B. degree from Morehouse College, followed by a B.D. from Crozier Theological Seminary in 1951, and a Ph.D. from Boston University four years later. Before completing his doctorate, King was appointed minister at the Dexter Avenue Baptist Church in Montgomery, Alabama, a move that would soon catapult him into the national spotlight.

In late 1955, King became the leader of the Montgomery Bus Boycott, which, after a favorable Supreme Court ruling, successfully integrated the public bus system of Alabama's capital city. Shortly after this victory, King and other southern ministers founded the Southern Christian Leadership Conference in Atlanta. King was elected its president, a position he would hold until his death. In 1960, King left Montgomery and returned to Atlanta where he became the co-pastor at his father's Ebenezer Baptist Church.

Through his leadership and advocacy of nonviolence in the campaign for civil rights, King spoke hundreds of times across the nation, not just in the South. In August 1963, he led the March on Washington, and delivered his most famous speech, "I Have a Dream," before a quarter of a million people. The following year, he received the Nobel Peace prize; at age 35, King was the youngest person to have been awarded this honor.

As the Civil Rights Movement began to achieve success with the 1964 Civil Rights Act and the 1965 Voting Rights Act, King began to turn his attention to the economic plight of African Americans and the poor in general. In April 1968, King was in Memphis helping to lead a city-wide strike of the garbage workers in their efforts to improve their working conditions and pay. King delivered his last speech, "I've Been to the Mountaintop," on April 3. He was shot and killed the next day as he stood on the balcony of the Lorraine Motel.

King's speech defending the bus boycott echoed the basic foundational tenets of the movement as it would develop over the next decade:

If we are wrong, then the Supreme Court of this Nation is wrong. If we are wrong, the Constitution of the United States is wrong. If we are wrong, God Almighty is wrong. If we are wrong, Jesus of Nazareth was merely a utopian dreamer and never came down to earth. If we are wrong, justice is a lie. And we are determined here in Montgomery to work and fight until justice runs down like water and righteousness like a mighty stream.

SPEECH AT HOLT STREET BAPTIST CHURCH[5]

Montgomery, Alabama
December 5, 1955

We are here this evening for serious business. We are here in a general sense because first and foremost we are American citizens, and we are determined to apply our citizenship to the fullness of its means. We are here because of our love for democracy, because of our deep-seated belief that democracy transformed from thin paper to thick action is the greatest form of government on earth. But we are here in a specific sense, because of the bus situation in Montgomery. We are here because we are determined to get the situation corrected.

This situation is not at all new. The problem has existed over endless years. For many years now Negroes in Montgomery and so many other areas have been inflicted with the paralysis of crippling fear on buses in our community. On so many occasions, Negroes have been intimidated and humiliated and oppressed because of the sheer fact that they were Negroes. I don't have time this evening to go into the history of these numerous cases. . . . But at least one stands before us now with glaring dimensions. Just the other day, just last Thursday to be exact, one of the finest citizens in Montgomery—not one of the finest Negro citizens but one of the finest citizens in Montgomery—was taken from a bus and carried to jail and arrested because she refused to get up to give her seat to a white person. . . . Mrs. Rosa Parks is a fine person. And since it had to happen I'm happy it happened to a person like Mrs. Parks, for nobody can doubt the boundless outreach of her integrity. Nobody can doubt the height of her character, nobody can doubt the depth of her Christian commitment and devotion to the teachings of Jesus. . . .

And just because she refused to get up, she was arrested. . . . You know my friends there comes a time when people get tired of being trampled over by the iron feet of oppression. There comes a time my friends when people get tired of being flung across the abyss of humiliation where they experience the bleakness of nagging despair. There comes a time when people get tired of being pushed out of the glittering sunlight of life's July and left standing amidst the piercing chill of an Alpine November.

We are here, we are here this evening because we're tired now. Now let us say that we are not here advocating violence. We have overcome that. I want it to be known throughout Montgomery and throughout this nation that we are Christian people. We believe in the Christian religion. We believe in the teachings of Jesus. The only weapon that we have in our hands this evening is the weapon of protest. And secondly, this is the glory of America, with all of its faults. This is the glory of our democracy. If we were incarcerated behind the iron curtains of a Communistic nation, we couldn't do this. If we were trapped in the dungeon of a totalitarian regime, we couldn't do this. But the great glory of American democracy is the right to protest for right.

My friends, don't let anybody make us feel that we ought to be compared in our actions with the Ku Klux Klan or with the White Citizens' Councils. There will be no crosses burned at any bus stops in Montgomery. There will be no white persons pulled out of their homes and taken out to some distant road and murdered. There will be nobody among us who will stand up and defy the Constitution of this nation. We only assemble here because of our desire to see right exist.

My friends, I want it to be known that we're going to work with grim and firm determination to gain justice on the buses in this city. And we are not wrong, we are not wrong in what we are doing. If we are wrong, then the Supreme Court of this Nation is wrong. If we are wrong, the Constitution of the United States is wrong. If we are wrong, God Almighty is wrong. If we are wrong, Jesus of Nazareth was merely a utopian dreamer and never came down to earth. If we are wrong, justice is a lie. And we are determined here in Montgomery to work and fight until justice runs down like water and righteousness like a mighty stream.

I want to say that with all of our actions we must stick together. Unity is the great need of the hour. And if we are united, we can get many of the things that we not only desire but which we justly deserve. And don't let anybody frighten you. We are not afraid of what we are doing, because we are doing it within the law. There is never a time in our American democracy that we must ever think we're wrong when we protest. We reserve that right. . . .

We, the disinherited of this land, we who have been oppressed so long are tired of going through the long night of captivity. And we are reaching out for the daybreak of freedom and justice and equality. . . . In all of our doings, in all of our deliberations . . . whatever we do, we must keep God in the forefront. Let us be Christian in all of our action. And I want to tell you this evening that it is not enough for us to talk about love. Love is one of the pinnacle parts of the Christian faith. There is another side called justice. And justice is really love in [application]. Justice is love correcting that which would work against love. . . . Standing beside love is always justice. And we are only using the tools of justice. Not only are we using the tools of persuasion but we've got to use the tools of coercion. Not only is this thing a process of education but it is also a process of legislation.

And as we stand and sit here this evening, and as we prepare ourselves for

what lies ahead, let us go out with a grim and bold determination that we are
going to stick together. We are going to work together. Right here in Montgomery when the history books are written in the future, somebody will have to say
"There lived a race of people, black people, fleecy locks and black complexion,
of people who had the moral courage to stand up for their rights." And thereby
they injected a new meaning into the veins of history and of civilization. And
we're gonna do that. God grant that we will do it before it's too late.

ROY WILKINS

If Martin Luther King Jr. was the charismatic leader recognized by most Americans as the voice and the symbol of the Civil Rights Movement, Roy Wilkins was the behind the scenes "party administrator, functionary, negotiator; the man who kept things together and helped make things happen."[6] Wilkins was born in St. Louis on August 30, 1901, but after his mother died when he was four, he grew up with his aunt in St. Paul, Minnesota. He received his A.B. degree from the University of Minnesota in 1923, where he majored in sociology and was an editor of the college newspaper. His first job out of college was as a reporter for an important black newspaper, the Kansas City, Missouri *Call*; he later became its managing editor. In 1931, he moved to New York and became the assistant to Walter White, the NAACP executive secretary. For the next forty-six years, Wilkins was a driving force in the NAACP, first as editor of the *Crisis*, then as acting executive secretary, administrator for internal affairs, finally, as executive secretary/director from 1955 to 1977.

His career as an activist started early, as he was a student member of the NAACP while in college and won an oratorical contest with an anti-lynching speech about the lynching of a black man in Duluth, Minnesota. While with the *Call*, Wilkins orchestrated a political campaign to unseat U.S. Senator Henry J. Allen and this successful effort brought him to the attention of White. Shortly after joining the national office, the NAACP sent him to Mississippi to investigate the racial conditions in a federally funded river levee building project. His report, *Mississippi Slave Labor*, was published by the NAACP and promoted a Congressional investigation that resulted in an improvement in the conditions in the labor camps.

Although Wilkins felt that the real avenue of approach for blacks was through the courts and by attaining the vote, he still actively led demonstrations; in the 1930s in protest against lynching, and in the 1950s across the South in support of the various causes for civil rights. He helped organize the 1963 March on Washington. As the 1960s moved along, and the black power advocates became disgruntled with the slower pace of the NAACP, Wilkins argued against their separatist and isolationist doctrine. Although vilified as an "Uncle Tom" by militant blacks, Wilkins stood staunchly against their rhetoric. Wilkins retired from the NAACP in 1977 and died on September 9, 1981, of kidney failure and heart trouble.

Wilkins received the NAACP Spingarn Medal in 1964 and President

Lyndon Johnson gave Wilkins the Presidential Medal of Freedom in 1969. He was also the receipient of more than thirty honorary degrees.

The Prayer Pilgrimage to Washington was organized by Wilkins, A. Philip Randolph, and Martin Luther King Jr. after it had been proposed by the Southern Christian Leadership Conference. The purpose of the rally was to demonstrate support for the Civil Rights Act of 1957, then before Congress. The meeting was held on May 17, 1957, on the third anniversary of the *Brown* decision. Wilkins' speech, along with the speeches by Randolph and King anthologized here, was only part of an extensive program of entertainment and oratory. Mahalia Jackson sang and other entertainers such as Sammy Davis Jr. and Harry Belafonte made appearances.

REMARKS AT THE PRAYER PILGRIMAGE FOR FREEDOM[7]

Washington, D.C.
May 17, 1957

With the permission of the dignitaries of the church and of the ministers of the faith who are leading us today, I wish to take as a text for my remarks the words of the great teacher, Paul, as found in his letter to the church in Ephesus. You will recall that after reminding the Ephesians of their blessings and their duties, the Apostle, in the sixth and final chapter of the letter, refers to the warfare of life. I have chosen as a guide the eleventh and twelfth verses of this chapter:

11. Put on the whole armor of God, that ye may be able to stand against the wiles of the devil.

12. For we wrestle not against flesh and blood, but against principalities, against powers, against the rulers of the darkness of this world, against spiritual wickedness in high places.

We have gathered here today because certain principalities of government in our own land, certain powers in the ascendancy in many communities, have not only turned their faces from us, but have attacked us with the weapons of wickedness: with slander, with economic oppression, with tailor-made laws, with guns and with bombs.

We are here because the rulers of the darkness of this world, the darkness of ignorance, arrogance, prejudice and hatred, have been permitted to rise up and ravage the peace of our nation, to recruit and inflame the wicked, and to browbeat the righteous.

We are here because spiritual wickedness in high places—in the mansions of certain Governors, in the law departments of certain states, in the legislative chambers of some state capitols, and under the dome of our nation's capitol—has caused a deaf ear to be turned to our plea for justice.

We have been given not bread, but a stone; not peace, but a sword.

And so we have come together not (as some have said) in a political rally, but in a sort of moral lobby; a lobby which is an effort to save not merely ourselves, but our country and its ideals, even to save our enemies. This meeting today calls to our fellow Americans of every station, region, faith, and race to return to the belief in, and observance of, the enduring principles of religion: truth, justice, forbearance, love, brotherhood. It calls, also, for renewed allegiance to the morality of the Founding Fathers who charted a government and wrote the words which have inspired mankind since first they were set down on paper:

"We hold these truths to be self-evident, that all men are created equal, that they are endowed by their Creator with certain unalienable Rights, that among these are Life, Liberty and the pursuit of Happiness."

We are Americans. We believe in these words. We believe in our Constitution and its Bill of Rights. We believe that men should have freedom of speech and of assembly. We believe they should be free to petition their government, that they should have government by consent of the governed. We believe they should have the right to seek redress in the courts of the land. We believe they must have equality before the law.

We have believed in these rights even when we have not always enjoyed their benefits. We believe in them today, at a time in which state governments in which we have been denied representation are snatching them from us.

Next door, in the State of Virginia, they are celebrating the 350th anniversary of the landing of the first white men at Jamestown. It is usually forgotten that this is also the 338th anniversary of the coming of the first black men to America. During all those 338 years we and our white fellow Americans have sweated, toiled, sacrificed, fought and died for our common country. Yet today, from some of the talk and the writing, one would think that we came here only yesterday, that out of a kind of charity we had been permitted to remain here but that this country is not ours as much as it is any man's.

Yes, we are Americans and as loyal Americans we believe that when the Supreme Court rules against a segregated public school system which has cheated our children these many decades, that ruling should be obeyed. Nine states have acted to comply, but eight states still are defying the Court and flouting the Constitution.

Since 1954 they have loosed the rulers of the darkness of this world, the crude mobs and the so-called "respectable" ones, to shoot and burn and terrorize white and black alike. Today in many sections of the South no white person is free to think or speak his mind unless he agrees with the mob. Let him raise but a small voice of dissent and he is cut down. On this question there is no more freedom for the individual than there was in Hitler's Nazi state, or is today in Communist Russia.

Three years of these tactics have not changed Negro Americans. We are steadfast in the face of the terror and the threats.

So now they have turned to passing new laws. In South Carolina, members of the NAACP are barred from state employment. In one Alabama county, the state must be paid $5.00 for every NAACP member enrolled. Mississippi has announced it will use secret police. In Louisiana teachers and school bus drivers may be fired for believing in integration.

Special laws aimed at the NAACP have been passed in many states, ranging from Virginia to Texas. These laws set up new regulations designed to make it so difficult for the NAACP to operate that the people will be left without legal advice or protection in their struggle against Jim Crow. The key sections of the new laws would hamper, if not completely prevent, citizens going to court to challenge discrimination. These laws also would prohibit citizens from lobbying for or against so-called "racial" bills in state legislatures.

The NAACP is under injunction in Alabama and Texas and in most of Louisiana, and, under the new laws is constantly faced with the possibility of swift action by states to put it out of business for any alleged violation of the many detailed regulations.

These laws deny basic American freedoms. They deserve the attention of every American, for they can and will be used against white citizens as well as colored. They are so oppressive that they may well force the NAACP to consider new methods of operation.

Not satisfied with hog-tying the Negro citizen on the local and state levels by denying him the vote, and by passing stringent laws in legislatures where he has no representation, the spiritual wickedness in high places has reached into the Congress of the United States and is now trying to choke the civil rights bill to death.

Certain Senators and Congressmen are using every trick to prevent the Federal government from protecting the right of citizens to vote. The need for this protection is found in Mississippi, for example, where only 8,000 out of 986,000 Negro citizens were permitted to register.

The civil rights bill has been buried since February in the Judiciary Committee of which Senator James O. Eastland of Mississippi is chairman. The committee is fooling no one. The Southerners are fooling no one. In the last election campaign it was charged that Senator Eastland, as chairman of the Senate Judiciary Committee, would block civil rights. His committee has done just that.

If a civil rights bill that has some meaning is not passed, voters in 1958 and 1960 will know where to place the responsibility. And remember, a civil rights bill that contains the phony "jury trial" amendment in contempt proceedings will not be a civil rights bill with meaning, and will not protect the Negro's right to vote. The mere fact that Eastland is for such an amendment tells the story.

Yes, we are in warfare for our rights, from local courthouses to the halls of Congress. Our opponents are "powers and principalities" and "rulers of the darkness of this world." We could have used some help. We can still use it, but we are holding up, but because of our own spirits, and because we know we are in tune with millions of our white fellow citizens, in and out of the South, who keep the faith, even though some must remain silent. With them, we turn to these other words of Paul, in Second Corinthians, the fourth chapter, eighth and ninth verses:

8. We are troubled on every side, yet not distressed; we are perplexed, but not in despair;

9. Persecuted, but not forsaken; cast down, but not destroyed . . .

For, to sustain us in our crusade, we have drawn from Leviticus 26:13 the inspiring admonition to the newly-freed people of Israel:

13. I am the Lord, your God, which brought you out of the land of Egypt that you should not be their bondmen; I have broken the bands of your yoke, and made you go upright.

Wrapped around with the whole armor of God, upright we shall go.

A. PHILIP RANDOLPH

Earlier in 1957, President Dwight Eisenhower had declined to meet at the White House with Randolph and other civil rights leaders. Randolph, Roy Wilkins, and Martin Luther King Jr. issued a call for the Prayer Pilgrimage to bring attention to Eisenhower's failure to meet with them. The purpose of the Pilgrimage soon expanded to show support and unity in the black community for the 1957 Civil Rights bill that Congress was considering. The three-hour demonstration was the largest civil rights gathering in the nation up to that time. The organizers claimed about 27,000 persons attended, other estimates ranged from 15,000 to 20,000. Randolph presided over the entertainment and speeches and gave the following address in which he rejects the support of "communists and communism as an illusion and a snare; a fraud and a menace.[8]

REMARKS AT THE PRAYER PILGRIMAGE[9]

Washington, D.C.
May 17, 1957

My honored colleagues and co-workers, the Rev. Dr. King and the Hon. Mr. Wilkins, Ministers of the Church and fellow Prayer Pilgrims for Freedom:

In the pattern of good American traditions, Negroes and whites, Jews and Gentiles, Protestant and Catholics, trade unionists, professional and educational leaders have assembled here in a great pilgrimage of prayer for freedom at the monument of Abraham Lincoln, the Great Emancipator, to tell the story of our long night of trial and trouble and our renewal of faith in and consecration to the sacred cause of a rebirth of freedom and human dignity.

Thus, we have come to memorialize the third anniversary of the historic United States Supreme Court decision for the desegregation of public schools, a veritable Emancipation Proclamation of the mind and the human spirit.

We have come to demonstrate the unity of the Negroes and their allies, labor, liberals and the church, behind the civil rights bills now before Congress, in order that they might not be strangled to death by committee maneuverings and the filibuster.

We have gathered together to proclaim our uncompromising support of the fight of the National Association for the Advancement of Colored People for civil rights and democracy under the able, resourceful and constructive leadership of Roy Wilkins, Executive Secretary. This is the agency which has been chiefly responsible for civil rights decisions in the courts of our land to eliminate second-class citizenship based upon race or color.

We are here to tell those who worship the false gods of white supremacy in the South to keep their evil hands off the NAACP.

And we have come to warn the liberal, religious, educational, labor and business forces of the North of the grave danger of a spreading sentiment in some sections of the South to deny the right of existence to the NAACP. It is a matter of common historical knowledge that the denial of free, voluntary association for the achievement of lawful, social, political and economic objectives of a particular group in our national community will, like the contagion of disease, spread to other associations of citizens which, for the present, may not be the objects of persecution. In very truth, it may be the NAACP which is banned by irrational racial legislation today, but the ban may come to the Knights of Columbus, B'nai B'rith, the AFL-CIO, and some of the sections of the National Council of the Churches of Christ in the USA, tomorrow.

We are here to make known our unqualified sanction of and cooperation with the magnificent, challenging and successful struggle against segregated buses in Montgomery, Alabama, the cradle of the old Confederacy, under the inspired leadership of a great church leader and prophet of our times, the Rev. Martin Luther King. This is one of the great sagas of the struggle for human decency and freedom, made effective by a veritable miracle of unity of some fifty thousand Negroes under the spiritual banner of love, noncooperation with evil and nonviolence.

We are assembled here to express our righteous indignation against and condemnation of the notorious Ku Klux Klan and White Citizens Councils. The revival of these agencies of hate and violence constitute a grave threat, not only to law and order in the South but to the democracy of our country, as well as a shock to the faith and confidence of peoples everywhere in the integrity of our moral leadership of the free world.

We have come to call upon President Eisenhower, our great national and world leader, who is undoubtedly possessed of a high sense of humanity, to speak out against the lawlessness, terror and fears that hang like a pall over the hearts of citizens of color in the South as a result of devastating bombings of their homes and churches, shooting and killing of citizens who have the courage to assert their constitutional rights, and the intimidation of white and colored people by cross burnings and the parades of hooded men and women.

As the highest expression of the moral and political authority of our country, we urge the President to help rebuild the shaken and shattered hopes of millions of Negroes and white peoples of the South, by raising his voice of counsel to the people to obey the laws of the land.

We have come to state our unshakable belief in the principles of human solidarity and the worth, value and dignity of the personality of every human being, regardless of race, color, religion, national origin or ancestry, and to point out the fallacy and mythology of the doctrine of white supremacy.

It is written in the Declaration of Independence of our country that all men are created equal and possess the inalienable right to life, liberty and the pursuit of happiness. These are natural human rights. They are God-given, not man-made. Every organ of government and official of State are required by constitutional fiat and the moral law to uphold these rights, not to conspire with anti-democratic forces to deny, nullify and destroy them.

Thus, civil rights have a moral and spiritual basis, for they are designed to implement and give reality and force to our human rights that exist as a result of our being human, and we are human because we have been created human beings by God. Since all men are the children of God, they are equal before God and should be equal before the laws of the state.

We are here to assert that the issue in the crisis of civil rights in our nation today does not involve opposition of Negroes to whites or whites to Negroes. There are leaders in certain circles who would like to make this the issue, but the real issue involves conflict between certain basic social and moral values, such as freedom against slavery, truth against error, justice against injustice, equality against inequality, love against hate, good against evil, the right to vote against disenfranchisement, law and order against mob rule.

One only has to witness this great demonstration of prayer pilgrims for freedom to note that they have come from various creeds, colors, countries, classes, callings and crafts.

We like to think that God is on the side of our American way of life but this will only be true to the extent that our American way of life is on the side of God, who said: "I am the way, the truth and the light." Hence, in the eyes of God there is neither black nor white, nor red nor yellow, nor Jew nor Gentile, nor barbarian nor Scythian, but all are brothers in Christ Jesus. "By this will all men know that you are my disciples, if you have love one for another."

We have come to assert our rejection of the promise and pattern and path to freedom by communists and communism as an illusion and a snare; a fraud and a menace, which can only lead to the dead end of chaos and confusion, frustration and fear, dictatorship, slavery and despair.

Finally, we have come to reaffirm our belief in and devotion and allegiance to the American constitutional system of government, within which citizens, though not fully free, are possessed of the priceless right to fight for their rights.

We reject the support and cooperation of communists in the fight for civil rights because we are opposed to the use of immoral means to attain moral ends. Further, we know that communists have no genuine interest in the solution of problems of racial discrimination but seek only to use this issue to strengthen the foreign policy of the Soviet Union.

But, to the end of achieving these civil rights and giving strength and integrity to our democratic order of government, it is the obligation and responsibility of every citizen of color, wage earner and lover of liberty to exercise his constitutional right to register and vote. We suggest no party or person to vote for, but we call upon every Negro, especially, not only to register and vote himself, but to serve as a missionary to get his neighbors in every house, in every block, in every hamlet, village, city and state of our country to register to vote, that we may build the power to help save the soul of America and extend and maintain the free world for free men.

Be not dismayed by the frightful wave of violence and persecution against persons of color now sweeping the South. It is written in the stars that the old order of southern feudalism, with its remnants and vestiges of lynching, peonage, vagrancy laws, mob violence, Ku Klux Klan, anti-labor union practices expressed in right-to-work laws, widespread illiteracy, low wages, is dying; its death will come as a result of the emergence of the dynamic impulse for freedom surging in the hearts of Negroes, together with the march of industrialization, urbanization, labor union organization, extension of education and the modernization of government through the spread of the ballot. These new forces will create and build a new South, free for the white and black masses to pursue a life of dignity and decency.

In conclusion, in the words of David, "I will lift up mine eyes unto the hills from whence cometh my help."

Yes, we have set our hands to the cause of a better and happier tomorrow for all men, and though we are beset by setbacks, persecution and trouble, the lot of all peoples who have won liberty and justice, may God grant that we may never falter.

MARTIN LUTHER KING JR.

The 1957 Prayer Pilgrimage organized by King, Randolph, and Wilkins, was important for several reasons. For one, it marked a combining of disparate forces that had not worked together before: the black labor unions, led by Randolph; the NAACP, led by Wilkins; and the southern black church, represented by King and the Southern Christian Leadership Conference. The 20,000-plus persons who attended came from around the country, some as far away as Los Angeles, and represented many of the constituencies of the black movement.

Another important result of the meeting was the demonstrated support for the Civil Rights Act of 1957. The act, although emasculated by southern Congressmen, passed and it set up an independent civil rights commission and a civil rights division in the Justice Department. These organizations played a central role in the 1960s as southern blacks worked for their voting rights.

An additional significant outcome of the rally was its exposure of Martin Luther King Jr. to a national audience. Up to this time, he was primarily known only in the South and among southern black church leaders. The speech presented here catapulted him to the national limelight as he repeatedly called for the vote for black Americans. Six days after the Pilgrimage, Randolph and King were granted an interview with Vice President Richard Nixon, thereby validating King's national leadership role.

KEYNOTE SPEECH AT PRAYER PILGRIMAGE FOR FREEDOM[10]

Washington, D.C.
May 17, 1957

Three years ago the Supreme Court of this nation rendered in simple, eloquent and unequivocal language a decision which will long be stenciled on the mental sheets of succeeding generations. For all men of good will, this May 17 decision came as a joyous daybreak to end the long night of enforced segregation. It came as a great beacon light of hope to millions of distinguished people throughout the world who had dared only to dream of freedom. It came as a legal and sociological deathblow to the old Plessy doctrine of "separate-but-equal." It came as a reaffirmation of the good old American doctrine of freedom and equality for all people.

Unfortunately, this noble and sublime decision has not gone without opposition. This opposition has often risen to ominous proportions. Many states have risen up in open defiance. The legislative halls of the South ring loud with such words as "interposition" and "nullification." Methods of defiance range from crippling economic reprisals to the tragic reign of violence and terror. All of these forces have conjoined to make for massive resistance.

But, even more, all types of conniving methods are still being used to prevent Negroes from becoming registered voters. The denial of this sacred right is a tragic betrayal of the highest mandates of our democratic traditions and it is democracy turned upside down.

So long as I do not firmly and irrevocably possess the right to vote I do not possess myself. I cannot make up my mind—it is made up for me. I cannot live as a democratic citizen, observing the laws I have helped to enact—I can only submit to the edict of others.

So our most urgent request to the president of the United States and every member of Congress is to give us the right to vote.

Give us the ballot and we will no longer have to worry the federal government about our basic rights.

Give us the ballot and we will no longer plead to the federal government for passage of an anti-lynching law; we will by the power of our vote write the law on the statute books of the southern states and bring an end to the dastardly acts of the hooded perpetrators of violence.

Give us the ballot and we will transform the salient misdeeds of bloodthirsty mobs into the calculated good deeds of orderly citizens.

Give us the ballot and we will fill our legislative halls with men of good will, and send to the sacred halls of Congress men who will not sign a Southern Manifesto, because of their devotion to the manifesto of justice.

Give us the ballot and we will place judges on the benches of the South who will "do justly and love mercy," and we will place at the head of the southern states governors who have felt not only the tang of the human, but the glow of the divine.

Give us the ballot and we will quietly and nonviolently, without rancor or bitterness, implement the Supreme Court's decision of May 17, 1954.

In this junction of our nation's history there is an urgent need for dedicated and courageous leadership. If we are to solve the problems ahead and make racial justice a reality, this leadership must be fourfold.

First, there is need for a strong, aggressive leadership from the federal government. So far, only the judicial branch of the government has evinced this quality of leadership. If the executive and legislative branches of the government were as concerned about the protection of our citizenship rights as the federal courts have been, then the transition from a segregated to an integrated society would be infinitely smoother. But we so often look to Washington in vain for this concern.

In the midst of the tragic breakdown of law and order, the executive branch of the government is all too silent and apathetic. In the midst of the desperate need for civil rights legislation, the legislative branch of the government is all too stagnant and hypocritical.

This dearth of positive leadership from the federal government is not confined to one particular political party. Both parties have betrayed the cause of justice. The Democrats have betrayed it by capitulating to the prejudices and undemocratic practices of the southern dixiecrats. The Republicans have betrayed it by capitulating to the blatant hypocrisy of right-wing, reactionary northerners. These men so often have a high blood pressure of words and an anemia of deeds.

In the midst of these prevailing conditions, we come to Washington today pleading with the president and the members of Congress to provide a strong, moral and courageous leadership for a situation that cannot permanently be evaded. We come humbly to say to the men in the forefront of our government that the civil rights issue is not an ephemeral, evanescent domestic issue that can be kicked about by reactionary guardians of the status quo; it is rather an eternal moral issue which may well determine the destiny of our nation in the ideological struggle with communism. The hour is late. The clock of destiny is ticking out. We must act now, before it is too late.

A second area in which there is need for strong leadership is from the white northern liberals. There is a dire need today for a liberalism which is truly liberal. What we are witnessing today in so many northern communities is a sort of quasi liberalism which is based on the principle of looking sympathetically at all sides. It is a liberalism so bent on seeing all sides that it fails to become committed to either side. It is a liberalism that is so objectively analytical that it is not subjectively committed. It is a liberalism which is neither hot nor cold, but lukewarm.

We call for a liberalism from the North which will be thoroughly committed to the ideal of racial justice and will not be deterred by the propaganda and subtle words of those who say, "Slow up for a while; you are pushing too fast."

A third area that we must look to for strong leadership is from the moderates of the white South. It is unfortunate, indeed, that at this time the leadership of the white South stems from the closed-minded reactionaries. These persons gain prominence and power by the dissemination of false ideas, and by deliberately appealing to the deepest hate responses within the human mind. It is my firm belief that this closed-minded, reactionary, recalcitrant group constitutes a numerical minority. There are in the white South more open-minded moderates than appear on the surface. These persons are silent today because of fear of social, political and economic reprisals. God grant that the white moderates of the South will rise up courageously, without fear, and take up the leadership in this tense period of transition.

I cannot close without stressing the urgent need for strong, courageous and intelligent leadership from the Negro community. We need leadership that is calm and yet positive. This is no day for the rabble-rouser, whether he be Negro or white. We must realize that we are grappling with such a complex problem there is no place for misguided emotionalism. We must work passionately and unrelentingly for the goal of freedom, but we must be sure that our hands are clean in the struggle. We must never struggle with falsehood, hate or malice. Let us never become bitter.

There is another warning signal. We talk a great deal about our rights, and rightly so. We proudly proclaim that three-fourths of the peoples of the world are colored. We have the privilege of noticing in our generation the great drama of freedom and independence as it unfolds in Asia and Africa. All of these things are in line with the unfolding work of providence.

But we must be sure that we accept them in the right spirit. We must not seek to use our emerging freedom and our growing power to do the same thing to the white minority that has been done to us for so many centuries. We must not become victimized with a philosophy of "black supremacy." Our aim must never be to defeat or to humiliate the white man, but to win his friendship and understanding, and thereby create a society in which all men will be able to live together as brothers.

We must also avoid the temptation of being victimized with a psychology of victors. In our nation, under the guidance of the superb legal staff of the NAACP, we have been able, through the courts, to remove the legal basis of segregation. This is by far one of the most marvelous achievements of our generation. Every person of good will is profoundly indebted to the NAACP for its noble work. We must not, however, remain satisfied with a court "victory" over our white brothers.

We must respond to every decision with an understanding of those who have opposed us and with an appreciation of the difficult adjustments that the court orders pose for them.

We must act in such a way as to make possible a coming-together of white people and colored people on the basis of a real harmony of interest and understanding. We must seek an integration based on mutual respect.

I conclude by saying that each of us must keep faith in the future. Let us realize that as we struggle alone, but God struggles with us. He is leading us out of a bewildering Egypt, through a bleak and desolate wilderness, toward a bright and glittering promised land. Let us go forth into the glorious future with the words of James Weldon Johnson resounding in our souls:

> God of our weary years,
> God of our silent tears,
> Thou who has brought us thus far on the way;
> Thou who has by thy might,
> Led us into the light,
> Keep us forever in the path, we pray.
> Lest our feet stray from the places, our God,
> where we met thee.

Lest our hearts, drunk with the wine of the world
we forget thee;
Shadowed beneath thy hand, may we forever stand
True to our God, true to our native land.

DAISY BATES

A long-time leader of the NAACP in Arkansas and the crusading co-publisher with her husband of the *State Press*, a weekly black newspaper in Little Rock, Daisy Bates gained national recognition in 1957 for her inspired participation in the Little Rock school integration crisis. Her planning, mentoring, communication skills, and overall leadership played a major role (along with the presence of the 101st Airborne Division troops and the federalized Arkansas National Guard) in the successful integration of Central High, despite the determined opposition of Arkansas Governor Orval Faubus, and the rabid segregationists of the state, backed up by their cohorts around the South.[11]

Daisy Gatson was born in 1914 in Huttig, a small town in southeast Arkansas just north of the Louisiana state line. She endured a typical segregated childhood, marked by several particularly bitter events that she chronicles in her autobiography. She never really knew her biological parents, having been taken in by friends of her family after her mother was murdered by a white man who was never brought to trial; her father left Huttig shortly after in fear of his own life. A run-in with a white storekeeper early in her life left a negative image in her mind's eye for years, and, as her foster father told her on his death bed, "You're filled with hatred. Hate can destroy you, Daisy. Don't hate white people just because they are white. If you hate, make it count for something. Hate the humiliations we are living under in the South. Hate the discrimination that eats away at the soul of every black man and woman. Hate the insults hurled at us by white scum—and then try to do something about it, or your hate won't spell a thing."

After finishing her schooling in Memphis, Tennessee, Daisy married L.C. Bates in 1941 and the couple settled in Little Rock. L.C. had been a journalist, but lost his job during the Depression and had turned to insurance. He had always harbored an interest in the newspaper business, so he and Daisy founded the *State Press*. She attended classes at Shorter College in Little Rock in order to learn more about the business side of the newspaper, and the couple was able to promote their newspaper into the leading black paper in the state. The *State Press* had a reputation from the start as a crusading publication and the Bateses were well-known for their advocacy of black causes. The *State Press* time and again exposed police brutality and oppression in Little Rock and central Arkansas, often at the expense of advertising revenue from white businessmen. When the time came in the mid-1950s to add another crusade to her portfolio, Daisy Bates was no stranger to controversy and advocacy.

The first round in the struggle to provide quality education for black southerners was marked in Little Rock by possibly the most important confrontation between state and federal authority since the Civil War, the spectacle of the state's governor calling out the National Guard to prevent the execution of the court's order, the reluctant order by the president of the United States federalizing that National Guard and calling in a seasoned paratroop unit of the U.S. Army to enforce the court's order, and the frenzied attempt of rabid segregationists to challenge the troops and keep the nine children out of the state's largest high school. Bates, in this speech, documents her perceptions of that year-long event.

THE NEW NEGRO[12]

Detroit, Michigan
May 2, 1958

Much has been written by some of the world's most renowned novelists of a new South, but the experience of the past few months in Arkansas shows clearly that we are not dealing with a new South. The attitude is still unchanged. But instead, we are dealing with a confused South and a new Negro. In spite of global conflicts of recent years, the South is still unable to disrobe herself of the cloak of ignorance, superstition and traditions which shielded her during the pre-reconstruction era.

How is the governor of Arkansas, the sage of Greasy Creek to know that in the South there was a new Negro? How was he to know that when he called out 270 Arkansas National Guards on that September morning to block the Negro children's entrance to a decent education, that the Negro would NOT run? How was he to know that he was exposing the South's role and her scandalous behavior that jolted the entire nation into shocked action?

The story of Little Rock was second in the world interest for 1957 to the Russian's landing a Satellite into space. The story of Little Rock was of world interest because it was disgraceful, and gave a picture to the world's peoples that refutes our ability to lay claim on the world's leadership.

LITTLE ROCK—BEFORE AND AFTER 1957

What was Little Rock like? I have often been asked, before she was discovered in September 1957? It was praise worthy, quiet, peaceful and rather aggressive—It gave the impression as a part of the new south. Little did I know then that it was not a changed Little Rock, Arkansas, but a new Negro who had appeared on the surface. Immediately following the governor's action in calling

out the Arkansas National Guards—against nine little teenage Negro children—
the horrors of the civil war, as if in a dream, only I was not asleep, arose before
me. I saw a little teenage Negro girl turned over to a mob of savage whites,
simply because she wanted a free education which was provided for her in a
free America. I saw black men going about their daily work being attacked from
the rear, kicked and unmercifully beaten. I saw Negro women on free streets in
a free America, stopped in automobiles, cursed and slapped. I saw men dressed
in the uniforms who had taken oaths to preserve law and order, turn their heads
when blacks were attacked. I saw the governor of Arkansas who had fled to his
friends in Georgia, basking in his ill won glory. I said to myself, that I would
rather be dead, than to be the governor of Arkansas who was trying to perpetuate
himself into an empire over broken oaths and human blood.

Many friends who were concerned with our safety before President Eisenhower sent troops—and even after the troops—what has often been referred
to—civil war in Little Rock, "Why don't you quit and give up?" "How do you
expect to succeed with so many odds against you?" We were reminded that the
governor, the attorney general, the state troopers, the county, city, school board,
all have joined hands with segregationists to block integration in Little Rock
schools. Our faith in God and the Constitution of the United States has given
us the courage to carry on, even though we have to sleep under the protection
of armed guards around my home. As we struggle daily I am reminded of
Thomas Paine in "The Crisis" when he said he did not believe God had relin-
quished the government of the world, and given us up to the care of the devils.

The struggle for human dignity is still being waged in Little Rock today. The
battle is far different from September 23, 1957, when the people so brilliantly
displayed their ignorance, prejudice and hate to the world. The battle lines are
drawn tight. The attacks are as deadly as those of the King Cobra. Those involved in the great human drama of all times never know where these destroyers
of young dreams will strike next.

YOUNG PIONEERS FOR FREEDOM—A TYPICAL DAY

Just to give you some idea of what these young pioneers have been facing,
trying to keep the spark of freedom alive in America, come with me to Little
Rock for one day for a visit with the family of a 15-year-old girl. We see the
mother quietly preparing breakfast, helping her daughter select the right dress
socks. It is important that she look nice, not daring to voice her real thoughts.
The mother, remembering the threats received on the phone the night before:
"There will be a nigger lynching if you send your daughter to school tomorrow."
She also remembers the last call to come in around midnite from a so-called
hysterical white mother stating that she just heard that the boys of Central High
will have water pistols loaded with acid to use on the children the next day, so
please keep your children home. As she watches her child join other children
in the special car to take them to school, she prays: "God, keep her safe today."
En route, the child wonders what will they try today. As she alights from the

car, she receives the daily greeting of "Go home, Nigger. You are not wanted." This does not bother her anymore. She only wonders why the principal, or any of the personnel in authority never corrected the children concerning them calling her "Nigger." Maybe they don't realize how deeply the word cuts as she enters the long hall. This same group falls in behind her stepping on her heels, "nigger—nigger—nigger." Another group will attempt to block her path and as she tries to side step them they close in and an elbow or a fist will shoot out and strike her in the side or back. She keeps moving, but turns slightly to see if she can identify any of the gang. Then she thinks, "What's the use, I have identified them before only to have the principal tell me 'You have to have a witness to the attack—or the attacker will have to admit it.' Otherwise it is just my word against his. So I continue on to my homeroom. I must be careful to watch my step, so I won't be tripped as I enter. In my classroom I only have to worry about tacks and glue in my chair, paper balls with small metal objects in them being thrown at me each time the teacher turns her head."

After class she sits for a few minutes, dreading the long walk down the hall. She remembers that she must be careful on the stairs. She recalls with horror what happened the previous day to her friends—two were kicked on the stairs, and had it not been for the alertness of one of the Negro girls when one of the so-called defenders of American democracy pushed her at the top of that long flight of stairs, serious injury could have been sustained. She thinks further, "I must be very watchful at lunch to keep hot soup from being poured down my back, or dirty objects from being thrown in my food." She tried to concentrate on the test that is coming up in the afternoon, and was thankful that she was able to finish the written assignment over the weekend, only to arrive at her locker to find it broken open and her assignments on which she spent so many hours completing, had been stolen.

On her way to the office to report the theft, she turned the corner—a boy faced her with a water pistol. In the split second before the water hit her she was cold with horror wondering whether the pistol contained water or acid as she had been told. Will the day never end? Nigger, Nigger—3:30 home to mother.

MINNIE JEAN BROWN FIGHTS BACK

Minnie Jean Brown, recently expelled from Central High, is a typical independent American girl, who held her head high in the face of insults, harassments and physical violence. For days, the white student had called her "Nigger looking b---" until Minnie lashed out on her with all the suppressed pent-up emotions of the previous months with "white trash," stating further that "If you were not white trash, you would leave me alone," with that, Minnie's tormentor struck her on the head with her bag—and for that Minnie was expelled, and advised by the democratic superintendent of the school, to take a correspondence course. We are deeply grateful to Dr. John L. Brooks, founder of the New

Lincoln High School, for giving Minnie the experience of a true democracy in America.

The seeds of freedom may lie dormant for a long time, and then they may sprout and their surge will begin to cause uneasy master to become more uneasy. The seeds of freedom are sprouting all over America today because of the courage of the nine children in Little Rock.

The road of "Jim Crow" in the South is stained by the blood of the Moores and Tills and drenched in the tears of humanity. Jim Crow is contrary to the basic American precepts of the Declaration of Independence. We hail the day as the most glorious in its dawning which would behold the black population of the United States placed under the rising sun of equal rights, clothed in the privileges and immunities of American citizens.

We have been asked numerous times, "how can you hold up under such tremendous pressure, such ridicule, threats and insults?" Inner strength and determination are drawn from faith in God, our fellow man, and the basic principle contained in the Constitution of the United States.

THE CRUCIAL TEST

September 1957, it was our only desire that the nine children selected by the school board would be able to walk to school as any other American citizen, and that the only time their names would appear in print would be in routine school news. The turn of events that followed that fatal day when the governor of Arkansas called out the National Guards to prevent nine children exercising their rights under the Constitution of the United States, far exceeded our wildest dreams, and started a chain of events that was felt around the world. Little did the nine children realize that their actions that morning would write a new chapter in American history. A lone, 15-year-old girl, Elizabeth Eckford, arrived early. Her grandfather and great-grandfather had participated in two major wars to make America safe for democracy. Thinking that the Guardsmen were there to protect her, she walked two long blocks with a vicious, jeering mob howling at her heels, without the slightest gesture of protection from the guards.

The morning of September 23, the nine Negro children gathered at my home for the entrance of school under the protection of the city and state police, who had assured us that every precaution would be taken to protect the children. We were notified by the city police the exact time to bring them in, and what route to take. While we waited, the radio gave a vivid description of the mob that has grown larger in number, and more vicious in its attitude. Yet, these children never once said, "Maybe we should not go today."

As the time grew nearer, I turned my attention to the parents, looking for a sign of weakening. A quietness had suddenly spread throughout the room. A mother or a father would lower his head as if in silent prayer. That morning, I observed courage rarely seen in a lifetime. I realized that these parents represented the spirit of the New South, and in a quiet, dignified manner, were serving notice on America that "We are a determined people, willing to pay the price that our children might enjoy true democracy." I have seen the hand of God throughout this crisis. If the Negro newsmen and photographers had not approached the school at the same moment, we were delivering the children to a side entrance, it would have been an entirely different story.

TRAGEDY—TERROR

About 11:30, it became apparent that the children would have to be moved from the building. This was done with all safety measures taken, and the children were delivered safely to their homes and parents. It was at that time that I realized that everything that we held dear and sacred in America was at stake, and if the actions of the mob were allowed to go unchallenged, the dreams and hopes of the Negro, and other freedom-loving peoples of the world would be completely lost. We tried hard not to cry out to the President, but the actions of the mob gave us no other choice. The people of America should be proud of their President for his patriotic actions preserving the principles of democracy.

The night of September 23, all available city and state police were pressed into action. The FBI blanketed the town: special police were assigned to the homes of the nine children, as well as to my home. Shortly before midnight, the police who were assigned to our home intercepted a caravan of more than 100 cars within two blocks from our home. In the cars were enough dynamite to blow the whole neighborhood to bits; and other weapons such as knives, guns, and clubs were also apprehended. There were several guests with us, who had to spend the night as no one was allowed to enter or leave the house.

A little later that night the telephone rang. Someone said: "We have just had our first killing in Little Rock, and you are responsible. There will be more before day." My heart stood still. I thought of Mr. Eckford, the father of Elizabeth, who would be returning from his night employment. I could envision his being shot down and his warm blood running in the streets; and at the same time, I pictured in my mind Arkansas's governor, gloating in his ill-famed glory.

FOR WHOM THE BELL TOLLS

In that moment I became bitter for the first time. I wondered who was to blame for this day and night of horror. I hated in that moment Faubus, the White Citizens Council, and all its kind. But something seemed to say, "No, Daisy, they are not to blame. You are responsible, along with all the freedom-loving people of America. You are responsible because you did not holler loud enough when policemen on the corner beat up the 'Wine-o'; when you failed to register to vote you were aiding and abetting the Faubuses all over the South." The sororities, fraternities, the professional group who failed to feel the plight of the little Negro when he was mistreated, denied, and harassed; yes—all of us share in this responsibility of September 23, 1957, in Little Rock, Arkansas.

GARDEN OF GETHSEMANE

I hated the people who had apparently burned the Constitution of the United States when they place fiery crosses on the lawn of our home; I hated the so-called liberals who were too afraid of their social positions to speak out clearly and firmly; I hated the moderates who were too cowardly to say: "This is the law of the land, and it must be obeyed. This kind of action should not only be stopped in Little Rock, but throughout the nation." Most of all I hated the frightened and complacent Negro of the South, and the contented Negro of the North and East. I walked into my bedroom and cried, "How much can a people stand." As these things were going through my mind, I was praying. Then something seemed to say to me: "You cannot spend your time hating, you must work and have faith." When the report was finally checked out and proved false, I felt like a person who had been given a new lease on life.

"SUFFER LITTLE CHILDREN TO COME UNTO ME . . . FOR SUCH IS THE KINGDOM OF HEAVEN"

On September 25, the children again assembled in my home, this time to be escorted to the school under the protection of federal troops. One of the children remarked, "They look so safe in their uniforms. For the first time in my life I feel like an American citizen." The children have been quizzed by some of the toughest newsmen around the world. I have seen reporters ask them the same question a hundred times, in as many different ways. They were all asking the same question, WHY! WHY! Would a parent allow his child, the most precious gift of life, to be used as a "pawn" as they had been informed by the opposition. I have watched them dig deeply into the lives and hearts and minds of these families. They could not understand this kind of courage, and so they dug deeper, and the deeper they dug, the brighter the courage shone. Their courage will shine around the world for centuries to come.

NO RETREAT

As the other eight students continue at Central High, the governor has repeatedly stated that, "The only solution to the integration problem at Little Rock is the removal of the Negro children from Central High School." He suggests that the Negro students could solve the problem by "voluntarily withdrawing from the school." The Negro children will NOT voluntarily surrender their hard-won civil rights in order to pacify the governor and the mob. Nor do I believe that the federal government will surrender to governor Faubus and the segregationist mob. It would be a great tragedy for the cause of justice, law and order if the federal government should ever surrender to the civil forces of prejudice and mob rule.

DEMOCRACY'S TESTING GROUND

Even though the children daily face adversities that would discourage the most hardened civil rights fighters, they have never lost their dignity, and the only time they have lowered their heads has been in prayer. They have awakened the conscience of America.

Little Rock is the testing ground for democracy in America today. The segregationists are using everything at their command—the courts, night riding, vandalism, cross burnings, and many other vicious types of intimidations and harassments. We are involved in eighteen law suits in an effort to kill the NAACP in Arkansas. The school board has petitioned the courts to delay integration in the public schools—"We need time to educate the public—you can't legislate love" are their contentions. We are not asking for love. We are DEMANDING the rights and privileges as guaranteed any American citizen under the Constitution of the United States—the right to move in a free society as free Americans, and it is the duty of the federal government down to the smallest town in Arkansas or Mississippi to protect these rights. Then and only then, can America command world leadership, and respect so badly needed throughout the world.

MEDGAR EVERS

One of the murdered martyrs of the Civil Rights Movement, Medgar Evers was a major figure in the struggle in Mississippi.[13] A veteran of the European campaigns in World War II, Evers was born in Decatur, Mississippi, on July 2, 1925. Returning to Mississippi after the war, he and his brother, Charlie, registered to vote. On election day, however, they were blocked from the polling place by an armed crowd of Mississippians. He graduated from Alcorn A&M College in 1952, then went into an insurance career. He joined the NAACP and in 1954 entered full-time work as the organization's state field secretary. By the late 1950s, he was on the hate lists of white supremacy groups in his home state.

During the late 1950s and early 1960s, Evers organized voter registration drives, demonstrations, sit-ins, and other active protests. An eloquent speaker, he traveled throughout the state advocating change and progress in race relations in what was doubtless the most racist state in the South.

On June 11, 1963, Evers was shot in the back just as he returned home from an NAACP meeting and died an hour later in a Jackson, Mississippi, hospital. It took three trials, but finally, in 1994, his killer, Byron de la Beckwith, a founding member of the Citizens Council, was found guilty of the murder. Eudora Welty's short story "Where Is the Voice Coming From?" is a fictionalized account of the murder.[14]

ADDRESS AT A MASS MEETING OF THE LOS ANGELES BRANCH NAACP[15]

May 31, 1959

Ladies and Gentlemen:

I count it a great honor to be with you today. May I take this opportunity to bring you greetings from the National Office, the Mississippi State Conference of NAACP Branches, its president, Mr. C.R. Darden, and fellow Mississippians, who share with you the aspirations of freedom, and the dignity and worth of individual Americans.

It is not my purpose here today to malign the state of my birth, but the many obnoxious bills passed by the state and local governments of Mississippi, for the obvious purpose of keeping me and my posterity second-class citizens, makes it compelling that I should, at this time, unfold the truth about the conditions under which Americans of African descent live here in this great country during the century of wonders—United Nations, sputniks, explorers, space, atoms—the twentieth century.

Certainly, many of the incidents mentioned herein will doubtless appear to be fantasies, but I can assure you that I shall not falsify against the state of my birth. To enumerate all of the injustices against Negro Americans in Mississippi would be next to impossible, so I shall make mention of injustices that are most prominent, along with others less prominent.

Many of the cries that are now heard echoing throughout the United States by white southerners, for more time to equalize schools, were never heard before the 1954 Supreme Court Decision, declaring segregation unconstitutional. There was hardly a whisper to give Negroes adequate schools, not to mention equal.

There is still in existence today, less than twenty-five miles from Jackson, the state capitol of Mississippi, a two-room school, with pot-bellied stoves, housing some forty-five students to the room, with most of the window panes out, and the responsibility of securing wood for fuel heat left to the students and teachers. There are many other such schools throughout the state. Doubtless, in each county the number could be doubled, certainly in most of them.

Mississippi started its ambitious equalization program after May 17, 1954, in an effort to get around the Supreme Court Decision. However, the $120,000,000 program is too little, and it has come too late. Negroes in Mississippi want for their children the quality of education that will help make them top scientists, top diplomats, and top engineers of tomorrow, and it cannot be done under the so-called "separate but equal" doctrine.

Negro teachers are brow beaten into acquiescence by being forced to sign an affidavit stating that they do not belong, nor contribute, to any organization whose purpose it is to overthrow the Constitution of the United States, or the Constitution of Mississippi and its customs. This requirement, passed by the Mississippi Legislature in 1956, was designed to prevent Negro teachers from working with or contributing to the NAACP. I hasten to say, it has served its purpose well, not that the purpose of the NAACP is to overthrow the Constitution of the United States or the State of Mississippi, except where the laws of the State of Mississippi do conflict with the Supreme laws of our land as it relates to the rights of Negro citizens.

The month of May, 1955, in the community of Belzoni, Mississippi, was probably the beginning of an intensified campaign of violence and economic pressure against Negro citizens who wanted the right to vote and be respected by their fellowmen. It was in this community that the Rev. G.W. Lee, a militant minister for civil rights, was shotgunned to death by unknown assailants, as he was enroute home on this particular Saturday night in May. Officers tried to claim that he lost control of his car and rammed into the porch of a house where a piece of 2×4 lumber was to have pierced the windshield, striking the Rev. Lee in the face, killing him almost instantly. During the coroner's inquest, there was an attempt made to say that the lead, which was discovered in Rev. Lee's jaw was filling from his teeth. This was later disproved, after sending several pellets to the FBI laboratory in Washington, which revealed that the lead was that of a buckshot and classified thusly.

In August 1955, there was the infamous Till case, while I am sure most of you are familiar, but to briefly recapitulate, a fourteen year old Negro boy in Chicago, Illinois came down to visit some relatives in Money, Mississippi, where he was alleged to have "wolf whistled" at a white woman, which irritated her husband and brother-in-law to the extent that young Till was taken from his home early one morning, beaten, shot and his weighted body dumped into the murky Tallahatchie River. The body was later discovered by a young white fisherman, who saw the form of a human being bobbing up and down in the water. The men responsible for the crime were apprehended, brought to trial and, as is typical of Mississippi justice, were released, and today are free.

During the same month of August 1955, in the County of Lincoln, the City of Brookhaven, a Negro citizen, Lamar Smith, was busily encouraging Negroes in his community to vote, either in person or by absentee ballot. As he proceeded to get more absentee ballot forms for neighbors, several white men accosted him on the lawn of the county courthouse, beat and shot him to death because of his activities. The guilty parties were apprehended later, released on $20,000 bond each, and never brought to trial, even unto this day.

Rev. Gus Courts, of Belzoni, Mississippi, was making change in his small grocery store late one Saturday evening in December when he heard a crashing window before him and felt a sting in his arm, only to look down and see blood streaming on the floor. It was then he knew that he had been shot by a load of buckshot, with only a portion of the load inflicting personal injury.

These acts of violence, coupled with economic pressure, have been the chief tactics used to discourage Negroes from seeking justice and equality in Mississippi. However, despite these and other acts of intimidation, people around the world have an unquenchable desire to be free men and women, even in the State of Mississippi.

Negro citizens in most Mississippi counties are barred from actively participating in local state and Federal elections by gestapo like actions similar to the ones referred to in the cases involving Rev. Lee, Courts and Lamar Smith, mentioned earlier, in addition to the legal barriers, such as poll tax and twenty-one questions, which are prerequisites to voting. Out of a potential 494,653 Negro voters there are less than 30,000 qualified Negro electors in the entire State of Mississippi. While the white man is responsible to a great degree for this one-sided situation, the Negro, himself, has not contributed all that he or she could to change the picture that has been brought before you. To illustrate, in cities like Jackson, Meridian, Laurel, Gulfport, Biloxi, Greenville, Clarksdale and a few others, where Negroes are permitted to register and vote without molestation, we find that there is a considerable amount of apathy, and reluctance on the part of Negroes to take advantage of the situation, which would make it easier for our fellowmen to live in places like Belzoni, Tylertown, Gloster, Money, and the like.

So often we find Negroes of means who could well afford to lead our people out of our present state but are nevertheless content with things as they are, because of the personal profit they receive from segregation and human misery. These people have been selected by whites as leaders of the Negro communities in an effort to stamp out any semblance of our fight for justice and equality by the more militant Negro people. Many of these "Uncle Toms" are given high educational posts, such as principals, superintendents, and even college presidents, to bolster their community prestige. In the case of principals, there seems to be a conspiracy, on the part of some state and county officials, to name all Negro schools that are now being built after the principal, to further his or her prestige in the community. A number of principals have assumed the role of community dictator to the extent that they have totally discouraged the formation of Parent–Teacher Associations to work with the schools; they have expelled students who expressed an opinion or action favorable to the Supreme Court Decision declaring segregation unconstitutional, and, in some instances, refused to permit student governments to function in school because of the political training it would provide some of the more aggressive students, making them "incorrigible" to the brainwashing techniques to which the curriculum subscribes.

During the Korean War, we often read in our newspapers how the Communists were brainwashing our troops. Well, if that technique was used, it could very well have been that such a scheme was a replica that was, and still is, used on southern Negroes by whites who attempt to make the Negro believe that he is nobody, or at best, inferior to every other racial group.

Charity begins at home and spreads abroad. The hypocrisy that is practiced at home and preached abroad has begun to fall on deaf ears, for as it is often said, "the things you do speak so loudly until the things you say cannot be heard."

The savagery dealt Mack Charles Parker, in a "civilized society," makes a mockery out of so-called cannibalism in the most remote areas of the world. It appears that the only time Mississippi makes national or international headlines is when a bunch of cowards like those at Poplarville, Mississippi take an unarmed Negro, who is already at their mercy, out of an unguarded jail cell, beat him, shoot him, and throw his lifeless body into the Pearl River, or some other large body of water. This is not to say that all white people in Mississippi are hoodlums, quite the contrary is true. There exist a predominance of white citizens of Mississippi who believe in law and order, justice and a semblance of fair play. However, this group does not have the Christian courage to stand up against the lawless elements of Mississippi and demand that the laws of God, the United States, as well as many of our state laws, be complied with as moral human obligations placed upon our democratic society. There is a tendency toward allowing the irresponsible to occupy high positions of public trust, which has nothing less than a disastrous affect in a state as backward as Mississippi.

Actually, the segregationists are losing, and they know it. The movement today for freedom cannot be pushed back any more than a tidal wave can be pushed back by hand. That which seeks to destroy the freedom of man seeks to destroy the soul of man. Man wants to be free, yes, even in Mississippi, and we will continue to struggle for freedom. The eyes of the world are upon America. To treasure the traditions of hate and fear and cling to traditional customs will surely lead to destruction of our democratic way of life. It is appalling to observe the unethical folly of men in government who think the outside world will continue to look up to America as a symbol of democracy. Theoretically, we are the greatest exponents of democracy of any nation in the world, but this is on paper, and not in the hearts of men who control the policies of this great country. We cannot wait until the hearts of men are changed to enjoy our constitutional rights.

We have been patient, and remain patient, because we believe enough in our country to press vigorously for our rights with the conviction that we will someday win first-class citizenship. We are confident that we will achieve victory, not through violence, but through the channels provided by the Constitution of the United States of America—through the courts, political action and education. If we work with sufficient dedication, we will be able to achieve, in the not too distant future, a society in which no one is discriminated against on the basis of his race, his religion or his national origin. Our faith is invested in a law that is over and above man made laws. We are dedicated to the cause of freedom, and will continue to fight under God's law, without fear of consequence. He hath saith, "Blessed are ye when men shall revile you, and shall persecute you and shall say all manner of evil against you falsely for my sake, rejoice, and be exceedingly glad, for great is your reward in heaven, for so persecuted they the prophets which were before you."

In closing, I am reminded of the writings of James Weldon Johnson, who wrote:

> God of our weary years, God of our silent tears,
> Thou who hast brought us thus far on the way;
> Thou who hast by thy might, led us into the light,
> Keep us forever in the path, we pray.
> Lest our feet, stray from the places our God where
>   we met thee,
> Lest our hearts, drunk with the wine of the world,
>   we forget thee,
> Shadowed beneath thy hand, may we forever stand
> True to our God, true to our native land.

NOTES

1. See Patricia Sullivan, *Days of Hope: Race and Democracy in the New Deal Era* (Chapel Hill: University of North Carolina Press, 1996).

2. This biographical sketch is taken from Charles D. Lowery and John F. Marszalek, eds., *Encyclopedia of African-American Civil Rights* (Westport, CT:

Greenwood Press, 1992), 198–99; and from Charles Moritz, ed., *Current Biography Yearbook 1963* (New York: H.W. Wilson Co., 1964), 139–41.

3. This speech was delivered by Franklin over the British Broadcasting Corporation's network in London on September 8, 1955. It was later printed in the BBC magazine *The Listener* September 15, 1955, 408–9. See text in *The Journal of Negro Education* XXV (spring, 1956), 95–100.

4. The main sources for this biographical sketch are: *The National Cyclopedia of American Biography* (Clifton, NJ: James T. White and Co., 1973), 1–2; and *Dictionary of American Biography*, supplement 8, 1966–1970, John A. Garraty and Mark C. Carnes, eds. (New York: Charles Scribner's Sons, 1988), 332–36.

5. Martin Luther King Jr., "Speech at Holt Street Baptist Church," Montgomery, AL, December 5, 1955. See text in Clayborne Carson et al., eds., *The Eyes on the Prize Civil Rights Reader* (New York: Penguin Books, 1991), 48–51.

6. Melvin Drimmer, "Roy Wilkins and the American Dream: A Review Essay," *Phylon* XLV (1984), 160–63. The primary sources for this biographical sketch are Barbara Carlisle Bigelow, ed., *Contemporary Black Biography*, vol. 4 (Detroit: Gale Research, Inc., 1993), 262–65; and John D'Emilio, *The Civil Rights Struggle: Leaders in Profile* (New York: Facts on File, 1979), 146–50.

7. Roy Wilkins, "Remarks at the Prayer Pilgrimage," Washington, DC, May 17, 1957. Roy Wilkins Papers, Manuscript Division, Library of Congress.

8. Paula F. Pfeffer, *A. Philip Randolph, Pioneer of the Civil Rights Movement* (Baton Rouge: Louisiana State University Press, 1990), 176–79; 185–86; 188–91; 193–94; 196; 197; 198–99.

9. A. Philip Randolph, "Statement at Prayer Pilgrimage," Washington, DC, May 17, 1957. A. Philip Randolph Papers, Manuscript Division, Library of Congress.

10. See Washington, James Melvin, ed., *A Testament of Hope: The Essential Writings and Speeches of Martin Luther King, Jr.* (San Francisco: HarperSanFrancisco, 1986), 197–200.

11. Major sources for this biographical sketch are Gayle J. Hardy, *American Women Civil Rights Activists* (Jefferson, NC: McFarland & Company, 1993), 32–38; and V.P. Franklin, "Daisy Lee Gatson Bates," in Darlene Clark Hine, ed., *Black Women in America: An Historical Encyclopedia* (Brooklyn: Carlson, 1993), 94–96.

12. Daisy Bates, "The New Negro." Speech delivered May 2, 1958, to the Detroit Branch of the NAACP at People's Community Church. See Daisy Bates Papers, State Historical Society of Wisconsin Library, Madison, WI.

13. The major sources for this sketch are Robert L. Jenkins, "Evers, Medgar W.," in Charles D. Lowery and John F. Marszalek, eds., *Encyclopedia of African-American Civil Rights* (Westport, CT: Greenwood Press, 1992), 172–73; and Barbara Carlisle Bigelow, ed., *Contemporary Black Biography*, vol. 3 (Detroit: Gale Research, Inc.), 62–65.

14. Suzan Harrison, " 'It's Still a Free Country': Constructing Race, Identity, and History," in Eudora Welty, 'Where Is the Voice Coming From?' " *Mississippi Quarterly* L (fall 1997), 631–46.

15. Medgar W. Evers, "Address at a Mass Meeting of the Los Angeles Branch NAACP," May 31, 1959. See Medgar W. Evers Papers, Coleman Library, Tugaloo University, Jackson, MS.

FOR FURTHER READING

John Hope Franklin

Estell, Kenneth, ed. *The African-American Almanac*, 6th ed. Detroit, MI: Gale Research, 1994, p. 743.

Henderson, Ashyia N., and Shirelle Phelps, eds. *Who's Who Among African Americans*, 12th ed. Detroit, MI: Gale Group, 1999, p. 146.

Martin Luther King Jr.

Branch, Taylor. *Parting the Waters: America in the King Years, 1954–63*. New York: Simon and Schuster, 1988.

———. *Pillar of Fire: America in the King Years, 1963–65*. New York: Simon and Schuster, 1998.

Calloway-Thomas, Carolyn, and John Louis Lucaites, eds. *Martin Luther King, Jr., and the Sermonic Power of Public Discourse*. Tuscaloosa: University of Alabama Press, 1993.

Garrow, David J. *Bearing the Cross: Martin Luther King, Jr., and the Southern Christian Leadership Conference, 1955–1968*. New York: William Morrow, 1986.

Patton, John H., "Martin Luther King, Jr." In Bernard K. Duffy and Halford R. Ryan, eds., *American Orators of the Twentieth Century: Critical Studies and Sources*. Westport, CT: Greenwood Press, 1987, pp. 263–70.

———. "Martin Luther King, Jr." In Richard W. Leeman, ed., *African-American Orators: A Bio-Critical Sourcebook*. Westport, CT: Greenwood Press, 1996, pp. 216–25.

Washington, James Melvin, ed. *A Testament of Hope: The Essential Writings of Martin Luther King, Jr.* San Francisco: Harper & Row, 1986.

Roy Wilkins

Wilkins' papers are in the Manuscript Division, Library of Congress.

Wilkins, Roy, with Tom Mathews. *Standing Fast, The Autobiography of Roy Wilkins*. New York: Viking Press, 1982.

Daisy Bates

Bates' papers are in the Special Collections Department, University of Arkansas Library, Fayetteville, Arkansas. A sizeable collection is also at the Wisconsin State Historical Society Library in Madison, Wisconsin.

Bates, Daisy. *The Long Shadow of Little Rock*. New York: David McKay, 1962.

———. "Report on Little Rock." Speech in New York City, November 3, 1957. In W. Stuart Towns, *Public Address in the Twentieth Century South: The Evolution of a Region*. Westport, CT: Praeger, 1999, pp. 84–88.

Blossom, Virgil. *It Has Happened Here*. New York: Harper, 1959.

Huckaby, Elizabeth. *Crisis at Central High School: Little Rock, 1957–1958*. Baton Rouge: Louisiana State University Press, 1980.

Medgar Evers

Donald, Cleveland, Jr. "Medgar Wylie Evers: The Civil Rights Leader as Utopianist." In Dean Faulkner Wells and Hunter Cole, eds. *Mississippi Heroes*. Jackson: University Press of Mississippi, 1980, pp. 217–28.

Moon, Henry Lee. "The Martyrdom of Medgar W. Evers." *The Crisis* 80 (June–July, 1973), pp. 186–89.

Sewell, George Alexander. "Charles and Medgar Evers: Leaders in Civil Rights." *Mississippi Black History Makers*. Jackson: University Press of Mississippi, 1977, pp. 331–45.

Diane Nash (far right). Courtesy of the National Archives and Records Center.

Fannie Lou Hamer. Courtesty of the National Archives and Records Center.

Daisy Bates. Courtesy of the Library of Congress.

W.E.B. Du Bois. Courtesy of the Library of Congress.

Lillian Smith. Courtesy of the Library of Congress.

President Dwight Eisenhower and Governor Orval Faubus, September 14, 1957. Courtesy of the Library of Congress.

Thurgood Marshall. Courtesy of the Library of Congress.

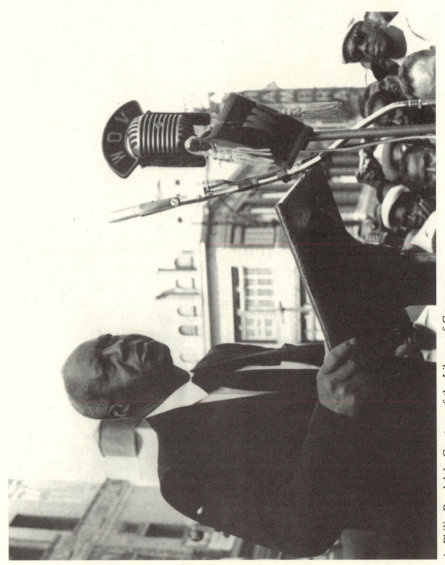

A. Philip Randolph. Courtesy of the Library of Congress.

Martin Luther King Jr. Courtesy of the Library of Congress.

Roy Wilkins. Courtesy of the Florida Photographic Collection, Florida State Archives.

CHAPTER 4

THE MOVEMENT HITS FULL STRIDE: THE 1960s

Brown v. Board of Education, the Montgomery Bus Boycott, the Prayer Pilgrimage for Freedom, and Little Rock Central High School were all 1950s preludes to the civil rights protest that exploded in the next decade. Beginning with the student sit-ins in the winter of 1960, the movement gained full speed, not to be slowed down until it gained its measure of success in the middle of the decade with the passage of the Civil Rights Act of 1964 and the Voting Rights Act of 1965. The first half of the 1960s was marked with incredible turmoil across the South as young black college students, militant black ministers, and white southerners who were ready for change faced the hatred of racial bigots who refused to grant first class citizenship to African Americans. The speeches in this chapter reflect and illustrate some of these events.

A major turning point in the movement was the infusion of college students into the fray with the activism of the sit-ins. Although there had been sporadic and relatively unorganized sit-ins at various locations around the South, the tactic did not receive much notice until February 1, 1960, when African-American students at North Carolina A & T College Ezell Blair Jr., Franklin McCain, Joseph McNeil, and David Richmond staged a sit-in at the Woolworth Store lunch counter in Greensboro, North Carolina. Within days, students were conducting sit-ins all over the downtown area in protest of the segregated facilities at the lunch counters. By February 5, 1,600 students attended a mass meet-

ing in which they agreed with city leaders to stop the sit-ins until negotiations could be carried out; these talks failed, and the movement
began again on April 1. A combination of sit-ins and an economic boycott forced the desegregation of the lunch counters by mid-summer of
1960. The Greensboro sit-ins sparked other student-led protests across
the South such as High Point, Charlotte, and Durham, North Carolina;
Albany, Georgia; Baton Rouge, Louisiana; Tallahassee, Florida; and
Nashville, Tennessee. Not only were many of the protests successful in
achieving their immediate goals of desegregating the lunch counters in
department stores and other public places, the students united and organized the Student Nonviolent Coordinating Committee (SNCC) at
Shaw University in Raleigh, North Carolina. This group quickly became
one of the key players in the Civil Rights Movement and provided much
of the leadership and the army of soldiers dedicated to tearing down the
barriers of racial inequality and injustice across the South.[1]

The Freedom Rides, sponsored at first by the Congress of Racial
Equality, and later picked up by SNCC, were the next major wave of
activism that swept across the region in 1961. The first rides began from
Washington, DC, on May 4 and were planned to cross the South to New
Orleans in order to protest the segregated facilities in interstate bus terminals. Met with violence in Anniston, Alabama, a bus was destroyed
and several riders were beaten by mobs. The Interstate Commerce Commission banned racially segregated accommodations in November 1961.[2]

Not all of the protests were successful. For example, the Albany
Movement in southwest Georgia met rebuff after rebuff and ground into
a stalemate in 1962. Because of the relative failure of the Albany protest,
the Birmingham campaign led by Martin Luther King Jr. and SCLC in
the spring of 1963 became a critical event. King had to gain a measure
of success in order to sustain the movement or see his support deteriorate.
Also in 1963, the high-water mark of the movement, the March on Washington was carried out in August of that year. The year was also marked
with the murder of a major leader in the movement, Medgar Evers, in
Jackson, Mississippi.

JAMES M. LAWSON JR.

Like several of the speakers included in this anthology, James M. Lawson Jr. has not often been given the credit he is due for his major leadership role in the Civil Rights Movement.[3] While a divinity student at Vanderbilt University in 1959–60, Lawson organized in November 1959 one of the first sit-ins of a segregated lunch counter that led in the next year to the prolonged and successful sit-in campaign known as the Nashville Movement. Lawson provided important leadership to the Nashville Movement, which later led to his expulsion from Vanderbilt. Later in 1960, he was one of the moving forces behind the founding conference of the SNCC and he took an active role in the organization until he accepted a pastorate in Memphis. Lawson's protest days were hardly over, however, as he was a major force in the 1968 Memphis garbage collectors' strike, which eventually led to Martin Luther King's fatal visit to Memphis in April 1968.

Lawson was born on September 22, 1928, in Uniontown, Pennsylvania. He received his undergraduate degree at Baldwin-Wallace College in 1952 and a theology degree from Boston University. His first teaching position was in India, where he taught from 1953 to 1956. From 1957 to 1969, Lawson was a field secretary in the South for the Fellowship of Reconciliation, and from 1962 to 1974 was pastor of Centenary United Methodist Church in Memphis. After leaving Memphis, Lawson continued his lifelong interest and involvement in human rights issues and concerns.

In this keynote speech to the two hundred or so college students gathered at Shaw University in Raleigh, North Carolina, in the spring of 1960, Lawson expresses the frustrations of the younger generation of black Americans who were yearning for progress in the quest for justice. He points out the barriers thrown up by an affluent society: "Already the paralysis of talk, the disobedience of piety, the frustration of false ambition, and the insensitiveness of an affluent society yearn to diffuse the meaning and flatten the thrust of America's first major non-violent campaign."

Lawson goes on to describe what the movement is really all about in the minds of the activists: "In the first instance, we who are demonstrators are trying to raise what we call the 'moral issue.' That is, we are pointing to the viciousness of racial segregation and prejudice and calling it evil or sin. The matter is not legal, sociological or racial, it is moral and spiritual. Until America (South and North) honestly accepts the sinful nature of racism, this cancerous disease will continue to rape all of us." For him and many of the young activists at Shaw, "the non-violent movement is asserting, 'get moving. The pace of social change is too slow. At this rate it will be at least another generation before the major forms of segregation disappear. All of Africa will be free before the American Negro attains first-class citizenship. Most of us will be grandparents before we can live normal human lives.' " In short, for Lawson, only nonviolent direct action could speed up the process of change.

SPEECH AT SNCC FOUNDING CONFERENCE[4]

Raleigh, North Carolina
April 1960

These are exciting moments in which to live.

Reflect how over the last few weeks, the "sit-in" movement has leaped from campus to campus, until today hardly any campus remains unaffected. At the beginning of this decade, the student generation was "silent," "uncommitted," or "beatnik." But after only four months, these analogies largely used by adults appear as hasty clichés which should not have been used in the first place. The rapidity and drive of the movement indicates that all the while American students were simply waiting in suspension; waiting for that cause, that ideal, that event, that "actualizing of their faith" which would catapult their right to speak powerfully to their nation and world.

The witness of enthusiastic, but mature young men and women, audacious enough to dare the intimidations and violence of racial injustice, a witness not to be matched by any social effort either in the history of the Negro or in the history of the nation, has caused this impact upon us. In his own time, God has brought this to pass.

But as so frequently happens, these are also enigmatic moments. Enigmatic, for like man in every age who cannot read the signs of the times, many of us are not able to see what appears before us, or hear what is spoken from lunchcounter stools, or understand what has been cried by jail cell bars.

Already the paralysis of talk, the disobedience of piety, the frustration of false ambition, and the insensitiveness of an affluent society yearn to diffuse the meaning and flatten the thrust of America's first major nonviolent campaign.

One great university equates the movement to simply another student fad similar to a panty raid, or long black stockings. Many merchants zealously smothering their Negro customers with courtesy for normal services, anticipated an early end to the unprecedented binge. Certainly no southern white person and few Negroes expected the collegiates to face the hoses, jails, mobs and tear gas with such dignity, fearlessness, and nonviolence. In fact, under any normal conditions, the mere threat of the law was sufficient to send the Negro scurrying into his ghetto. Even astute race reporters accentuate the protest element as the major factor.

Amid this welter of irrelevant and superficial reactions, the primary motifs of the movement, the essential message, the crucial issue raised are often completely missed. So the Christian student who has not yet given his support or mind to the movement might well want to know what the issue is all about. It is just a lot of nonsense over a hamburger? Or is it far more?

To begin, let us note what the issue is not. Many people of good-will, especially Methodists and Nashvillians, have considered my expulsion from Vanderbilt University and the self-righteousness of the press attack as the focus of attention. But nothing could be further from the truth. The expulsion, three months before the completion of the Bachelor of Divinity degree, drastically alters certain immediate personal plans. The press attack tended to make me a symbol of the movement. But such incidents illustrate an ancient way of escaping an existential moment. Call him "the son of the devil," or one of the "men who turn the world upside down," and there are always the gullible who will "swallow the camel."

Police partiality is not the issue. Nashville has been considered one of those "good" cities where racial violence has not been tolerated. Yet, on a Saturday in February, the mystique of yet another popular myth vanished. For only police permissiveness invited young white men to take over store after store in an effort to further intimidate or crush the "sit-in." Law enforcement agents accustomed to viewing crime, were able to mark well-dressed students waiting to make purchases, as loitering on the lunch counter stools, but they were unable even to suspect and certainly not to see assault and battery. Thus potential customers, quietly asking for service, are disorderly, breaching the peace, inciting riots, while swaggering, vilifying, violent, defiant white young teenagers are law-abiding. The police of the nation have always wreaked brutality upon minority groups. So our Nashville experience is nothing new, or even unexpected. We hold nothing against these hard-pressed officers. Such partiality, however, is symptomatic of the diagnosis only—an inevitable by-product—another means of avoiding the encounter. But the "sit-in" does not intend to make such partiality the issue.

Already many well-meaning and notable voices are seeking to define the problem in purely legal terms. But if the students wanted a legal case, they had only to initiate a suit. But not a single city began in this fashion. No one planned to be arrested or desired such. The legal battles which will be fought as a consequence of many arrests never once touch on the matter of eating where you normally shop, or on segregation *per se*.

The apparent misuse of local laws requires new legal definitions which can only be made in the courts, under the judgment of the Constitution of the United States. Old laws and ordinances originally written to hamper labor have been revived to stop or crush the sit-in; disorderly conduct codes which could be used against almost every conceivable peaceful demonstration; conspiracy to block trade charges. Obviously these have no relation to the Bill of Rights and are but gimmicks designed to impede civil liberty.

Let us admit readily that some of the major victories gained for social justice have come through the courts, especially the Supreme Court, while other branches of government were often neglecting their primary function to sustain the American experiment. The Negro has been a law-abiding citizen as he has struggled for justice against many unlawful elements.

But the major defeats have occurred when we have been unable to convince the nation to support or implement the Constitution, when a court decision is ignored or nullified by local and state action. A democratic structure of law remains democratic, remains lawful only as the people are continuously persuaded to be democratic. Law is always nullified by practice and disdain unless the minds and hearts of a people sustain law.

When elements of good-will called for law and order during the crisis in Little Rock, their pleas fell on deaf ears. In many sections of the country where law no longer sustains and enforces segregation, the segregation persists because it is etched upon the habits of mind and emotions of both Negro and white. Separate but equal in transportation has by the Supreme Court been judged as impossible and unconstitutional. Yet in many cities like Nashville the buses more or less remain segregated

Both Negro and white sustain the custom because their basic inner attitudes and fears remain unchanged. Eventually our society must abide by the Constitution and not permit any local law or custom to hinder freedom or justice. But such a society lives by more than law. In the same respect the sit-in movement is not trying to create a legal battle, but points to that which is more than law.

Finally, the issue is not integration. This is particularly true for the Christian oriented person. Certainly the students are asking in behalf of the entire Negro community and the nation that these eating counters become places of service for all persons. But it would be extremely short-sighted to assume that integration is the problem or the word of the "sit-in." To the extent to which the movement reflects deep Christian impulses, desegregation is a necessary next step. But it cannot be the end. If progress has not been at a genuine pace, it is often because the major groups seeking equal rights tactically made desegregation the end and not the means.

The Christian favors the breaking down of racial barriers because the redeemed community of which he is already a citizen recognizes no barriers dividing humanity. The Kingdom of God, as in heaven so on earth, is the distant goal of the Christian. That Kingdom is far more than the immediate need for integration.

Having tried to dispel the many smokescreens spewed to camouflage the purpose and intent of the "sit-in," let me now try as carefully as possible to describe the message of our movement. There are two facets to that message.

In the first instance, we who are demonstrators are trying to raise what we call the "moral issue." That is, we are pointing to the viciousness of racial segregation and prejudice and calling it evil or sin. The matter is not legal, sociological or racial, it is moral and spiritual. Until America (South and North) honestly accepts the sinful nature of racism, this cancerous disease will continue to rape all of us.

For many years Negroes and white have pretended that all was well. "We have good race relations." A city like Nashville has acquired national fame about its progress in desegregation. Yet when the "sit-ins" began, the underlying hatred and sin burst to the surface. A police department with a good reputation for impartiality swiftly became the tool of the disease always there. A mayor, elected with overwhelming Negro support, made the decisions which permitted mob rule. If Nashville had "good race relations," why did such violence explode? The fact is that we were playing make-believe that we were good. All the while Negro and white by pretension, deliberate cooperation and conscious attitudes shared in such a deluded world.

The South and the entire nation are implicated in the same manner. True, there has been progress. For example, lynching has virtually disappeared (although there are many signs that even it might break forth again with unprecedented fury); but the real lynching continues unabated—the lynching of souls, persons (white and Negro) violating its victims absolutely, stripping them of human traits. This actual lynching goes on every day even while we make-believe that lynching is a phenomenon of the past. What's more, the masses of people, including most moderates of both "races," are glibly unaware of the lynching.

The nonviolent movement would convict us all of sin. We assert, "Segregation (racial pride) is sin. God tolerates no breach of his judgment. We are an unhealthy people who contrive every escape from ourselves." Thus a simple act of neatly dressed, non-violent students with purchases in their pockets, precipitated anger and frustration. Many "good" people (white and Negro) said, "This is not the way. We are already making adequate progress." Nonsense! No progress is adequate so long as any man, woman or child of any ethnic group is still a lynch victim.

That the nonviolent effort has convicted us of sin, and thus appealed to consciences is attested by the new found unity and direction now established in Negro communities in places like Durham and Nashville. Witness further the many white people who say, "I never thought the problem was so serious. I feel so ashamed." Many of these people now support the movement.

In the second instance, the nonviolent movement is asserting, "get moving. The pace of social change is too slow. At this rate it will be at least another generation before the major forms of segregation disappear. All of Africa will be free before the American Negro attains first-class citizenship. Most of us will be grandparents before we can live normal human lives."

The choice of the nonviolent method, "the sit-in," symbolizes both judgment and promise. It is a judgment upon middle-class conventional, half-way efforts to deal with radical social evil. It is specifically a judgment upon contemporary civil rights attempts. As one high school student from Chattanooga exclaimed, "We started because we were tired of waiting for you adults to act."

The sum total of all our current efforts to end segregation is not enough to do so. After many court decisions, the deeper south we go, the more token integration (and that only in public schools) we achieve. *Crisis* magazine [published by the NAACP] becomes known as a "black bourgeois" club organ, rather than a forceful instrument for justice. Interracial agencies expect to end segregation with discussions and teas. Our best agency (the NAACP) accents fundraising and court action rather than developing our greatest resource, a people no longer the victims of racial evil who can act in a disciplined manner to implement the constitution. The Negro church and minister function as in an earlier day and not as God's agents to redeem society.

But the sit-in is likewise a sign of promise: God's promise that if radically Christian methods are adopted the rate of change can be vastly increased. This is why nonviolence dominates the movement's perspective. Under Christian nonviolence, Negro students reject the hardship of disobedient passivity and fear, but embrace the hardship (violence and jail) of obedience. Such nonviolence strips the segregationalist power structure of its major weapon: the manipulation of law or law enforcement to keep the Negro in his place.

Furthermore, such an act attracts, strengthens and sensitizes the support of many white persons in the South and across the nation. (The numbers who openly identify themselves with the "sit-in" daily grow.)

Nonviolence in the Negro's struggle gains a fresh maturity. And the Negro gains a new sense of his role in molding a redeemed society. The "word" from the lunch counter stool demands a sharp re-assessment of our organized evil and a radical Christian obedience to transform that evil. Christian nonviolence provides both that re-assessment and the faith of obedience. The extent to which the Negro joined by many others apprehends and incorporates nonviolence determines the degree that the world will acknowledge fresh social insight from America.

MARTIN LUTHER KING JR.

On May 21, 1961, shortly after the Freedom Riders were attacked and beaten in Birmingham as they attempted to break down the segregated interstate transportation system, a rally was held in support of their efforts. King flew into Montgomery and spoke to the rally, praising the Freedom Riders: "The Freedom Ride grew out of a recognition of the American dilemma and a desire to bring the nation to a realization of its noble dream. We are all deeply indebted to CORE for this creative idea. These courageous freedom riders have faced ugly and howling mobs in order to arouse the dozing conscience of the nation." He urges the federal government "to assure every citizen his constitutional rights," otherwise, "we will be plunged into a dark abyss of chaos." King concludes with a call for an all-out campaign to end segregation in Alabama, but one that will be nonviolent, following the "magnificent example of strong courageous action devoid [of] violence. . . . This I am convinced is our most creative way to break loose from the paralyzing shackles of segregation."

SPEECH AT A RALLY TO SUPPORT THE FREEDOM RIDERS[5]

Montgomery, Alabama
May 21, 1961

The words that I will utter tonight were written this morning as I flew at an altitude of 38,000 feet on a jet plane from New York to Atlanta, Georgia. As that gigantic instrument stretched its wings through the air like an eagle and moved smoothly toward its destination, many thoughts ran through my mind. On the one hand I thought of how the technological developments of the United States had brought the nation and the world to an awe-inspiring threshold of the future. I thought of how our scientific genius had helped us to dwarf distance and place time in chains. I thought of how we had carved highways through the stratosphere, and how our jet planes had compressed into minutes distances that once took days. On the other hand I thought of that brutal mob in Alabama and the reign of terror that had engulfed Anniston, Birmingham and Montgomery. I thought of the tragic expressions of man's inhumanity to man that still exist in certain sections of our country. I could not help being concerned about this glaring contrast, this tragic gulf. Through our scientific and technological developments we have lifted our heads to the skys and yet our feet are still firmly planted in the muck of barbarism and racial hatred. Indeed this is America's chief moral dilemma. And unless the Nation grapples with this dilemma forthrightly and firmly, she will be relegated to a second rate power in the world.

The price that America must pay for the continued oppression of the Negro is the price of its own destruction. America's greatest defense against communism is to take the offense for justice, freedom and human dignity.

The Freedom Ride grew out of a recognition of the American dilemma and a desire to bring the nation to a realization of its noble dream. We are all deeply indebted to CORE for this creative idea. These courageous freedom riders have faced ugly and howling mobs in order to arouse the dozing conscience of the nation. Some of them are now hospitalized as a result of physical injury. They have accepted blows without retaliation. One day all of America will be proud of their achievements.

Over the past few days Alabama has been the scene of a literal reign of terror. It has sunk to a level of barbarity comparable to the tragic days of Hitler's Germany.

Now who is responsible for this dark night of terror in Alabama? Certainly the mob itself must be condemned. When people sink to such a low level of hatred and evil that they will beat unmercifully nonviolent men and women, they should be apprehended and prosecuted on the basis of the crime they have committed. But the ultimate responsibility for the hideous action in Alabama last week must be placed at the doorsteps of the Governor of this State. His consistent preaching of defiance of the law, his vitriolic public pronouncements, and his irresponsible actions created the atmosphere in which violence could thrive. When the governor of a state will urge people to defy the Law of the Land, and teach them to disrespect the Supreme Court, he is consciously and unconsciously aiding and abetting the forces of violence.

Among the many sobering lesson that we can learn from the events of the past week is that the deep South will not impose limits upon itself. The limits must be imposed from without. Unless the Federal Government acts forthrightly in the South to assure every citizen his constitutional rights, we will be plunged into a dark abyss of chaos. The federal government must not stand idly by while blood thirsty mobs beat nonviolent students with impunity.

The familiar cry of state rights will certainly come up at this time. The South will argue that Federal intervention is an invasion of the Rights of States. We must answer this argument by making it clear that we too believe in State Rights. We are committed to Jeffersonian democracy and would not want to see a complete centralization of government. But although States must have rights, no State must have the right to do wrong. We must not allow state wrongs to exist under the banner of State Rights. To deny individuals the right to vote through threats, intimidations and other insidious methods is not a State Right, but a State Wrong. To trample over a people with the iron feet of economic exploitation is not a State Right, but a State Wrong. To keep a group of people confined to nasty slums and dirty hovels is not a State Right, but a State Wrong. To confine certain citizens to segregated schools and deprive them of an equal education is a State Wrong moving under the guise of a State Right. To allow hooded perpetrators of violence and vicious mobs to beat, kick and even kill people who only want to be free is a State Wrong without one scintilla of right. We are for *State Rights* when they are *Right.*

The other familiar cry that we will hear is that freedom riders, the federal government and no other agency can force integration upon the South. Morals, they argue, cannot be legislated. To this we must answer it may be true that morals cannot be legislated, but behavior can be regulated. It may be true that laws and federal action cannot change bad internal attitudes, but they can control the external effects of those internal attitudes. The law may not be able to make a man love me, but it can keep him from lynching me. The fact is that the habits, if not the hearts of men have been, and are being changed everyday by federal action.

The recent developments in Alabama should challenge us more than ever before to delve deeper into the struggle for freedom in this State. There must now be a full scale nonviolent assault on the system of segregation in Alabama. In a few days I will call a meeting of the executive board of the Southern Christian Leadership Conference to map plans for a massive campaign to end segregation in Alabama. This will include an intensified voter registration drive, a determined effort to integrate the public schools, lunch counters, public parks, theaters etc. In short, we will seek to mobilize thousands of people, committed to the method of nonviolence, who will physically identify themselves with the struggle to end segregation in Alabama. We will present our physical bodies as instruments to defeat the unjust system.

We cannot in all good conscience sit complacently by while Alabama has no respect for law and order and while it continues to impose upon the Negro the most inhuman form of oppression. We must stand up now not for ourselves alone, but in order to carry our nation back to those great wells of democracy which were dug deep by the founding fathers in the formulation of the Constitution and the Declaration of Independence. If Alabama continues to follow its present course of defiance, lawlessness, and Hitlerism, the image of the United States will be irreparably scarred and the results may be fatal in terms of our national survival.

As I close may I strongly urge you to continue to follow the path of nonviolence. The freedom riders have given us a magnificent example of strong courageous action devoid [of] violence. This I am convinced is our most creative way to break loose from the paralyzing shackles of segregation. As we intensify our efforts in Alabama, Mississippi, and the deep South generally, we will face difficult days. Angry passions of the opposition will be aroused. Honesty impels me to admit that we are in for a season of suffering. I pray that recognizing the necessity of suffering we will make of it a virtue. To suffer in a righteous cause is to grow to our humanity's full stature. If only to save ourselves, we need the vision to see the ordeals of this generation as the opportunity to transform ourselves and American society.

So in the days ahead let us not sink into the quicksands of violence; rather let us stand on the high ground of love and noninjury. Let us continue to be strong spiritual anvils that will wear out many a physical hammer.

DIANE NASH

Diane Nash was a significant figure in the sit-in movement of the early 1960s and played a major role in the SNCC that grew out of the sit-ins.[6] Born in Chicago in 1938, Diane enrolled at Howard University in Washington, DC, but transferred to Fisk University in Nashville where she majored in English. She participated in James Lawson's workshops on nonviolence in late 1959. The workshop students became the first sit-in group attempting to integrate Nashville's downtown stores. Diane was the unofficial leader of the group as they tested their sit-in tactics in December 1959, before launching the full-blown effort on February 7, 1960. The sit-ins continued through the month of February and eighty-two students were arrested. Many of the students decided to stay in jail rather than pay the bail and eventually Mayor Ben West agreed to release the students and establish a biracial committee to make recommendations to desegrate the stores. Nash served as a member of the committee and ultimately the students were successful as the lunch counters and other facilities in Nashville were integrated. By June 1960, lunch counters in seven Tennessee cities had been opened to black citizens as well.

In April, the organizing meeting of the SNCC was held in Raleigh, North Carolina, and Nash played a significant role in that meeting. The next event was in Rock Hill, South Carolina, when students were arrested at a CORE meeting and jailed. Their response was the "jail, no bail" strategy. SNCC members, led by Nash and others, such as Ruby Doris Smith, Charles Sherrod, and Charles Jones, were arrested and served thirty-seven days in jail. After her release, Nash left school and went to work full time for SNCC. The "jail, no bail" strategy worked all over the South, as jails filled to overflowing and put increased pressure on white authorities.

Nash also took an active role in the Freedom Rides of May 1961. After the Freedom Riders were attacked in Anniston, Alabama, on May 14, Nash organized her Nashville students and they went to Birmingham to pick up where the original group had stopped. Later in 1961, SNCC, acting on the advice of Ella Baker, developed a two-prong approach, one for direct action, which was headed by Nash, and one for voter registration campaigns, which was directed by Charles Jones. Some time later, Diane went to work for SCLC in Atlanta, where she married James Bevel, and in April 1962, she was jailed in Jackson, Mississippi for teaching nonviolent protest techniques to young black children. She insisted on staying in jail, even though she was four months pregnant;

sentenced to two years in prison, she was released after a short stay in jail.[7]

As the movement gained success and reached its major goals with the passage of the Civil Rights Act of 1964 and the Voting Rights Act of 1965, Diane left her activism with SNCC and SCLC, but she continued to work against racial oppression and for social change. She was active in the antiwar protest, and after divorcing Bevel, she taught in Chicago and lectured on women's rights issues.

The speech included here was presented at a symposium in Detroit in August 1961, sponsored by the National Catholic Conference for Interracial Justice. The symposium focused on the topic of the "New Negro" in American life.

INSIDE THE SIT-INS AND FREEDOM RIDES: TESTIMONY OF A SOUTHERN STUDENT[8]

Detroit, Michigan
August 1961

I see no alternative but that this text must be a personal interpretation of my own experience within the region known as "Dixie."

My participation in the movement began in February 1960, with the lunch counter "sit-ins." I was then a student at Fisk University, but several months ago I interrupted my schoolwork for a year in order to work full time with the movement. My occupation at present is coordinating secretary for the Nashville Nonviolent Movement.

I should not wish to infer that I speak for the southern movement, for I think that there is no single person who can do that. Although many of the following statements can be generalized for the entire movement in the South, I shall refer largely to Nashville, Tennessee, for that is where I have worked.

I submit, then, that the nonviolent movement in that city:

1. is based upon and motivated by love;

2. attempts to serve God and mankind;

3. strives toward what we call the beloved community.

This is religion. This is applied religion. I think it has worked for me and I think it has worked for you and I think it is the work of our Church.

One fact occurs to me. This is that the problems of the world lie within men and women; yes, within you, me, and the people with whom we come in contact daily. Further, the problems lie not so much in our action as in our inaction. We have upon ourselves as individuals in a democracy the political, economic, sociological, and spiritual responsibilities of our country. I'm wondering now if we in the United States are really remembering that this must be a government "of the people" and "by the people" as well as "for the people." Are we really appreciating the fact that if you and I do not meet these responsibilities then our government *cannot* survive as a democracy?

The problems in Berlin, Cuba, or South Africa are, I think, identical with the problem in Jackson, Mississippi, or Nashville, Tennessee. I believe that when men come to believe in their own dignity and in the worth of their own freedom, and when they can acknowledge the God and the dignity that is within every man, then Berlin and Jackson will not be problems. After I had been arrested from a picket line about three weeks ago, I jotted down the following note, with this meeting in mind:

> If the policeman had acknowledged the God within each of the students with whom I was arrested last night, would he have put us in jail? Or would he have gone into the store we were picketing and tried to persuade the manager to hire Negroes and to treat all people fairly? If one acknowl- edges the God within men, would anyone ask for a "cooling off period," or plead for gradualism, or would they realize that white and Negro Amer- icans are committing sin every day that they hate each other and every day that they allow an evil system to exist without doing all they can to rectify it as soon as they can?

Segregation reaches into every aspect of life to oppress the Negro and to rob him of his dignity in the South. The very fact that he is forced to be separated obviously implies his inferiority. Therefore the phrase "separate but equal" de- nies itself. The things non-black Americans take for granted, such as a movie and dinner date for college students, or a coffee-break downtown, are usually denied the black American in the South. Sometimes he may obtain these services if he wishes to compromise his dignity. He might, for example, attend a down- town movie if he would enter through the alley entrance and climb to the bal- cony to be seated.

But these are not the most important things. The purpose of the movement and of the sit-ins and the Freedom Rides and any other such actions, as I see it, is to bring about a climate in which all men are respected as men, in which there is appreciation of the dignity of man and in which each individual is free to grow and produce to his fullest capacity. We of the movement often refer to this goal as the concept of the redeemed or the "beloved" community.

In September 1959, I came to Nashville as a student at Fisk University. This was the first time that I had been as far south as Tennessee; therefore, it was the first time that I had encountered the blatant segregation that exists in the South. I came then to see the community in sin. Seeing signs designating "white" or "colored," being told, "We don't serve niggers in here," and, as happened in one restaurant, being looked in the eye and told, "Go around to the back door where you belong," had a tremendous psychological impact on me. To begin with, I didn't agree with the premise that I was inferior, and I had a difficult time complying with it. Also, I felt stifled and boxed in since so many areas of living were restricted. The Negro in the South is told constantly, "You can't sit here." "You can't work there." "You can't live here, or send your children to school there." "You can't use this park, or that swimming pool," and on and on and on. Restrictions extend into housing, schools, jobs (Negroes, who provide a built-in lower economic class, are employed in the most menial capacities and are paid the lowest wages). Segregation encompasses city parks, swimming pools and recreational facilities, lunch counters, restaurants, movies, drive-in movies, drive-in restaurants, restrooms, water fountains, bus terminals, train stations, hotels, motels, auditoriums (Negro college students usually attend the most important formal dances of the year in the school gymnasium), amusement parks, legitimate theaters, bowling alleys, skating rinks—all of these areas are segregated. Oppression extends to every area of life.

In the deeper South, Negroes are denied use of public libraries, they are denied entrance even to certain department stores, are discriminated against on city buses, in taxicabs, and in voting. Failure to comply with these oppressions results in beatings, in house-burnings and bombings, and economic reprisals, as we saw in Fayette County, Tennessee, and in Montgomery in the case of the Freedom Riders. Significant, however, are the many countless incidents that the public never even hears about.

As can easily be imagined, all this has a real effect upon the Negro. I won't attempt to analyze here the effect of the system upon the Negro, but I should like to make a few observations. An organism must make some type of adjustment to its environment. The Negro, however, continues to deny consciously to himself, and to his children, that he is inferior. Yet each time he uses a "colored" facility, he testifies to his own inferiority. Many of the values that result from this dual selfconcept are amazing to note. Let me relate to you one very interesting incident.

I spent thirty days in the jail in Rock Hill, South Carolina. For the first few days the heat was intense in the cell. Breathing was difficult. Everyone was perspiring profusely. We couldn't understand why the women in the cell hesitated to ask that a window be opened or the heat be turned down. It turned out that it was because they were so often cold in their homes, and had come to value heat so highly, that they were willing to suffer from it if they could just have it.

A further example of these curious values is given by the Negro who has received several college degrees or who has a profession and who can consider himself a successful and important man, but who, at the same time, will still attest to his own inferiority by cooperating with segregation. What value, or lack of it, accounts for the fact that so many faculty members at Negro colleges have not disassociated themselves from universities which have expelled student demonstrators? Why are the faculty members and administrators of southern Negro colleges not on the picket lines and sitting at the lunch counters? I think the answer lies within the answer of what Jim Crow does to the Negro. For one thing, it stymies his ability to be free by placing emphasis on the less important things, but on things, nevertheless, which Negroes have been denied.

Segregation has its destructive effect upon the segregator also. The most outstanding of these effects perhaps is fear. I can't forget how openly this fear was displayed in Nashville on the very first day that students there sat-in. Here were Negro students, quiet, in good discipline, who were consciously attempting to show no ill will, even to the point of making sure that they had pleasant and calm facial expressions. The demonstrators did nothing more than sit on the stools at the lunch counter. Yet, from the reaction of the white employees of the variety stores and from the onlookers, some dreadful monster might just as well have been about to devour them all. Waitresses dropped things. Store managers and personnel perspired. Several cashiers were led off in tears. One of the best remembered incidents of that day took place in a ladies restroom of a department store. Two Negro students, who had sat-in at the lunch counter, went into the ladies restroom which was marked "white" and were there as a heavy-set, older white lady, who might have been seeking refuge from the scene taking place at the lunch counter, entered. Upon opening the door and finding the two Negro girls inside, the woman threw up her hands and, nearly in tears, exclaimed, "Oh! Nigras everywhere!"

So segregation engenders fear in the segregator, especially needless fear of what will happen if integration comes; in short, fear of the unknown. Then Jim Crow fosters ignorance. The white person is denied the educational opportunities of exchange with people of a race other than his own. Bias makes for the hatred which we've all seen stamped upon the faces of whites in newspaper pictures of the mob. The white hoodlum element is often provoked and egged on by the management or by onlookers; this is a type of degradation into which the segregator unfortunately slips.

Police departments can also sink to a sorry state. Bias lets the police turn their heads and not see the attacks made against demonstrators. In Nashville, police permissiveness has served to make the hoodlum element more and more bold, with incidents of real seriousness resulting, even a real tragedy, as was the case in the bombing of a Negro attorney's home last year during the sit-ins.

An unhappy result of segregation is that communications between the races become so limited as to be virtually nonexistent. The "good race relations" to which segregators in the South often refer, is nothing more than a complete breakdown in communication so that one race is not aware of any of the other race's objections or of interracial problems. This has been clearly exemplified in cities where race relations have been called "good" and where the masses of Negroes have rallied behind students in boycotts of downtown areas that have been, reportedly, up to 98 per cent effective among the Negro population.

By not allowing all its citizens to produce and contribute to the limit of their capacities, the entire city, or region, or country, will suffer, as can be seen in the South's slow progress in industrial, political, and other areas today and in the weakening of American influence abroad as a result of race hatred.

Segregation, moreover, fosters dishonesty between the races. It makes people lie to each other. It allows white merchants to accept the customers' money, but to give them unequal service, as at the Greyhound and Trailway Bus Lines, where all customers pay the same fares but some are not free to use all the facilities in the terminals and at restaurants where rest stops are made. Fares are equal, but service is not. The system forces the Negro maid to tell her employer that everything is all right and that she's satisfied, but when she is among her friends she talks about the injustice of the system.

Worst of all, however, is the stagnancy of thought and character—of both whites and Negroes—which is the result of the rationalization that is necessary in order that the oppressed and oppressor may live with a system of slavery and human abasement.

I can remember Nashville in this stage of sin when I first came there in September 1959, a few months before the sit-in movement was to begin. As a new student at Fisk University that September, I was completely unaware that over the next few months I would really experience segregation; that I would see raw hatred; that I would see my friends beaten; that I would be a convict several times and, as is the case at the moment, that there would be a warrant out for my arrest in Jackson, Mississippi. Expecting my life to pursue a rather quiet course, I was also unaware that I would begin to feel part of a group of people suddenly proud to be called "black." To be called "Negro" had once been thought of as derogatory and had been softened by polite company to "colored person." At one time, to have been called "nigger" was a gross insult and hurt keenly. Within the movement, however, we came to a realization of our own worth. We began to see our role and our responsibility to our country and to our fellow men, so that to be called "nigger" on the picket line, or anywhere, was now an unimportant thing that no longer produced in us that flinch. As to the typical white southerner who compromises with "nigra" we only secretly wish for a moment when we could gracefully help him with his phonetics, explaining that it's "knee—grow."

The revolution in the Negro student's concept of the name of his own race is really important only as it is indicative of change in the Negro's concept of himself and of his race.

Through the unity and purposefulness of the experience of the Nashville Negro, there was born a new awareness of himself as an individual.

There was also born, on the part of whites, a new understanding and awareness of the Negro as a person to be considered and respected.

I think an outstanding example of this latter change was revealed by the negotiations which took place between Negro students and leaders and the white merchants who were the managers of downtown lunch counters. It became apparent to me during the negotiations that the white southerner was not in the habit of taking the Negro seriously. During the initial stages, the attitude of the merchants was one of sort of patting us on the head and saying, "Yes, we've listened to your story and maybe segregation is bad, but you can't have integration now, because it'll ruin our business." And they closed the matter there. However, after the sit-ins continued and after the moral weight of the community was felt, through our 98 per cent effective boycott; after a number of talks in which the merchants got to know us as people and saw our problem (and we saw theirs), there was indeed a beautiful type of awareness born, to the extent that one of the merchants, who incidentally was a white southerner, made what I think was a real concession: "Well, it was simply that we didn't see they were right and we were wrong."

I think we can also see this awareness of Negro and white for each other as individuals, in the attitudes of the crowds who watched the demonstrations. In the beginning, as I mentioned, there was mostly fear. However, after the violence was allowed to go on and after the police protection broke down and officers insisted on looking the other way while people were beaten, not infrequently there was a white person in the crowd who would see someone about to tear up one of the picket signs or about to hit someone, and would go up and stop this person and say, "No, no! You can't do that." And often they would get into a discussion which sometimes looked constructive. I hope it was.

There also has been a real change in the temper of the crowd, a change from fear to, I think, just curiosity and watching because something is going on. There is not the hatred and the serious fear and emotional tension that there once was. In Nashville, since the integration of the lunch counters and dining rooms and department stores, we've been fortunate enough to have movies also integrated. As I mentioned earlier, in the downtown area Negroes could not attend movies unless they entered through an alley entrance and sat in the balcony. However, after several weeks of standing-in, they are now allowed to use the theaters' facilities on a fully integrated basis.

Swimming pools in Nashville have been closed this summer under very strange circumstances. It seems that on one particular day a group of Negroes attempted to integrate the city's swimming pools, which incidentally, of course, are tax-supported. On the next day, the park commissioners closed all the swimming pools in the city, for financial reasons. Now it seems that the mayor did not know anything about the park commission being in serious financial difficulty, nor did any of the other city officials, and strangely enough the park commissioners could not be reached for comment. But I'm afraid our swimming pools are closed for financial reasons.

The H.G. Hill food stores are currently being picketed. This is our local project for the moment. This company hires Negroes only for warehouse work and as truck drivers and, of course, pays them below union standards. Many stores are in completely Negro neighborhoods and even in these stores we cannot have Negro cashiers or personnel.

I am eager to talk with you about the Freedom Rides because I think that they denote a new and important level of effort. And I feel that more such projects will be necessary for the ultimate success of the southern movement, especially in states of the deep South, such as Alabama and Mississippi. As you know, the idea of a Freedom Ride was conceived and the project was begun by the Congress of Racial Equality. The first trip originated in Washington, DC, in May of this year (1961). From Washington, the group traveled through most of the southern states and was repeatedly beaten and jailed as the bus made its way across Dixie. As you remember, at Anniston and Birmingham, Alabama, the bus met with mob violence; the CORE members were beaten and the bus was burned. Most of the riders were hospitalized for a short time. Mr. James Peck, who was one of the whites along with the group, had fifty stitches taken in his head as a result of the repeated beatings that he had to take. Attempting to get a bus to their destination, which was Montgomery, the riders were told that no driver would take them further. In a state of exhaustion then, after traveling hundreds of miles under tremendous tension, repeated jailings and beatings, they took a plane to New Orleans, which was the last stop of the planned itinerary.

In Nashville, the students had been closely following the Freedom Bus as it moved from town to town, for the people on the bus somehow were ourselves. Their dream of freedom in travel was our dream also. Their aspirations were our own aspirations. There is a tremendous bond between people who really stand up or ride for what they feel is just and right. You see, the CORE members were riding and being beaten for our freedom, too. Therefore, it was quite simple. Mob violence must not stop men's striving toward right. Freedom Rides and other such actions must not be stopped until our nation is really free.

In Nashville then, we were faced with a grave situation. We called a meeting of the students and adults within the movement. Talking by phone with persons who had been at the scene of the tragedies in Birmingham and Anniston, we were told, "Don't come. It's a bloodbath. Be assured, someone will be killed if you do come." Upon hearing this, the Nashville group set about preparing themselves for the fact that someone of them would be killed when they took the trip.

You see, these people faced the probability of their own deaths before they ever left Nashville. Several made out wills. A few more gave me sealed letters to be mailed if they were killed. Some told me frankly that they were afraid, but they knew that this was something that they must do because freedom was worth it. I, incidentally, feel very blessed and very grateful for knowing such people and for being able to call most of them my friends.

The purpose of any nonviolent demonstration is to focus the attention of people on how evil segregation really is and then to change their hearts. Some people have been confused about the objectives of the Freedom Rides, and I've heard it said that "the point has been made," so there is no use in going on. The objective of the Freedom Ride from Birmingham was not just to point out that people cannot ride freely but to make it possible for all persons to ride and use terminal facilities without being discriminated against. Until that objective has been attained there *is* reason for going on.

So the drama continued. The bus left Nashville about 6:00 A.M. en route to Birmingham, Alabama. My own role was to stay at the telephone, to keep contact with Birmingham, to hear from the riders as often as they could call, to make arrangements ahead in Montgomery, to keep the Justice Department advised—in short, to coordinate.

The students were held on the bus for some time when they reached Birmingham, and subsequently were taken into "protective custody." The next morning at 4:25, I received a call from them. They said that they'd been driven by the police to the Alabama-Tennessee border and had been put out of the car there on the highway and told to cross the border. At the moment they were on the open highway and felt unsafe. They did not know where shelter was, but would call again as soon as possible. They had been fasting since they had been in jail the day before.

We immediately sent an automobile to get them, and the next time we heard from them, they advised us that they were returning to Birmingham and were determined to board a bus for Montgomery. The police chief wasn't going to get off that easily.

The next night was an all-night vigil for them at the bus station. They were told, again, that no driver would drive the bus. Finally, next morning they were able to get a driver and the bus moved on to Montgomery, Alabama. We all read about that morning, I think, in Montgomery, Alabama. I wish I could have shared with you the moments in our office when that violence was taking place. It seemed that when the bus arrived and the mob attacked the students, they were immediately dispersed. People put a few of them in their cars and took them home. Within a very short time the group was scattered throughout the city.

We listed all the names of the persons who had left Nashville and began trying to account for them. We would ask the students as they called in, "When did you last see _____?" The reports we got that morning were: John Lewis was bleeding profusely from the head; another student seemed unconscious; Jim Swirg had been cornered by about sixteen or seventeen men and was being beaten. They had lead pipes, knives, and guns. In a relatively short time, however, we were able to account for all of the students. Miraculously, no one was dead.

Shortly afterwards, in the job of coordinator, I went down to Montgomery to help with the work there. I think you probably read about the meeting which took place in the church in Montgomery that night, at which Martin Luther King, the Freedom Riders, and a number of other people were present. When the police would not afford the church protection, a car was burned. There were incidents of violence and a mob of thousands, I understand, gathered outside.

People in the church that night didn't know how close they were to real tragedy. This was the night martial law was declared in Montgomery. That night everyone remained in the church throughout the night.

Now something very interesting took place in the church that night. I think it can almost be a generalization that the Negroes in Alabama and Mississippi and elsewhere in the deep South are terribly afraid until they get into the movement. In the dire danger in which we were that night, no one expressed anything except concern for freedom and the thought that someday we'll be free. We stayed there until dawn and everyone was naturally tired, but no one said so. There were about three thousand people there that night, representing all walks of life, from young children to the elder people in the community. I don't think I've ever seen a group of people band together as the crowd in the church did that night.

Finally at dawn, we were escorted home by the troops. The students boarded the bus for Jackson, along with a second bus that had come from Nashville carrying five ministers. The buses left for Jackson, Mississippi, and I think we pretty well know the story from there on. Immediately upon arrival, the people were jailed. Since then there have been roughly three hundred people jailed for doing nothing more than riding a bus.

It interests me that the Freedom Riders have been called "trouble makers," "seekers of violence," and "seekers of publicity." Few people have seen the point: here are people acting within their constitutional and moral rights; they have done nothing more than ride a bus or use a facility that anyone else would normally expect to use any day of the year, but they have been confined and imprisoned for it. And somehow the Attorney General and the President of the United States and the Justice Department of the United States can do nothing about such a gross injustice. As far as being seekers of violence and publicity, the students have, at all times, remained nonviolent. Are not the committers of violence responsible for their own actions? To date, as I've said, there have been approximately three hundred people jailed as Freedom Riders. All were returned within the last two weeks for arraignment. There stood to be lost five hundred dollars for each person who did not return to Jackson. And out of 189 who were on bond, all except nine were returned. The riders had been convicted in the city court and are currently appealing on the county court level. Their appeal trials have been set at the rate of two per day between now and January. The first trial took place yesterday. The result of that trial is that Mr. Henry Thomas was convicted of breach of peace, sentenced to four months imprisonment, and his bond was set at two thousand dollars.

Now I think that this is a serious question for the American public to consider. Is this really the country in which we live? This is a serious moment, I think, for those who take democracy and freedom seriously. Remember now that these Freedom Riders are citizens of the United States who can be called on to go to war and who are receiving treatment of this type.

If so harsh a treatment is involved for an action as right as riding a bus, perhaps one as unimportant as riding a bus, can we not draw from that an inference of what life in the South for the Negro must really be like?

I think that it is most essential that the government move at a rate of progress adequate to meet the needs of the governed. Not being able to do so has resulted in the tragedies of Little Rock, New Orleans, and Montgomery. It might be interesting to note that we have not had incidents such as New Orleans and Montgomery where there has been adequate government. There always needs to be a Faubus or a Patterson.

The Negro must be represented by those who govern. Without this representation, there is moral slavery, if not physical. No person or country can have a clear conscience and a noble mien with such a sin on its conscience. I'm interested now in the people who call for gradualism. The answer, it seems to me, is to stop sinning and stop now! How long must we wait? It's been a century. How gradual can you get? Montgomery has shown how far it has advanced on its own; we've seen this from the mob to the governor. As for the legal position about the right to serve whom one pleases, I would say that this position does not alter the fact that segregation is wrong. Segregation on the bus lines, trains, and planes is wrong *intra*state as well as *inter*state. The press has made much of the interstate passage. However, the Freedom Riders are just as concerned with intrastate travel, because we're concerned with the injustice of segregation.

The Negro is seeking to take advantage of the opportunities that society offers; the same opportunities that others take for granted, such as a cup of coffee at Woolworth's, a good job, an evening at the movies, and dignity. Persons favoring segregation often refer to the rights of man, but they never mention the rights of Negro men.

I would like to say also that the students and the adults who have taken part in this movement and who are doing so now are dead serious. We're ready to give our lives. It is a slight miracle, I think, that in the almost two years since February of 1960 there has not been a fatality. But we have come amazingly close to it several times. Let me mention the case of William Barbee who was on the Freedom Ride when it arrived at Montgomery and met with mob violence. Barbee had gone on a few hours ahead to arrange for cars and other necessities before the riders arrived. When they did get there and were attacked, he was busy trying to get them into taxi cabs or ambulances and take them where they could receive medical attention. Just as about all of them had gotten into cabs, the mob attacked him.

At that moment a Negro man was passing by. He was on his way to pay a bill. It was just a regular day in his life until he saw one of the mobsters with his foot upon William Barbee's neck. Mr. Nichols, who had lived in the South all his life, said that he started to go ahead about his business. But, he said, he knew that he would never be able to live with his conscience again if that man killed Barbee. So he turned around and pulled the man off. Well, Mr. Nichols landed in the hospital next to Barbee. But even after he had pulled the man off, the crowd went back to William Barbee, and he was again in danger of death when the head of the highway patrol came along and was able to get the mob off with a gun. This student, William Barbee, is back in the movement, has been beaten up on a picket line and jailed again. I think that this is indicative of some of the determination and the seriousness with which we take the cause.

I think that quite often today you can hear the strains of a very old spiritual that's sung quite seriously. Some of the words are: "Before I be a slave I would be buried in my grave and go home to My Lord and be free."

From those who say they approve the ends, not the means, I would be interested in suggestions for a means which would yield freedom without delay. Let us look at the means. The students have chosen nonviolence as a technique; there is no reason why they couldn't have taken up guns. It was a responsible choice, I think. We have decided that if there is to be suffering in this revolution (which is really what the movement is—a revolution), we will take the suffering upon ourselves and never inflict it upon our fellow man, because we respect him and recognize the God within him.

Let us see now what the movement needs. The movement is very much in need of a major federal decision that will result in enforcement of the Constitution and federal law. (You might be interested to know that during the Freedom Rides Governor Ross Barnett of Mississippi informed me of two very interesting things by telephone: He said (1) that he did not feel that Supreme Court decisions applied to his state, and (2) that he intended to enforce Mississippi law over and above any federal law that conflicted with it.) Along with a major federal decision to follow through on civil rights, there is needed a major decision on the part of the people. There is needed a realization that the problem lies as much in Jackson or Nashville as it does in Berlin or anywhere in the world. The problem, I think, centers around the questions of truth, honesty, justice, and democracy. What is needed is concern for human rights—not just white human rights. Until such time as this realization comes, Freedom Rides and similar such south-wide projects are necessary. Count on more of them.

As far as the Catholic student and the Catholic Church are concerned, from our pulpits we need directness and we need emphasis. If this is not an area in which the Church must work, what is? It seems that our role must necessarily be leadership. And anything but outspoken and direct leadership in this movement is immoral. Newman Clubs and campus organizations in the South can certainly revitalize themselves by contacting local movements or starting one, pledging their support and participation. And the same is true for the problems which exist in the North.

There are roles for all of us to play. First, of course, is the role of the participant, who really pickets or sits in. Then there is the role of the observer. I don't know if you have heard, but a number of whites are being utilized effectively as observers. In the integration of lunch counters and movie theaters, many of the older church women who have been sympathetic with the cause for a long time, but who haven't had an opportunity to speak out, have helped by doing such things as sitting next to Negroes at the lunch counters or at movies and thus creating an appearance of normalcy. These people have become quite enthusiastic about their new role. There have been several cases of—well, real "bigness." One lady is known to have drunk countless cups of coffee and gained ten pounds in sitting at lunch counters all day for several days in a row and looking normal. Several have been known to see the same picture over and over again. Also looking normal. For those in the North, as I mentioned, there are local problems, and we also need groups that we can call upon to support the southern movement.

Finally, this movement has been called one of passive resistance. But it is not that at all. Rather it might be called one of active insistence. In regard to our own roles and the role of our Church, I think we need to understand that this is a question of *real* love of man and love of God. Is there such a thing as moderate love of God or moderate disdain for sin? I think we need radical good to combat radical evil. Consider the South. It can be the answer for the free world; it can be the pivot. The problem there is a vital challenge for truth; for respect for man. In a word, it is a question of dignity.

MARTIN LUTHER KING JR.

This speech by King was given at a particularly difficult time in the 1963 Birmingham campaign led by King and the SCLC. The Birmingham Project C (for confrontation) campaign had been developed by King and his SCLC associates such as Andrew Young and Wyatt Tee Walker after the failure of the Albany protest, which resulted in a stalemate in that Georgia city. Fred Shuttlesworth had asked SCLC to come into Birmingham; after Albany, SCLC and King saw a need for a dramatic success in the movement. They went into Birmingham determined to get it. James Lawson came from Memphis to help train protesters willing to go to jail and King himself spent many days in prison, during which he composed his stirring and important "Letter from the Birmingham Jail." The ensuing protests were met with bitter attacks from the public safety commissioner, "Bull" Connor, who ordered police dogs and fire hoses into the fray against the protesters—many of whom were children.[9] The end result was an agreement that broke down segregation in Birmingham. The brutality of the opposition led the Kennedy Administration to propose what became the Civil Rights Act of 1964 and its passage, some say, marked the high-water mark of the Civil Rights Movement. This speech was given by King on May 3, 1963, in the evening of one of the most brutal days of the protest.

SPEECH AT SIXTEENTH STREET BAPTIST CHURCH[10]

Birmingham, Alabama
May 3, 1963

Thank you, my dear friends and fellow citizens of Birmingham, Alabama. At points, today was a dark day in Birmingham. The policemen were mean to us. They got their violent, angry dogs and turned them loose on nonviolent people. Unarmed people. But not only that, they got their water system working. And here and there we saw the water hose with water pouring on young boys and girls, old men and women, with great and staggering force. Birmingham was a mean city today. But in spite of the meanness of Birmingham, we must confront her with our kindness and our goodness and our determination to be nonviolent. As difficult as it is, we must meet hate with love. As hard as it is, we must meet physical force with Soul Force. And let us keep going down the path of nonviolence because somebody must have sense in this world.

The reason I can't advocate violence is because violence ultimately defeats itself. It ultimately destroys everybody. The reason I can't follow the old eye-for-an-eye philosophy is that it ends up leaving everybody blind. Somebody must have sense and somebody must have religion. I remember some years ago, my brother and I were driving from Atlanta to Chattanooga, Tennessee. And for some reason the drivers that night were very discourteous or they were forgetting to dim their lights, and every time we passed a car for some reason the lights stood there with all their force. And finally A.D. looked over at me and said, "I'm tired of this now, and the next car that comes by here and refuses to dim the lights, I'm going to refuse to dim mine." And I said, "Wait a minute, don't do that. Somebody has to have some sense on this highway, and if somebody doesn't have sense enough to dim the lights, we'll all end up destroyed on this highway." And I'm saying the same thing for us here in Birmingham. We're moving up a mighty highway toward the city of Freedom. There will be meandering points. There will be curves and difficult moments, and we will be tempted to retaliate with the same kind of force that the opposition will use. But I'm going to say to you, "Wait a minute, Birmingham. Somebody's got to have some sense in Birmingham." And we are the ones that must prove to be the spiritual anvils that will wear out many a physical hammer. This is what we can do right here in Birmingham. Just let them get their dogs, and let them get the hose, and we will leave them standing before their God and the world splattered with the blood and reeking with the stench of their Negro brothers. And then they will have to say, "We're going to have to bring an end to our excesses for this can't stop these people. We tried to use water on them and we soon discovered that they were used to water for they were Methodists or Episcopalians or other denominations and they had to be sprinkled. And even those who hadn't been sprinkled happened to have been Baptists and not only did they stand up in the water, they went under the water." And dogs—well, I'll tell you, when I was growing up I was dog bitten for nothing, so I don't mind being bitten by a dog for standing up for freedom. And I was down there going to court the other day when we were in jail and they took us into City Hall for court under Brown. And I looked over there and saw a tank. A tank was sitting over there, and I don't know what—and I said, "What is that?" Somebody said, "Well, that's Bull Connor's tank." And you know it's a white tank. Now, I want to say tonight that they can bring their dogs out, they can get his white tank, and our black faces will stand up before the white tank.

Now, we're not alone in this. Don't let anybody make you feel that we are alone. Already we have support of friends from all over the country. If you listened this afternoon to the Huntley-Brinkley program, you saw three distinguished leaders from Washington saying that they were calling for a pilgrimage to Birmingham, Alabama. They are coming here. They are coming here by the busloads to aid us in this struggle. Now yesterday was a D-Day. And tomorrow will be a double D-Day.

Now, briefly I want to tell you what we're asking for because we need to know this. We need to know the things we are requesting. So that these things will be in our minds over and over again. Number one, we are asking the merchants to desegregate all of the facilities in the stores downtown and over the city. The lunch counters, the rest rooms, the water fountains, and the fitting rooms. We are requesting that desegregation will take place in these stores. Now, you know for a long time you have been shopping and you have been spending big money at times in these stores. And yet, you can't even get a cup of coffee at a lunch counter. And you look across the seas and you see men and women of the nations of Asia and Africa moving with jet-like speed toward political independence and we are still moving at horse and buggy pace trying to get service at a lunch counter. Now, this is nothing unusual. We're not asking for anything extreme. Since the sit-in movement started in 1960, more than 210 cities have integrated their lunch counters. You had some in Alabama, Huntsville, Alabama for instance. And Birmingham must face the realities of life, and we've got to get it over to the officials of this community that when they stand up against integration, it is like standing up on the beaches of history trying to hold the tides back—it just isn't possible. So we're trying to end segregation.

Now, the other thing we see is this. The second thing is this. We are tired of Negroes being employed only in menial areas. We're tired of Negroes only being employed to sweep floors in the stores downtown. Did you know—you should know that the annual income of the average Negro family of Birmingham, Alabama, is fifty percent less than the average white family. The average Negro family makes just a little above $2,000. The average white family earns an average of $4,854. Now, I am here to say to you tonight that we are God's children, and that we deserve the opportunity to have jobs that are decent like anybody else. We are making it clear now that we are not going to spend our money anywhere that we can't get jobs on an equal basis. So you can see we are simply asking that they will up-grade Negroes and give them some jobs that will pay well and that will be an expression of our various abilities.

Third, we are urging them to recommend to the city government that they will drop the charges against all of these people who have been arrested for only seeking their constitutional rights. We don't live in Russia. We don't believe in communism. We don't believe in a system of government which says that the state is the end. The great glory of democracy is the right to protest for rights. Embedded deep down in the Constitution of our Nation is the First Amendment—freedom of speech, freedom of press, freedom of assembly. If we lived in Russia, we would understand all this mess they're carrying on down in Birmingham, Alabama. But we live in the United States. And somewhere it is said to us that all of us have certain rights that are neither derived from nor conferred by the State. In order to discover where they came from it is necessary to move back behind the dim mist of eternity. They are God-given. This is what we believe. Organized labor has demonstrated over and over again our right to picket and yet in Birmingham, Alabama, we can't picket. We can't engage in an orderly nonviolent protest. But our rights—our basic constitutional rights— [*sic*]. But we believe in democracy. We are devoted to democracy. We love America, and we love democracy. And while we're struggling down here in Birmingham not to save ourselves alone, but we're struggling to save the soul of this nation. And so we're telling them to urge the city government to drop these charges.

Fourth, we're asking them to appoint a good-faith biracial committee. I say "good-faith" because too many biracial committees are nothing but window-dressing committees. Now, we've passed the stage now where white people in the power structure can pick our leaders. We don't want any leaders they're going to pick. The Negroes who are to be represented on this biracial committee must be selected by the Negroes and approved by the mayor. The committee is to deal with the question of a time-table for integrating the schools. Several years ago, the Supreme Court rendered a decision outlawing segregation in the public schools. That Brown decision said in substance that separate facilities are inherently unequal and to segregate a child on the basis of his race is to deny that child equal protection of the law. And then in 1955, it rendered its implementation decision. And it is said that every community was to work under the scrutiny of the local federal judge and move with all deliberate speed toward implementing it. Alabama hasn't even started moving toward it. She isn't much less talking about all deliberate speed; she hasn't even developed an all deliberate crawl. And we're saying now that something must be done about school integration. Now, the parks, they're closed all over this city. Samuel Johnson said once that parks are lungs of a city, and it's high time that Birmingham would start breathing again. It's time for these parks to open and we want this committee to deal with that and all of the other problems of segregation.

Now, these are the four things. Keep them in your mind. They're very simple. Desegregating all of the facilities, up-grading Negroes in employment in the stores, the dropping of the charges, and the appointment of a good-faith biracial committee. Now, there isn't anything extreme about this. These are things we should have had a hundred years ago.

Now, finally, your children, your daughters and sons are in jail, many of them. And I'm sure many of the parents are here tonight. Don't worry about them. They are suffering for what they believe, and they are suffering to make this nation a better nation. And you see the eyes of the world are on Birmingham, and I'm not saying that they want to treat them so nice, but they have to treat them nice. You see they are political prisoners. And it's a little different when you are a political prisoner. See, they're not in there for being drunk. They're not in there for stealing some chickens. They're not in there for embezzlement. They are political prisoners and it's a little different. And we're going to keep in touch with the jails, and we're going to see that they are treated right. I've been in jail about thirteen times in this struggle, and every time I go, it's a new spiritual experience. You can get a lot of things done that you need to do and you can't get done in the hurly-burly of everyday life. Jail helps you to rise above the miasma of everyday life. You can think about things. You can meditate a little. You can read a little. If they want some books, we will get them. I catch up on my reading every time I go to jail. I have a book that is just being published. The publication date is June 5th, but they sent me a copy yesterday or day before stating that this was the first copy that they had printed. And I looked in it, and I started reading the Preface. And I thought about the fact that I had written in this Preface several months ago something that was a real experience. That was the fact that three chapters in this book, three of the sermons in this book were written in the Albany, Georgia, jail. So if they put me in jail again in Birmingham I'll have time to write another book. Don't worry about jail, for when you go in jail for a cause like this, the jails cease to be jails, they become havens for freedom and human dignity.

So, we need everybody. We need your support. And we're going on in spite of the dogs, in spite of the hose, in spite of the tank. We can't stop now. We've gone too far to turn back. And somebody here tonight is still standing in the valley of decision. We need your support. We need you in this movement. And I hope that every Negro citizen of this city, and every white person of good-will will join in this movement as we move to democratize Birmingham and to make this nation a better place in which to live. I ask you to decide now, not tomorrow, not later on tonight, but I urge you to start to decide at this minute— remembering a tiny little minute, just sixty seconds in it. I didn't choose it, I can refuse it, it's up to me to use it. A tiny little minute, just sixty seconds in it, but eternity is in it.

MEDGAR EVERS

This speech by the NAACP leader in Mississippi was delivered over radio and television in Jackson, Mississippi, on May 20, 1963, in response to the Jackson mayor, Allen Thompson, who had claimed in a televised speech that black Mississippians were content and had a good standard of living. Thompson even went so far as to deny that racial discrimination existed in Mississippi's capital city. After praising Jackson as a "progressive, beautiful, friendly, prosperous city with an exciting future," he proclaimed, "You will not find anything that will breed discontent."[11] Evers appealed to the radio and television stations that broadcast Thompson's speech and received equal time for a response. He was forced to tape the speech at a studio away from the station, due to threats on his life, but the first statewide television address by a black man in the history of Mississippi went forward without a hitch. Evers' speech triggered a massive wave of protests, demonstrations, sit-ins, and boycotts. Many black students from Tougaloo College and Jackson State were arrested and the cost of bail became so high that Evers' NAACP branch was unable to cover the cost. Evers called on Lena Horne, the black entertainer, who sponsored a benefit concert to raise money for the bail expenses. Evers was murdered less than three weeks later.

In this speech, Evers urges the mayor to use a representative biracial committee to explore solutions to the problems in Jackson—a solution that Thompson had rejected in his speech.

REMARKS OF MR. MEDGAR EVERS FOR DELIVERY OVER WLBT AND WJTV[12]

Jackson, Mississippi
May 20, 1963

I wish to express appreciation for this time, which has been made available to the NAACP, to comment on the speech of Mayor Allen Thompson on May 13, in which the NAACP was criticized by name.

I speak as a native Mississippian. I was educated in Mississippi schools, and served overseas in our nation's armed forces in the war against Hitlerism and Fascism.

I mention this because I believe I am typical of many loyal Mississippians of color, who are equally devoted to their State and want only to see it assume its rightful place in the democratic scheme of our country.

First, I wish to explain a bit about the NAACP.

Most Southern white people, whether they are friendly or hostile, usually think of the NAACP as a "Northern outside group." The facts do not bear this out. At least one-half of the NAACP membership, is in the South. There have been branches in Mississippi since 1918. The Jackson, Mississippi branch was organized in 1926—37 years ago.

Therefore, when we talk of the NAACP we are also talking about fellow Mississippians, local home-grown Negro citizens, born and reared in communities such as Jackson. They know the communities in which they live. They know the white people here. They have worked and bought homes. Some own businesses, belong to churches and lodges, rear their families and try to educate their children. They pay taxes, and their trade helps support business in Mississippi.

Now the Mayor says that if the so-called outside agitators would leave us alone everything would be all right. This has always been the position of those who would continue to deny Negro citizens their constitutional rights. The history of race relations in the South refutes this thesis. Never in its history has The South as a region, without outside pressure, granted the Negro his citizenship rights. The right to vote in Democratic Party primaries; to attend State-supported institutions of higher learning; and more recently, the right to attend all public schools; the right to use interstate travel facilities without being segregated; and the right to live in public and private housing and to use, without discrimination, public facilities, such as parks, playgrounds, swimming pools, golf courses, public libraries—these rights were won in the courts with the aid and assistance of the NAACP and similar organizations. All of these gains were obtained through use of the courts, the American way, which has been the policy and practice of the NAACP for 54 years.

Despite these legal precedents, one hundred years after Emancipation, there are many cities including our own, which have failed to acknowledge these rights.

It is also in the American tradition to demonstrate, to assemble peacefully and to petition the government for a redress of grievances. Such a petition may legitimately take the form of picketing, although in Jackson, Negroes are immediately arrested when they attempt to exercise this constitutional right.

We believe that it is not helpful to the solution of problems in race relations for a public official to state that he will not discuss matters with members of the NAACP. Why not? These people are Mississippians. They have chosen not to move elsewhere, but to stay here at home and do their bit toward making things better for all the people, white and colored.

The NAACP is *not* subversive. It has never been on any official subversive list. In fact, FBI chief, J. Edgar Hoover, in his book, "Masters of Deceit," commended the NAACP for its stand against communism.

We feel that Mayor Thompson will help Jackson if he will consult with a Democratically selected biracial committee, some of whose members may be members of the NAACP. He would profit from the experience of other Southern cities such as Nashville, Knoxville, and Memphis, Tennessee, Jacksonville, Fla.,

New Orleans, La., Dallas, Texas, Atlanta, Ga., and more recently Raleigh, N.C. and Anniston, Alabama.

In view of the success of the cooperative efforts of public officials, business men and Negro leaders in these cities, such a good faith move here would be a step in the right direction. Public officials cannot afford to turn their backs on representative committees of white and colored citizens in favor of hit-and-miss discussions with hand picked colored citizens personally known and approved by them. Such a method is not likely to get to the heart of the problem. The hand-picked representative seldom represents or speaks for the Negro community.

Flexibility is needed in the present situation. We stand ready to consult in good faith and to offer our honest views and suggestions on objectives and procedures.

On last Wednesday, Astronaut Gordon Cooper, a southerner, orbited the globe twenty-two times. By this feat, he helped America close the space gap with Russia. A few years ago, such a feat was inconceivable. But American scientists, with open minds and by prodigious effort, marshalled our country's abilities and resources to achieve the impossible. They were not afraid of changes.

The world has moved forward in the past twenty years. Racial concepts have changed. Many southern communities have changed.

Tonight the Negro plantation worker in the Delta knows from his radio and television what happened today all over the world. He knows what black people are doing and he knows what white people are doing. He can see on the 6:00 o'clock news screen the picture of a 3:00 o'clock bite by a police dog. He knows that Willie Mays, a Birmingham Negro, is the highest paid baseball player in the nation. He knows that Leontyne Price, a native of Laurel, Mississippi, is a star with the Metropolitan Opera in New York. He knows about the new free nations in Africa and knows that a Congo native can be a locomotive engineer, but in Jackson he cannot even drive a garbage truck. He sees black prime ministers and ambassadors, financiers and technicians.

Then he looks about his home community and what does he see to quote our Mayor, in this "progressive, beautiful, friendly, prosperous city with an exciting future"?

He sees a city where Negro citizens are refused admittance to the City Auditorium and the Coliseum; his children refused a ticket to a good movie in a downtown theater; his wife and children refused service at a lunch counter in a downtown store where they trade; students refused the use of the main public libraries, parks, playgrounds and other tax-supported recreational facilities.

He sees Negro lawyers, physicians, dentists, teachers and other professionals prevented from attending meetings of professional organizations.

He sees a city of over 150,000, of which 40% is Negro, in which there is not a single Negro policeman or policewoman, school crossing guard, fireman, clerk, stenographer or supervisor employed in any city department or the Mayor's office in other than menial capacities, except those employed in segregated facilities—the College Park Auditorium, Carver Library and the segregated schools.

He sees local hospitals which segregate Negro patients and deny staff privileges to Negro family physicians.

The Mayor spoke of the twenty-four hour police protection we have. Well, there are questions in the minds of many Negroes whether we have 24 hours of protection, or 24 hours of harassment. We do appreciate and expect protection, but are alarmed by the numerous reports which come to our office of unnecessary police brutality.

Mayor Thompson said last Monday and I quote, "You will not find anything (here in Jackson) that will breed discontent."

I ask you this evening, if you suffered these deprivations, were often called by your first name "boy," "girl," "auntie," and "uncle," wouldn't you be discontent?

What then does the Negro want? He wants to get rid of racial segregation in Mississippi life because he knows it has not been good for him nor for the State. He knows that segregation is unconstitutional and illegal. While States may make laws and enforce certain local regulations, none of these should be used to deprive any citizen of his rights under the Constitution.

The Negro citizen wants to register and vote without special handicaps imposed on him alone and we are encouraging him to do so.

The Negro Mississippian wants more jobs above the menial level in stores where he spends his money. He believes that new industries that have come to Mississippi should employ him above the laboring category.

He wants the public schools and colleges desegregated so that his children can receive the best education that Mississippi has to offer. He believes additional Negro students should be accepted at Ole Miss and at other colleges. He feels strongly about these and other items although he may not say so publicly.

Mayor Thompson said that when he was president of the Conference of Mayors he travelled to other cities. Naturally and properly he remained convinced that his own city of Jackson is the greatest. But when Mayor Thompson went to these cities he saw Negro State legislators in their State capitals. He saw Negro city councilmen, judges and commissioners. In municipal and State universities he found not only Negro students, but also Negro faculty members. He found Negro physicians in unsegregated facilities open to all citizens. He could have been waited on by a Negro clerk in a big department store. He could have seen Negro white-collar workers in public offices and private business. He saw Negro policemen directing traffic and Negro firemen putting out fires. All people used the libraries and museums. No one had to sit in the back of the bus.

Not all of this happens in the North. The Mayor knows that many southern cities have altered their old policies and have moved into new ways of living. In spite of these evidences of change, Mayor Thompson persists in deluding the people that conditions are going to remain the same in Jackson.

The NAACP believes that Jackson *can* change if it *wills* to do so. If there should be resistance, how much better to have turbulence to effect improvement, rather than turbulence to maintain a stand-pat policy. We believe there are white Mississippians who want to go forward on the race question. Their religion tells them there is something wrong with the old system. Their sense of justice and fair play sends them the same message.

But whether Jackson and the State choose change or not, the years of change are upon us. In the racial picture things will never be as they once were. History has reached a turning point, here and over the world. Here in Jackson we can recognize the situation and make an honest effort to bring fresh ideas and new methods to bear, or we can have what Mayor Thompson called "Turbulent times." If we choose this latter course, the turbulence will come, not because of so-called agitators or presence or absence of the NAACP, but because the time has come for a change and certain citizens refuse to accept the inevitable.

Negro citizens want to help all other good citizens bring about a meaningful improvement in an orderly fashion. As Mayor Thompson said, the two races have lived here together. The Negro has been in America since 1619, a total of 344 years. He is not going anywhere else; this country is his home. He wants to do his part to help make his city, State and nation a better place for everyone regardless of color and race.

Let me appeal to the consciences of many silent, responsible citizens of the white community who know that a victory for democracy in Jackson will be a victory for democracy everywhere.

In the words of President John F. Kennedy, speaking at Vanderbilt University, Saturday, May 18, 1963:

> This nation is now engaged in a continuing debate about the rights of a portion of its citizens. That will go on and those rights will expand until the standard first forged by the nation's founders has been reached—and all Americans enjoy equal opportunity and liberty under law. . . . All Americans must be responsible citizens—but some must be more responsible than others, by virtue of their public or their private position, their role in the family or community, their prospects for the future or their legacy from the past. Increased responsibility goes with increased ability— for of those to whom much is given, much is required.

To these words, one can only say—Amen.

ROY WILKINS

Four days after Evers' murder, Roy Wilkins, the executive director of the NAACP, spoke at the funeral for the organization's Mississippi field secretary. In his eulogy for Evers, Wilkins places the blame for the assassination squarely on white southern leadership:

> The Southern political system put him behind that rifle: the lily-white Southern governments, local and state; the Senators, governors, state legislators, mayors, judges, sheriffs, chiefs of police, commissioners, etc. Not content with mere disfranchisement, the office holders have used unbridled political power to fabricate a maze of laws, customs and economic practices which has imprisoned the Negro.

For Wilkins, Evers "was the symbol of our victory and of their defeat . . . he was a constant threat to the system, particularly in his great voter registration work. In the manner of his death he was the victor over it."

REMARKS AT FUNERAL SERVICES FOR MEDGAR W. EVERS[13]

Jackson, Mississippi
June 15, 1963

There have been martyrs throughout history, in every land and people, in many high causes. We are here today in tribute to a martyr in the crusade for human liberty, a man struck down in a mean and cowardly fashion by a bullet in the back.

The NAACP has had its share of sufferers: John R. Shillady, one of the earliest NAACP executive secretaries, who was badly beaten by a mob in Austin, Tex., in 1919; Elbert Williams, secretary of the Brownsville, Tenn., NAACP, who was lynched in 1940; Rev. George W. Lee, officer of the Belzoni, Miss., NAACP, who registered to vote and was assassinated in 1955; Harry T. Moore, NAACP state secretary for Florida, and his wife, both murdered in their beds in Mims, Fla. by a bomb on Christmas night, 1951.

Now in 1963, Medgar W. Evers, NAACP state secretary for Mississippi, shot June 12, 1963.

We tend to forget pioneer fighters. We say, unfeelingly and thoughtlessly, "No one really acted before now." "These marches were the first." "This death shot in the dark was the first." The truth is that through all the years before our time men have fought for freedom. Now it is our turn, not to re-write the record, but to add to it, not to preach that there never was a Columbus because there is now a Gordon Cooper.

The lurking assassin at midnight June 11–12 pulled the trigger, but in all wars the men who do the shooting are trained and indoctrinated and keyed to action by men and by forces which prod them to act.

The southern political system put him behind that rifle: the lily-white southern governments, local and state; the senators, governors, state legislators, mayors, judges, sheriffs, chiefs of police, commissioners, etc. Not content with mere disfranchisement, the office holders have used unbridled political power to fabricate a maze of laws, customs and economic practices which has imprisoned the Negro.

When at times it appeared that the rest of the nation might penetrate the Kingdom of Color, there were those ready always to beat back the adherents of decency and justice. Speaking of the U.S. Supreme Court's public school decision of 1954, Senator James O. Eastland told a 1955 Senatobia, Miss., audience: "You are obligated to disobey such a Court."

In far-away Washington, the southern system has its outposts in the Congress of the United States and by their deals and maneuvers they helped put the man behind the deadly rifle on Guynes Street this week. The killer must have felt that he had, if not an immunity, then certainly a protection for whatever he chose to do, no matter how dastardly.

Today as Americans and their President try to recover from their horror and to devise ways to correct the evils now so naked in our national life, these men in Congress, abetted by the timorous, the technical and the selfishly ambitious are raising the familiar—and by now sickening—chorus of negation. With surgery required, they talk of ointments and pills. With speed the essence, they cite their rituals of procedure. Men may die and children may be stunted, but the seniority system and the filibuster rule must remain inviolate.

There appears to be a very real question as to whether the white man, so long an exemplar of bold and venturesome ingenuity in many fields, is not committing spiritual suicide here in the land he fashioned as the home of free men. "All men" he said in his Declaration of Independence. But today he is shocked at the eruptions on every hand against his amendment of the "all men" doctrine to mean "all white men."

In their moment of truth our opponents are striving frantically to drive away the reality of their decline. In something of the manner of the Maginot Line strategy, their defenses have been breached or by-passed. A Southern state hires a retired professor to write a book setting forth the inferiority of the Negro race—twenty years after a Negro mathematician had helped in the calculations for the first atomic bomb! The opposition has been reduced to clubs, guns, hoses, dogs, garbage trucks and hog wire compounds.

Obviously, this opposition is nearing bankruptcy. Fresh material is in short supply and strategy is stale and ineffective. Obviously, nothing can stop the drive for freedom. It will not cease here or elsewhere. After a hundred years of waiting and suffering, we are determined, in James Baldwin's language, not upon a bigger cage, but upon no cage at all.

Medgar Evers was the symbol of our victory and of their defeat. Contrary to the view of a Jackson city official, Medgar was more than just an opponent. In life he was a constant threat to the system, particularly in his great voter registration work. In the manner of his death he was the victor over it.

The bullet that tore away his life four days ago tore away at the system and helped to signal its end.

They can fiddle and they can throw a few more victims to the lions of repression and persecution, but Rome is burning and a new day is just over yonder.

At his arrest with me two weeks ago today, Medgar found that the man in the fingerprint room was from his home town, Decatur, Miss. There they were, the one home town boy carrying out the routine of the old order, unaware, perhaps, that the other, calm and smiling, was the herald of that future day when no man, white or black, even in Mississippi, will be fingerprinted and photographed under a felony charge merely for seeking his manhood rights as an American citizen.

We in the NAACP loved him for himself, for his sincerity and integrity. We mourn him, but we are not cast down. For a little while he loaned us and his people the great strength of his body and the elixir of his spirit. We are grateful for this blessing. For him we shall all try harder to hold our nation to the concept of "all men." If he could live in Mississippi and not hate, so shall we, though we will ever stoutly contend for the kind of life his children and all others must enjoy in this rich land.

Many years ago an NAACP executive secretary, James Weldon Johnson, wrote the words to the anthem, "Lift Ev'ry Voice and Sing."

These words belong here today to this heroic fallen NAACP officer who believed in his people and fought each waking hour for the realization of their destiny; who believed in his country and in its high principle of individual freedom and human dignity:

> Stony the road we trod
> Bitter the chast'ning rod.
> Felt in the days when hope unborn had died;
> Yet with a steady beat,
> Have not our weary feet
> Come to the place for which our fathers sighed?
> We have come over a way that with tears has been watered,
> We have come, treading our path through the blood of the slaughtered,
> Out from the gloomy past,
> Till now we stand at last
> Where the white gleam of our bright star is cast.
>
> Lift ev'ry voice and sing
> Till earth and heaven ring.

Ring with the harmonies of Liberty;
Let our rejoicing rise
High as the list'ning skies,
Let it resound loud as the rolling sea.
Sing a song full of the faith that the dark past has taught us,
Sing a song full of the hope that the present has brought us.
Facing the rising sun of our new day begun,
Let us march on till victory is won.

JOHN R. LEWIS

One of the key leaders of the student protesters during the 1960s, John Lewis made a major impact on the history of civil rights in America.[14] Despite more than forty arrests, many physical attacks, and several serious injuries, Lewis continually advocated the nonviolent approach to social protest. Lewis was born the son of sharecroppers on February 21, 1940, on a farm near Troy, Alabama. As a young boy, Lewis aspired to be a preacher, practicing diligently his skills before his family chicken flock, and later before local Baptist churches in the area around Troy. He attended American Baptist Theological Seminary in Nashville, Tennessee, but he left after a year with plans to try to integrate Troy State College, near his home. Those plans did not materialize, and Lewis returned to Nashville and enrolled at Fisk University where he became a leader in the 1960 Nashville sit-ins. He went on the next year to participate in the Freedom Rides and was severely beaten by mobs as the riders challenged segregation at interstate bus terminals.

Recognized by his peers for his leadership, from 1963 to 1966 Lewis served as the chairman of the SNCC, which he had helped found at Shaw University in 1960. In 1964, Lewis coordinated SNCC efforts in the "Mississippi Freedom Summer" project and in March 1965, Lewis led marchers across the Edmund Pettus Bridge in Selma, Alabama, in the "Bloody Sunday" tragedy.

After leaving SNCC in 1966, Lewis remained active in the protest movement as he worked in the Southern Regional Council's (SRC) voter registration programs, serving as the executive director of the SRC Voter Registration Project from 1970 to 1977. In 1977, President Jimmy Carter appointed Lewis to direct the federal volunteer ACTION program and in 1980 he became community affairs director of the National Consumer Co-op Bank in Atlanta. The next year, Lewis was elected to the Atlanta City Council, where he remained until successfully running for Congress in 1986. He has since served in Congress, representing the city of Atlanta and parts of Fulton, DeKalb, and Clayton counties, running unopposed in 1996.

The speech published here is the original text that Lewis had planned to deliver at the Lincoln Memorial at the 1963 March on Washington. The night before the event, however, a copy of his speech circulated to various persons, including the archbishop of Washington, Patrick O'Boyle, who was scheduled to deliver the opening invocation the next day. The archbishop reacted strongly to the speech, saying he would not present the invocation if Lewis was allowed to deliver this speech. After a tense negotiating session in a room behind Lincoln's statue in the moments before Lewis' appearance on the platform, including an impassioned plea from A. Philip Randolph for Lewis to tone down his remarks, the SNCC chairman agreed to do so. His speech as delivered still had "sting" to it, as Lewis described it himself, but it left out the reference to Sherman's march to the sea and a few other more harsh words.[15]

". . . A SERIOUS REVOLUTION"[16]

Washington, DC
August 28, 1963

We march today for jobs and freedom, but we have nothing to be proud of. For hundreds and thousands of our brothers are not here. They have no money for their transportation, for they are now receiving starvation wages, or no wages, at all.

In good conscience, we cannot support the administration's civil rights bill, for it is too little, and too late. There's not one thing in the bill that will protect our people from police brutality.

This bill will not protect young children and old women from police dogs and fire hoses, for engaging in peaceful demonstrations. This bill will not protect the citizens of Danville, Virginia, who must live in constant fear in a police state. This bill will not protect the hundreds of people who have been arrested on trumped-up charges. What about the three young men—SNCC field secretaries—in Americus, Georgia, who face the death penalty for engaging in peaceful protest?

The voting section of this bill will not help thousands of black citizens who want to vote. It will not help the citizens of Mississippi, of Alabama, and Georgia, who are qualified to vote, but lack a 6th-grade education. "One man, one vote," is the African cry. It is ours, too. It must be ours.

People have been forced to leave their homes because they dared to exercise their right to register to vote. What is there in this bill to insure the equality of a maid who earns $5 a week in the home of a family whose income is $100,000 a year?

For the first time in 100 years this nation is being awakened to the fact that segregation is evil and that it must be destroyed in all forms. Your presence today proves that you have been aroused to the point of action.

We are now involved in a serious revolution. This nation is still a place of cheap political leaders who build their careers on immoral compromises and ally themselves with open forms of political, economic and social exploitation. What political leader here can stand up and say "My party is the party of principles?" The party of Kennedy is also the party of Eastland. The party of Javits is also the party of Goldwater. Where is *our* party?

In some parts of the South we work in the fields from sun-up to sun-down for $12 a week. In Albany, Georgia, nine of our leaders have been indicted not by Dixiecrats but by the Federal Government for peaceful protest. But what did the Federal Government do when Albany's Deputy Sheriff beat Attorney C.B. King and left him half dead? What did the Federal Government do when local police officials kicked and assaulted the pregnant wife of Slater King and she lost her baby?

It seems to me that the Albany indictment is part of a conspiracy on the part of the federal government and local politicians in the interest of expediency.

I want to know, which side is the Federal Government on?

The revolution is at hand, and we must free ourselves of the chains of political and economic slavery. The nonviolent revolution is saying, "We will not wait for the courts to act, for we have been waiting for hundreds of years. We will not wait for the President, the Justice Department, nor Congress, but we will take matters into our own hands and create a source of power, outside of any national structure that could and would assure us a victory."

To those who have said, "Be Patient and Wait," we must say that, "Patience is a dirty and nasty word." We cannot be patient, we do not want to be free gradually, we want our freedom, and we want it *now*. We cannot depend on any political party, for both the Democrats and the Republicans have betrayed the basic principles of the Declaration of Independence.

We all recognize the fact that if any radical social, political and economic changes are to take place in our society, the people, the masses, must bring them about. In the struggle we must seek more than civil rights; we must work for the community of love, peace and true brotherhood. Our minds, souls and hearts cannot rest until freedom and justice exist for *all people*.

The revolution is a serious one. Mr. Kennedy is trying to take the revolution out of the streets and put it into the courts. Listen, Mr. Kennedy. Listen, Mr. Congressman. Listen fellow citizens. The black masses are on the march for jobs and freedom, and we must say to the politicians that there won't be a "cooling-off" period.

All of us must get in the revolution. Get in and stay in the streets of every city, every village and every hamlet of this nation, until true Freedom comes, until the revolution is complete. In the Delta of Mississippi, in southwest Georgia, in Alabama, Harlem, Chicago, Detroit, Philadelphia and all over this nation—the black masses are on the march!

We won't stop now. All of the forces of Eastland, Barnett, Wallace, and Thurmond won't stop this revolution. The time will come when we will not confine our marching to Washington. We will march through the South, through the Heart of Dixie, the way Sherman did. We shall pursue our own "scorched earth" policy and burn Jim Crow to the ground—nonviolently. We shall fragment the South into a thousand pieces and put them back together in the image of democracy. We will make the action of the past few months look petty. And I say to you, WAKE UP AMERICA!

MARTIN LUTHER KING JR.

On Sunday morning, September 15, 1963, a roar of dynamite shattered the Sixteenth Street Baptist Church in Birmingham and ended the lives of four young children: Adie Mae Collins, Denise McNair, Carole Robertson, and Cynthia Wesley. The hours of rioting and chaos that followed left Johnny Robinson, a black youth, dead from a police officer's buckshot to the back as the youngster was running down a street away from the officer. Another black youngster, Virgil Ware, was dead from a senseless shooting by a white youth. Fred Shuttlesworth and Martin Luther King Jr. demanded that President Kennedy send military force to the beleaugered city. In that mileau, King delivered this eulogy to the slain girls on September 18, before eight thousand mourners, including eight hundred Birmingham pastors of both races—the largest by far of any interracial gathering of ministers in the history of Birmingham.[17]

EULOGY TO VICTIMS OF BIRMINGHAM CHURCH BOMBING[18]

Birmingham, Alabama
September 15, 1963

THIS AFTERNOON we gather in the quiet of this sanctuary to pay our last tribute of respect to these three beautiful children of God. They entered the stage of history just a few years ago, and in the brief years that they were privileged to act on this mortal stage, they played their parts exceedingly well. Now the curtain falls; they move through the exit; the drama of their earthly life comes to a close. They are now committed back to that eternity from which they came.

These children—unoffending; innocent and beautiful—were the victims of one of the most vicious, heinous crimes ever perpetrated against humanity.

Yet they died nobly. They are the martyred heroines of a holy crusade for freedom and human dignity. So they have something to say to us in their death. They have something to say to every minister of the gospel who has remained silent behind the safe security of stained-glass windows. They have something to say to every politician who has fed his constituents the stale bread of hatred and the spoiled meat of racism. They have something to say to a federal government that has compromised with the undemocratic practices of southern Dixiecrats and the blatant hypocrisy of right-wing northern Republicans. They have something to say to every Negro who passively accepts the evil system of segregation, and stands on the sidelines in the midst of a mighty struggle for justice. They say to each of us, black and white alike, that we must substitute courage for caution. They say to us that we must be concerned not merely about *WHO* murdered them, but about the system, the way of life and the philosophy which

PRODUCED the murderers. Their death says to us that we must work passionately and unrelentingly to make the American dream a reality.

So they did not die in vain. God still has a way of wringing good out of evil. History has proven over and over again that unmerited suffering is redemptive. The innocent blood of these little girls may well serve as the redemptive force that will bring new light to this dark city. The Holy Scripture says, "A little child shall lead them." The death of these little children may lead our whole southland from the low road of man's inhumanity to man to the high road of peace and brotherhood. These tragic deaths may lead our nation to substitute an aristocracy of character for an aristocracy of color. The spilt blood of these innocent girls may cause the whole citizenry of Birmingham to transform the negative extremes of a dark past into the positive extremes of a bright future. Indeed, this tragic event may cause the white south to come to terms with its conscience.

So in spite of the darkness of this hour we must not despair. We must not become bitter; nor must we harbor the desire to retaliate with violence. We must not lose faith in our white brothers. Somehow we must believe that the most misguided among them can learn to respect the dignity and worth of all human personality.

May I now say a word to you, the members of the bereaved families. It is almost impossible to say anything that can console you at this difficult hour and remove the deep clouds of disappointment which are floating in your mental skies. But I hope you can find a little consolation from the universality of this experience. Death comes to every individual. There is an amazing democracy about death. It is not aristocracy for some of the people, but a democracy for all of the people. Kings die and beggars die; rich men die and poor men die; old people die and young people die; death comes to the innocent and it comes to the guilty. Death is the irreducible common denominator of all men.

I hope you can find some consolation from Christianity's affirmation that death is not the end. Death is not a period that ends the great sentence of life, but a comma that punctuates it to more lofty significance. Death is not a blind alley that leads the human race into a state of nothingness, but an open door which leads man into life eternal. Let this daring faith, this great invincible surmise, be your sustaining power during these trying days.

At times, life is hard, as hard as crucible steel. It has its bleak and painful moments. Like the ever-flowing waters of a river, life has its moments of drought and its moments of flood. Like the ever-changing cycle of the seasons, life has the soothing warmth of the summers and the piercing chill of its winters. But through it all, God walks with us. Never forget that God is able to lift you from fatigue of despair to the buoyancy of hope, and transform dark and desolate valleys into sunlit paths of inner peace.

Your children did not live long, but they lived well. The quantity of their lives was disturbingly small, but the quality of their lives was magnificently big. Where they died and what they were doing when death came will remain a marvelous tribute to each of you and an eternal epitaph to each of them. They died not in a den or dive nor were they hearing and telling filthy jokes at the time of their death. They died within the sacred walls of the Church after discussing a principle as eternal as love.

Shakespeare had Horatio utter some beautiful words over the dead body of Hamlet. I paraphrase these words today as I stand over the last remains of these lovely girls.

"Good-night sweet princesses; may the flight of angels take thee to thy eternal rest."

FANNIE LOU HAMER

Fannie Lou Hamer was one of the many lesser known heroes and heroines of the Civil Rights Movement.[19] Often called on to sing at civil rights rallies and meetings, the Mississippi sharecropper was also a powerful speaker whose heartfelt oratory resounded from the small towns of the Mississippi Delta to the National Democratic Party Convention and to the committee rooms of the U.S. Congress.

Hamer was born on October 6, 1917, as the twentieth child of sharecropper parents. A prime example of the results of segregation, Hamer finished only six years of school, and in 1942 she married Perry Hamer, a tractor driver on a Delta plantation. The Hamers were unable to have children, but they adopted two girls, one of whom died in 1967.

In 1962, Hamer was introduced to students from SNCC and workers from SCLC and she became involved in the movement and interested in Mississippi politics. After hearing a sermon by James Bevel that challenged black Mississippians to register to vote, Hamer volunteered to register. On August 31, she and seventeen others attempted to register, but failed the literacy test that required them to interpret a section of the Mississippi state constitution. The plantation owner where she worked forced her off his plantation because of her efforts and she moved to another plantation, where night riders fired into her home. She attempted to register again in December 1962, failed the test again, but passed on the third attempt in January 1963. She became an SNCC supervisor in Sunflower County and was an active worker in voter registration drives. Returning to Ruleville from a civil rights workshop in South Carolina, Hamer and others who attempted to eat at a segregated bus terminal in Winona, Mississippi, were beaten brutally by city police, an event she describes in this speech.

Hardly deterred, Hamer became vice chairperson of the Mississippi Freedom Democratic Party (MFDP) in 1964 and campaigned for the U.S. Congress. She was defeated, of course, but gained national attention for her remarks at the Democratic Party National Convention that summer, as the MFDP challenged the white Mississippi delegates for seats on the convention floor.[20] That, too, failed, but Hamer was now nationally recognized.

After her involvement in the Civil Rights Movement, Hamer continued her activism. She helped to bring a Head Start program to Ruleville; organized the Freedom Farm Cooperative; helped to get several hundred low-income housing units built in her hometown; started a day-care center; and helped bring a factory to Ruleville to provide jobs. For her years of inspiration and hard work on the behalf of poor people, Hamer was awarded honorary degrees from several universities, among them, Morehouse College and Howard University. She died of heart trouble, breast cancer, and diabetes on March 15, 1977.

The remarks anthologized here were presented to a Congressional Committee in Washington, on June 16, 1964.

TESTIMONY OF FANNIE LOU HAMER, RULEVILLE, MISS.[21]

Washington, DC
June 16, 1964

MR. FREEDMAN: Mrs. Hamer, what is it that brings you before the panel today?

MRS. HAMER: To tell about some of the brutality in the State of Mississippi. I will begin from the first beginning, August 31, in 1962. I traveled 26 miles to the county courthouse to try to register to become a first-class citizen. I was fired the 31st of August in 1962 from a plantation where I had worked as a timekeeper and a sharecropper for 18 years. My husband had worked there 30 years.

I was met by my children when I returned from the courthouse, and my girl and my husband's cousin told me that this man my husband worked for was raising a lot of Cain. I went on in the house, and it wasn't too long before my husband came and said this plantation owner said I would have to leave if I didn't go down and withdraw.

About that time, the man walked up, Mr. Marlow, and he said, "Is Fannie Lou back yet?"

My husband said, "She is."

I walked out of the house at this time. He said, "Fannie Lou, you have been to the courthouse to try to register," and he said, "We are not ready for this in Mississippi."

I said, "I didn't register for you, I tried to register for myself."

He said, "We are not going to have this in Mississippi, and you will have to withdraw. I am looking for your answer, yea or nay."

I just looked. He said, "I will give you until tomorrow morning. And if you don't withdraw, you will have to leave. If you do go withdraw, it's only how I feel. You might still have to leave." So I left that same night.

On the 10th of September, they fired into the home of Mr. and Mrs. Robert Tucker 16 times at me. That same night, two girls were shot at Mr. Herman Sissel's. Also, they shot Mr. Joe Maglon's house. I was fired that day and haven't had a job since.

In 1963, I attended a voter registration workshop and was returning back to Mississippi. At Winona, Miss., I was arrested there. Some of the folks had got off the bus, Miss Annelle Ponder, June West Johnson, Euvester Simpson, Rosemary Freeman, and James West got off the bus to go into the restaurant to get food. Two of the people decided to use the restroom. I saw them come right straight out of the restaurant. I got off the bus to see what had happened. Miss Ponder said, "They won't let us eat." She said, "There was a chief of police and a highway patrolman inside, and they ordered us out." I said, "Well, this is Mississippi."

I got back on the bus, and about the time I just got sat down good, I looked out the window, and they were getting Miss Ponder and the others into the highway patrolman's car.

I stepped off the bus to see what was happening, and one screamed, "Get that one there." I was picked up, the police, Earl Wayne Patric, told me I was under arrest. He opened the door, and as I started to get in, he kicked me. They carried me to town to this county jail.

We were carried to the booking room. Soon as we walked inside, I was in the car with Earl Wayne Patric and one plain clothesman. I don't know whether he a policeman or not. He didn't have on police clothes, had a crew haircut. They would ask me questions going on to jail, and as I would go on to answer, they would curse me and tell me to hush.

I was carried on to the booking room and carried from the booking room to a cell. After I was locked up in a cell with Miss Euvester Simpson, I began to hear the sounds of licks, and I could hear people screaming. I don't know how long it lasted before I saw Miss Ponder, the southside supervisor for SCLC, pass the cell with both her hands up. Her eyes looked like blood, and her mouth was swollen. She passed my cell. Her clothes was torn. She backed and they carried her again out of my sight.

After then, the State highway patrolman, because it was on the insignia on his arm and another silver plate across his pocket, walked into my cell with two other white men. He asked me where was I from, and I told him. He said, "I am going to check."

They left my cell, and it wasn't too long before they returned, and he said, "You damn right, you are from Ruleville," and he called me a bad name. He said they would make me wish I was dead.

I was carried out of the cell into another cell where there were two Negro prisoners. The State highway patrolman gave the first Negro a long blackjack that was heavy. It was loaded with something, and they had me to lay down on the bunk with my face down, and I was beat. I was beat by the first Negro until I was exhausted.

After I was beaten by the first Negro, the State highway patrolman ordered the other Negro to take the blackjack. The second Negro, he began to beat. The State highway patrolman ordered the first Negro that had beat me to sit on my feet. One of the white men that was in the room, my dress would work up because it had a large skirt, but I was trying to keep it down and trying to shield the licks from the left side, because I had polio when I was a child. During the time that I was trying to work my dress down and keep the licks from the left side, one of the white men walked over and pulled my dress up.

At this time I had to hug around the mattress to keep the sound from coming out.

MR. FREEDMAN: Mrs. Hamer, you referred to the woman from the SCLC. Is that a religious organization, as I understand it?

MRS. HAMER: Yes, Southern Christian Leadership Conference.

MR. FREEDMAN: Is there anything that you would like to add to your statement before you are questioned?

MRS. HAMER: We have a curfew in our town, Ruleville. Also, the night police there is a brother to J.V. Milan, that lynched Emmett Till in Sunflower County, the boy that was 14 years old and put in the Tallahatchie River. We have a curfew only for Negroes. It was a little before Christmas. My husband got up at 5 o'clock to go to the washroom. As he walked out, he heard a knock at the door, and he opened the door. He said, "Come in." Two policemen walked in, Mr. Milan and Mr. Dave Fleming, and asked him, what was he doing up at this time of night?

Not only have I been harassed by the police. I had a call from the telephone operator that I qualified to run as congresswoman. She told me, "Fannie Lou, honey, you are having a lot of different callers on your telephone. I want to know do you have any outsiders in your house? You called somebody today in Texas. Who was you calling, and where are you going? You had a mighty big bill." I said the bill was paid. "Well, I wouldn't let no outsiders come into my house."

I said, "What do you mean outsiders?"

"Well, we are going to check on this, and we just don't want no people from outside your house coming in and making outside calls."

I would like to add right now, the people I was with in Boston had to call the doctor to get some relief for my back that I still suffer with.

CHAIRMAN TAYLOR: Mrs. Hamer, may I ask, what was the charge on which you were arrested on the bus incident?

MRS. HAMER: Well, during the time I asked the jailer, "Would you leave the door open so I could catch air." During the time the door was open, I heard discussion: "Now, what is we going to charge them with?" Somebody said something. He said, "Well, you are going to have to get up something better than that. Man, that is the end of the wire."

So, I actually didn't know what we were charged with until they got ready to have our trial, and we were charged with resisting arrest and disorderly conduct.

DR. SYKES: We are all concerned about what might possibly happen in Mississippi this summer. Can you tell us about some things that have happened, what is going on now? But what do you think might happen with people going to Mississippi this summer?

MRS. HAMER: Well, I can say there will be a hot summer in Mississippi, and I don't mean the weather. Because the people are really getting prepared. They have been riding with the guns. But Ruleville is a very small town. There are about 2,000 people in there. I see now they have a tank, and they are keeping the dog riding on the back of the truck so if the truck stops, the dog won't have anything to do but jump off.

And the mayor he would ride around and tell folk don't let the outside people come into their homes, because after they stay awhile, they would just beat them up. But they say, "Don't say nothing to old Fannie Lou Hamer about it."

I am not even going on that street. My husband was fired the day after I qualified to run as Congresswoman in the Second Congressional District. Last week he had gotten a second job. The mayor went out on this job on which he was working, so he will probably be fired by the time I get back home.

DR. COLES: First of all, this curfew, is this legally done, or is this done—how is this known that there is a curfew?

MRS. HAMER: As long as there is a white man says that a Negro violated, it is legal with them.

DR. COLES: There is no public statement?

MRS. HAMER: No, you just get arrested, a Negro, if you are out after 12 o'clock.

DR. COLES: What do they say?

MRS. HAMER: They say you have broke the curfew hour. Violated the curfew hour.

DR. COLES: Is it a local ordinance? That is what we want to know? Is there a local law that says that if you are on the streets after 12 o'clock, you are violating the law?

MRS. HAMER: It must be, because I know you do get arrested.

DR. COLES: Has anyone challenged this?

MRS. HAMER: No.

DR. COLES: The other thing I would like to find out is, who do you pay your telephone bills to? Is this the Southern Bell Telephone Co.?

MRS. HAMER: That is right.

DR. COLES: Now, this is the town telephone operator, is it?

MRS. HAMER: The long distance operator—they operate out of Cleveland, Miss., because I asked her her name. She told me her name, and she said that it was just too much. And also, they take the telephone wire loose from the telephone post and got it right in front of the house and clipped on the main line.

DR. COLES: All I can say is I lived in a town in Georgia, and no telephone operator ever talked to me like this.

MRS. HAMMER: Well, it was the first time for me, but it did happen. One of the other things that happened in Sunflower County, the North Sunflower County Hospital, I would say about 6 out of the 10 Negro women that go to the hospital are sterilized with tubes tied. They are getting up a law said if a woman has an illegitimate baby and then a second one, they could draw time for 6 months or a $500 fine. What they didn't tell us is that they are already doing these things, not only to single women but to married women.

CHAIRMAN TAYLOR: Thank you very much.

AARON HENRY

Aaron Henry spent a third of a century as the leader of the Mississippi state branch of the NAACP and was a dominant figure in civil rights activism in his home state.[22] Henry was born in Coahoma County on July 2, 1922, the son of a sharecropper, but when he died on May 19, 1997, his obituary was published in *The New York Times*.[23]

Henry participated in his first protest in Hawaii, where he was stationed in the U.S. Army, when he and other soldiers demanded integrated housing on military bases. Returning from the service, Henry attended Xavier University in New Orleans on the G.I. Bill, where he received a B.S. degree in politics and government and a pharmaceutical degree and served as president of the junior and senior classes and of the student body his senior year. After graduating, he opened a drug store in Clarksdale, Mississippi, and quickly became a leader of civil rights protest. In 1953, he organized the Coahoma County branch of the NAACP and in 1960 he was elected president of the Mississippi state organization. He served on the national board of directors of the NAACP and its executive committee and was on the national boards of dirctors for the SCLC, the Southern Regional Council, and the Mississippi Council on Human Relations. He was chairman of the Freedom Democratic Party that challenged the national Democratic Party to include blacks in the Mississippi party. In 1962 Henry was elected president of the Council of Federated Organizations (COFO), a coalition of civil rights groups which conducted a voter registration campaign in 1963. COFO also organized the 1964 Mississippi Freedom Summer Project, a movement that brought more than one thousand volunteers to the state to establish community schools and work on voter registration. After the Voting Rights Act passed in 1965, Henry and Charles Evers pushed even harder for voter registration of Mississippi blacks and increased the proportion of voting-age blacks from 6.7 percent in 1964 to 32.9 percent in 1966. By 1967, twelve black Mississippians had won election to state offices.

As a result of his activism, Henry's home and business were bombed on several occasions and he was often harassed and intimidated by white authorities in Clarksdale and around the state. He was arrested on various charges thirty-eight times.

Aaron Henry died of congestive heart failure in Clarksdale, after suffering a stroke.

This speech was delivered at the state meeting of the NAACP in Jackson, just after the 1964 national election, during which Henry toured the nation speaking in support of the Lyndon Johnson presidential ticket.

KEYNOTE ADDRESS TO MISSISSIPPI STATE CONVENTION OF NAACP[24]

Jackson, Mississippi
November 6, 1964

Fellow members and friends of the National Association for the Advancement of Colored People. We have come together at this Convention after what has been perhaps the most interesting summer in Civil Rights Activity for our State. This summer has seen a tremendous effort in Voter Registration where more than ten thousand Negro Citizens of our State have tried to become registered voters. The tragedy of this is, however, that only about 400 new Negro voters were added to the voting rolls of the State. When we contrast this with the great results in Negro Registration with other states all over the nation, there immediately becomes a sadness in our hearts. This difficulty of becoming registered to vote in our home state is greatly discouraging. When we remember, however, that a few years ago the States of Florida, Georgia and Tennessee were no better off than we are now, this sadness turns to hope. For in the States of Georgia and Tennessee, Negroes were elected to political offices in the election, just over. Although Negro Registration was a big part of this success, it follows that when Negroes are Registered in large numbers, white citizens conduct themselves a little bit differently and candidates who are best qualified begin to win elections with many white persons supporting them. When Negroes become registered to vote, this seems to have an effect for good on the entire community. We are hopeful that Mississippi will immediately try this experiment.

The great victory just won by President Johnson and Senator Humphrey was a joy to behold. The great contribution of thousands of Negroes in Mississippi, was only desire; desire to participate in the Democratic Party and desire to vote for President Johnson and Senator Humphrey. A few of our citizens were to give a bit more than desire to this campaign for some travelled all over the nation in support of the Johnson Humphrey Ticket. We also recognize the great job done by members of the Mississippi Freedom Democratic Party [MFDP], inside the State in its efforts for the National Democratic Ticket. In trying to support President Johnson and Senator Humphrey, several persons were arrested in many parts of the state for distributing literature bearing the photographs of President Johnson and Senator Humphrey. Many were physically abused and intimidated, yet the members of the MFDP never lost the faith. When we remember that Medgar Evers gave his life for trying to encourage Negroes to become first class citizens and the death of Michael Schwerner, Andrew Goodman, and James Chaney was a direct result of their efforts in Registering and voting, we knew that the mandate we have to keep on is too great to surrender.

There were several lessons taught in this election. The Republican Party was able to carry Mississippi so overwhelmingly, because the state and congressional leaders of the Democratic Party would not support the Democratic Party. We got absolutely no help from Senator Stennis, or Senator Eastland, Congressman John Bell Williams, Congressmen Abernathy, Congressman Colmer, Congressman Winstead nor Congressman Whitten. We recognize with appreciation the giant effort expended by Attorney Douglass Wynn and a few of his supporters in behalf of the National Ticket of the Democratic Party. Besides them the MFDP was alone in this effort. We fail to understand why the National Democratic Party and the National Democratic caucus can not see the liability that these men heap upon the party. It was because of the negative action of the party greats that 64 Citizens of Mississippi went to Atlantic City to the National Democratic Convention in an effort to produce a change in the identity of those representing the Democratic Party. We informed the National Democratic Party that the representatives of the Party of Mississippi would not support the party in this election and we have been proven absolutely right. Our position has been completely vindicated by their negative action in the election just held.

We believe there is still a way to be found to correct this deplorable situation. The chore now falls to the Democratic Caucus in the House and the Senate. We call upon the caucus of the House and the Senate to refuse to grant seniority to the members of the congress and the Senate from the state of Mississippi within the Democratic Party. This seniority must be denied because these men have done nothing to identify themselves with the party. If they will not support the National Party, then they should be men enough to identify themselves with another party, other than the Democratic Party. If they will not do this voluntarily, then the caucus of the Democratic House and Senate should do it for them. The Congress and Senate must also seriously consider the fact that at least the seven members of the house and senate in Mississippi are illegally elected, because they come from districts where a great number of Negro Citizens are denied the right to vote. If we were allowed to vote in these districts most likely, the men who represent us, would not be the representative from the areas they are now identified with. We agree with Attorney Douglass Wynn that in the present election, we, "Lost the battle of Mississippi, but we won the war for America."

We call upon the Administration and the Department of Justice to become dedicated to the cause of securing the right to vote for all of America's Citizens. With the right to vote we can resolve many of the other problems that beset us here in Mississippi. These problems in addition to the right to vote are reflected in other areas. The question of economics is a major factor. In Mississippi 26% of our population, according to the 1960 census earns less than $3,000.00 per year; 32% of us earn less than $2,000.00 per year, and in the Mississippi delta, where I come from 51% of the people earn less than $1,000.00 per year. With this great economic blot in our state, yet every member of our federal delegation, senate and house, voted against the Poverty Bill. In the area of Education, the only reason Mississippi is not 51st in terms of academic attainment, is because America has only 50 states. When we had 48 states we were 48th, when Alaska and Hawaii came in, we moved progressively to 49th and 50th.

When the Virgin Islands come in, we will, in all probability move to 51st because we seem to have an affinity for the bottom. Yet, every member of our Congressional and Senate Delegations voted against Federal aid to Education. Injustice in the courts remains one of our most menacing evils. Never in the History of Mississippi, has a white man been convicted of a Capital Crime against a Negro; never in the History of the state. When a lesser crime is committed against a Negro and the white man pleads guilty, the judge suspends his sentence and says he needs a second chance, because he is so young and is just starting out in life, although the white man may be 46, 36, 35 or 34 years of age. With this kind of injustice going on in our State, still every member of our senate and Congressional delegation voted against the Civil Rights bill. This bill, in addition to securing equal protection of the laws in this instance, also guarantee the right to vote to all of America's Citizens. While we have a right to rely upon the Federal Government to secure for all of America's Citizens these rights and privileges, we have come to know too well that America has given its Negro Citizens a "do it yourself kit" to carve out for ourselves those rights and privileges that our state Government and National Government so jealously guards for all our other citizens.

Therefore, my friends and lovers of the NAACP, we call attention to our unfinished task. Before we are going to be able to secure the energetic support of the Federal Government, in helping to resolve our problems, there are many things that we can and must do. The freedom program now going on in Mississippi must have the support of all of us. We congratulate branches of Hattiesburg, McComb, Biloxi, Gulfport, Clarksdale, Moss Point, Meridian, Jackson, Vicksburg and Laurel. Here the NAME of the NAACP has been held high as the Freedom Movement has progressed. We cannot expect these few branches to continue to carry the load for all of us. We must each share in the work. These branches under tremendous odds have supported the Mississippi Freedom Summer Programs. Each conducted a Freedom School, a Community Center and carried on a very difficult Voter Registration Campaign. A bulk of those going down to try to register came from these areas.

Members from these areas were prominent in the delegation of the Mississippi Freedom Democratic Party in Atlantic City. It is very important for all of us to become aware and to understand that the political era is just beginning for us in Mississippi. Decisions of great importance have been made and are to be made. Every member of the NAACP should be a participator in the Mississippi Freedom Democratic Party. This party is going to be the political spokesman for the Negroes in Mississippi. It needs the assistance and the wisdom of all who will work with it. If we are going to have any say in the political decisions to be made, we must be participators all along, not just when the television cameras are present. The Mississippi Freedom Democratic Party has no positions open for prestige seekers, nor ornaments. To be a member of the Freedom Democratic Party, one needs only fill out the forms provided. But for one to hope to be a part of the machinery of the party, one must work for the party in every way; seeking other members, coming to meetings, precinct, county, district and State, and be willing to take your chances along with the others of us in every way. Over 70,000 of the members of the MFDP have just participated in a Freedom Vote Campaign, that should have a great effect upon future politics and politicians in and from our State; did you cast a Freedom Vote, or get someone else to cast one?

Until we become so interested in being free, that no one will doubt our sincerity we are going to continue to be plagued with the status of second class citizenship. There is much to be done. Too many schools in Mississippi still remain segregated, without a lawsuit being filed to do away with segregation. Too many hotels and restaurants remain segregated with no effort being made to cause them to comply with what is now the law of the land, ex-senator Goldwater, not withstanding. Too many courtrooms still remain segregated too many service stations along the highways continue to have rest rooms designated by race. As long as we in Mississippi permit these things to continue, all America soothes her conscience because of us. They can all point a self righteous finger at themselves and say, "We are not as bad as Mississippi." Mississippi is going to remain the dumping ground of America as long as we permit it to remain as it is. We realize that Mississippi is no mutation in this Country. Racial prejudice is alive all over the land, but nowhere as blatant as it is in Mississippi. When we correct this situation in Mississippi, we change the image of America, both within the country and in the international world.

The Presidential election just concluded bared some interesting facts. The racial bigotry so associated with the campaign of Senator Goldwater was so attractive to the white race prejudice in Mississippi that Senator Goldwater not only carried Mississippi, but he carried every county in the State of Mississippi. The white vote in Mississippi is around 500,000 as compared to about 20,000 Negroes. There dwell in Mississippi however, over 450,000 Negro Citizens over the age of 21 who desire to vote. At this time it is without a doubt these unregistered voters will lean toward the Democratic Party. This is a wonderful time for a democratic administration to show to these persons desiring the right to vote that it is as anxious to have them within the democratic fold as they are to become identified with the Democratic Party. Our problems are mutual, our desires are mutual. The Negro citizens of Mississippi this day pledge to do all we can toward changing the image of Mississippi, and thus the image of America, to one that we all can be proud of. Our question to you America, with all our wealth, all of our sky scrapers, with all our armies and navies, and now that the "election is behind us," and with all our great and good citizens, are you now as ready to do for America as much as our Negro Citizens of Mississippi are to make this great nation of ours truly the land of the free and the home of the brave? As much as we recognize that our problems are mutual and our desires are mutual, our destiny is the same. It is not a question of our efforts and our methods being violent or nonviolent. On both the national and the local scene the issue becomes now, nonviolence or nonexistence.

But America, you must become as willing to challenge Mississippi as its Negro Citizens are.

During the presidential campaign just concluded, I heard a story told by a candidate, who was a candidate for the senate in the state of Pennsylvania. The story goes, that on a cold winter day, a farmer who was the father of a two year old child, suddenly realized that the child was no where to be found. He began to search for the child, but could not locate the child. He called 50 or more of his neighbors to help him search in a vacant field for the child. This plot of ground was heavy with dead vegetation. They searched for almost two days in this fashion for the child. Then someone suggested that all the men join hands and stretch the length of the field. As they joined hands and began to cover the entire field, they soon came upon the child dying of exposure. The father lifted the child to his breast and the child breathed his last breath. The father then in anguish, turned to the other men and asked, "Why didn't we join hands sooner." America, let us not wait too late to join hands with your Negro Brothers in Mississippi.

STOKELY CARMICHAEL

Stokely Carmichael was one of the most dynamic young leaders of the Civil Rights Movement in the South as he made a major impact on SNCC and with his radical rhetoric helped to drive Martin Luther King Jr. and other more moderate leaders further to the left.[25] He was born in Trinidad on June 29, 1941, and emigrated to New York in 1952. By 1960, Stokely was participating in demonstrations, sit-ins, and picketing while a student at Howard University. He was a Freedom Rider in 1961 and as a result served time in Parchman Prison in Mississippi. Carmichael worked with fellow SNCC members on various projects in the South and was active in the 1964 Freedom Summer voter registration project in Mississippi. In 1965, he directed a voter registration project in Lowndes County, Alabama, which was able to register more than 2,600 black voters in a county which previously had only 70 registered African Americans. His efforts led to the Lowndes County Freedom Organization (LCFO), a political party that challenged white candidates in 1966. The LCFO adopted the black panther as its symbol, a foreshadowing of the use of that theme by the radical group, the Black Panther Party, which Stokely later joined.

Sometime during his activist career, Carmichael began to tire of the slow pace of progress in the movement and began to distance himself from King's and SNCC's nonviolent approach. He advocated that SNCC throw out all white members and began to talk about "Black Power" and social revolution. Carmichael was elected chairman of SNCC in 1966, and during the Meredith March in Mississippi, he made his famous "Black Power" speech that ultimately led to the changing direction of the movement from King and SCLC's nonviolent approach that sought integration, to a support of self-defense in the face of white attack, and a black nationalism approach that sanctioned violence. He began to connect the struggle in the rural South and the urban ghettos of the North and West with the worldwide struggle of non-white people against imperialism and colonialism. As part of this new approach, he began to attack U.S. involvement in the Vietnam War and began to link the black struggle with the various student protests and peace movements which swept the country in the mid to late-1960s. He left the country and traveled around the world denouncing the United States. As a result, he become one of the most reviled Americans in that era.

After he returned to the United States in 1968, his passport was seized and many politicians threatened to have him jailed. The Black Panther Party named him its honorary prime minister and he continued to speak around the country. In 1969, he left for the Republic of Guinea, in West Africa, where he took up residence and changed his name to Kwame Ture and continued his call for revolution as the only answer to racism.

Stokely Carmichael died of prostate cancer in Conakry, Guinea, on November 15, 1998. Unrepentant to the end, he was still answering his telephone with the phrase, "Ready for the revolution!"

SPEECH AT MORGAN STATE UNIVERSITY[26]

Baltimore, Maryland
January 28, 1967

It's good to be back here at Morgan. I used to party here when I was at school—after we sat-in in Baltimore on Route 40.

I hope some of the people who have been disagreeing with the concept of Black Power are here. I would suggest they read two articles—one that I wrote for the *New York Review of Books* in September [1966] and one that appeared in the *Massachusetts Review* in 1966.

They explain the theoretical concept of Black Power; they criticize the exponents of the coalition theory and those who say that integration is the only route to solving the racial problem in this country.

I would think that at a black university it would be absurd for me to talk about Black Power, that rather I should talk to black students about what their role is to be in the coming struggle. And so my remarks today are addressed to you, black students of Morgan, to give you a chance to hear some of the things that you never hear about, your need to stop being ashamed of being black and come on home. Though there are many members of the press here, you should pay them no mind because they will not be able to understand what we are talking about.

When I was supposed to speak at this university in October, they canceled the speech. Now I understand there were all sorts of bureaucratic tieups for canceling the speech. We know that elections were close at hand in Maryland and there was a feeling—on my part, I am not saying that anyone really said this—that the people were scared, and so they canceled the speech. They were scared that if I spoke here on the "your house is your castle" concept, Mahoney would win. One of the reasons I want to talk about that is that I think it is important to understand what that means. What I think the country is trying to do is kill the free speech of the Student Nonviolent Coordinating Committee.

I'd like to read from one of my favorite men, Frederick Douglass—I hope he is yours. You know Baltimore was his home spot, where he spent his early age. It was from Baltimore that he escaped to freedom.

I want to read it because I think it is crystal clear in our minds what we must do in this generation to move for Black Power. Our mothers scrubbed floors.

Our fathers were Uncle Toms. They didn't do that so we could scrub floors and be Uncle Toms. They did it so that this generation can fight for Black Power—and that is what we are about to do and that is what you ought to understand.

Mr. Douglass said:

> Those who profess to favor freedom, yet deprecate agitation, are men who want crops without plowing up the ground; they want rain without thunder and lightning; they want the ocean without the awful roar of its many waters.
>
> Power concedes nothing without demands—it never did and it never will. Find out just what any people will submit to and you have found out the exact amount of injustice and wrong which will be imposed upon them; and these will continue till they have resisted with either words or blows or with both. The limits of tyrants are prescribed by the endurance of those whom they suppress.

Following in Mr. Douglass's footsteps we intend to strike our first blow for our liberation, and we will let the chips fall where they may. We do not wish to earn the good will of anybody who is oppressing us. They should rather try to earn our good will, since they have been oppressing us.

This country has been able to make us ashamed of being black. One of the first recognitions of a free people is that we must be united as a people; we must understand the concept of peoplehood and not be ashamed of ourselves. We must stop imitating white society and begin to create for ourselves and our own and begin to embody our own cultural patterns so that we will be holding to those things that we have created, and holding them dear.

For example: it is nonsensical for black people to have debutante balls. It is nonsensical because you are imitating that which white society has given to you and that which you know nothing about. Your fathers slaved for one year to save $500 so that you can walk up in some white dress for one night talking about virginity. Wouldn't it be better to take that $500 and give it to Morgan so that you could develop a good black institution?

Imitation runs deep in the black community in this country. It runs very deep. You know, when we first got people to go to college and they went to the first white university in this country, there were things called fraternities and sororities. Our black brothers and sisters could not get into these fraternities. They were kept out because of the color of their skin. So what did our brothers do? They turned around and formed something called Alphas, and only light-skinned Negroes could get in. Our black sisters, not to be outdone, formed AKA, for bluebloods only. The other dark-skinned brothers, not to be outdone, set up Omega and Kappa. And then, of course, we had the counterparts, the Deltas.

Now, wouldn't it have been far better if those people, instead of imitating a society that had been built on excluding them, had turned around and built a fraternity that included everybody, light-skinned and dark-skinned?

Perhaps that is the greatest problem you, as black students, face: you are never asked to create, only to imitate.

Then we come to the question of definitions. It is very, very important, because people who can define are the masters. Understand that. You remember a couple of years ago when our black leaders would talk about integration. They would say we want to integrate. They would be talking about good houses, good schools, good neighborhoods. White people would say, You want to marry my daughter. They would say, No, I don't want to marry your daughter; we just want to be your brother, we don't want to be your brother-in-law. Or: We want to live next door to you, we don't want to live in your bedroom. What the white people were doing was defining integration for those black leaders, and those black leaders allowed them to. By the time those cats finished reacting to a definition by a white man, they were out the window. And by the time they came back to being aggressive the black community said later for those cats. They allowed white people to define their reaction.

Now when we get asked that question in SNCC you know what we say: Your daughter, your sister, and your mama. The white woman is not the queen of the world, she is not the Virgin Mary, she can be made like any other woman. Let's move on, let's move on.

They try the same things now. These days, I say Black Power and someone says, you mean violence. And they expect me to say, No, no, I don't mean violence, I don't mean that. Later for you, I am master of my own term. If Black Power means violence to you, that is your problem, as is marrying your daughter.

I know what it means in my mind. I will stand clear. And you must understand that, because the first need of a free people is to be able to define their own terms and have those terms recognized by their oppressors. It is also the first need that all oppressors must suppress. I think it is what Camus talks about. He says that when a slave says no, he begins to exist. You see you define to contain. That's all you do. If we allow white people to define us by calling us Negroes, which means apathetic, lazy, stupid, and all those other things, then we accept those definitions.

We must define what we are—and then move from our definitions and tell them, Recognize what we say we are!

We all watch cowboy movies all the time. You know, there would be a fight and there would be Indians and they would be coming from the hills and Chief Crazy Horse would have a million Indians and they would be yelling, "Wha, wha, wha," and they would be killing the good white women. And at last here comes the cavalry. They would come riding in and they would get out their guns and shoot up everybody—men, forward march, forward, shoot. Look out, that one on the right. Boom, we've got him, he's dead. They would come back and they would say, we had a victory today. We killed the Indians.

The next time the Indians would win; they would beat the hell out of the cavalry and the white man would come back and say, Those dirty Indians, they massacred us.

See what they were doing. They were putting connotations in our minds. A massacre is not as good as a victory because in a victory you shoot people and you kill them in an honorable way, but in a massacre you kill with a knife and everybody knows that's foul.

But the Indians had victories too. That we must begin to recognize. That's very important.

You ever listen to the news? Every day now, Viet Cong terrorists bomb and kill fifty women and children, what a shame. In the meantime, United States jet bombers have been flying heavily over Hanoi, dropping bombs.

The power to define is the most important power that we have. It is he who is master who can define; that was cleared in the McCarthy period. If McCarthy said you were a communist, you had to get up and say, No I am not a communist. Who the hell is McCarthy? I mean who is he? He had the power to define. It is the same thing. "My fellow Americans, the communists, the slant-eyed Viet Cong are our enemy. You must go kill them." You don't have the right to define whether or not that cat is your enemy. The master has defined it for you. And when he says "jump," you say, "how high, boss?" We must begin to define our own terms and certainly our own concept of ourselves and let those who are not capable of following us fall by the wayside.

You must begin to understand the nature of this country called America, which exploits all other, non-white countries. You know what they are talking about—you see that's the thing with definitions—you know, we are fighting for freedom, democracy, for peace. Nobody questions it. Yes, we are going to kill for freedom, democracy, and peace. These little Chinese, Vietnamese yellow people haven't got sense enough to know they want their democracy, but we are going to fight for them. We'll give it to them because Santa Claus is still alive.

I want to read a quote made August 4, 1953, before the United States Governors' Convention in Seattle. Incidentally, I highly recommend this book. It is *Vietnam, Vietnam*, by Felix Green.

I think the trouble with our black students is that they just don't read enough. If we could get books like we could boogaloo we would be uptight.

"Now let us assume," the quote says, "that we lost Indochina . . ." Now that is in 1953, the U.S. was not fighting the war, the French were fighting it for the United States. America was just giving them the money.

Now let us assume that we lost Indochina, the tin and tungsten that we so greatly value from that area would cease coming. So when the United States votes $400 million to help that war we are not voting a give-away program. We are voting for the cheapest way that we can to prevent the occurrence of something that would be of a most terrible significance to to the United States of America, our security, our power and ability to get things we need from the riches of the Indo-Chinese territory and from Southeast Asia.

That quote was made by President Dwight D. Eisenhower—now we may say that Dwight wasn't too smart. But that was in 1953. So, well, we figure, you know Dwight wasn't too smart and that was a long time ago and we have become more civilized.

I want to read you a statement now by Henry Cabot Lodge. He's the good-looking one, you know—tall, blond hair, blue eyes. He said, a year ago:

Geographically, Vietnam stands at the hub of a vast area of the world— Southeast Asia—an area with a population of 249 million persons. . . . He who holds or has influence in Vietnam can affect the future of the Philippines and Formosa to the east, Thailand and Burma with their huge rice surpluses to the west, and Malaysia and Indonesia with their rubber, ore and tin to the south . . .

Vietnam thus does not exist in a geographical vacuum—from it large storehouses of wealth and population can be influenced and undermined.

He is absolutely right. That's what that war is all about. And that's why we are not going.

Those are the words of the ambassador to Saigon, they are not my words. And he outlines very clearly what the war is being fought for.

If you understand anything about this country, you know that 75 per cent of the budget is spent on war materials. That means that for this country to survive it must always be at war.

You will not get a victory for this country if you win in Vietnam. That's no victory. The country must keep fighting. You do not invent things that have no use. You invent them so that they have a use. And every time you invent a better bomb, you must drop it. So you invent another bomb. That is why this country keeps going at the breakneck speed it is going in terms of its military might. We are told that it is civilized—another word to define.

You know Rudyard Kipling defined civilization for us. He talked about the white man's burden. Pick up your whiteness and go to Africa to cultivate the savages and illiterates. So all these nice, white people of good will who wanted to do well, they got in their little black robes and they went to Africa and they saw these little black savage women, man, running around with no shirts on. "Why, you dirty thing, cover yourself up." Africans were never excited, so it must have been the nice, white people who were excited because they wanted them to cover it up. Africans didn't even know what breasts were for except to feed their young.

But the white people brought their concepts. When they left they had the land and we had their religion. And that was civilization for them. Indeed, what is civilization? To be able to drop bombs on Hiroshima? To be able to drop bombs on Hanoi? Is that civilization? Do we want to be civilized too?

This country has said that civilization is at stake and there is no other solution but war. So what they do is train us in ROTC. You dig it? All they do in ROTC is teach you how to kill. You may try to justify it all you want, but your job is to kill. The job of the army is to kill. ROTC doesn't teach you how to become anything. If you want me to be taught something, build a school in my neighborhood and let me go there. Don't tell me about going to Vietnam to learn anything.

I have to be appalled at the president of the university who stands up and says that Black Power is about violence while at this very campus he encourages institutionalized violence—compulsory ROTC—and does not speak about that. Who does he think he's kidding? There is nothing wrong with violence. It is just who is able to control it. That's what counts. Everybody knows that. You have institutionalized violence on your campus. You have to dress up in a monkey suit and train how to kill once a week. And what is your response to that as black students, coming to a university where they are supposed to teach you civilization? Is that civilization too? That one must kill?

Is that what you are imitating? Is it for you not to reason why at a university, but to do and die? Do you not have the guts to say: Hell, no. Do you not have the guts to say, I will not allow anyone to make me a hired killer.

When I decide to kill, since it is the greatest crime that man can commit, I alone will make that decision, and I will decide whom to kill.

You are now at a vast black university where they have already incorporated violence in your thinking. And here you are marching around every Friday, or Thursday, or Wednesday or whatever it is, with your shoes spit-shined, until three o'clock in the morning—marching with a gun in your hand, learning all about how to shoot.

And somebody talks about violence. No, I am not violent, I don't believe in violence. I don't want no Black Power. I ain't got nothing to do with violence. Over in Vietnam they put you on a front line and you are shooting. But that is not violence because you can't define for yourself. You ought to tell the school that if you wanted to learn how to kill you would have gone to West Point. You came here to learn how to help your people in Baltimore in the ghettos, and then you turn your backs on them as soon as you get a chance.

What can you tell a black man who lives in the ghettos in Baltimore about killing? Hasn't he been subjected to it all of his life? What is your analysis about the rebellions that have been occurring all around the state?

Are you like everybody else? Are you against violence? Do you analyze? Do you recognize what it means?

The reason they say that we preach violence isn't because we preach violence, but because we refuse to condemn black people who throw rocks and bottles at policemen. That is why. And I say that is the only reason why. Look at all the other Negro leaders—so-called leaders—every time there is a riot:

We deplore violence, we avoid use of violence, it is very, very bad, there is only a small group of vagabonds, they don't represent our community, and violence never accomplishes anything.

Yes, we are training our boys to go to Vietnam. We think it is a good thing to send them to Vietnam, but violence never accomplishes anything at all.

Now, you have got to understand this very clearly. If you know anything about the ghetto, you know that on any given Friday or Saturday night there is more violence inside the ghetto than anyplace else in any given city. You know that we cut and butcher and shoot each other. And do you also know that in any given ghetto there is more police power, that is, in terms of numbers, there are more police per block, per square inch, than in any other area of the city? What does that mean to you? On Friday night while there are more police, there is still more violence among black people. Obviously, they don't give a damn about the violence among black people.

What it points out is the problem between property rights and human rights in this country—a problem the country is not capable of facing up to. Let one black boy throw one rock at some filthy grocery store and the whole damned National Guard comes into our ghetto. Property rights mean more than human rights and we in the ghetto do not own the property. If we get robbed, you can call the policemen till you turn white. He ain't coming. You know it as well as I do. But just hit a grocery store, just throw a Molotov cocktail through a window and see how quick they come in. They deplore violence.

It's all right with them when we cut each other in the street on Friday and Saturday nights. We need nonviolence in the black community, that's where we need it. We have to learn to love and respect ourselves. That's where it should begin. That is where it must begin. Because if *we* don't love us, ain't nobody going to love us.

The people who have power in our ghettos are the property owners and when their stores are touched they call the National Guard.

But analyze that one step further. Everybody in our ghettos knows that we are charged higher prices for rotten meat. Everybody knows that, but nobody says, "We deplore the high prices they charge the Negro for rotten meat." Nobody moves to readjust the problems black people are facing in the ghetto like the slumlord. And if they try, they would find out that the people who own the property are the people who make the laws.

Property rights, that's what the United States Constitution is based on. You should know that. You are three-fifths of a man until this very day. Property rights. People who didn't own property could not vote when this country was first founded, not until years afterwards. So the analysis is the question of property versus property-less people.

That's what those rebellions are about, nothing else, nothing less. And what appalls me about the black leaders is they do not have the guts to condemn the grocery store owner. Anytime a man has been charging us all that money for fifteen years, his store should have been bombed five years ago. It should have been out of the neighborhood five years ago. And if nobody wants to do it, then you can't blame people when they move to do it for themselves.

If you want to stop rebellion, then eradicate the cause.

It is time for you to stop running away from being black. You are college students, you should think. It is time for you to begin to understand that you, as the growing intellectuals, the black intellectuals of this country, must begin to define beauty for black people.

Beauty in this society is defined by someone with a narrow nose, thin lips, white skin. You ain't got none of that. If your lips are thick, bite them in. Hold your nose; don't drink coffee because it makes you black. Everybody knows black is bad. Can you begin to get the guts to develop criteria for beauty for black people? Your nose is your boss, your lips are thick, you are black, and you are beautiful. Can you begin to do it so that you are not ashamed of your hair and you don't cut it to the scalp so that naps won't show?

Girls, are you ready? Obviously, it is your responsibility to begin to define the criteria for black people concerning their beauty. You are running around with your Nadinola cream. The black campuses of this country are becoming infested with wigs and Mustangs and you are to blame for it. You are to blame for it. What is your responsibility to your fellow black brothers? Why are you here? So that you can become a social worker or so that you can kick down a door in the middle of the night to look for a pair of shoes?

Is that what you want college for? So that you can keep the kid in the ghetto school, so that you can ride up in a big Bonneville with an AKA sign stuck on the back? Is that your responsibility? What is your responsibility to black people of Baltimore who are hungry for the knowledge you are supposed to have?

Is it so that you can just get over? Do you forget that it is their sweat that put you where you are? Do you now know that your black mothers scrubbed floors so you can get here—and the minute you get out, you turn your back on them? What is your responsibility, black students? What is it? Is it to become a teacher so you can be programmed into a ghetto school? So that you can get up and say, "It's a shame how our children are culturally deprived?"

What do you know about culturally deprived? What is your definition of culture? Is it not anything man-made? How the hell can I be culturally deprived? You deny my very existence, to use that term.

Do you question what they tell you at school? Or do you only accept, carry it back, get over, go out to further stymie black people in the ghetto?

I blame you for the rebellions across the country this summer. And I will blame you again when they increase this summer. It is your obligation to be back in the ghetto helping out black people who are looking, who are acting, begging, and thinking a way to solve their problems. And you are running out of the ghetto as fast as your sports cars and Mustangs can carry you.

What is your responsibility, black students of Morgan? Do you know about

Du Bois? Have you read Douglass? Do you know Richard Wright? Can you quote J.A. Rogers? Do you know Claude McKay?

Can you understand, can you understand LeRoi Jones? There is a young man with me now. His name is Eldridge Cleaver. He just spent eight years in jail. He is writing some of the most profound writing that has come out in the country from black men. Do you know him? Have you read his stuff? Why haven't you read his stuff? Is it because you are too busy trying to find out where the Kappas are partying Friday night?

Why is it that you haven't read his stuff? Is it that you are spit-shining your shoes so that you can become a lieutenant colonel to go to Vietnam when you graduate?

Why is it that you haven't read his stuff? Is it that you don't want to read anything about being black because you, too, are ashamed of it and are running from it? So you want to run to your debutante ball. So you want to run to your Kappa fraternity ball and forget all else.

When the ghettos rebel you are going to be the buffer, and you are the ones who are going to be caught in the middle. The gate is swinging open. Brothers and sisters, you had better come home early this summer. You had better take what knowledge you have and use it to benefit black people in the ghetto.

You had better recognize that individualism is a luxury that black students can no longer afford. You had better begin to see yourself as a people and as a group and therefore, you need to help to advance that group.

Can you be aggressive? Can you say that Baltimore is almost 52 percent black, and black people should own it, run it, lock stock and barrel? Or are you afraid?

Can you not go out and organize those people to take the political power that they have been denied and by which they've been oppressed and exploited? Can you not help? Are you too busy trying to be a doctor and lawyer so that you can get a big car and a big house and talk about your house in the suburbs? Am I the only one out there?

Can you begin to say that James Brown is us, that he is a musical genius as much as Bach or Beethoven? Can you understand your culture? Can you make them teach it to you here in college, rather than teach you Bach and Beethoven, which is only one-sided? Why can't you also have James Brown so that you can begin to know what culture is all about?

I want to finish with one quote—actually there are two quotes I want to finish with.

I want to read it because I don't want to make a mistake. The quote I want to read before I close is from Bertrand Russell. You know about the war tribunal. You should. Bertrand Russell is calling the war tribunals to judge the leaders of this country for their actions in Vietnam. I have been asked to serve on it and I am greatly honored. I want to read a quote he calls "An Appeal to My Conscience." The war in Vietnam should have interest for you not only personally, but also because it is very political for black people. When McNamara says he is going to draft 30 per cent of the black people out of the ghettos, baby, that is nothing but urban removal. You should realize you are going to be the fellows leading the charges of your black people. Do you have the guts to stand up now and say I will not follow law and order, I will follow my own conscience. That's what they sent Eichmann to jail for, you know, because he followed law and order.

The choices are very clear. You either suffer or you inflict suffering. Either you go to the Leavenworth federal penitentiary in Kansas or you become a killer. I will choose to suffer. I will go to jail. To hell with this country.

Mr. Russell:

Just as in the case of Spain, Vietnam is a barbarous rehearsal. It is our intention that neither the bona fides nor the authenticity of this tribunal will be susceptible to challenge from those who have so much to hide. President Johnson, Dean Rusk, Robert McNamara, Henry Cabot Lodge, General Westmoreland and their fellow criminals will be brought before a wider justice than they recognize and a more profound condemnation than they are equipped to understand.

That is a profound statement.

The last statement that I want to leave you with is by John Donne. He said the "death of any man diminishes me because I am involved in mankind."

This generation is not involved in mankind. When we began to crawl, they sent six million people to an oven and we blinked our eyes. When we walked, they sent our uncles to Korea. And we grew up in a cold war. We, this generation, must save the world. We must become involved in mankind. We must not allow them the chance to kill everything and anything that gets in their way. We must not become part of the machine.

I want to read my favorite quotation to conclude.

"If I am not for myself, who will be? If I am for myself alone, who am I? If not now, when? And if not you, who?"

NOTES

1. For a thorough overview of the sit-ins, see William Chafe, *Civilities and Civil Rights: Greensboro, North Carolina, and the Black Struggle for Freedom* (New York: Oxford University Press, 1980); Aldon D. Morris, *The Origins of the Civil Rights Movement: Black Communities Organizing for Change* (New York: Free Press, 1984); Harvard Sitkoff, *The Struggle for Black Equality: 1954–1980*, rev. ed. (New York: Hill & Wang, 1993).

2. August Meier and Elliott Rudwick, *CORE: A Study in the Civil Rights Movement, 1942–1968* (Urbana: University of Illinois Press, 1975).

3. This biographical sketch is taken largely from James R. Chumney, "Lawson, James M., Jr." in Charles D. Lowery and John F. Marszalek, eds., *Ency-*

clopedia of African-American Civil Rights (Westport, CT: Greenwood Press, 1992), 311; and "Lawson, James M., Jr." in Iris Cloyd, ed. *Who's Who among Black Americans*, 6th ed., (Detroit: Gale Research, Inc. 1991), 763. There has been little else of a biographical nature written about Reverend Lawson.

4. Delivered in Raleigh, North Carolina, April, 1960. See text in August Meier, Elliott Rudwick, and Francis L. Broderick, eds., *Black Protest Thought in the Twentieth Century*, 2nd ed. (Indianapolis: Bobbs-Merrill Co., 1971), 308–15.

5. Delivered at Montgomery, Alabama, May 21, 1961. See text in the Martin Luther King Jr. Library and Archives, Atlanta, Georgia.

6. This biographical sketch is taken largely from Reavis Mitchell and Jessie Carney Smith, "Diane Nash," in Jessie Carney Smith, ed., *Notable Black American Women* (Detroit: Gale Research, Inc., 1992), 796–800.

7. See Nash's statement about her jail sentence in W. Stuart Towns, *Public Address in the Twentieth-Century South: The Evolution of a Region* (Westport, CT: Praeger, 1999), 95–98.

8. Delivered in Detroit, Michigan, August 1961. See text in Mathew H. Ahmann, ed., *The New Negro* (Notre Dame, IN: Fides Publishers, 1961), 43–60.

9. For a thorough discussion of the Birmingham crisis, see Taylor Branch, *Parting the Waters: America in the King Years, 1954–63* (New York: Simon and Schuster, 1988), chapters 18, 19, and 20.

10. Delivered in Birmingham, Alabama, May 3, 1963. See text in *The Black Experience in American Politics* (New York: G.P. Putnam & Son, 1973), 159–64.

11. Allen C. Thompson, "Speech over Radio WJDX and TV WLBT," Jackson, Mississippi, May 13, 1963. Text from Medgar Evers Papers, Tougaloo University Library, Jackson, MS.

12. Delivered in Jackson, Mississippi, May 20, 1963. See text in Medgar W. Evers Papers, Tougaloo University, Jackson, Mississippi.

13. Delivered in Jackson, Mississippi, June 15, 1963. See text in Roy Wilkins Papers, Manuscript Division, Library of Congress.

14. Most of this biographical sketch is from Michael E. Mueller, "John Lewis," in Barbara Carlisle Bigelow, ed., *Contemporary Black Biography*, vol. 2 (Detroit: Gale Research, 1992), 137–39; and John D'Emilio, *The Civil Rights Struggle: Leaders in Profile* (New York: Facts on File, 1979), 92–94.

15. For a thorough description of the writing of the speech and the reaction it received, and the negotiations that led to its slight modification, see Lewis' wonderful autobiography, *Walking with the Wind: A Memoir of the Movement* (New York: Simon & Schuster, 1998), 214–27.

16. Text as planned to be delivered in Washington, DC, August 28, 1963. See John Lewis, *Walking with the Wind: A Memoir of the Movement* (New York: Simon & Schuster, 1998), 216–18.

17. For descriptions of the bombing and its aftermath, see Taylor Branch,

Parting the Waters, 889–92; and Glenn T. Eskew, *But for Birmingham* (Chapel Hill: University of North Carolina Press, 1997), 318–22.

18. Delivered in Birmingham, Alabama, September 15, 1963. See text from King Library and Archives, Atlanta, Georgia.

19. This biographical sketch is taken largely from an autobiographical sketch on Ms. Hamer in the Amistad Research Center, Tulane University, New Orleans, LA, where her papers are housed; from Liza Featherstone, "Fannie Lou Hamer," in Barbara Carlisle Bigelow, ed., *Contemporary Black Biography*, vol. 6 (Detroit: Gale Research, Inc., 1994), 107–10; and from Jacquelyn Grant, "Fannie Lou Hamer," in Jessie Carney Smith, ed., *Notable Black American Women* (Detroit: Gale Research, Inc., 1992), 441–44.

20. For a text of her remarks, see W. Stuart Towns, *Public Address in the Twentieth-Century South: An Evolving Region* (Westport, CT: Praeger, 1999), 110–13.

21. *Congressional Record*, 88th Cong., 2nd sess., June 16, 1964, 14001–14002.

22. Most of this biographical sketch is from John D'Emilio, *The Civil Rights Struggle: Leaders in Profile* (New York: Facts on File, 1979), 67–69; and George Alexander Sewell, *Mississippi Black History Makers* (Jackson: University Press of Mississippi, 1977), 244–47.

23. Robert McG. Thomas, Jr., "Aaron Henry, Civil Rights Leader, Dies at 74." *The New York Times*, May 21, 1997.

24. Delivered at Pratt Memorial Methodist Church, Jackson, Mississippi, November 6, 1964.

25. Most of the material for this biographical sketch is from Charles D. Lowery and John F. Marszalek, eds., *Encyclopedia of African-American Civil Rights: From Emancipation to the Present* (Westport, CT: Greenwood Press, 1992), 89–90; John D'Emilio, *The Civil Rights Struggle: Leaders in Profile* (New York: Facts on File, 1979), 37–39; and Barbara Carlisle Bigelow, ed., *Contemporary Black Biography*, vol. 5 (Detroit: Gale Research, Inc., 1994), 46–50.

26. Delivered January 28, 1967. See text in *Stokely Speaks: Black Power Back to Pan-Africanism* (New York: Random House, 1971), 61–76.

FOR FURTHER READING

Halberstam, David. *The Children*. New York: Random House, 1998.

Proudfoot, Merrill. *Diary of a Sit-In*, 2nd ed. Urbana: University of Illinois Press, 1990.

Scott, Robert L., and Wayne Brockreide. *The Rhetoric of Black Power*. New York: Harper & Row, 1969.

Smith, Arthur L. (Molefi K. Asanti). *Rhetoric of Black Revolution*. Boston: Allyn and Bacon, 1969.

Wolff, Miles. *Lunch at the 5 & 10*. Rev. ed. Chicago: Ivan R. Dee, 1990.

James M. Lawson Jr.

Conkin, Paul K. *Gone with the Ivy: A Biography of Vanderbilt University.* Knoxville: University of Tennessee Press, 1985. See especially Chapter 18, which describes the Lawson affair and the furor created by his expulsion from Vanderbilt.

Tucker, David M. *Black Pastors and Leaders: Memphis, 1819–1972*, Memphis: Memphis State University Press, 1975. See especially chapter 9, "Reverend James M. Lawson, Jr. and the Garbage Strike."

Martin Luther King Jr.

For readings on King, see chapter 3.

Diane Nash

Hine, Darlene Clark, ed. "Diane Nash," *Black Women in America: An Historical Encyclopedia.* Brooklyn: Carlson Publishing Inc., 1993, pp. 834–36.

Nash, Diane. "Statement at Jackson, Mississippi." April 30, 1962. In W. Stuart Towns, *Public Address in the Twentieth-Century South: The Evolution of a Region.* Westport, CT: Praeger, 95–98.

Medgar Evers

For readings on Evers, see chapter 3.

Roy Wilkins

For readings on Wilkins, see chapter 3.

John R. Lewis

Ritter, Kurt, and Garth Pauley. "John Robert Lewis." In Richard W. Leeman, ed., *African-American Orators: A Bio-Critical Sourcebook.* Westport, CT: Greenwood Press, 1996, pp. 226–38.

Fannie Lou Hamer

Lee, Chana Kai. *For Freedom's Sake: The Life of Fannie Lou Hamer.* Urbana: University of Illinois Press, 2000.

Mills, Kay. *This Little Light of Mine: The Life of Fannie Lou Hamer.* New York: NAL/Dutton, 1991.

Price, Bernice, and Annie Pearle Markham. "Fannie Lou Townsend Hamer." In Karlyn Kohrs Campbell, ed., *Women Public Speakers in the United States, 1925–1993, A Bio-Critical Sourcebook.* Westport, CT: Greenwood Press, 1994, pp. 424–435.

Hamer, Fannie Lou. "Statement to the Democratic Party Credentials Committee." August 22, 1964. In W. Stuart Towns, *Public Address in the Twentieth-Century South: The Evolution of a Region.* Westport, CT: Praeger, 1999, pp. 110–13.

Aaron Henry

Jenkins, Robert L. "Henry, Aaron." In Charles D. Lowery and John F. Marszalek, eds., *Encyclopedia of African-American Civil Rights.* New York: Greenwood Press, 1992, pp. 253–54.

Sewell, George A., and Margaret L. Dwight. *Mississippi Black History Makers,* rev. and enlarged ed. Jackson: University Press of Mississippi, 1984, pp. 84–87.

Woodley, Richard A. "It Takes Guts to Work for LBJ in Mississippi." *The New Republic,* October 10, 1964, pp. 6–7.

Stokely Carmichael

Carmichael, Stokely, and Charles V. Hamilton. *Black Power: The Politics of Liberation in America.* New York: Vintage Boooks, 1967.

DeWitt, Karen. "Formerly Stokely Carmichael and Still Ready for the Revolution." *The New York Times,* April 14, 1996.

Kaufman, Michael T. "Stokely Carmichael, Rights Leader Who Coined 'Black Power,' Dies at 57." *The New York Times,* November 16, 1998.

Parks, Gordon. "Whip of Black Power." *Life,* May 19, 1967, pp. 76–80.

Stewart, Charles J. "The Evolution of a Revolution: Stokely Carmichael and the Rhetoric of Black Power." *Quarterly Journal of Speech* 83 (1997): 429–46.

CHAPTER 5

"BETRAYERS OF THEIR RACE": SOUTHERN WHITE LIBERALS

Despite the appearance to the world of a monolithic white South, totally and irrevocably opposed to racial integration, there was a tiny cluster of white men and women whose moral commitment led them to speak out for racial justice. Often the more vocal were the subject of venomous attacks, firebombing of their homes and businesses, ostracism from their white neighbors, and crosses burned on their lawns. But they persevered and provided support for black activism. They were important to the movement for a number of reasons; as David Chappell points out, often, they were the only source of financial support, legal training, and inside information that the movement needed.[1]

This cadre of white liberals had a long history. Elements of liberalism can be traced back even to the last decades of the nineteenth century, when men like Atticus G. Haygood, the president of Emory College; writer George W. Cable; Andrew Sledd, a professor and one-time president of the University of Florida; and Lewis Harvie Blair, a Virginia businessman who attacked repression of the Negro, sought to educate the newly freed slaves and to improve their economic conditions.[2] Their liberalism was tinted with the colors of segregation, however, as they advocated a better place for southern Negroes—but a "place" below the ranks of the white race and in a clearly segregated world. Their liberalism was offset by the much more dominate segregation mindset of the James Harpers and James Griggs heard from in the first chapter of this anthology. The racial etiquette and the segregated South established by the white supremacists around the turn of the century was the norm. The white liberals who wanted "to improve the Negros' lot," as they put it, were always relegated to the background and their minority role almost disappeared in the early decades of the twentieth century.

But not quite. In the 1920s and 1930s, a small handful of whites began to agitate for better conditions in education, health, and other human services for southern blacks. Organizations were formed such as the Commission on Interracial Cooperation, the Southern Sociological Congress, and the Association of Southern Women for the Prevention of Lynching; they all provided a home for the small band of whites whose conscience had been stirred to attempt to ameliorate conditions in the benighted South. Again, however, their positions regarding race were conditioned by their almost universal belief in improving the conditions, but only within the restrictions of a segregated society. Even the liberals generally did not want to upset the system.

It was not until the Southern Regional Council was established in Atlanta in 1944 that a forum was created for white liberals to attack segregation, but it took this organization five more years before it openly attacked segregation in the South.[3]

The speeches in this section reflect the thinking and convictions of this small group of whites who were morally committed to speaking out against the bigotry of southern racism.

CLARK FOREMAN

Clark Foreman was one of the most determined of the small band of liberals who advocated change in the racial mores of the segregated South.[4] Born in Atlanta, Georgia, on February 19, 1902, Foreman was from a distinguished Georgia family. His grandfather, Clark Howell, was the long-time editor of the Atlanta *Constitution*, and both of his grandfathers had fought for the Confederacy. He graduated from the University of Georgia, where he was a champion debater and class orator. While in Athens, Foreman witnessed a lynching that led him to begin to question the racial environment of the South. Foreman studied for a time at the London School of Economics, then returned to Georgia where he worked for the state committee of the Commission on Interracial Cooperation. He then earned a master of arts degree from Columbia University with a thesis on interracial cooperation in the South. In 1932, he completed a Ph.D. from Columbia and the next year he joined the New Deal administration as a staff member for Secretary of the Interior Harold L. Ickes, where he served as an advisor on the economic status of the Negro. For the next several years, Foreman served in various capacities with the Department of the Interior, always promoting racial nondiscrimination in government agencies and in contracts with builders of power plants. He was the editor of the landmark *Report on Economic Conditions in the South*, which was published in 1938. A result of this report was the establishment of the Southern Conference for Human Welfare (SCHW), which was founded in Birmingham, Alabama, to deal with the problems defined in the report; Foreman was elected treasurer of this new group. The purpose of the SCHW was to "promote the general welfare and to improve the economic, social and political, cultural and spiritual conditions of the people of the South, without regard to race, creed, color, or national origin." In 1942, he was elected president of the organization and he served in that role until 1947. During the years after that, he was associated with the Emergency Civil Liberties Committee and continued to promote equal rights and racial harmony. Foreman died in Atlanta on June 15, 1977.

This speech was presented to the Keynote Session of the Southern Youth Legislature in Columbia, South Carolina, on October 19, 1946.

KEYNOTE ADDRESS TO SOUTHERN YOUTH LEGISLATURE[5]

Columbia, South Carolina
October 19, 1946

Nearly three hundred years ago, Pierre Robert, my grandfather ten generations back, settled in what is now the state of South Carolina, to escape the persecution of Protestants which was then prevailing in France. As the first Huguenot minister in America, Pierre Robert came to build a free country, where all people, of whatever faith or origin, could live in harmony, free from the persecutions of the old world. Thousands of other early settlers in the South set out to make this country free and democratic. Freedom and liberty are just as important in the heritage of the South as the puritan tradition in New England. The best Southerners have always been true to that tradition of freedom.

The freedom and liberty-loving Southerners were overwhelmed several generations ago by the growing power of the small minority of plantation owners. We were pushed into slavery and secession by these big-business men of the old South because then, as now, the majority of the people of the South were not allowed to vote.

The period of slavery, secession and bloody civil war would not be in our history books today if all the Southerners had had the vote in the seventeen- and eighteen-hundreds. So long as a handful of people are allowed to speak for an entire state, we shall not have democracy in the nineteen-hundreds. I know that one of South Carolina's newspapers is editorially opposed to democracy, but it can hardly be said to speak the sentiments of many citizens of South Carolina. The democracy which the Charleston *News and Observer* and its Northern industrial friends are against is the true expression of the Southern people.

The sooner the people of the South elect their own officials and have a real voice in the running of their government, the better off the South and the whole nation will be.

Just as slavery, secession and civil war would never have happened if all Southerners, or even all free Southerners, had been able to vote, so that long list of notorious lynchings would never have taken place if the Federal Constitution had ever been properly enforced and the rights of our citizens in elections had not been abridged.

The recent post-war wave of lynching and terror has focused the eyes of the Nation on the corruption of much of our democracy machinery in the South. Almost without exception the victims of lynching have been guilty only of standing up for their rights. Decent people throughout the South and through the nation hang their heads in shame while Bilbo, Talmadge and the other minority-elected products of disfranchisement continue their outrages against decency and democracy. These petty dictators of the South continue to encourage violence by their mere presence in office.

Just as the plantation-owners profited from slavery in the South that many Americans like to think is a thing of the past, their present-day successors still hope for greater profits through labor at little better than slave prices. Unfortunately, slavery has not disappeared from the South. One look into the Southern part of the United States will tell any observer that now not only the Negroes, but the whites as well, are enslaved. Enslaved to a system of taxation without representation, enslaved to a system which knows little economic security, enslaved to a combination of Northern industrial overseers and modern plantation-owners whose Simon Legrees are the Bilbos, and Talmadges and their tools among the police who shoot up Negro communities as in Columbia Tennessee, or wink at lynching as in Monroe, Georgia, or who gouge out the eyes of a Negro veteran as in Batesburg, South Carolina.

The rulers of this feudal minority can call upon money from the North and the South to maintain their control. They can buy a large corrupt segment of the press. Wherever the masses of the people are unable to vote, there rulers can buy into office their state, county and municipal officials and even legislators in Washington. They can also confuse many people by spreading false information and inflaming prejudice.

These feudalists endanger the whole country, because their minority-elected stooges in the Senate and the House of Representatives can be depended upon to block every piece of progressive legislation introduced in Congress.

The racist propaganda put out by these would-be Hitlers deceives many people into crimes they never would commit if they had economic security. The Southern white worker is very often the victim of poverty and prejudice. Under the goading of the demagogue, the white worker is driven by that age-old enemy of logic—fear. The white worker, constantly in a state of insecurity, is afraid that he will lose his job to a Negro, and rationalizes the sinister lies and distortions of the demagogue.

Lynching is no racial matter. All of us are endangered when the mob strikes at any one of us. The organization of prejudice is the prelude to fascism. It is a tool used by Northern and Southern owners of industries in the South, who, like the German industrialists, realize that economic fear can be profitable to them.

I have seen in my native Atlanta the shops of a Northern corporation which employed both Negroes and white workers on a fifty–fifty basis but kept them segregated and allowed very little communication. Whenever either group asked for some remedy or better working conditions, the standard answer was that if they didn't like what the company was doing, the company would be glad to employ more of the other group. This answer was given with equal facility to a grievance from a white person as to a grievance from a Negro. The separation of the two groups made it difficult, if not impossible, to present a united demand.

Segregation, prejudice and discrimination are all part and parcel of the economic issue in the South. So long as the workers of the South are kept divided by economic fear they cannot have security; they cannot have the basic protections of our Constitution.

The Northern and Southern mill-owners who think of their profits and not of the security and prosperity of the people of the South are doing everything in their power to keep the South divided into two groups which are constantly fighting each other. They will use any means at their disposal to keep the workers of the South unorganized and working for low salaries. During the recent primary campaign in Georgia one of the largest mill-owners there offered to support Carmichael, Talmadge's opponent for governor, if Carmichael would guarantee him the same protection against labor troubles that Talmadge had given him during the previous Talmadge administration. That protection meant arresting strikers and imprisoning them behind barbed-wire enclosures. Carmichael refused to have any part of this corrupt bargain—so Talmadge had the support of this mill-owner and of practically every large mill in Georgia, whether owned in the North or in the South.

We blame the German people because they did not resist more effectively the growth of fascism in Germany. We cannot sit idly by and watch the familiar pattern take shape in our country. There are people in the South who would welcome the way of fascism. But organizations like the Southern Negro Youth Congress and meetings like this Youth Legislature are proof that many of the people of the South are aware of the menace, and that they are determined to fight it regardless of danger of intimidation.

The day of Uncle Tom is over. More and more the people of the South are realizing that complacency and subservience are not the answers to segregation and discrimination. To those who say, "the Negro must keep his place," there can be but one reply: the only possible meaning that phrase can convey is that the Negro must take his place as an equal along side his fellow white citizens under the Constitution of the United States.

The United States has always assured the civil liberties of Americans abroad even to the extent of threatening war when an American's rights have been threatened in a foreign country. And yet we have second-class citizenship for millions of people in our own country. Now Mr. James Byrnes of South Carolina is insisting that European nations guarantee to their nationals the civil rights that this same Mr. Byrnes has insisted should be denied the citizens of his home state.

The South has strayed far from the precepts of Pierre Robert and the early founders. The United States is governed by the most comprehensive document ever drafted to safeguard human rights. And yet in the South the United States Constitution has been deliberately and continually and habitually violated time after time, with the responsible officials making little attempt to enforce it.

In Lawrenceburg, Tennessee, the curtain went down this month on the second act of a gruesome spectacle called "Dixie Justice." Twenty-five Negro citizens were on trial for the crime of standing up for their American rights. Tennessee's politicians are protecting the real culprit, Safety Commissioner Lyn Bomar, who ordered his storm troopers to destroy the Negro community in Columbia, Tennessee, and who let the mob of vandals, looters and potential murderers. The trial of twenty-five Negroes for "attempted murder" was conducted under a biased judge by a court which allowed little evidence to be presented on behalf of the defendants. Even so, an all-white jury registered a verdict which the attorney for the defense called "a victory for Americanism." Twenty-three of the defendants were freed.

The tragedy of the Columbia cases is that the wrong parties were on trial. There, as in so many of the recent lynchings in the South, the state, county and municipal officials have entered into a conspiracy with the murderers. By not entering these cases, and upholding the Bill of Rights, the Department of Justice is placing the Government of the United States in tacit approval of these conspiracies.

There exists today a law known as the Civil Rights Statute which provides for the punishment of violators of the civil rights Amendments of the Constitution. Since V-J Day, the Department of Justice has applied that statute to one case—the case of police chief Linwood Shull of Batesburg South Carolina, who brutally blinded and tortured Isaac Woodard, a Negro veteran just out of the service. The people of the United States, rather than the Department of Justice, deserve credit for the arrest. Public opinion all over the country—North and South—demanded that Shull be apprehended. Apparently only public opinion can force the Department of Justice to apply the statute to the hundreds of other cases of violations of the Constitutional rights of American citizens.

In my opinion, and in the opinion of many qualified lawyers, the existing Civil Rights Statute is broad enough to apply to *all* violations of Constitutional rights. However the Government has chosen to give it a very narrow interpretation. For that reason, the Southern Conference for Human Welfare has initiated and is cooperating in the drafting of a Federal Civil Rights Bill which will be introduced when Congress reconvenes. This bill will leave no doubt that the civil rights granted in the Constitution are to be enforced by the Federal government. The Federal Civil Rights Bill will, for the first time, give a real meaning to the Constitution in many Southern states.

We all know how sorely this bill is needed under present Federal practice to guarantee protection from the lynch-mob, Federal punishment for lynchers, insurance of free elections and fair justice for all. To some of the South's demagogues this will seem like the end of the world—and it may be to their world. The Federal Civil Rights Bill will merely enforce what has been the law for 160 years.

We are determined that this bill shall not be filibustered to death by the reactionary Senators and Congressmen. Just as public opinion demanded that the Department of Justice arrest Batesburg's local storm-trooper, an aroused public opinion will demand that Congress pass this bill guaranteeing to *all* citizens the rights Americans have been so proud of for more than a century.

I do not want to give the impression that the picture in the South is wholly dismal. Politically, we have made good progress in the recent elections. As a result of the Supreme Court decision, Negroes voted in the Democratic primaries in five new states. While it is true that Rankin, Bilbo, McKellar and Byrd have been re-elected, many other Southern Congressmen potentially as bad have been defeated.

In Florida, the people elected ex-Governor Spessard Holland Senator over a man who made his chief campaign against Negroes. Also in Florida, Congressman Cannon of Miami, one of the worst in Congress, was defeated by a young veteran, George Smathers.

In North Carolina, Congressman Folger, one of the best from the state, was re-elected over a well-financed reactionary. In Virginia, Congressman Daughton was turned out because of his sorry record. In Alabama, the people chose for Governor, Jim Folsom, a man with a very liberal platform including the abolition of the poll tax and opposition to an amendment to the state constitution which would have caused many Negroes to be disfranchised. In Alabama also, John Sparkman was chosen for Senator over two of the most reactionary people in that state, Congressman Boykin and Jim Simpson—both of whom had bad records with respect to agitation against Negroes.

In Georgia's first gubernatorial election since the abolition of the poll-tax, the people voted overwhelmingly against Talmadge, but he claims the nomination on the basis of a clearly unconstitutional system of county unit-votes. I am glad to say that the people of Georgia are challenging the validity of that election in the Supreme Court. In Georgia also, three of the most reactionary of our Congressmen have been retired—Paterson, Taryer and Gibson. The local machines in Augusta, Brunswick and Savannah have been turned out. In Augusta, the speaker of the Georgia House of Representatives was defeated after a campaign almost entirely devoted to an attack on Negro voting. His opponent never once gave in to this demagoguery and was overwhelmingly elected. Significantly, he would have been elected even if the Negro vote had not been counted, which shows that the white people of Augusta are not duped by bigotry.

In McMinn County, Tennessee, the people showed how dearly they treasured democracy. When the machine politicians refused to count the ballots openly and squarely, the non-partisan citizen's committee were forced to meet violence with violence to insure free elections. The citizens' slate in McMinn won an overwhelming victory when the ballots were counted.

The encouraging signs in the South are not limited to the field of politics. Probably the brightest light in the South today is the progress being made in the organizing of Southern labor. Organized labor has long realized that discrimination and prejudice are means of keeping Southern workers divided and in a state of subservience through low wages, poor conditions and inequal educational, housing and medical facilities. The labor organizations realize that so long as Negro and white are kept divided by prejudice and ignorance the South will continue to be the most unhealthy, most disadvantaged and most oppressed region of the country.

All progressive labor organizations know, too, that so long as we are denied free elections, the South will be represented in Washington by the enemies of labor, by men who thrive on the division and poverty of the South. Labor knows that the South will never be either democratic or prosperous while it is represented in the nation's capital by Bilbos, Byrds, Rankins and McKellars.

The Southern Conference for Human Welfare was founded eight years ago on the basis that all the people of the South must attack their problems together—because they are common problems. So long as the Negro in the South is voteless and intimidated, the white worker will never have security. The Southern Conference for Human Welfare is composed of forward-looking Southerners, both colored and white, who know that the welfare of the South is a problem for all Southerners. We work for a prosperous South and a democratic South. We believe that this goal can be accomplished only when the people of the South join together to achieve it, regardless of race, creed or color.

We have state committees in Virginia, North Carolina, Georgia, Alabama, Tennessee and Louisiana and members in all the Southern states. By 1948 we hope to have a committee in each of the thirteen Southern states. We know that we can never hope to match the money that the machines use in elections. We know that the reactionaries of the South get support from the reactionaries of the North. We need money but we need it not to buy votes and steal elections. We need it for organizations.

The lack of democracy in the South is not a problem for the South alone. Franklin D. Roosevelt said in 1938, "the South represents the Nation's number one economic problem—the Nation's, not merely the South's." Economically and politically the low standards in the South affect the entire country. Roosevelt's words are just as true today as they were eight years ago.

The rising tide of fascism in the South must be turned back before it has the chance to engulf the whole Nation. In this fight for democracy no one can sit idly by. Wherever you are, seek out those people of both races who are willing to stand up for their rights, and join with them in the fight. The forces of reaction are solidly organized and well financed. Only through organization of all the people who cherish liberty and freedom and are willing to work for it can American fascism be prevented from doing what Hitler and Tojo failed to accomplish in the United States.

SARAH PATTON BOYLE

Sarah Patton Boyle was another southerner, like Foreman, born into one of the elite southern white families, whose history dated back to before the Revolutionary War era.[6] She was convinced by her mother that she was from the best family in the best state and she inherited the typical white southerner's perspective on racial relationships. She vividly describes her perception of the racial etiquette of the South in her autobiography: "My thoughts became saturated with the assumption that Negroes belonged to a lower order of man than we . . . I quickly learned not to judge them by our standards, but by a segregated, separate standard."[7] It was not until 1950, when Gregory H. Swanson sued the University of Virginia Law School, that she came face to face with the reality of segregation. Swanson won his suit and Boyle began a campaign to convince white southerners that integration was possible and desirable.

Boyle immediately began to write letters to various Virginia newspapers and had an article published in the *Saturday Evening Post*, titled "Southerners Will *Like* Integration."[8] Naturally, white southerners did *not* like it, and she quickly became an outcast. Crosses were burned on her yard in Charlottesville, where she was the wife of a University of Virginia professor of speech and drama. At the outset of her campaign, Boyle believed she was only one of many white southerners who would stand up for Negro rights. As she put it in *The Desegregated Heart*:

> I thought of myself as a finger-in-the-dike until help came. I had to keep back the withering brine of hatred and fear only until Virginia's brave thousands came quickly forward with sandbags, determined that there should be no innundation of our green land. But down the miles of dikes where I had thought to see hordes at work, I saw only scattered individuals who like myself were thrusting numbing fingers and arms into holes in the crumbling dike. The good people of Virginia rushed, not for sandbags, but for safety, while chill, brackish waters flooded in. . . . All my beliefs that I had been in a position to test had been proven untrue.[9]

This speech was given to the Virginia Voters League when Boyle received the organization's 1956 annual award for "relentless, consistent, unselfish, untiring efforts on behalf of all citizens."[10] Boyle continued her civil rights efforts for several years, picketing for open seating in Charlottesville restaurants in 1963. The following year, she marched in a protest in St. Augustine, Florida, at the request of Martin Luther King

Jr. She was arrested for this protest at the Monson's Motor Lodge. She gradually removed herself from the battle as the years passed and she died February 20, 1994, in Arlington, Virginia.

DEMOCRACY DEPENDS ON YOU[11]

Ashland, Virginia
September 23, 1956

As colored Southerners you have an obligation to yourself, your group, the whole South, the nation and the world to set a standard of what an American citizen is supposed to be. Why does this obligation fall on you? It falls on you because the colored Southerner is carrying the banner for democracy today.

Our oppressed minorities are the only living Americans who are really in a position to know what this nation is all about. Colored Southerners are now living through the kind of experience which gave birth to our Constitution and our Bill of Rights.

Southern Negroes are now being faced with what is probably the heaviest responsibility ever laid upon a minority—that of realizing the brotherhood of man and the democratic ideals of our nation. For in America the light of these principles now shines chiefly through our largest minority.

Until six years ago I was a typical white Southerner, which is to say that I lived in an all-white world. Like most Southerners I had the warmest feelings toward Negroes, but accepted the status quo without the faintest realization that it was contrary to the principles for which we all stand.

If it hadn't been for the NAACP I'd still be in my white prison. For it was through the admission of our first Negro student to the University of Virginia, where my husband teaches, that I became aware that I was really in a prison and that I might be able to escape.

Listen carefully now, for this is important: The very first thing that confronted me when I stepped out of my white prison was the *modern Negro's superior grasp of democracy*. As I began to know the educated Negroes in my community I realized that here are people who understand the American ideal much better than the people of my own understand it.

All the struggles and agonies of Negroes have been like fertilizer and workings in a garden of their humanity. Stepping as I did from a group which has been kept childishly unthinking by easy living, I was confronted by the virile idealism and human understanding of most of the colored leaders of today. *The modern Negro has a firm grasp of American Ideas which white America has not enjoyed since Jeffersonian days.*

Did you ever stop to think that the situation of the Negro almost parallels that of white Americans before the Revolution? England discriminated against the colonists and oppressed them in the same ways in which whites now discriminate against and oppress Negroes.

And the result has been the same. Negroes today are swept with a realization of the dignity of man, the rights of every individual and the certainty that brotherhood is the destiny of the human race.

It was the realization of these dynamic truths, a realization born of oppression and hardship—which gave to Jeffersonian Americans the spiritual brawn which has made our nation great. The virility of this vision, however, has become sadly weakened in the white group. As our memory of oppression faded, our vision faded, too.

But happily there is one group of Americans to whom these ideals are still dynamic. Because our colored citizens are oppressed just as our colonies were once oppressed, these truths have for them the powerful thrust which originally drove them in the Constitution. *Of all the peoples of our nation colored Southerners are in the best position to understand what the fathers of our Republic were talking about.*

White Americans are like protected children. Having always had their basic needs supplied, they give their attention chiefly to superficialities. The average white never thinks about the innate dignity of man because he has never had his dignity challenged. He has never even known a man who has had his dignity challenged. Since such a thing is completely outside of his experience, it cannot be for him a living issue.

But when such a childlike white man is given the opportunity to know a superior Negro, for whom the dignity of man is a vital truth, this truth comes alive for the white man also. It's the same with the principles of freedom, equality and the right to chosen pursuits. White Americans are not aware of the nature of these right fulfillments, because their experience has never included a lack of them.

If the United States is to recapture a realization of the principles upon which she was founded, it must be with the help of and guidance of our colored people of the South.

The American Vision of the rights of man is like a two-stage rocketship. The first rocket of this vision plunged upward, powered by our releases from British oppression. We've reached a great height but I think the power of our first rocket is nearly spent. We need our second, smaller rocket if we are to escape the gravity pull of outgrown custom and reach the outer space of true democracy. As they point toward liberty and discharge their wrongs, Southern Negroes can be our nation's second rocket.

What can you as an individual do to help this rocket? Give your money, time, and loyalty regularly to the cause of freedom, but I'm going to make a very specific suggestion about what to do *first.* I hope, if there is anybody here who is not now a voter, he will go straightway tomorrow morning and pay his poll tax and register, so he'll be in position to vote. And I hope that every one here who is a voter will go straightway tomorrow morning and find someone who is not a voter and will go with him to pay his poll tax and register.

Do you realize that if every Negro in the South voted, discrimination would become almost impossible? Not only are a high percentage of our Southern people Negroes, but also many White Southerners vote on the Negro's side. Look at all the white people who voted against constitutional amendment. If all our colored citizens had voted with them there would have been a different ending to that story.

If you study voting records throughout the South you will find, to my knowledge, no Negro candidate who has ever run for office in the South, even the deep south, who has failed to draw a large white vote. Then why aren't more of them elected? Because so few Negroes vote. In most Southern communities a colored candidate can expect little help from his own people.

Worst still perhaps, white candidates know that they can count on little support from the minority. Can you blame them, then, if they don't go to bat for minority rights? A white politician recently said, "I believe in everything that the NAACP believes in, but it would be political death for me even to hint such a thing."

I said, "If you believe in minority rights, don't you think it's your duty to make convictions known, no matter what it costs you?"

His reply was vitally significant. I want you to listen carefully to what he said. He said:

"I certainly do—just as soon as the minority will support me *when* I do. But until colored people show themselves ready to help themselves by voting, I don't think they are ready to be helped. And I don't think that any politician should be asked to help them at such a sacrifice."

His statement gives you in a nutshell the attitude of many good-willed white Southerners. They see no reason to make a large effort and a large sacrifice— and I assure you that this is what it requires a white person to make a stand against the official position of his own group. They are not willing, I say, to do this until Negroes show themselves glad to make at least the small effort and sacrifice of becoming voters and giving their support to those who try to help them.

Imagine yourself in this position:

You are driving along a paved road in your shiny Buick, when you are flagged down by a man whose car had run off the road and is stuck. He says to you, "Hey, Mr. Another Buick just like yours, ran me off the road. Will you give me a push and help out?"

You reply, "Well, friend, it surely will get my nice car muddy but if you'll get over there on the other side and push, I'll see what I can do."

But he shakes his head. "Ho, no! That would be too much trouble, and besides, I'd get muddy myself."

If you had this experience, do you think that you would go ahead and push this man out, just because it was another Buick which ran him off the road? Or would you drive away with a clear conscience?

I suspect you'd drive away. Anyhow, that's what most good-willed Southern politicians do, and don't you think they are justified? I don't think you can blame them. The fact that other white people are responsible for the colored citizen's present position does not seem to them sufficient reason for sacrificing themselves to help him unless he is prepared to make every possible effort to help himself.

This voting situation is rather like the kind of offers often made by rich people to charity organizations. That is, "You raise $1,000 and I'll double it." They won't give a nickel unless those organizations get out and hustle for that first $1,000, but if the hustling is done, they're glad to match it with a fat check. There are many good willed and fair minded white citizens who have no intention of helping us in our fight until Negroes as a group prove more ready and willing to help themselves through their vote.

And do you realize that every Negro who doesn't vote is lending his support to the most evil and destructive forces in the nation? Every Negro who doesn't vote is an argument against equality of opportunity. He is a living statistical proof that Negroes are not ready for full citizenship.

Do you think you're entitled to be a first class citizen? Not if you don't vote, you're not. The very first qualification of a first class citizen is that he be in a position to protect himself and his supporters by his vote.

I realize that for a colored citizen to become a qualified voter is troublesome, expensive and sometimes embarrassing. But he'll never have either the respect or the support of many fair minded white citizens until he votes.

And remember that no one has to bear this trouble and possible embarrassment alone as long as you have this organization and your NAACP. Any of the responsible leaders of either organization will accompany anyone who wishes to become a voter while he pays his poll tax or registers or votes for the first time.

He has only to let them know that he is ready to assume his citizenship responsibilities and he'll get all the cooperation he can use.

But speaking of the NAACP, you know I strongly support that some colored citizens listen to, and even believe propaganda of the opposition that the NAACP's methods do more harm than good. Sisters and brothers, don't you believe it! The NAACP is a legal organization, not a public relations organization, but the o'er-all position of NAACP leadership is sound and irreproachable, and the over-all progress it has made has been solid and irreversible.

The simple truth is that the good willed whites of the South—the people who were willing to be fair—didn't even know that there was a need for desegregation until the NAACP kept forcing the facts upon their attention. Take myself, for example. I'd never given the matter of integration the very first thought until Gregory Swanson, our first Negro student, sued for admission to the University of Virginia.

Southern whites have been raised to take segregation laws and customs for granted. They would have gone on taking them for granted from yesterday to dooms day if it hadn't been for the NAACP.

There's much talk about the stiffening opposition. Nobody breathes a word about the stiffening support. Nevertheless it is there. More and more civic and religious groups are quietly integrating month after month. More and more groups and individuals are quietly admitting among themselves that integration must and should come, and also that the South should yield more gracefully. In the midst of all the fuss and fume that has been going on in Florida, for instance, a large hospital in Miami was given an award for having completely integrated its colored nurses, with no discrimination whatsoever in any form.

With the one exception of Louisville, Ken., just about all we've heard or read in the daily papers on the school integration question are stories of opposition, riots, and boycotts by white students. But the true picture is considerably different.

For instance, not just Louisville, but more than a hundred counties have integrated peacefully in Kentucky—Clay and Sturgis being the only schools which had any trouble.

In Texas, again more than 100 school districts integrated peacefully, but Mansfield is the only one we've heard much about.

In Delaware, 63, and in Oklahoma, 161 school districts have integrated.

In Maryland, 85%, and in Missouri, 88% of the Negro pupils are in integrated schools.

If you want the truth about the progress of integration, pay little attention to the headlines, and train yourself to look for inconspicuous items, often placed near the end of the story. The person who reads only the large print in his newspaper today gets an utterly false impression of the trend of events. From the moment our colored citizens began to step boldly out on their constitutional rights we have never for a moment stopped winning. But the speed of our winning depends on you.

Colored citizens too often think of the successes of the NAACP as drops of equality in a bucket of discrimination. Actually, its successes are like the broadcasting of seeds. Each springs up to bear many seeds of its own. A few law suits have resulted in the voluntary opening of many organizations and many institutions, and in the awakening all over the nation of millions of white people to a new understanding of the needs and problems of the nation's largest minority.

Southern Negroes are no longer alone in their struggles for equality. With exception of a few states, the nation is with you, and the world is with you. Even in the resisting Southern states, far more white people are on the side of justice than many of us think. These Southern whites, who are silently with us now, will step forward when Southern Negroes themselves step forward and claim their right to vote.

I urge you to remember that not only do colored citizens need full liberation, but also the nation needs their full liberation, and the world needs their full liberation. America can neither realize her own great ideals nor take her place in world leadership until her colored citizens are altogether free.

I don't like it when people present this struggle for equality as a bloodless battle between Negroes and the South. This movement is not to be thought of entirely in terms of the Negro's own welfare. His welfare is at stake, it's true, and his welfare is important. But there is a larger need and a larger truth involved here even than the welfare of 18,000,000 human beings.

There is the need of every Christian to see the brotherhood of man enacted by the nation which contains this ideal in the blueprint of its charter. There is the need of every upright American, regardless of his color, to have his nation become in fact, the thing it claims to be.

And there is the need of every human being, whether he is aware of it or not, to see the just, the decent, the fair, the warm hearted way of life triumph quickly and cleanly in any contest where goodness and right are pitted against the forces of evil and wrong.

As I said in the beginning, Southern Negroes are now being faced with perhaps the heaviest responsibility ever laid upon a minority. Do you think they are equal to it? Many people don't but I do.

I always close my talks with a portion of a prayer by St. Francis of Assisi. Please join me in praying it aloud.

> Lord,
> Make me an Instrument of thy peace
> Where there is hatred let me sow love.
> Where there is injury,
> Pardon;
> Where there is discord,
> Union;
> Where there is doubt,
> Faith.
> O Divine Master,
> Grant that I
> Shall not so much seek
> To be consoled,
> As to console;
> To be understood
> As to understand;
> To be loved,
> As to love,
> AMEN

LILLIAN SMITH

Historian Joel Williamson characterized Lillian Smith as "perhaps the best example in the twentieth century of one able to make the intuitive leap to a more equitable racial posture."[12] In her autobiography, *Killers of the Dream*, Smith wrote a description of her growing up years that was similar to what Sarah Boyle and many other southern whites could have written about their maturing years:

> The mother who taught me what I know of tenderness and love and compassion taught me also the bleak rituals of keeping Negroes in their "place." The father who rebuked me for an air of superiority toward schoolmates from the mill and rounded out his rebuke by gravely reminding me that "all men are brothers," trained me in the steel-rigid decorums I must demand of every colored male.[13]

But she, too, grew out of this stifling environment and became a major spokesperson for racial equality and decency. Harry Ashmore, himself a crusading white journalist, portrayed Smith as "an outright evangel for the black cause."[14]

Smith was born in Jasper, Florida, on December 12, 1897, the daughter of a businessman.[15] After World War I, Smith's father moved his family to the north Georgia hills where he opened a camp for girls. Smith went to Piedmont College in Georgia, then studied to be a concert pianist at the Peabody Conservatory in Baltimore, followed by a year at Columbia University. In 1921, she went to China to teach music at a Methodist mission school. Returning to the United States in 1924, Smith took over the operation of the summer camp.

She and Paula Snelling began to publish a little magazine, *Pseudopodia*, which later became the *North Georgia Review* and eventually *South Today*. Their magazine provided an opportunity for black and white writers to publish about the various elements of southern culture.

Her first novel, *Strange Fruit*, a story of a tragic love affair between a white southern male and a black female in a small southern town, became a best seller and was the object of an obscenity lawsuit in Boston and an effort to ban it in Detroit. Her home in Georgia was burned in protest.

Smith was active in the Civil Rights Movement, speaking frequently to college groups and other liberal organizations. Her book, *Now Is the Time*, was a challenge to the South on the issue of segregation and was published in 1955 in the wake of the Supreme Court decision in the

Brown case.[16] After the sit-in movement started in 1960, the four students at Greensboro credited their reading of Smith's work as a catalyst for their activism.[17] She was a member of the advisory committee of the Congress of Racial Equality, but resigned in the mid-1960s over the black power issue. Smith also was a supporter and defender of the SNCC until it came under the militant control of Stokely Carmichael. She was on the national board of the American Civil Liberties Union.

Smith's writing brought her a special citation from the National Book Award Committee for her distinguished contribution to letters and she received the Southern Authors Award in 1950 and the Sidney Hillman Award for magazine writing in 1962.

Smith died of cancer in Atlanta on September 28, 1966.

THE MORAL AND POLITICAL SIGNIFICANCE OF THE STUDENTS' NONVIOLENT PROTESTS[18]

Washington, D.C.
April 21, 1960

I am going to talk tonight of the spiritual crisis which the South and its people are facing. We have been in an ordeal a long time and have had outbursts of violence and localized crises again and again: in Little Rock, in Montgomery, Clinton, Nashville, Tallahassee, and in other spots in the South.

But what we are now facing is not localized and cannot be. It is something different, something that has not happened in this country before; it has a new quality of hope in it; and is, I believe, of tremendous moral and political significance. Somehow it is involving not only students but all of us, and there is a growing sense that what we say or fail to say, do or fail to do, will surely shape the events that lie ahead.

This hour of decision—and it is that for the South, certainly—was precipitated on February 1, by a Negro student, age eighteen, a freshman in a college in Greensboro, North Carolina. He had seen a documentary film on the life of Gandhi; he had heard about Montgomery and the nonviolent protests made there; he had probably listened to Dr. Martin Luther King—certainly he knew about him; he had his memories of childhood and its racial hurts; and he had his hopes for the future. But millions of southerners, young and old, and of both races, have had similar experiences. What else was there in this young student that caused him to be capable of his moment of truth? Courage, of course; and imagination, and intelligence—and enough love to respond to Gandhi's love of mankind, and enough truth-seeking in his mind to realize the meaning of Gandhi's teaching of nonviolence and compassion and their redemptive and transforming power. Was this all the young man had? No, there was more: an indefinable, unpredictable potential for creating something new and lasting, and doing it at the right time. Every leader and every hero, and many artists and scientists, possess this talent for fusing their lives with the future. And yet, I doubt that the young man knew he possessed this special quality, or even now knows it.

In some strange way, however, his thoughts and memories and hopes came together and he talked about what was on his mind with three young friends. And a short time afterward, the four of them went on their historic journey to a Greensboro ten-cent store.

From this small beginning, this almost absurd beginning, so incredibly simple and unpretentious that we Americans—used to the power of big names and money and crowds and Madison Avenue and Gallup polls—can scarcely believe in it, there started the nonviolent students' protests which have caught the imagination of millions of us.

Why are we stirred so deeply? What is it we feel? What are we hoping for? I cannot answer for you. For me, it is as if the NO EXIT sign is about to come down from our age; it is almost as if a door is opening in a wall where there was no door. The older generations, to which I belong, have found decisions so hard to make; they have wobbled this way and that in their beliefs; they have postponed the right action until the right time for it has passed. And now suddenly, completely unexpectedly, the students' sit-in protests began, spreading from college to college, school to school. It is exciting to watch them discover a freedom and purpose within themselves that they have not experienced in the outside world; to see them acting out actually living, their beliefs in human dignity and democracy and in the redemptive power of love and non-violence, and going to jail for their beliefs.

* * *

Wait now, you say: You are giving these students quite a build-up. Do you actually think they are so extraordinary? No, I don't. I think they are probably quite ordinary young people in most ways: they are extraordinary only in their awareness that the hour we live in is an hour calling for courage and commitment, and they are making their commitment, and in doing so they are finding their courage. Actually, I suspect they were pretty shaky, those first ones who walked in the stores with their books and their Bibles to make their protest. They probably didn't have one grand, noble thought in their heads; they had made their decision in all earnestness and they were going through with it; and they were probably praying that they'd find the strength just to sit there; just sit there, that's all. But afterward, they must have felt an exaltation; a sudden rush of both pride and humility.

* * *

But even as I say this, I know the new life that is beginning, this spiritual renascence, can be snuffed out by you and me; by our apathy and stupidity and lack of imagination. I know police measures can become so cruel and massive and overwhelming that the students may not be able to take it. I am aware that a terrific effort will be made by certain powerful groups in the South who have close economic ties with the North to smother the movement by hushing the national press and the TV networks. I know that a few men in strategic places, by saying irresponsible things, as Mr. Truman did a few days ago, can throw pretty big obstacles in the students' path. There will be accusations of the most vicious kind, and misinterpretations, idiotic and dangerous, and there will be persistent persecution.

And it may be that these young students won't have the stamina to hold out. They may not find within themselves enough moral resources, enough psychic strength to carry them through the bitter and bleak days ahead of them. I know, too, that the white students of the South may not be able to break out of their apathy and moral paralysis in large enough numbers to help the young Negroes in this struggle for a new life, and without help the burdens may prove too heavy.

But I believe the movement *can succeed* if enough of us have the imagination to see its significance and its creative possibilities and to interpret these to others who do not see; and if we give the students the moral support and the money they are going to need. There is a tremendous power in the nonviolent protest that the sensitive southern conscience and heart will find hard to resist; but even so, the students may have to struggle a long time. They will need friends during their ordeal. Americans in other sections can help them and should, for this not only concerns the South, it concerns the entire nation and the nation's relationships with the rest of the world. It also concerns each person's relationship with himself and his beliefs.

But there are some things that only the South can do. Things that only good, responsible, decent southerners can accomplish. Only they can create a new climate of opinion in which mob violence and the hoodlums and the police and the White Citizens Councils can be controlled; and they can do this only by breaking their silence and speaking out. To speak out for law and order is not enough, today; there is a higher law which we southerners must take a stand on, that concerns justice and mercy and compassion and freedom of the spirit and mind. Thousands of us must also speak out against segregation as a way of life; not simply racial segregation but every form of estrangement that splits man and his world into fragments. The time has come when we must face the fact that only by speaking out our real beliefs, and then acting on them, can we avoid a bitter time of hate and violence and suffering.

But will the southerners do it? I don't know. I hope so but I do not know. They let Little Rock happen when they could have kept that debacle out of the history books simply by taking a stand for the right things. They are now, in Birmingham, letting even worse things happen.

Our responsible people's silence is not because they are in the minority: they outnumber the demagogues and Klans and hoodlums and crackpots twenty to one. In their hands are the media of communication: the pulpits, the TV and radio stations, the newspapers. They have the power and the money, the education and the technics to create an atmosphere of vigorous, healthy-minded concern wherein good words can be heard and the good act carried through; an atmosphere where people can plan, think clearly, and find ways to do what is right.

Why, then, are they silent? Why do they evade their responsibility at this time of crisis?

Is it fear? I don't think so. I think it is anxiety. There is a vast difference between the two.

It is difficult to analyze a complex state of mind in just a few minutes but let me try: We white people of the South think of ourselves as free but we are chained to taboos, to superstitions; tied to a mythic past that never existed; weakened by memories and beliefs that are in passionate conflict with each other.

The tragedy of the South lies just here: Segregation has made psychic and moral slaves of so many of us. We think we are a free people but we have lost our freedom to question, to learn, to do what our conscience tells us is right, to criticize ourselves. We are torn apart inside by a conflict that never lets up, and we wall our minds off into segregated compartments. How can a man believe simultaneously in brotherhood and racial discrimination? In human freedom and forced segregation? How can he fight Communist dictatorship and surrender himself to the dictatorship of an idea like White Supremacy? How can he do and think these things and fail to see the moral inconsistency, the intellectual absurdity of his position?

But many southerners can. And some of them are educated men who think of themselves as the community's moral and civic leaders. The psychic result has been that a deep anxiety possesses them and they feel that any change would be only for the worse. When they are asked why they fear the crumbling of segregation they cannot tell you that what they really fear is the crumbling of the walls inside themselves. Instead, they talk about intermarriage. It makes poor sense but they think it explains their acute anxiety.

But there are other southerners who have changed, who don't like discrimination, who don't believe in segregation. And I am often asked, Why don't they say so? Some are speaking out, of course; hundreds of them; others want to but are afraid they will do "more harm than good." Here, once again, we have the result of a rigid, inflexible training in early childhood, given to us during a time of panic and dread. I was born at the turn of the century when the first segregation statutes were being put on the law books of the southern states. During the first ten years of my life there were almost a thousand lynchings in the South. It was in this atmosphere of terror and brutality, of internal and external disorder, that we were taught our lessons in segregation. No wonder so many southerners of my age cling to it. We were told as children never to question it, never to talk about it. This silence that is today so dangerous to us and so puzzling to others is a built-in silence; its foundations go down to babyhood; to our mother's hushed whispering; there is a hypnotic quality about such learning and only the rebellious mind, the critical intelligence, or the loving heart can defy it.

The truth is that our parents and grandparents paid a terrible price for a security which they believed segregation could give them. When they permitted the system to be set up, they did not foresee that emergency measures would be frozen permanently into state laws. They did not dream that segregation would become a ritual so sacred that it would be given priority over the teachings of Christ in our churches. They did not know a time was ahead when the politician would exert more influence than the preacher. The history of the political and social and psychological pressures that caused our fathers to blunder in so tragic a way is too complex to go into here. Let us settle for this: that the price they paid for security was exorbitant and their white children are still paying today. For they have been as surely injured in mind and spirit by segregation as have Negro children: Both have been warped, both have been kept from a free, creative life; both find it difficult to be courageous, strong individuals who can defy conformity and find their own responses to the world.

But some white southerners are speaking out; and more would if they could hear others do so. There is a serious lack of communication between liberal southerners. We can't hear each other speak because there are so few places where the person who opposes segregation can speak in the South. The local radio and TV forums have not as yet been opened up to many white southerners who oppose segregation; nor have the national forums been opened to them. Again and again, on TV, the nation sees Senator Talmadge and Senator Eastland and other racial demagogues and hears them say the same old things they've said for years about mongrelization. Why can't we have a change? There are eloquent and courageous young ministers in the South who oppose segregation, and have something fresh to tell the country. To hear them on networks would give encouragement to those in the South who have never heard any southerner state in a public speech that he is opposed to segregation. This is one way to help break the taboo of silence.

Once the silence is broken the South will change quickly. More quickly than we think. There are so many ready for change: thousands of ministers who have taken a good stand; hundreds who preach strong eloquent sermons against segregation; there are close to a hundred thousand women in Georgia alone, who are willing to give up segregation in public places including the schools; and there are hundreds of them working hard every day to rid our state of a system that has hurt everybody. These women are informed; they have thought and studied and examined their own souls, many of them, and have given their children better training in human relations—certainly in terms of race—than my generation had.

It is important for us to break the word "South" into a thousand pieces: not only geographically, but economically; not only culturally but in terms of the sexes, not only vocationally, not only psychologically; but also into generations: there are gradations of opinion in all of these groups, and gradations of moral strength. What is terrifying to the older generation (those born when segregation was being set up in the South) doesn't bother the young students; the southerner over forty is likely to suffer from taboos the eighteen-year-old does not feel; what paralyzes the men often releases the women; what seems easy to do for the twenty-five-year-old seems impossible to the fifty-year-old; the poor and ignorant often feel a psychic and social hunger to belong "to the white race" as if it were a club, while the more sophisticated, the more secure economically and culturally do not have this need; their sense of "belonging" has come to them in other ways. In certain areas of work, there is no racial competition; in others the competition is severe and exacerbates race feelings. And too, differences go beyond the groups; the South is chock-full of individuals each with his own ideas—this, despite our somewhat totalitarian training and our one-party political system. People may act the same under pressures and not feel the same or believe the same or have the same values. (This may be as true of Russia as it is of the South.) The false lumping of all southerners together by those who speak and write of us is not a good thing and makes for identifications which we don't feel, or accept.

* * *

These differences among our people are potentially good; this lack of conformity in feelings and beliefs keeps the door cracked. What we need to know is that these differences exist. We need to know that millions of people are no longer for segregation. That is why I have such hopes for the students' nonviolent protests. They are encouraging responsible people to speak out. If white students will join in large numbers with Negro students, their experiences of suffering together, their self-imposed discipline and philosophical training will create a fine reservoir of new leadership for the South. We cannot change the South until we change our leadership, and we cannot change leaders until we change ourselves. We, as a region, can have our moment of truth only when we begin to think of ourselves not as members of races but as persons; we can take the walls down outside only by taking the walls down within us. Then it will come. And it will be a healing time for us, and perhaps the whole world, for we are so sensitized to one another, so closely related by the common purpose of creating a future, that whatever brings wholeness to us will bring wholeness to millions of others across the world.

Perhaps, even now, our moment of truth is near; let's pray that it does not turn into an agonizing time of sin and error.

ANNE BRADEN

Anne Braden was a journalist born in Louisville, Kentucky on July 28, 1924, but grew up in Anniston, Alabama, after living for a short time in Mississippi as a child. She received an undergraduate degree from Randolph-Macon College in 1945. She was a reporter for two newspapers in Alabama, the Anniston *Star* and the Birmingham *News and Age Herald* in the mid-1940s, and for the Louisville (Kentucky) *Times* in the late 1940s. She became field secretary of the Southern Conference Education Fund (SCEF) and editor of its publication, *Southern Patriot*, and eventually the SCEF co-director, along with her husband, Carl.[19] In 1975, she began working with the Southern Organizing Committee for Economic and Social Justice. In all of these roles, she spoke for social equality and justice on many platforms across the country

Anne's first exposure to national notoriety came during the spring of the 1954 *Brown* case. In May, the Bradens sold their house to a black man, Andrew Wade. Within days, the house was fire-bombed, a cross was burned on the man's lawn and rocks were thrown through the windows. The Bradens were indicted for sedition—attempting to overthrow the government of Kentucky—and later were indicted for conspiring to blow up the house.

ADDRESS TO ANNUAL CONVENTION OF SCLC[20]

Birmingham, Alabama
September 27, 1962

I am happy to be here today and to be a part of this meeting. I am happy because when I come to Alabama, it is coming home. I used to work in Birmingham, just after I finished school some 16 years ago, and I grew up just 60 miles from here in the town that has recently become infamous, Anniston. Coming back to my home state and my home town is not always a happy experience—I rarely have occasion to be proud of them and what they are doing, and it would be the understatement of the year to say that among certain elements of the population I am welcomed back with something less than open arms. But when I come home to attend a meeting of this kind, I am both proud and happy because I believe that it is the people attending this meeting and organizations like the Southern Christian Leadership Conference which is sponsoring it that offer an almost miraculous hope that someday—and that not too far off—Alabama is going to be a decent state to live in. In fact, I would go even further and say what to some might seem an extreme statement: I believe it is entirely possible that because of the work groups like this one, Alabama and other Deep

South states, so benighted now, may someday become a force for good that will influence the whole course of man's history by showing to the world a new kind of relationships among men. I think the possibility of this development is greatest here precisely because, paradoxically, it seems the most remote here.

I will come back to this idea in a few moments and try to explain more exactly what I mean. First, however, before I get to the main topic of my remarks, I would like your indulgence for one more personal comment.

I don't know whether this meeting here today will be covered by the Birmingham newspapers or not. If it is, I'm sure they will have some very uncomplimentary things to say about me. That does not bother me too much, because I am quite accustomed to having uncomplimentary things said about me. Trouble is they never give you a chance to answer such things in print—so any answer I want to make, I'd best make right now.

I mention this because the last time I made a public speech in Alabama was a couple of years ago at a meeting of the Tuskegee Civic Association. On that occasion, the *Birmingham News* was so upset about my being in the state that they wrote an editorial about it. I don't know where the *Birmingham News* presumes to get the right to advise Negroes in Alabama as to what they should do, but that's what they attempted to do in this editorial. The head on it was "Tuskegee Group Makes a Mistake," and the editorial, complete with a picture of myself and my husband, went on to say that the Negroes of Tuskegee would be well advised not to invite people like me to visit them. They said I was a quite dangerous character and had been accused of being a communist. Well, this sort of thing doesn't bother me very much; it's been said so often and I get used to it and I consider the source which is the committee of Sen. James Eastland of your neighboring state of Mississippi. But one thing in that editorial really hurt me: They not only called me a communist which is a tired old charge I'm used to; they described me as an outside "agitator."

I don't usually bother to answer such attacks. But this time I did. I sat down and wrote the *Birmingham News* a letter and asked them to publish it. I asked them why they had neglected to mention in the editorial that I used to be a reporter for their newspaper and that I lived in Alabama all my life until I was 24 years old, and had never lived outside the South yet. I said to them—I believe this was the wording, I am quoting from memory: "All I know about the evils of segregation I learned in Alabama, a great deal of it, I might add, while working as a reporter for your paper. In fact, if there was any one thing that more than anything else made an integrationist out of me, it was the stark injustice and inhumanity that I saw while covering the Birmingham courthouse for the *Birmingham News*. I saw that this was the final horrible fruits of segregation, that it was destroying the soul of white Alabamians as it was destroying the bodies of Negroes—and I had to do something about it."

As you might imagine, the *Birmingham News* did not print this letter. I don't guess they'd print it now if I wrote it again. So I'm saying it here. I guess this somewhat constitutes my credentials to speak to you: When I talk about segregation in Alabama and the Deep South, I know whereof I speak. Nobody can tell me I don't know, because I grew up with it. As a white person, I may never be able to completely understand what segregation does to the Negro, but I know what it does to white people: It destroys them utterly and completely.

I have gone into this incident with the *Birmingham News* for two reasons: First, of course, just to set the record straight in case they call me an outside agitator again, but also because I think all this ties in with the topic I am to discuss this afternoon.

I have been asked to speak on "The Deeper Meaning of Nonviolent Direct Action." To go back just a minute, I have sometimes wondered why the segregationists—and their newspapers—become so frenzied in attacking people like me. Why can't they just express their differences with us in reasonable, rational terms? Why do they have to try to explain us away—as communists, as outside agitators, as the devil incarnate?

I've been watching these people operate now—from my present vantage point within the integration movement—for more than 15 years. I used to wonder but I don't anymore. I think I understand.

These people simply can't admit that people like us—and we are becoming more numerous all the time, white Southerners who have decided unequivocally that the fight for integration is our fight—they just can't admit that we exist. Because once they admit that, they've got to examine their whole world; the same world that produced us produced them; the same evil that we escaped from imprisons them. If they look at us honestly, they've got to look at themselves and their world honestly—and once they do that, they've got to admit to themselves that their whole world is wrong and evil and corrupt. That's not an easy thing to do. The human organism builds up every kind of defense it can to avoid a showdown of this kind, to avoid a face-to-face confrontation with stark ugly truth. No one likes to admit that his whole world and the people he loves are evil; when he has to face this, it tears his insides out—until he can once get over that hump of facing it and then he is free. But he'll postpone the moment of truth as long as he can by every device of self-deception. And that is what has been going on in communities all over the South in recent years.

But some of the truest words ever spoken are those that tell us it is the truth that will make us free—the truth no matter how painful, no matter how ugly. I think it is herein that lies one of the most significant aspects of the nonviolent direct action movement in the South today. It is this movement that is presenting to the white population, in mass—and in a way that could never have occurred without the direct action movement—the necessity, the burden if people want to see it that way but I would rather call it opportunity, to face the truth about themselves and their society. When I was growing up, only a relative few of us ever came to that point of necessity to face the truth; we were the lucky ones; the necessity came to me, I think, by chance—the details are not pertinent to this discussion, but I could so easily have missed the opportunity and gone in a different direction. Others also found their way by chance—more perhaps than are generally realized. But no longer today is it a matter of chance. There is not a white person in the South today who does not have the opportunity to find the truth and be set free. And this situation exists because the nonviolent direct action movement has carried this issue into the glaring light of the public marketplace—and into the secret recesses where each man lives with his own conscience; into the schools, the churches, the public park, into the streets with picket-lines and marches and into jails; into the front pages of every newspaper (which when I worked on the Birmingham ones were ignoring the issue in every way they could), and to the doorstep of every white Southerner.

And the frenzied attacks—the ones that I feel, the ones that every person in the nonviolent movement has felt in some form or another—all come from the same source: They are the defense mechanisms of those who are fighting off the pain and liberation that comes with facing Truth.

There are two aspects of the deeper meaning of nonviolent direct action that I want to discuss specifically. One is related to what it seems to me direct action means to the people who participate in it, and the other to what it means to those who see themselves at this moment as its opponents.

First, to define some terms as I am using them. I should make it clear that I do not see direct action as the only form of nonviolent action or the only channel for nonviolent revolution. I realize we could get into some fine-point discussion on this, but other means of social action can if they are carried out in certain ways come within my definition of nonviolence. I have a friend who says her favorite form of nonviolence is political action—and certainly it is theoretically possible to have a nonviolent revolution at the ballot box. Court action is also a nonviolent way of attacking a social evil.

But while both of these methods are nonviolent and *could* be revolutionary, they have in life very rarely been revolutionary—and the reason they have not is that traditionally too few people have participated in them. When you file a law suit and do nothing else, a lawyer does it and the rest of the people who are interested can go home and forget it—or just hope it comes out right. Everybody can theoretically go to the polls, but even in the areas of our country where there are no limitations on the ballot by terror or other devices, how many, Negro *or* white, do? Relatively few.

This is all related to what it seems to me is one of the real tragedies of our modern age. So many people feel—often unconsciously—that there is really nothing significant that they personally can do about the society and the world in which they live. The problems look too big, too complex—the evil too monstrous, big impersonal things like bombs that can kill the whole human race with one blow, complex problems that supposedly only "experts" understand. What, many have been led to ask, can the individual conscience of one man or woman mean in this vast impersonal fabric of human affairs? And so we have the sense of futility that grips so much of mankind—with each individual withdrawing into his own life, into his own backyard, into a position of moral neutrality, into ultimate alienation from his fellowman.

The use of nonviolent direct action as a mass social weapon was introduced into the Western World by the integration movement in the South. In this, I believe history will record that this movement made a contribution to our times and our society that actually transcends the issue of segregation. For nonviolent direct action cuts through this shield of moral neutrality and this sense of futility that grips modern man. Nonviolent direct action says the individual conscience does matter, it says the individual *can* do something about his fate and the future of his society. If a mass movement exists you can go faster, but no man moved by conscience need wait for a mass movement. One individual acting, may move mountains. One small woman, Mrs. Rosa Parks, refused to move back on a bus, and a whole movement resulted. Four lone students sat down at a lunch counter in North Carolina, and the South has never been the same since. One could go on and on with the examples. And when a mass movement develops, such as we've seen in Albany and elsewhere, every person who cares has a part to play; no one need sit back and think the problems must be solved by experts.

Once people have come together and become involved in their society through direct action, they are changed people. I am not speaking here just of what it gives the Negro in terms of a new sense of dignity and strength—as important as that is—but what I'm talking about happens to all participants in direct action, Negroes and the white people who identify with the cause. They realize that they are not just helpless pawns in the hands of fate or forces too complex for them; they realize they are making themselves felt. They become active participating members of the human race, not passive neutralists.

After this sort of awakening has occurred, then if you go into court action and political action, these weapons for social change also take on a new character. It is in this context that they also become a part of a nonviolent revolutionary struggle—because they involve the participation and allegiance of individuals who felt futile before. The whole matter involves the difference between paternalism and democracy—the difference between people having something done for them and doing it themselves. The only changes that really go deep are the ones people bring about themselves. Democracy means doing it yourself. Democracy has been at a low ebb throughout America in recent years, precisely because too many people have lost faith that—they *can* do anything for themselves. The nonviolent direct action movement may be seen in history to have revitalized democracy in the Western World by giving people faith again that they can organize and change things for themselves.

But this important new situation that comes with a wide feeling of participation could also come in a violent revolution; for violent revolution too requires that many individuals participate in shaping their fate and the world they will live in. And so we should look at another deeper aspect of what the current direct action movement means in the South: What is this nonviolence and what does it mean?

To me, the most important thing about the nonviolent philosophy is not just its refusal to use physical violence. That's essential to it, of course. But the aspect of nonviolence which provides the real hope in human affairs is the implicit faith of the one who practices nonviolent protest that there can and will be an ultimate reconciliation with people who are now the opponents, or the enemy.

I'll tell you what nonviolence means to me. It is something I heard Fred Shuttlesworth say a few years ago. Someone in a workshop asked him what he was working for in Birmingham; he thought a minute and said: "The day when I can sit down and talk as a friend with the man who attacked me and my family with chains at Phillips High School." Fred Shuttlesworth—this man who has suffered from the actions of white men as much as anybody I know—and this is what he said. I believe he meant it. I don't think he literally believes the day will come when he and that particular man will sit down as friends—maybe he does, maybe I'm the one who does not have enough faith, I don't know—but what I'm sure he believes is that the day will come when Negroes will be able to sit down as friends with the children of that man or people like him.

Now I am fully aware that not everyone in the nonviolent movement has this perspective, or this hope, or this faith. But I know that some do, and to me this is simply a miracle, and I use the word advisedly. I think that statement of Fred's which I just quoted—and I've quoted it all over America—is a miracle of the human spirit, pure and simple.

As a white person, I'm not sure I understand how any Negro could ever want to reach a reconciliation with white people, but for some reason it has been given to us in the Southern United States that in this year of 1962 this is so. Because of this, we on this little spot on the map may have the opportunity that exists in few places in the world—to prove that people of different colors can live together on this planet in peace and brotherhood. The very survival of our planet may depend on this—and so we here in this small corner of it may have been born to the age and the location which can decide the future of humanity.

But let us think for just a moment about what is involved when we speak of reconciliation between Negro and white Southerners. Reconciliation, as I understand it, does not mean compromise—or just peaceful co-existence. Reconciliation means an entirely new relationship. And to reach new relationships, you have to have new people, profoundly changed people.

When Fred Shuttlesworth said he was working for the day when he could sit down as friends with the man who beat him—or someone like that—he didn't mean he wanted to sit down with that man as he is now, or even that man slightly "moderated." You can't talk about integration with the white South as it has been. These people—all of us, and I include myself in this—have got to become new people. This is why the movement we are engaged in is in a very literal sense a revolution. We are working for a complete and radical change in the structure of our society *and* in its people. This is both an outer revolution and an inner revolution—and they are both going on simultaneously.

Now, I think it is axiomatic that revolutions don't come easy. Not if we are talking about real change. Sometimes, when there are direct action protests and

a whole white community doesn't have a change of heart overnight, you hear
people say that the nonviolent faith is a futile dream, that it doesn't work. Or
you hear them say that things are worse than they've been before, that new
hatreds have been generated in a place, for example, like Albany, Georgia.

I think people who say these things simply don't understand the true revolutionary nature of this movement and its goals. If we are truly working for new
relationships among men, the changes can't come painlessly to the white South.
If it were just surface changes we wanted; it might be easy. You can get a few
court decisions, you can get a few bad laws off the books, you can get a little
token desegregation, you can force a system of law and order and restrain the
really crude forms of discrimination—you can do all that, and we should do it—
and you can do it without too much turmoil if you ease the pain of the segregationists by tacitly assuring them things really aren't going to change much.
But if that's all we are going to do, we are going to end up with more sophisticated forms of discrimination and a society not too different from what the
world has had for a long time and which has brought us to a stage where the
human race may well destroy itself.

I think of a discussion I had a year or so ago with a group of white ministers
in a Border city. All of them were from northern cities except one, and he was
from Birmingham. He was the one-man minority in the room, because he was
the only one of them who did not classify himself as an integrationist. He was
really suffering. He was not defending segregation, but he was saying: "I know
it's wrong, but I don't know what to do—if I go to Birmingham and say these
things, I know what will happen. There will be turmoil. I don't know what to
do." He wasn't on the right side from our point of view—but he was suffering,
he was probing, into himself and his society. The others in the room weren't
suffering at all; they had all the answers, it seemed. It all began to seem a little
too glib to me, and finally I realized why when one of the other ministers said
to the man from Birmingham: "Look here, I don't see why this has you so
upset. You are making a mountain out of a molehill. You could get rid of all
those silly segregation laws you have in Birmingham, and it's really not going
to hurt anybody because things wouldn't change too much. It wouldn't be very
different from the town I come from." And I interrupted to say to the man who
was speaking: "That is just the point—this man doesn't want things to go unchanged in Birmingham, he knows in his heart that to have a town like yours
as you describe it is not the answer to the evil that has corrupted Birmingham.
He is afraid of the future, but he is realizing he can't live with the past. He's
looking for something new." I told the Birmingham man later that for all his
hesitation at this moment I'd put my money on him ahead of that other minister
who had not yet even recognized the evil we are fighting.

This man—and people like him all over the South—have got to go through
this inner turmoil—and society has got to through an outer turmoil if there is
to be any real change. They have got to recognize the evil in themselves and
their society for what it is. To go back to the point I was making in the beginning

this afternoon, it seems to me that it is the nonviolent direct action movement that is providing them with the necessity to face it. If a mass conversion does not come to a white community in a sudden flash of light, this does not mean we are failing. It simply means that people do not face Truth within themselves and become reborn without turmoil. First all their defense mechanisms go up, all the hatred and hostility that has been latent before boils to the surface. When things seem to get worse instead of better, I think we are witnessing the birth pangs of a new set of relationships among men.

Recently I talked with some old friends of mine in Anniston, a couple I grew up with. They are now parents of young children. These people consider themselves somewhat "moderate" and civilized. They've learned how to pronounce the word "Negro" fairly well, which their parents didn't know when we were all growing up, so they feel they are a part of the "New South." And this young father said to me: "I'm worried about what is happening. I know segregation is wrong—but all this agitation for integration, it's creating hatred, hatred you and I never knew when we were children. Take our children, for example, we've tried to rear them without prejudice (as if this were possible in a segregated society) and the other day our nine-year-old son came in using the old ugly word for Negro and saying he'd never go to school with them. He hasn't heard that at home—but he's getting it because of all the turmoil."

This father was sincerely concerned. I said to him: "I don't think you need to worry about your son; you can talk this thing out with him. He's got a better chance than you or I had at that age—because there was no opportunity for talk to reach us. We didn't hear this kind of open hatred, to be sure. But we grew up in a world which simply took for granted the assumption that some people should be separated from others. This was hatred in the worst form, we accepted it, we lived with it and it corrupted us—until long afterward when we were grown, we had to dig it out, piece by piece. With your son, with the people who are hearing these things now, it's on a conscious level—and there it can be cured, and so much more easily."

I'm not sure this father understood then—or now. He is one of those who has not yet faced the Truth. Often we divide white Southerners into neat categories—we talk about segregationists, moderates, liberals, integrationists, etc. For the purpose of this discussion, let me suggest different categories. Let's classify people on where they stand in this thing I've been talking about, this basic encounter with Truth, recognition of the fact that their society is evil and the evil is within them. Some of us who have faced the Truth, rejected all of the values of our old world and identified our lives with the movement for change are the most fortunate white Southerners today. We are free; we have escaped from the prison segregation places around the soul of the white man. We have our difficulties, but they all come from the outside, not from within. Then there are great numbers who have honestly faced the Truth but for various reasons have not yet come to the point of identifying openly and completely with the movement for change. They are more numerous than is sometimes realized, and of all the people in the South today they are the most miserable, I think. Many white Ministers, I believe, fall into this category. When the prison to which they still consign themselves becomes unbearable, more and more of them will break loose. But then there is the great third category: of people who have simply not yet faced the truth. Obviously segregationists are in this category. But what is not so obvious is that many quote "moderate" unquote people are also in this third category: People who say sure segregation is wrong, but wait a minute now, don't go so fast, you are going to stir up too much turmoil, there's an easy way to work this out—all this: These people too are evading the truth and finding defense mechanisms. Because if they had really faced the truth of the evil of segregation and what it does to all of us, they would not suggest to anyone, white or Negro, that he live with it another day. Nor would they suggest, if they had faced the truth of how deep the evil goes, that a real change can come without pain and turmoil, both outer and inner.

I don't think there's really any question as to whether the nonviolent direct action movement in the South is succeeding or not. Direct action, along with other nonviolent techniques that have been fired with new meaning *because* of mass involvement in direct action, has *already* made many surface changes that some thought were impossible a few years ago. It has also already effected an inner revolution in more white people than is sometimes realized—the inner changes that can make possible the real substantive changes outside. If it has not yet changed enough people in this fundamental way, the present tumult is a sure sign that it has cracked through the hard shell of complacency and made a beginning. And I think we can soon see a quickening of the tempo of real conversion.

I think this will occur, given certain important conditions within the nonviolent movement itself. Number 1, I think the nonviolent movement must continue to be radical. I don't think it can succeed if it begins to listen to those who say go slow, or those who say we must try to ease the pain of change for the white South. The nonviolent direct action movement has got to recognize, as it has in the past, that it would not be doing any white person a favor to try to make things easy for him or to compromise on the old terms. The real favor that can be done the white Southerner is to present him the challenge so sharply that he can't avoid meeting it, to present him with the opportunity to turn himself inside out.

And Number 2, I think the nonviolent movement has got to continue to work for civil liberties as well as civil rights. If nonviolence depends on reaching the opponent with what we have to say, we've got to have the right to say it. We've got to have the right to speak, to picket, and to protest—these are all civil liberties, and as we all know they don't exist in many parts of the South. Nonviolence as a weapon of social change depends on a civil libertarian atmosphere. Civil liberties have been at a low ebb in recent years not only in the South but all over America, and the national civil liberties crisis results from the after effects of McCarthyism and the hysteria over "communism." This has had a profound effect in the South because it has provided the white Southerner with one of the best defense mechanisms against truth—he can tell himself and the world that there is no real problem, it's just all the communists trying to stir up trouble. He couldn't use that defense mechanism so effectively if the rest of the nation weren't using it too, every time they want to avoid a real problem our world faces. I see no real fundamental solution to this in the South unless the whole nation can establish a civil libertarian atmosphere where the scare word communist cannot be used so effectively.

If we in the nonviolent movement can do these things—if we can maintain our radicalism without compromise and if we can help establish a civil libertarian atmosphere in the nation—I believe we are going to accomplish a real nonviolent revolution in the South. The tumult we are witnessing now is not because things are worse but because a new society is struggling to be born. It is not coming easily, because we are asking of the future a society which is different from any ever established among men before. We want more than surface changes. Racial segregation is just one aspect of the separation of man from man that has plagued humanity everywhere—but it is the aspect of it that is on our doorstep. If we can solve it in a fundamental way, creating new relationships among men, we will be setting an example the whole world can look to. And we may be able to do it here, where it looks the most hopeless, *precisely* because man's alienation from his fellowman here is so deep that it *can't* be alleviated by any short-cut measures, by anything but the most fundamental revolution of man's inner being and his outer institutions. That, I think, is the opportunity that history has given us, and the direct action movement gives to each of us a way to have a part in the seizing of this opportunity.

NOTES

1. David Chappell, *Inside Agitators: White Southerners in the Civil Rights Movement* (Baltimore: The Johns Hopkins University Press, 1994), p. xxiii.

2. Charles E. Wynes, ed. *Forgotten Voices: Dissenting Southerners in an Age of Conformity* (Baton Rouge: Louisiana State University Press, 1967).

3. See W. Stuart Towns, *Public Address in the Twentieth-Century South: The Evolution of a Region* (Westport: Praeger, 1999), Chapter Six, "Taking a Stand for Justice: White Southerners Who Battled for Racial Change," for speeches by Lillian Smith, Ralph McGill, LeRoy Collins, Charles Morgan Jr., and James McBride Dabbs.

4. See biographical sketch in Anna Rothe, ed., *Current Biography* (New York: The H.W. Wilson Company, 1948), pp. 218–20.

5. Columbia, South Carolina, October 19, 1946.

6. The source for most of the biographical sketch is a brief description of Boyle's life found in her papers in the University of Virginia Library, and from her autobiographical best-seller, *The Desegregated Heart: A Virginian's Stand in Time of Transition* (New York: William Morrow & Co., 1962).

7. *The Desegregated Heart*, p. 14.

8. *Saturday Evening Post*, p. 27 (19 February 1955).

9. *Desegregated Heart*, pp. 297–98.

10. *Desegregated Heart*, p. 273.

11. Sarah Patton Boyle, "Democracy Depends on You," Speech to the 16th annual convention of the Virginia Voters League, September 23, 1956. Ashland, Virginia. Sarah Patton Boyle Papers (MSS 8003-a), Special Collections Department, University of Virginia Library.

12. Joel Williamson, *A Rage for Order: Black-White Relations in the American South Since Emancipation* (New York: Oxford University Press, 1986), p. 258.

13. Lillian Smith, *Killers of the Dream*, rev. and enlarged ed. (Garden City, New York: Anchor Books, 1963), p. 17.

14. Harry S. Ashmore, *Hearts and Minds: A Personal Chronicle of Race in America* (Cabin John, MD: Seven Locks Press, 1988), p. 96.

15. This biographical sketch is from *Current Biography, 1944*, Anne Rothe, ed. (New York: H.W. Wilson Co., 1944), 635–38; and from Will Brantley, *Feminine Sense in Southern Memoir* (Jackson: University Press of Mississippi, 1993), 38–85.

16. Lillian Smith, *Now Is the Time* (New York: Viking Press, 1955).

17. Pat Watters, *Down to Now: Reflections on the Southern Civil Rights Movement* (Athens: University of Georgia Press, 1971), 73.

18. Lillian Smith, "The Moral and Political Significance of the Students' Non-Violent Protests." Speech given at All Souls Unitarian Church, Washington, DC, April 21, 1960. See text in Michelle Cliff, ed., *The Winner Names the Age: A Collection of Writings by Lillian Smith* (New York: W.W. Norton & Company, 1978), 91–99.

19. This biographical sketch is from *Who's Who of American Women*, 8th ed. (Chicago: Marquis Who's Who, Inc., 1973), 103; and from Sue Thrasher and Eliot Wigginton, "You Can't Be Neutral," *Southern Exposure* 12 (November/December 1984), pp. 79–85.

20. Anne Braden, "Address to Annual Convention of Southern Christian Leadership Conference." September 27, 1962. Birmingham, AL. Text in Southern Christian Leadership Conference Papers, King Center, Atlanta, GA.

FOR FURTHER READING

Egerton, John. *Speak Now Against the Day: The Generation Before the Civil Rights Movement in the South*. New York: Alfred A. Knopf, 1994.

Hobson, Fred. *But Now I See: The White Southern Racial Conversion Narrative*. Baton Rouge: Louisiana State University Press, 1999.

Clark Foreman

Bamberger, Werner. "Clark H. Foreman, 75; Former Head of Emergency Civil Liberties Group." *The New York Times*, June 16, 1977.

Kirby, John B. "Foreman, Clark H." In Charles D. Lowery and John F. Marszalek, eds. *Encyclopedia of African-American Civil Rights*. Westport, CT: Greenwood Press, 1997, pp. 195–96.

McWilliams, Carey. "Clark Foreman." *The Nation*, July 2, 1977, pp. 5–6.

Sullivan, Patricia. *Days of Hope: Race and Democracy in the New Deal Era*. Chapel Hill: University of North Carolina Press, 1996, pp. 24–40.

Sarah Patton Boyle

Dierenfield, Kathleen Murphy. "One 'Desegregated Heart': Sarah Patton Boyle and the Crusade for Civil Rights in Virginia." *The Virginia Magazine of History and Biography* 104 (spring 1996), pp. 251–84.

Egerton, John. *A Mind to Stay Here*. New York: Macmillan, 1970, pp. 128–45.

Lillian Smith

Blackwell, Louise, and Frances Clay. *Lillian Smith*. New York: Twayne Publishers, 1971.

Gladney, Margaret Rose, ed. *How Am I to Be Heard?: Letters of Lillian Smith*. Chapel Hill: University of North Carolina Press, 1993.

Loveland, Anne C. *Lillian Smith: A Southerner Confronting the South*. Baton Rouge: Louisiana State University Press, 1986.

Anne Braden

There are no biographical studies of Anne Braden, other than those cited in note 19.

CHAPTER 6

"There Always Has to Be a Faubus": White Resistance and the Rhetoric of Fear

As Diane Nash pointed out, "there always has to be a Faubus." The Civil Rights Movement in the South was inevitable, given the white leadership of the South. The demagogues of the 1950s and 1960s were direct descendants of the rabble rousers of the 1880s and 1890s. That earlier generation was working to create and enhance the system of segregation; at the middle of the century, Eastland, Brady, Faubus, and Coleman were trying to preserve, protect, and defend it. The earlier generation was completely successful, the later generation failed—but only after creating much bitterness, hatred, and violence.

The rhetoric of the white resistance of the 1950s and 1960s created a culture that condoned and, in some cases, no doubt encouraged, the climate of hatred and fear that led to the 1955 murder of black minister George W. Lee in Belzoni, Mississippi; the shooting of activist Gus Courts in his store in Belzoni; the bloody murder of Lamar Smith, whose crime was trying to persuade other blacks to register to vote; and the murder of a teenager, Emmett Till.[1] These were only a few of the many beatings, murders, lynchings, and threats of violence against both black and white Americans that drove Mississippi, and many parts of the South, into what has been called "the closed society."[2]

It is easy to characterize the public communication of these white leaders as a rhetoric of fear. The white South was afraid of the unknown; the region's social relationships between white and black had been controlled by the white man for more than two centuries. First, there was slavery, then there was segregation. What would happen when segregation was overturned? Many southerners still recalled the mythologies of the days of Reconstruction—Black Reconstruction in the minds of many who could see those old stories coming back to life. White political figures were afraid of losing power. In county after county in Mississippi, and to a lesser extent, in Arkansas, Alabama, Louisiana, and South Carolina, a black majority was a frightening ghost, waiting in the wings. If blacks were allowed to vote, surely they would vote in a block, and what white politician would have a chance, went the reasoning.

A strong fear, and one that echoed across the centuries, was the fear of "outside influences," shaping or dictating what southern culture and society should be. First, it was the abolitionists in the antebellum years, then the invading Northern armies during the "War of Northern Aggression," as many southerners characterized it for decades. After Appomattox, it was the Carpetbaggers, the occupying Army, and the "Yankees," with their materialistic, mercantile, idealistic outlook on life. With this history of "outside influence," it was easy for the white southern leadership of the Civil Rights era to play on southern fear of "Northern liberals," the "NAACP from New York," and as the Cold War grew hotter and hotter in the 1950s and 1960s, "the Commies." Yet another fear, and one played to the hilt by the Citizen's Councils and the Ku Klux Klan, was that of "mongrelization" of the races, should blacks and whites be forced to mix and mingle on buses, in theaters, at water fountains, and, especially, in public schools. The speeches in this chapter rely on all these fears as the basis of their rhetoric.

JAMES O. EASTLAND

Long-time U.S. Senator James O. Eastland was born in 1904 in Dodds-ville, Mississippi. After attending the University of Mississippi, Vander-bilt, and the University of Alabama, he returned in 1927 to his home state to practice law and operate a six-thousand acre plantation near Doddsville. From 1928 to 1932 he served in the state legislature, and in 1941, after the death of Senator Pat Harrison, he was appointed to fill Harrison's vacant seat in the U.S. Senate. He won election in 1943, and served in the upper house until 1978. Eastland never faced serious op-position; he won his closest Senate campaign with 66 percent of the vote. While in the Senate, he served for six years as the president pro tem, which made him third in line of succession to the Presidency under Presidents Nixon, Ford, and Carter. As chairman of the Senate Judiciary Committee for twenty-two years, Eastland was a powerful opponent of civil rights legislation. He died in Greenwood, Mississippi, on February 19, 1986.[3]

Eastland was not only a rabid opponent of integration, he was one of the Senate's strongest advocates for the anti-Communist point of view. He saw the threat of Communism in government agencies, schools, and newspapers, and often characterized the Supreme Court under Earl War-ren as the "greatest threat to our Constitution," especially after the *Brown* decision. Unlike George Wallace and other defenders of the segregated way of life in the South who eventually recanted their positions and attempted to gain the support of black southerners, Eastland said as late as 1984, when asked if he regretted his opposition to civil rights legis-lation, "Nope."[4]

In this 1954 Senate speech, delivered only days after the *Brown* de-cision, he makes his first of many attacks on the nation's highest court:

> In these broad and sweeping decisions, the Court has overruled fundamental principles of the Constitution which have been settled and determined for generations. The Court has determined to strike down all State laws which provide for racial segregation, and upon which the institutions, the culture, and the civilization of the South are built.

This theme was one of the major foundations undergirding the region's opposition to integration for the next decade. Ironically, Eastland calls attention to the successful leadership of Mahatma Gandhi in his cam-paign to overthrow British rule, whose "hunger strikes and professions of piety, drove imperial Britain from India. He mobilized the spirit of his people. Southern spirit is mobilized. Southern people will stand firm." Hardly did the Mississippi Senator know that less than two years later, Martin Luther King Jr. would use Gandhian teachings as his model to mobilize another group of Southern people to overthrow white supremacy and segregation on the buses in Montgomery, Alabama.

THE SUPREME COURT, SEGREGATION, AND THE SOUTH[5]

U.S. Senate
May 27, 1954

Mr. President, last week the Supreme Court held that racially segregated schools were in violation of the 14th amendment to the Constitution. Last Monday, the Court further extended its new doctrine by holding that segregation of the races in public housing, municipally owned golf courses, and entertainment in a municipally owned theater, though operated by a private corporation, was in violation of the 14th amendment. What the Court has done has been to legislate additional civil rights, which were admittedly not heretofore authorized by the Constitution or by Congress. The Court has overturned a great principle of law and has made illegal the acts of States which the great judges who have heretofore composed the Court had held for generations did not violate the 14th amendment to the Constitution.

The Court, in violation of its power and in disregard of its duty, has legislated these new Federal civil rights: First, the right of any race to attend an unsegregated school, second, the right to live in unsegregated houses if publicly owned, and third, the right to use an unsegregated golf course, if publicly owned. By the same decision there can be no such thing as segregation in publicly owned swimming pools, parks, or any publicly owned recreational facility. In these broad and sweeping decisions, the Court has overruled fundamental principles of the Constitution which have been settled and determined for generations. The Court has determined to strike down all State laws which provide for racial segregation, and upon which the institutions, the culture, and the civilization of the South are built. This attack upon the South is not concluded. We are witnessing only the beginning.

These decisions go far beyond any heretofore contemplated civil rights. The Court has entered the social field in violation of the Constitution, the laws of nature, and the law of God. It is an attempt to put the races together, physically, upon a plane of social equality. The Court contemplates doing this irrespective of the reaction of either race involved. In reality these decisions do not create civil rights. They create social rights.

Mr. President, a court cannot enforce its will in these fields. Racial instincts are normal, natural, human instincts. It is natural that persons of every race, hybrids only excepted, desire to associate with their own kind, and to maintain the purity of their own race. To do the things which the Court is attempting to do is beyond the power of the government. It will justly cause, in my judgment, evasion and violation of the law and contempt for law, and will do this country great harm.

These decisions, coming at a time of grave world crisis, when there should be unity in the United States, will cause great dissension and will weaken us internally. . . .

The Supreme Court could not find the authority for its decisions in the wording of the 14th Amendment, in the history of the amendment, or in the decision of the court. Instead, the Court was forced to resort to the unprecedented, unsound, and irrelevant authority of a group of recent partisan books on sociology and psychology. If this is the judicial calibre of the Court, what can the Nation expect from it in the future? What is to prevent the Court from citing as an authority in some future decision the works of Karl Marx?

The Court holds that the segregation of white and colored children in public schools has a detrimental effect upon the colored children. What about the white children? Do they not, also, have rights? Will not the commingling of the races in public schools have a detrimental effect upon white children? The rights of our children have been trampled upon by the Court. Everyone knows, Mr. President, that the school atmosphere, the tension, and frictions generated in interracial schools will have a detrimental effect upon the children of both races, will lessen their ability to learn, and will retard the progress of education.

Creation of mixed schools would aggravate the teacher shortage by making the teaching profession far less desirable.

The Supreme Court, therefore, in its alleged concern for Negro "feelings" in segregated schools, while ignoring fundamental questions of great significance, has strained at a gnat and swallowed a camel. It has created the greatest crisis in the history of American education. . . .

The tragic part of this unwarranted decision is that the thinking people of neither race want the abandonment of segregation. Radicals and rabblerousers and race agitators are in great glee of course but all persons in both races who use their heads for something other than loafing places for hair well realize the gravity of the situation and the tragic consequences to which it may lead.

The doctrine of separate but equal facilities upon which southern civilization is built has been the law of the land since the beginning of the Republic. The Constitution of the United States permits racial segregation. The Constitution would not have been adopted, the United States would not have been created, if anyone had dreamed that the Constitution would deprive the States of their power to segregate the races, and invade, therefore, the police powers of the States.

The 14th amendment to the Constitution, upon which these decisions are based, did not prevent segregation, and it was so understood at the time the courts had uniformly, until last week, so interpreted the 14th amendment. Mr.

President, the meaning of the Constitution or an amendment is fixed when it is adopted. It cannot conceivably have one meaning at one time, and another meaning in later years.

Apparently, the present Supreme Court has based its decision upon psychological and sociological concepts in the light of what it considers changed social conditions of the present day. In doing so, this Court has introduced a new principle which heretofore was unknown to the law, and that is that a constitutional provision may have a flexible meaning and a flexible interpretation.

The 14th amendment could not have one meaning in 1896, when the Supreme Court decided Plessy against Ferguson, and a different meaning when the present Court has occasion to pass upon it. . . .

COURT CANNOT COERCE SOUTH

Mr. President, let me make this very clear: The South will retain segregation. This means that public facilities of recreation and amusement now owned by the public must be transferred to private hands. I think that in the future this Court will go even further, and will hold that the act of a State in licensing certain private businesses, such as hotels and restaurants, to operate on a segregated basis, as heretofore, would also be in violation of the 14th amendment. In other words, I do not believe that in the future the Court will permit a State to charge a privilege tax to theaters, hotels, restaurants, places of amusement, or any other facility in which segregation is practiced. All our institutions were built upon the interpretation of the 14th amendment as announced in the case of Plessy against Ferguson, from which I have quoted; and one is naive, indeed, to think that southern people will permit all their social institutions to be swept away on the distorted and, in my judgment, politically inspired decision of the nine men who now occupy the Supreme Court.

Mr. President, in the exercise of their police power, the legislatures of the Southern States have established separate schools for white and colored children. Similarly the Congress has enacted legislation establishing separate schools for white and colored children in the District of Columbia. The legislatures of Southern States and many others under their police power have enacted laws forbidding the intermarriage of the 2 races and requiring separation of the 2 races in public conveyances, theaters, hotels, public parks, swimming pools, and other recreational facilities owned by the public. Long prior to the decision of the Supreme Court in 1896, in the case of Plessy against Ferguson, and continuously thereafter, the legislature of the Southern States have enacted segregation legislation harmonious with established usages, customs, traditions, and the general sentiment of the people of both races. They have enacted such legislation with a view to the promotion of public comfort and the preservation of public peace and good order. The legislatures of the Southern States and the southern people, both white and colored, know that social equality can neither be accomplished nor promoted by laws or court decisions which conflict with the general sentiment of the community upon which they are designed to operate. Southerners know that legislation and court decrees are powerless to eradicate racial instincts or to abolish distinctions based upon physical differences; and any attempt to do so can only result in accentuating the difficulties of the present situation.

The principle of segregation of the white and colored races in the institutions of the South is not and has never been based upon the concept that one race should be inferior to the other before the law. On the other hand, if the colored race is considered socially different from the white race, there is no power whatsoever in the Constitution and laws of the United States or in the Supreme Court which can put the two races upon the same social plane.

SOCIAL, NOT CIVIL, RIGHTS AT ISSUE

If the policy of separating the races is interpreted as denoting the inferiority of the Negro race, such inferiority cannot be legally inferred as arising from a denial of a civil right. These are not civil rights. They are social rights. In addition, they are social obligations which each individual owes to his race. It therefore follows that the reasoning of the Supreme Court that the Negro child is psychologically harmed in a segregated school is based upon the social differences, rather than the denial of a civil right. The Supreme Court is attempting by its present decision not to grant to the Negro child a civil right, but to put the Negro child and the white child upon the same social plane by integration of the races in the same school.

Mr. President, the southern white people are peaceful, law-abiding citizens. They do not desire any form of lawlessness; but, on the contrary, they desire public peace and good order. But southern people, both white and colored, know that they cannot in the foreseeable future meet upon terms of social equality by voluntary consent. They know that social equality conflicts with the general sentiment of both races. They know that the established usages, customs, and traditions and general sentiment of the people would have to be changed, in order to provide social equality of the races. They consider that the requirement to integrate the white and colored children in the public schools will break down and destroy their established usages, customs, and traditions. Such a requirement does violence to the sentiment of both races. Southern people know that if the Supreme Court attempts to impose such a requirement upon them by force, stern resistance and lawlessness will inevitably result, regardless of whether the requirement is invoked forthwith or gradually. . . .

JEFFERSON'S WARNING

The great Thomas Jefferson wrote a prophetic letter to Charles Hammond dated August 18, 1821, in which he describes the present Court in accurate terms:

It has long, however, been my opinion, and I have never shrunk from its expression (although I do not choose to put it into a newspaper, nor, like a Priam in armor, offer myself its champion), that the germ of dissolution of our Federal Government is in the Constitution of the Federal judiciary. An irresponsible body (for impeachment is scarcely a scarecrow) working like gravity by night and by day, gaining a little today and a little tomorrow, and advancing its noiseless step like a thief, over the field of jurisdiction until all shall be usurped from the States and the government of all be consolidated into one.

To this I am opposed, because when all government, domestic and foreign, in little as in great things, shall be drawn to Washington as the center of all power, it will render powerless the checks provided of one government on another, and will become as vernal and oppressive as the government from which we separate. It will be as in Europe where every man must be either pike or gudgeon, hammer or anvil. Our functionaries and theirs are wares of the same workshop, made of the same materials and by the same hand. If the States look with apathy on this silent descent of their government into the gulf which is to swallow all, we have only to weep over the human character formed uncontrollable but by a rod of iron; and the blasphemers of men as incapable of self-government, become his true historians.

Mr. President, the dual system of government, the Federal Republic itself, is in jeopardy if this Court is not curbed. . . .

DE TOCQUEVILLE: EVIL COURT CREATES CONTEMPT FOR LAW

Jefferson was not the only expert in political philosophy who feared the outcome of concentrated judicial power. More than 100 years ago, that shrewd French traveler and observer of American institutions, Alexis De Tocqueville, commenting upon our Supreme Court as a unique governmental institution, described the vital necessity of maintaining its reputation for integrity and impartiality in the following memorable words:

The peace, the prosperity, and the very existence of the Union are vested in the hands of the seven Federal Judges. Without them, the Constitution would be a dead letter: the Executive appeals to them for assistance against the encroachments of the legislative power; the Legislature demands their protection against the assaults of the Executive; they defend the Union from the disobedience of the States, the States from the exaggerated claims of the Union, the public interest against private interests, and the conservative spirit of stability against the fickleness of the democracy. Their power is enormous, but it is the power of public opinion. They are all-powerful as long as the people respect the law, but they would be impotent against popular neglect or contempt of the law. The force of public opinion is the most intractable of agents, because its exact limits cannot be defined;

and it is not less dangerous to exceed, than to remain below, the boundary prescribed.

The President, who exercises a limited power, may err without causing great mischief in the state. Congress may decide amiss without destroying the Union, because the electoral body in which the Congress originates may cause it to retract its decision by changing its members. But, if the Supreme Court is ever composed of imprudent or bad men, the Union may be plunged into anarchy or civil war.

Such, Mr. President, is the importance attached to the integrity and impartiality of the Supreme Court by the most famous European analyst of the American system of government. Happily for America, the highest standards of impartiality, propriety, and honesty have generally been adhered to by members of this Court.

PRESENT COURT BRAINWASHED

Today, however, a trend away from traditional standards of propriety begins to be in evidence. Our Court has been indoctrinated and brainwashed by left-wing pressure groups. The Court is out of step with the American people. We see Justices of the Supreme Court banqueted and honored by left-wing Communist-front organizations militantly interested in legislation on which the Supreme Court must pass.

Permit me to quote from the Washington *Afro-American* of April 14, 1945:

"JUSTICE HUGO L. BLACK HONORED AT INTER-RACIAL BANQUET BY HUMAN WELFARE GROUP—JUSTICE BLACK, JEFFERSON AWARD WINNER, LAUDED FOR ROLE IN CIVIL RIGHTS STRUGGLE—DR. CHARLES H. HOUSTON EXTOLS FORMER ALABAMA SENATOR, GIVEN AWARD SECOND TIME, FOR PRACTICAL BELIEF IN DEMOCRACY—FIRST LADY HEARD"

"Justice Hugo Black has grown to be a great stabilizing force in the colored race's struggle for equal rights," said Dr. Charles H. Houston, on March 27 at the Statler Hotel where the Jefferson award was presented to the Supreme Court Justice.

The presentation of the award, given for work in public affairs by the Southern Conference for Human Welfare, was the second to Mr. Black, who has been similarly honored when a Senator.

Justice Sherman Minton, at that time a judge of the Seventh Circuit Court of Appeals, was also a speaker at this dinner.

Accompanying the news article are several pictures of these Justices sitting at the banquet table with various Negro leaders.

Mr. President, the so-called Southern Conference for Human Welfare was not only aggressively interested in anti-segregation cases appearing before our courts, including the Supreme Court, but was a notorious Communist-front organization.

The extreme impropriety of Federal justices accepting awards and testimonial dinners from Communist-front organizations that are vitally interested in court cases according to their own declarations must be apparent to all. Such a prima facie exhibition of bias disqualifies a judge in the public eye, and rightly so.

DOUGLAS ACCEPTS $1,000 FROM CIO

Nor is this the only matter in which the Supreme Court has been brought into dispute. The CIO, which, as everyone knows, is up to its neck in politics, is also vitally interested in numerous Court decisions, including the question of segregation. Yet Supreme Court Justice William O. Douglas has become virtually the protege of the CIO.

Thus, we find Justice Douglas, in November 1948, stepping down from the bench and doffing the toga of judicial impartiality to deliver the principal address at the National CIO Convention at Portland, Oreg. While in Portland, Justice Douglas was the honored and flattered guest of the CIO. His strongly partisan speech brought down the house.

Mr. President, page 11 of the *New York Times* of November 13, 1950, carries an article entitled "Aid in Revolutions Urged by Douglas." The same page of the *New York Times* reports Justice Douglas receiving the civil rights award of the B'nai B'rith Metropolitan Council in 1950.

Mr. President, page 1 of the *New York Times* of September 1, 1951, carries an Associated Press article beginning:

"Supreme Court Justice William O. Douglas proposed today that the United States recognize Red China, and in the ensuing uproar Senator Tom Connally, Democrat, of Texas, accused him of making 'fool statements.' "

What a spectacle it is, Mr. President, for a man who sits on the highest tribunal of our country and interprets the laws of this free Nation, openly to espouse the cause of our greatest enemy which has destroyed freedom and made a mockery of law in every country where it has seized power. . . .

Mr. President, not long ago Supreme Court Justices Reed and Frankfurter broke all precedents of the Supreme Court to become character witnesses for Alger Hiss, later convicted of perjury in a case involving espionage for Soviet Russia.

Everyone knows that the Negroes did not themselves instigate the agitation against segregation. They were put up to it by radical busybodies who are intent upon overthrowing American institutions.

With so many Supreme Court Justices accepting testimonial dinners from Communist-front organizations like the Southern Conference for Human Welfare, or taking outright cash awards from the very organization, the CIO, that is itself providing legal talent to work up the antisegregation cases at issue, what kind of justice can we expect?

SOUTH FREER FROM RACIAL TENSION

Mr. President, the decision of the Supreme Court of the United States in declaring the segregated school system to be in violation of the 14th amendment to the Constitution has created an extremely grave problem for the Southern States. This problem in all of its ramifications is much graver than many Americans realize. People from other sections of the country do not comprehend the racial problem of the South. Several millions of people there of both races live side by side in peace and harmony. We do not have the riots and racial tensions which exist in other areas of the country. The racial troubles and racial tensions which exist in northern cities are due to the fact that the people there have not had the experience in racial affairs which southern people of both races have acquired over the years. Northerners who move South immediately acquire the same viewpoint as Southerns on the segregation problem. This proves the naturalness and necessity of segregation as a means of securing racial peace and goodwill.

The southern institution of racial segregation or racial separation was the correct, self-evident truth which arose from the chaos and confusion of the reconstruction period. Separation promotes racial harmony. It permits each race to follow its own pursuits, to develop its own culture, its own institutions, and its own civilization. Segregation is not discrimination. Segregation is not a badge of racial inferiority, and that it is not is recognized by both races in the Southern States. In fact, segregation is desired and supported by the vast majority of the members of both of the races in the South who dwell side by side under harmonious conditions.

The Negro has made a great contribution to the South. We take pride in the constant advance he has made. It is where social questions are involved that Southern people draw the line. It is these social institutions with which Southern people, in my judgment, will not permit the Supreme Court to tamper.

Let me make this clear, Mr. President: There is no racial hatred in the South. The Negro race is not an oppressed race. A great Senator from the State of Idaho, Senator William E. Borah, a few years ago said on the floor of the Senate:

"Let us admit that the South is dealing with this question as best it can, admit that the men and women of the South are just as patriotic as we are, just as devoted to the principles of the Constitution as we are, just as willing to sacrifice for the success of their communities as we are. Let us give them credit as American citizens, and cooperate with them, sympathize with them, and help them in the solution of their problem, instead of condemning them. We are one people, one Nation, and they are entitled to be treated upon this basis."

Mr. President, it is the law of nature, it is the law of God, that every race has both the right and the duty to perpetuate itself. All free men have the right to associate exclusively with members of their own race, free from governmental interference, if they so desire. Free men have the right to send their children to schools of their own choosing, free from governmental interference, and to build up their own culture, free from governmental interference. These rights are inherent in the Constitution of the United States and in the American system of government. It is the duty of Government both State and National to promote and protect this right. . . .

The white people of the South do not have race prejudice. They have race consciousness, and they are proud to possess this awareness of the significance of race. Had they not possessed it, the South would have been mongrelized and southern civilization destroyed long ago. The South is historically justified in its unflinching stand for racial integrity.

PROGRESS IN NEGRO EDUCATION

Mr. President, as poverty has diminished in the South, great progress has been made in the fields of public health and Negro education. In the school year of 1939–40 the States of Mississippi, Alabama, Florida, Arkansas, Georgia, and North Carolina spent an aggregate total of $22,703,000 on Negro education. Twelve years later, in the school year of 1951–52, these same States spent an aggregate total of $117,551,000—an increase of 520 percent. Rapid progress is thus being made voluntarily in providing Negroes with equal educational facilities. I do not have available the figures on public health, but in my judgment equal progress percentagewise has been made there too.

Mr. President, there has been no responsible demand in the South from either race for the elimination of the segregated school system. The agitation for it is of northern origin, and the suits on which the Court based its decision were instigated and promoted by organized minority pressure groups from the North.

White people of the South prefer that their children be taught by white teachers; likewise colored people of the South prefer that their children be taught by colored teachers. If the schools are integrated, neither white nor colored parents will have any choice whatsoever as to their children being taught by white or colored teachers. What folly this is. Mr. President, no one can legislate or enforce a decision in these fields of close human relationships. . . .

We desire friendly racial relations. We desire progress and racial understanding. I believe that without the intervention of northern meddlers, segregated schools would continue by mutual agreement of the leaders of both races.

The Negro will receive just treatment. His children will be educated. His standard of living has increased, and will continue to increase. But the racial questions which confront the South are social and not economic. This grave question should be settled with justice to both races.

SOUTH WILL NOT GIVE AN INCH

Mr. President, I know southern people. I know conditions in the South at first hand. Our people are peaceful, law-abiding citizens. They do not desire any form of lawlessness, but, on the contrary, desire public peace and good order. I know that southern people by and large, will neither recognize, abide by, nor comply with this decision. I know that in the foreseeable future, they will not permit their schools to be racially integrated. I know that there will be no compromise. In my judgment, southern people will not give an inch. Segregated schools will be maintained by the proper and legitimate use of the police power inherent in every State, regardless of what the Supreme Court says. After all, power rests in the hands of a united people.

Many people realize that the South will retain segregated schools, if necessary, by means which the Court will say are illegal. Many persons think that, if necessary, the South will defy the Court. I know that people in local communities in the South will for a long time in the future, handle their local problems to the best advantage of the community, regardless of the nine men who now compose the Court....

SOUTH WILL BE VICTORIOUS

We are witnessing the beginning of a great controversy—one which will last for years. The issue is: Shall the white man and the Negro retain their racial identities? The future greatness of America depends upon racial purity and the maintenance of Anglo-Saxon institutions, which still flourish in full flower in the South. Who says the South will not win?

Mr. President, the British Empire was entrenched in India for 100 years. It had an army stationed there. Britain had invested billions of dollars in that country. Yet old Mahatma Gandhi, ill, in the last stages of high blood pressure, dressed in a loin cloth, leading a nanny goat and carrying a spinning wheel, with his hunger strikes and professions of piety, drove imperial Britain from India. He mobilized the sentiment of his people. Southern sentiment is mobilized. Southern people will stand firm.

Again we saw the fortitude of little Ireland in her fight for freedom from the British yoke. Imperial Britain was defied. The fight for independence went on, by both legal and illegal means, until the Irish were victorious.

We, in the South, have seen the tides rise before; when we refuse to be engulfed, they recede. The present campaign against segregation is based upon illegality. The South will therefore prevail.

THOMAS PICKENS BRADY

Thomas Pickens Brady was born in Brookhaven, Mississippi, on August 6, 1903. He was educated at Lawrenceville Preparatory School in New Jersey, received a B.A. degree at Yale University, and a law degree from the University of Mississippi. For two years before beginning his law practice in 1930, Brady taught sociology at the University of Mississippi. During the unsuccessful 1948 third-party presidential campaign of the States Rights Party, Brady was the party's speaker's bureau chairman. In 1950, he was appointed judge of the Circuit Court, Fourteenth Judicial Circuit of Mississippi, a post he held until 1963, when he became an associate justice of the State Supreme Court where he served until his death. He was vice president of the Mississippi Bar Association in 1954–55 and in the following year, Brady received a Distinguished Service citation from the Mississippi Legislature. He died in Jackson, Mississippi, on January 31, 1973.[6]

SEGREGATION AND THE SOUTH[7]

San Francisco, California
October 4, 1957

> Segregation in the South is a way of life. It is a precious and sacred custom. It is one of our dearest and most treasured possessions.

It is indeed an honor to be invited to address the distinguished membership and the guests of the renowned Commonwealth Club of California.

I have been asked to speak on Segregation and the South, and I have been requested to do in twenty seven minutes that which cannot be adequately done in several hours. I will do my best to present the case for the South. I know you will give me a fair hearing. I shall try to be objective, but if I fail in this regard, I assure you that I can and will be truthful. I earnestly hope that no one will be offended, but let me assure you, I will not sacrifice truth on the altar of courtesy.

Segregation is defined by Webster: "To separate or set apart from the others or from the rest; to isolate."

It is essential that you realize that in the twelve Southern States, segregation means something quite different than what it means in the other States. In the South, segregation is something more than a definition in the dictionary. It is something more than a political program. It supersedes a philosophical conception. It is more than a sociological platitude. Segregation in the South is a way of life. It is a precious and sacred custom. It is one of our dearest and most treasured possessions. It is the means whereby we live in social peace, order and security. It is the guarantee whereby our wives and children are afforded the common decency and protection which is essential if any harmonious relationship is to exist between two different races. Segregation exists not simply because we prefer it, but because we must maintain it. For over a hundred and fifty years, we have been maintaining and protecting this sacred custom. Self-preservation, the first law of life, has required that we do so. It is the first commandment and not the last. It is our shield and buckler. Segregation, moreover, is preferred by both the white and the Negro races in the South. Ninety-eight percent of both races desire it. It does not work any hardship upon the Negro, nor does it deprive him of any of his constitutional rights. It should be admitted that a white man and a white woman have the same equal right to associate with whom they please as does the Negro man and the Negro woman.

Historically, our problem today dates back to the passage of the 14th Amendment. In 1866, after one of the world's bloodiest wars was ended, the South lay prostrate at the feet of a Northern victor, devoid of mercy and gallantry. Full of hatred and determination to forever crush the South, Congress submitted to the States the 13th, 14th and 15th Amendments, hoping upon the passage of said Amendments to enact legislation which would forever weaken the Southern States so that the Federal Government could dominate the South through Negro Carpetbag rule. The 13th and 15th Amendments, which prohibited slavery and provided that the power to vote should not be denied on account of race or color, were promptly ratified by a three-fourths majority of the States. The Southern States, with an all-white electorate and all-white legislatures, voted for these amendments which were promptly passed. The 14th Amendment, however, loaded with the dynamite of social integration, was completely rejected. The 14th Amendment was lawfully submitted and lawfully rejected under the constitutional procedure. That should have ended the matter, but Congress became infuriated and from thenceforth adopted high-handed measures. It proclaimed military rule in the South and took over the Southern States by military occupation. The white people were disfranchised, the ballot was put into the hands of the illiterate Negro, coached by carpetbaggers.

In 1868, the 14th Amendment was re-submitted and, of course, ratified almost unanimously by the Southern States, the white people being denied the right to vote. The United States Army attended to the details. This last ratification was unlawful and in violation of the Constitution. Now hear this. In so far as the Negro is concerned, the 14th Amendment, the creature of unending hate against the South, has never been of any moral force in the South. This may sound fantastic but it is true, as every white child in the South fully knows. The ultimate results of this Amendment of hate and corruption, I prophesy, in the future will not only operate against the South but will ultimately be one of the principal means whereby the rights of all the sovereign states will be usurped or destroyed by a totalitarian inclined government, if the government continues on its present course.

My grandfather was a Captain in the Mississippi Rifles. He fought for four years in the War Between the States. He buried his brother who was killed by his side at Vicksburg. From my grandfather's lips, as millions of other Southerners heard from their grandfather's lips, I obtained a vivid description of the first Reconstruction Era. The homes, cotton and corn fields which had escaped the scourge of war were destroyed under the Negro Carpetbag military rule which lasted 3½ years in Mississippi. Drunken, marauding bands of crazed Negroes shot and broke into homes, raping and killing the women and children whom they dragged screaming from their flaming homes. The crackle of the flames and the groans and screams of the helpless victims, though not loud, are still audible in the minds of Southerners. The Negro gangs now operating in South Chicago, Harlem, Pennsylvania and Washington are mildly reminiscent of that First Reconstruction. We know what unbridled Negro rule can produce, and the South is never going to relinquish into the hands of the ignorant, the unqualified, the unscrupulous, the primitive and uncontrolled the rein of our Government. To do so is simple suicide.

I want it distinctly understood that the South does not hate the Negro. You know little, if anything, about the true Southern Negro. As a matter of fact, there is a great deal of genuine affection and understanding between the races. We have lived harmoniously together, with a minimum of violence and bloodshed. We have nurtured the Negro, taught him, provided for him, educated him and endeavored to make him a worthwhile citizen. He has made great strides. Though he pays about only 12 percent of the taxes, we have in the last twenty years given him equally of the benefits to be afforded from taxation. I realize that this statement may provoke disagreement, but the fact nevertheless remains that in Mississippi, and in other Southern States, Negroes, who desired to do so, have become well educated and wealthy. Millionaires are included in this group. This group has within its numbers, doctors, lawyers, teachers, business men and plantation owners. There is no field of economic endeavor which has been barred to the Negro. It is only in the social sphere that the barrier is raised.

There are many reasons why the Southerner flatly refuses to permit integration with the Negro in the social sphere of our life. Time will not permit an analysis of all of them but the basic ones can be enumerated. First, the high percentage of Negroes in the South is of grave importance. The national average which the Negro bears to the white man in America is 10 percent. In Mississippi, however, it is 45.3 percent. In Georgia, it is 38.8 percent. In South Carolina it is 38.8 percent. In Louisiana, it is 32.9 percent. In Alabama, it is 32 percent. In Arkansas, it is 22.3 percent, and in Florida, it is 21.7 percent. The great State of California has but 4.4 percent. The State of New York, that yearns so for the welfare of the Negro in Mississippi, has but 6.2 percent. New Jersey has 6.6 percent, and Pennsylvania has 6.1 percent. Ohio has 6.5 percent, Oregon has but eight-tenths of one percent. Montana and Nevada have but two-tenths of one percent. South Dakota has .01 of one percent. If the State of New York, where so much turmoil has arisen over the desegregation in the public schools, or in Pennsylvania and Illinois, where similar mass demonstrations of violence have taken place, had 45.3 percent of their population Negro, I shudder to think what would have taken place between the Negroes and whites. If, in this county, as in many counties in Mississippi, and other Southern States, the Negroes outnumbered the whites five and six to one, I wonder whether or not you would be willing to have or consent to complete educational and social integration?

There is, as every sociologist knows, a distinct correlation between the degree of segregation of the races and the numerical strength of the Negro. The reason for this, I will later conclusively show. If in the South the Negro was permitted, as he is in some Northern States to obtain the ballot by simply reaching 21 years of age, it would mean that no white man in many counties would ever hold public office. It would also mean that in the Halls of Congress, as is earnestly desired by the Communists of America, the seats now occupied by our representatives would be held by incompetent, illiterate and ignorant Negroes.

While I regret that I must do so, I must nevertheless comment upon the intellectual and moral aspects of the reason why the South must remain segregated socially. The average vocabulary of the Negro in the South consists of approximately 650 words. The reason for this is that the average Negro boy quits school around the age of 13 or 14 years. The average Negro girl generally goes through high school, and has a larger vocabulary. I hesitate to estimate the I.Q. of the average Negro of the South since I could not obtain from the Federal Government the results of the intelligence tests given in World War Two and in the Korean conflict. The NAACP objects, but I can safely say that based upon the tests which were available from World War One, there is a great gulf of difference between the I.Q. of the Negro of the South, as well as in America, and the average white man. Northern left-wing educators and sociologists explain this deficiency by saying that it is caused by an inefficient and inferior educational setting for Negroes. This is wholly false. It is because of a deficiency in mental ability; it is due to indifference and indolence on the part of the Negroes. That fact cannot be disputed, and that is that of all the races that have ever been on this earth, assuming that they all started out at approximately the same time in God's calendar, the Negro race is the only race that lacked the imagination and mental ability to put its hopes, dreams and thoughts in writing. The Negro race was the only race that was unable to invent even picture writing.

Exhaustive study of the program of integration in the schools of Washington, D.C., which the NAACP and other groups fostering integration said would be an example for the rest of the United States to follow, clearly indicates that the average white student who was integrated in the classes with the Negroes has been retarded two to three years in his educational progress. This, in itself, should convince the most dubious that it is not to the best interest of America that the white children in certain congested sections be retarded two years, or more, in their educational advancement. Remember that the left-wing socialistic groups of this country are always grading down, never grading up the intelligence, the industry and the genius of this country.

While there is undoubtedly fear of ultimate intermarriage between a small segment of the whites and Negroes if complete social integration should take place, still, this is not yet a major concern. The late Walter White, Secretary of the NAACP for many years, when questioned as to whether integration in the schools would lead to intermarriage, was forced to admit that association leads to friendship and friendship leads to love and marriage. He said, however, without any explanation, that he doubted if this would happen. There is certainly less than one percent of the white people of the South who would agree to marry a Negro. Miscegenation had largely taken place, I am glad to say, North of the Mason and Dixon line, and whatever laxity has existed in Southern mores permitting clandestine relationships between Negroes and whites had almost entirely disappeared. The rule is now hard and adamant. Such is taboo in the South.

The main objection to social integration of the races by Southerners is for moral reasons. As revealed by Representative John Bell Williams, of Mississippi, in his remarkable treatise, WHERE IS THE REIGN OF TERROR, it is shown that the white boys and girls were subjected to untold vulgarity, immorality and filth because of the integration which has taken place in Washington. The truth is often brutal, but I must speak it. As revealed in the treatise of Representative Williams, the white children of Washington, D.C., were retarded two to three years in their educational advancement. The obscenity, the vulgarity and brutality which existed required the constant maintenance of policemen in the halls and corridors of many of the schools. Obscene notes and pictures were placed on the desks of white girls by Negroes. The radiators, stairs and halls were utilized as urinals and toilets by the Negroes. The carrying of concealed weapons and aggravated assaults and the rape and attempted rape of white girls and even teachers are some of the results found in the model example of what integration in our high schools can do. Make no mistake about this, the Southern fathers and mothers are not going to permit their daughters to be insulted by Negroes, or anyone else! They are not going to permit their daughters to have to resist the advances of Negro boys. They are not going to permit their sons and daughters to be subjected to the vulgarity of Negro boys and girls who are urged to take every possible advantage of the white children that can be taken. Possibly I cannot speak for the South, but I can speak for Mississippi, and I can tell you this, we have already, by constitutional amendment, authorized our Legislature to abolish the public school system in Mississippi if the Negro and white children are integrated therein. Make no mistake about it, we will abolish our public school system and establish private schools for children. We will have private academies for the white children only, and we will still see that the Negro is educated separately. It will cost dearly, but we will do it!

There have been but few isolated cases in either the white or Negro schools in Mississippi where assaults with deadly weapons have taken place. Such assaults are numerous in Washington and other places where the Negroes and white children have been integrated. The Negro, in so far as sex is concerned, is not immoral, he is simply non-moral. He merely obeys his natural instincts. The pregnancies and illegitimate births which have occurred among the Negro girls in the schools of Washington is not abnormal, merely astounding. In the South there is a double standard in so far as sex morals are concerned. The white man has his standard and the Negro has his standard. Perhaps we are responsible, because we have not and do not punish the Negro except in rare instances for desertion, illegitimacy or bigamy. The white race laid aside cannibalism thousands of years before the Negro race was forced to do so. The white race is on the verge of forever abolishing incest. The Negro race is far behind. We punish the Negro for incest and there is now on my docket, as is frequently the case, indictments for incest by Negroes. Negro men who beget children by their daughters are tried.

We cannot count for naught the natural indolence and indifference of the Negro's tendencies to immorality and violence and subject our children to the terrible consequences resulting from such traits, notwithstanding the socialist mouthings by socialist preachers.

In California, the Negro constitutes 4.4 percent of your total population, yet 19 percent of all crimes committed in California were committed by Negroes. In the State of New York, the Negro constitutes 6.2 percent of the total population, and yet 40.1 percent of the prison population of New York is Negro. In Mississippi, the Negro constitutes 45.3 percent of the population and commits 73.4 percent of the crimes. In the District of Columbia, the Negro's mecca of America, according to the 1950 census, the Negro constituted 35 percent of the total population, and the Negro prison population is 70 percent, or twice the ratio of Negro population to that of white population. This is a national disgrace. The District of Columbia has more Negro convicts than either Louisiana, Mississippi, Arkansas, Alabama, Florida, Texas, Kentucky or Maryland. The pattern seems to be the larger concentration of Negro population, the higher the incidence of crime. This conclusion is further established in the Northern and Eastern States where the crime rate percentages have taken another advance. In this group, California fits very well also. The exception of this pattern is in the Southern States where we have the largest concentration of Negro population, but in spite of the great concentration, the incidence of crime among the Negroes is considerably less than in the Northern and Midwestern States. . . .

The passage of the Civil Rights bill of August 29, 1957, marks the beginning of another Reconstruction Era in the South. It is as dark a day as was May 17, 1954, the date of the illegal, unconstitutional and Communistic Black Monday decision. The Black Monday decision was a total usurpation of the rights of Congress. The Supreme Court, by edict, has sought to pass a law which only Congress had the authority to do.

The South is the citadel of conservatism. It is a fortress for constitutional government. Throughout Mississippi and the other Southern States, a feeling of concern over the socialist trend of our Federal Government has been constantly growing. Beginning with the administration of F.D.R., the South viewed with alarm the birth of the welfare state, and the growth of the 130 Communist-front organizations which nourish it. It was greatly concerned over the prodigal give-away program to the socialist countries abroad. It resented the competing by the Federal Government with private industry. It deplored the tolerance shown the Communist and left-wing groups in America. None of these stimuli were suf-ficient to precipitate a wholesale grass roots movement, though Mississippi, South Carolina and Louisiana did cry protest in 1948 when these States walked out of the National Democratic Convention in Philadelphia, organized the States Rights Party, nominated and voted for Strom Thurmond of South Carolina and Fielding L. Wright of Mississippi as its Presidential and Vice-Presidential nom-inees. The people of the United States had an opportunity then to vote for two men who were opposed to the gradual socialization of America and the destruc-tion of the sovereign rights and powers of the 48 States by a totalitarian-inclined Federal Government. Our protest provoked only ridicule and abuse.

It was only when the Supreme Court of the United States, on May 17, 1954, handed down its Black Monday decision that the people of the South realized that the "Rubicon had been crossed," and that they had no alternative except to organize completely and resist this infamous sociological, unconstitutional de-cision. Thus it was that the Citizens' Councils were born. Membership therein, however, is restricted. The Citizens' Council is a good cross-section of that city or county it represents. Lawyers, doctors, ministers, industrialists, merchants, employees, farmers, plantation owners and laborers compose the Councils. Jews, Catholics, and Protestants alike become members when they subscribe to an oath of nonviolence and pledge themselves to support in every legal way pos-sible the maintenance of segregation and the preservation of the sovereign rights of the States of this Union. We have no Ku Klux Klans in Mississippi, and we want none. The Klan is negligible in the South.

There are in Mississippi 360 Councils with approximately 85,000 members, and throughout the South, though some States utilize different names such as The Defenders of State Sovereignty in Virginia, there are more than 300,000 members. Each Council is completely autonomous and has a State Charter. In each State, however, there is a State Board of Directors which represents every Council in that State, and there is a South-wide coordinating agency in which eleven of the twelve Southern States are represented. This organization is known as the Citizens' Councils of America. . . .

Primarily, the Councils are dedicated to the preservation of segregation and the sovereign rights of the States of this Union. The Councils are unalterably opposed to the socialization of our basic industries, including transportation, banking, agriculture, electric power, medicine and education. They are opposed to the communizing and socializing of our labor organizations, schools and churches. The Citizens' Councils are determined to do everything possible to prevent the broadening of the powers of the executive branch of our Government and the usurpation by the judiciary of powers which are under our Constitution vested solely in the Congress. The Citizens' Councils are determined to resist the enormous and unwarranted pressure which is brought to bear on all branches of our Government by the aforesaid left-wing minority groups. Last, but not least, the Councils are opposed to the proposed welfare state and all of its destruction of the responsibilities and liberties of the citizens of this country, and above all, the Citizens' Councils are dedicated to nonviolence. The Councils firmly believe that within the Constitution of the respective States, an orderly, peaceful and legal means exist whereby these objectives can be secured and maintained.

In conclusion, we in the South realize and firmly believe that the resurgence of demand and effort for the advancement of the Negro politically and socially in the last thirty years was conceived and promoted by world-wide communism. Though there are many facets to the movement to completely integrate the Negro in the South, the basic cause we know is of Communist origin and Socialist plan. We know also that the drive for integration of the races in the South is but a small segment in the overall checkerboard plan to first socialize and then communize America. The proof of this can be found in the Workers (Communist) Party National Platform adopted on May 25, 1928, which included every demand for Negroes which is found in *Target for 1963*, a pamphlet published by the NAACP in 1956. As a matter of fact, the World Communists at one time actually and fantastically contemplated having the Negroes in the South violently overthrow the Southern States. Russia proposed to recognize the Negro Republic. It must be said to the lasting credit of the Negro that his loyalty to the white Southerner and to his country made this ridiculous plan impossible. Subsequently, the Communists then decided that every Negro in the South must be franchised so that the Negroes would hold political offices in the State Legislatures and would occupy the Southern seats in Congress.

Much of what has been done to advance and strengthen the fight against the South in recent months is directly in line with suggestions made in a statement on Negro Rights issued by the National Committee of the Communist Party of October 5, 1955, which concluded with this advice, "Most important is the further strengthening of a great united movement based on the maximum mobility of the Negro people and organization with the united support of the labor movement. Simultaneously, the Communists will play their part in helping to guarantee the participation and the militant initiative of the Left. Pass Civil Rights Legislation! End Segregation! Full equality for the Negro people—now!"

The February number of the Red Magazine, *Party Voice*, said: "Victory would mean desegregation, majority rule and Negro representation. Victory would mean the replacement of the Dixiecrat delegations to the State and National Legislatures by the spokesmen for the Negro people, labor and the poor farmers."

I cannot help but wonder what would happen to this country if the 24 Southern Senators were replaced by ignorant Negro or Communist labor leaders. I cannot help but wonder how the rights of Californians and the people of all the States would fare if the seats of the United States Senate which have been filled by such men as Cordell Hull, Walter George, Harry Byrd, James F. Byrnes, Strom Thurmond, Ellender, Lyndon Johnson, Jim Eastland were usurped by communistic Negroes or labor leaders. What would happen if one hundred-odd Southern members of the House of Representatives in Congress were replaced by Angelo Herndons? It cannot be disputed that the Communist Party has infiltrated and dominates many of our great labor parties. It is a fact that Communist sympathizers and Communist-front organizers founded the NAACP and largely control it. It cannot be disputed that the left-wing groups have infiltrated our colleges and our churches. A war is on to capture the American mind. The South above all other sections of the country has stubbornly resisted and opposed these groups which would communize our Government. The NAACP knows this, labor knows this, and the Communists know this, and we are, therefore, the target of their resentment and unending hate. We have grown accustomed to the vicious misrepresentations, the vituperation and abuse that is daily heaped upon us by means of the northern left-wing newspaper, radio and television. We have taken it and we can still take it. We are waiting for that day, and believe that it is not far distant, when conservative Americans in all the States will unite, when all constitutional Americans in this country will rise up in our defense and join hands with us in waging our lonely fight to protect and preserve America from Godless Communism!

We sometimes weary in fighting the four great lies which are being deliberately fostered upon an unsuspecting public by the Communists, the NAACP and the Marxian Christians of this country. Just as Goebbels, Minister of Propaganda in Germany, the greatest exponent of mass psychology the world has ever known, perpetuated his great lie of Germanic superiority on an unsuspecting public, so are the people of America being subjected to the merciless barrage of the four great lies calculated to produce integration of the races in America. They are: 1. No racial differences save that of our skin, hair and eyes, which are unimportant. 2. That laws create second-class citizenship. 3. That segregation is unChristian. 4. That all men are created equal. Four greater lies cannot be imagined. . . .

In an address in the United States House of Representatives, Congressman William Colmer of Mississippi stated:

> The Civil Rights Bill recently enacted by Congress, which inaugurates a Second Reconstruction in the South, will, however, affect not only the South. The sovereign rights of every State in this Union have been violated. August 29, 1957, is a day of infamy. This iniquitous act, like a loaded pistol, is aimed at the South which had contributed to so much of the foundation and perpetuation of our Republic. It is not the South, the Democratic Party or the Republican Party which will suffer most. The real victim in the tragedy which was concluded will be the Republic itself, for once the trigger is pulled, the freedom and real rights of the citizens of the sections of this country will be further curtailed. The powerful arm of an already powerful Federal Government will be further stretched out into

every metropolitan center as well as every hamlet of this great country, North, South, East and West, for the further regimentation of our citizens. The existing election machinery of the Southern States which they were granted under the 10th amendment, the right to create and utilize will be henceforth conducted under the scrutiny and intimidation of armed marshals of the Central Government in Washington. This could well be the final step next to achieve the goal of the true proponents of this legislation: The complete destruction of the sovereignty of the States and the centralization of all power of the people in one strong centralized government under the dome in the Capitol in Washington. . . .

Finally, so that there may be no vestige of doubt in your minds, I now fervently say, "Dum vivamus tum segrebimur et post mortem—deo volente, etiam nunc sic erit," which literally translated means, As long as we live, so long shall we be segregated, and after death, God willing, thus it will still be! Though you may not agree with what I have said, it is indeed a great honor and sacred right for you to have permitted me to say it.

ORVAL E. FAUBUS

Orval Eugene Faubus never intended to be a symbol of the white supremacist South, but his actions and speeches as governor of Arkansas during the Little Rock Central High School integration crisis of 1957 and 1958 branded him as one of the leading exponents of segregation.[8]

His political career did not start out that way; in fact, he had a reputation as a moderate at least, and even a somewhat liberal and progressive politician. He was born in the Ozark Mountains, in the small town of Combs on January 7, 1910; his father, Sam Faubus, was a Socialist and named his son after his Socialist hero, Eugene Debs. The younger Faubus taught school from 1928 to 1938, was elected to his first office in 1938 as the Madison County circuit clerk, was re-elected in 1940, then served in the U.S. Army during World War II. While on active duty, Faubus reached the rank of major and was awarded the Bronze Star. After the war, he returned to Arkansas and bought the Madison County *Record* and edited that home-town newspaper until 1949 when Governor Sidney McMath brought Faubus into state government as the state highway director, a post he held throughout the McMath administration, earning the reputation as the most liberal member of the McMath team. In 1954, he unexpectedly won a two-year term as governor, defeating the incumbent, first-term governor, Francis Cherry. Faubus' victory was somewhat of an upset, as normally Arkansas governors were re-elected to their second term.

In his first term, Faubus was a populist with a strong program of economic and social development. He pushed through the state legislature a reform of welfare laws, established a conservation commission, increased mental health facilities and formed the Arkansas Industrial Development Commission to promote industrialization of the state. Also during that first term, Faubus began complying with the 1954 Supreme Court decision and supported the desegregation of six out of seven state colleges and the schools in Fayetteville, Hoxi, and Charleston. His stand began to change, however, in 1956 when he ran for a second term against a strong segregationist, Jim Johnson. Knowing that a statewide poll indicated that 85 percent of Arkansans opposed integration, Faubus openly opposed forced integration and supported local option on the question.

In 1957, the Little Rock School Board decided to begin integration in the capital city with Central High School as the first target. Faubus did not take a stand on the issue until late in the summer, when he called on the Justice Department for help, a plea that was turned down. On September 2, the governor ordered the National Guard to prevent desegregation at Central High. After a several week stand-off, on September 23, integration began with nine students attempting to enter the school, only to be turned away by a hostile mob. President Eisenhower federalized the Arkansas National Guard and ordered units from the 101st Airborne Division to Little Rock. On September 25, the students were escorted into school by the federal troops.

Throughout the year, Faubus continued to oppose integration and in September 1958 the governor closed all the Little Rock schools. In the same month, Little Rock citizens voted more than 70 percent against reopening the schools on an integrated basis. The speech published here is Faubus' statewide address explaining his position on closing the schools.

Faubus served six terms as governor, finally retiring in 1967. He died in Conway, Arkansas, on December 14, 1994.

SPEECH OF GOVERNOR ORVAL E. FAUBUS[9]

Little Rock, Arkansas
September 18, 1958

Those who would integrate our schools at any price are still among us. They have seized upon the present situation to promote and foment concern and discontent, because of the temporary closing of the schools.

They have spread wild rumors and attempted to organize demonstrations. These are the same people and the same forces who have all along been opposed to the majority will of the people of Little Rock and Arkansas. The only difference at the moment is that they have substituted the cry "Open the schools" for the well-worn "Law and Order" phrase.

It can also be again noted, as it has been in the past, that they always say: "It isn't worth the fight. The result is inevitable. We might as well surrender now." The aim, of course, is to destroy the will to resist those efforts to destroy our way of life—a way of life which has brought more progress and more good to the members of all races than has been attained anywhere else in the world.

Last year, I stated during the September crisis that I was not elected Governor of Arkansas to surrender all our rights as citizens to an all powerful Federal autocracy. I repeated this statement many times during the campaign of the past summer, and I re-emphasize it now. It is my responsibility, and it is my purpose and determination, to defend the constitutional rights of the people of Arkansas to the full extent of my ability.

We find now that our boys and girls are being used in this struggle. They are being urged to demonstrate and to issue statements which the adult instigators themselves do not have the courage to do.

I am fully aware of the deep concern of the parents for the continued proper education of their children, and I am fully aware of the inconvenience to the students in the interruption of the proper educational processes. To them, both parents and students, I express my sympathy and understanding.

To the students who are concerned, I say that in the years to follow, when you have come to realize the importance of maintaining our form of government, and the importance of preserving the great freedoms and privileges which we have known, you will be happy and proud to remember that you suffered inconvenience and personal sacrifice, and thereby made a worthwhile contribution to the maintenance of our dual system of government.

Thomas Jefferson once wrote:

> But it is not by the consolidation, or concentration of powers, but by their distribution, that good government is effected. Were not this great country already divided into States, that division must be made, that each might do for itself what concerns itself directly, and what it can so much better do than a distant authority. Were we directed from Washington when to sow, and when to reap, we should soon want bread. It is by this partition of cares, descending in graduation from general to particular, that the mass of human affairs may be best managed, for the good and prosperity of all.
>
> They (the people) are the only sure reliance for the preservation of our liberty. After all, it is my principle that the will of the majority should prevail.

In this dual system of government, with its checks and balances, lies the strength of the United States of America. Once this form of government is destroyed, we would live under the constant threat of dictatorship. One-man rule, or the rule of a small group of men, as the Presidium in Moscow, in a centralized government, would mean the same rule in the entire country and in all facets of government and human affairs.

To you people in this struggle who seek to preserve our form of government, I am proud of my role as a leader in the fight, I did not seek this role. It was thrust upon me in the course of events. I did not, nor do I now, shrink from my responsibilities in what is perhaps the greatest struggle for constitutional government during this century.

To you who oppose the great majority of Arkansas people in this fight, I urge you to think lest, in your consuming desire to gain your ends, among them the destruction of Orval Faubus, you destroy also the very principles of government that enable you and all others to live as a free people, and to rear your children under the high standards of living and freedom which prevail in this State and Nation.

It was with a heavy heart that I found it necessary to sign the bills of the Extraordinary Session of the General Assembly and to close the High Schools in the City of Little Rock. I took this action only after the last hope of relief from an intolerable situation had been exhausted.

The Supreme Court shut its eyes to all the facts, and in essence said—integration at any price, even if it means the destruction of our school system, our educational processes, and the risk of disorder and violence that could result in the loss of life, perhaps yours.

This price, you as a people are unwilling to pay. This price, I could not see you pay without first offering to you a legal plan whereby such a catastrophe can be avoided, and still provide the opportunity of an education for our children.

This plan I now explain to you in detail. This plan is within the law. Even the Supreme Court, in the so-called school integration cases, has not ruled to the contrary. This plan is based upon our own State Constitution, written and adopted in 1874, and Arkansas Statutes enacted in 1875.

First. The Federal Government has no authority to require any State to operate public schools.

Second. The Federal Government has no authority to tell a State Government for what purposes it may levy taxes, or how the tax money may be expended.

Third. In all the cases involving the public schools and integration, the Federal Courts have said only that an agency of the State cannot maintain segregated schools. This ruling does not apply in any way to private schools. Private schools are not affected by these decisions, even though the schools receive aid from State and Federal sources.

In 1875, the General Assembly enacted two laws which give us a legal way to maintain a private system of education, at a time when a part of our public educational system cannot be maintained in a suitable and efficient manner.

Our own educational people have testified that a suitable educational system at Little Rock cannot be maintained on an integrated basis. Why, then, should we even attempt to keep these schools open as public schools when, based upon this sworn testimony, they clearly do not meet our constitutional provisions for a suitable and efficient system of education? We have a perfect right to close these schools as public institutions, and once closed and found to be not needed for public school purposes, the School Board has the right and the authority under a law that has been on our statute books for 83 years, to lease these buildings and facilities to a bona fide private agency.

A bona fide private school system appears to be the only answer to the Federal Government's Order to integrate at any price.

Let me read this law, enacted by the General Assembly, and signed by the Governor in 1875.

80–518. DIRECTORS MAY PERMIT PRIVATE SCHOOL TO USE SCHOOL HOUSE. The Directors may permit a private school to be taught in the district school house during such time as the said house is not occupied by a public school, unless they be otherwise directed by a majority of the legal voters of the district. (Act December 7, 1875).

Now, it is crystal clear that if the voters of the Little Rock School District vote against integration on September 27th, these facilities will become surplus and not needed for public school purposes.

This will leave the School Board free to lease the buildings to a suitable private agency. In this connection, I am sure that you are already aware that such an agency has been organized under another law that was enacted in 1875.

I have been informed by its organizers that they formed this private, bona fide, nonprofit corporation for the purpose of being prepared to accept any offer that may be made by the Little Rock School Board to lease its unused high school facilities for private school purposes—if the vote is against integration on September 27th.

In this connection, here is a letter I received from the School Board:

Little Rock, Arkansas
  September 12, 1958
  Hon. Orval E. Faubus
  Governor of Arkansas
  Little Rock, Arkansas

Dear Governor Faubus:
It has come to our attention that you have stated as follows:
'Central High School can be operated on a private basis as a segregated school if the School Board wants to take such action.'

We are unaware that such is possible, but if this be true, we would like very much to have an opportunity for our attorneys to explore this possibility with your attorneys.

We are as anxious as anyone for our educational program to continue uninterruptedly and stand ready to explore every conceivable avenue with you.

Very truly yours,
LITTLE ROCK SCHOOL BOARD
By: (Signed) Wayne Upton
President

I accept this letter as having been written in good faith, and I call upon the Board to demonstrate their good faith by immediately offering to a private group these unoccupied school buildings after the election. I say immediately after the election, because I have no doubt that the people of this school district will never voluntarily integrate their schools. I am confident that the vote on September 27th will be against integration. I say a private group, because I understand that others may be formed.

Once again, I am compelled to point out to the people of this city, this State, this nation, and the world, if you please, that our objective has been to maintain the peace and good order of the community. As long as there is a legal way, as I have outlined, to maintain the peace and good order and a suitable educational system, I will not shirk from my duty and responsibility.

What are some of the questions that will be raised, or have been raised, regarding this plan?

First. Is there legal authority for the operation of private schools in a publicly owned facility?

I have cited the authority in our own State laws, and it is something that has been done many times in the past years.

Second. Can State-aid be legally furnished to a privately-operated educational institition?

Both State funds and Federal funds have been and are now being furnished to such private institutions in the form of transportation and lunch programs. Many other forms of aid are flowing to private schools from State and Federal sources.

Also, the Federal Government, by Acts of Congress, subsidized a private educational institution for Negroes in Washington, D.C., over a period of 91 years. If the Federal Government can do this, how can it prohibit a State from so doing?

Third. What about accreditation of the privately-operated schools?

Any informed person knows there are thousands of private schools throughout the nation which are accredited.

Let me emphasize that the State Board of Education is the accrediting agency for Arkansas. If the private schools are properly conducted, there will be no difficulty in this respect.

Fourth. What about funds with which to pay the expenses of the private schools?

Under Act 5 of the Second Extraordinary Session of the 61st General Assembly, a student seeking an education in another school, either private or public, because of a situation such as exists here now, will have the benefit of all funds to be expended for his education. The funds follow him to the school of his choice anywhere within the State.

The plan is sound and workable. It is all legal. To this the advocates of the so called "law of the land" can have no objection.

Perhaps it would be well to review here the reasons for the wide spread and adamant opposition to the forcible integration of schools, not only here, but also in other sections of the nation. This, of course, is a difficult undertaking. Books can be written on the subject; in fact, many books have been written and the streams of editorial comment from the presses throughout the nation are so great in volume that no one person can even attempt to keep abreast of all that is said or written on this subject.

Behind all this is the basic issue which should be and is of concern to people throughout the nation, and that is the gradual, constant, and forcible usurpation of the powers of the States and the people, by the Federal Government and the United States Supreme Court. Were it not for this violation of the rights guaranteed to the States by the Constitution, then the segregation-integration controversy would be a moral or political issue, and would not have become a legal battle which has spilled over to a great extent into the field of the military.

We are, of course, convinced that the use of force is arbitrary, illegal, and unwise. The use of the military has startled the people like a firebell in the night. And there is ample cause for this alarm. In every case in the history of the world where democracy has been supplanted by dictatorship, the dictatorial powers have clothed their actions in the pious cloak of legality and "acting in the best interest of the people."

If the control of the public schools is left to the States, as envisaged by the founding fathers and guaranteed by the Tenth Amendment to the Constitution, then the controversy will at most be only State-wide, and States can have, as their people choose, either segregated or integrated schools, or both.

Some so-called "do-gooders" cannot seem to understand the reasons for the strong belief of many people in segregation. There are many reasons. First: There can be found no example throughout this nation where the change from segregated schools to integrated schools has improved the quality of education, or has made for better relations between the races. On the contrary, the reverse is true, and you need but to go into the integrated areas in this nation to find clear and indisputable evidence.

All of us were made aware some time ago, by the widespread publicity, of the terrible conditions that exist in the integrated schools of New York City.

For concrete, factual examples of what happens to the students and teachers and to the quality of education in general following integration, I quote some excerpts from the report of "Investigation of Public School Conditions" by the Committee on District of Columbia, House of Representatives, Eighty-Fourth Congress.

The schools of Washington, D.C. were integrated in 1954. There was a public admonition by the President of the United States that they should serve as a model of integrated schools to be copied by the rest of the country.

In the beginning, the Committee Report reads:

> Washington, D.C., is the most favorable choice as an integration experiment most likely to succeed. Our best educated Negroes are migrating to the Capital in great numbers. The Negro per capita income in the District of Columbia is higher than the White income in some areas of the nation. As residents of the Nation's Capital, the people of the District of Columbia enjoy more cultural advantages than people of any other city in America. The District of Columbia Negroes have had school facilities superior to most other school districts in the nation. No other place in the nation offers such superior advantages for a successful integration program.

What has been the result?

The first result was the exodus of White people from Washington. The records show conclusively that the elementary population was increasing after World War II, until the first steps into integration were taken in public housing and other fields. At the first threat of integration, the White residents began to leave. A few years ago, there were 59,582 White students and 33,498 Negro students in Washington. The school census of October 21, 1955, disclosed that there was a school membership of 38,768 White students, and 68,877 Negro students. The school census of October, 1956, showed 34,750 White students, 32 per cent and Negro students, 68 per cent. (Since the completion of this report, the percentage of Negro students in the Washington, D.C., schools is now 78 per cent and White students 22 per cent.)

Another result of integration of the schools in Washington has been to lower the educational standards city-wide. A number of nationally recognized and used educational achievement and I.Q. tests, quoted extensively in the report, reveals that the school population as a whole in the public schools of Washington is now two grades lower than the national norm. Test after test revealed in this report makes known the fact of deterioration in the quality of education on every grade-level and in every field of educational activity. I quote from this report prepared by the Committee of Congress:

Prior to the integration of the schools in the District of Columbia there were very few unusual disciplinary problems in either of the school systems. Since the integration of the schools there have been very unusual disciplinary problems in the predominately segregated schools. Disciplinary problems in the predominately integrated schools have been described as appalling, demoralizing, intolerable, and disgraceful. Fighting, lying, stealing, vandalism, obscene writing, vulgar talking, absenteeism, tardiness, and truancy have increased to an amazing degree. Mental and physical suffering has affected the health and morale of many white teachers as a reaction to these unexpected disciplinary problems that arose in the predominately integrated schools.

Some white teachers have resigned, some have retired before the fixed date for their retirement, and some have indicated they will leave the school system as soon as possible for them to do so.

For the first time in the history of some of the schools, teachers were required to police the corridors and playgrounds and cafeterias. Disorder in the classrooms greatly reduced teaching efficiency, and retarded the ability of students to learn. Police were called on numerous occasions to the various integrated schools.

The overwhelming majority of those interviewed mentioned the following items: Stealing . . . Lying . . . Cheating . . . Fighting . . . Vandalism . . . Obscene language . . .

The following are quotes from teachers and others who testified before the Committee:

> I found it necessary to require that all teachers leave their desks when the bell rang and keep order in the corridors. . . .
>
> At times, I heard colored girls at the school use language that was far worse than I have ever heard, even in the Marine Corps. . . .
>
> White children manifested a spirit of cooperation to help the colored children become acclimated, but these efforts were not particularly successful. . . .
>
> There have been more thefts at Eastern in the last 2 years than I had known in all my thirty-odd years in the school system. . . . Never, in all of my experience, have I observed such filthy and revolting habits. . . .
>
> There was constant fighting in the classrooms between colored and colored, and sometimes between colored and white. . . . After integration disciplinary problems increased in number and type. It had a frustrating effect on teachers. . . .
>
> During 1955, I imagine we called the police about 50 times. However, the newspapers claimed only 4 incidents in 3 years. . . .
>
> I have had requests from colored parents to take their children out of my schools and put them back in all-colored schools. They thought they could get a better education there than they could by being mixed up. I have had to call the police a number of times. We have had to call them maybe 25 or 30 times. . . .
>
> We have had a number of fires set on purpose during school hours. . . . I would say last year our books took what would be the normal wear of 10 years in using those books. . . .
>
> A fight took place outside my classroom. There was a knifing out there and somebody got badly cut. It touched his heart but the knife was too short to kill him. . . .
>
> We did not have any social activities after integration. We just cut it out. . . .
>
> We have not had dances since integration. We felt it better in order to avoid any situation. . . .
>
> We do not have dancing, dramatics, or operettas since integration.

And the following excerpt is from the minority report of two Northern Congressmen on the Committee:

> The facts brought to light by this investigation seem to indicate that Negro leaders, and those actively interested in the advancement of the Negro people, have much work to do among the Negro people, and that all of the difficulties attended with integration are not caused by the seemingly uncompromising attitude of the white people.

There are many things in this report which I cannot, in good taste, mention on this television program. Write to your Congressman and secure a copy of this report and read for yourself the revolting and shocking developments in the Washington, D.C., schools, following integration.

Now, what will you be voting on at the Special Election, September 27th?

It will not be just to open the school or to keep it closed, although that is a part of it.

It will not be the question of whether or not seven Negro students may or may not attend Central High School, although that is a part of it.

It will not be deciding the question of segregation versus limited integration. In the ultimate, there can be no such thing as limited integration, so far as the public schools of Little Rock are concerned.

The choice you make on Saturday, September 27th, is whether to continue to fight our constitutional rights, and the opportunity to find an acceptable solution to this problem, or you vote for the beginning of complete and total integration. And if the latter be your decision, it will come sooner than you think.

I have read to you only a small part of the results of such integration, carried out under what was said to be the most favorable conditions in the nation.

Some people dread, shrink from, and grow weary of the struggle in which we are now engaged. I grow weary also but is there any choice? Once integration is effected totally and completely, will the peace and harmony you desire be attained? If we are to judge by the results elsewhere, anywhere, once total, or near total integration is effected, the peace, the quiet, the harmony, the pride in our schools, and even the good relations that existed heretofore between the races here, will be gone forever.

Perhaps the conditions will not be completely intolerable, but the lowering of educational standards, the rise in immorality and juvenile delinquency, and strife, will be the order of the day, just as it is now in every extensively integrated area of the nation.

And then some weak and fearful individual cries out, "But we cannot win! The Federal Government is all powerful!"

That may be true. It could well be that the rights guaranteed to us by the Constitution will be taken from us by the use of billy clubs, pistol barrels, and bayonet points. But we do not have to be parties to such methods or efforts. We can carry on the struggle in the legal and political arenas. We have that right as free citizens.

If we lose the struggle, then we have done all that we possibly can do, and the guilt for the harm that may come cannot be charged to us.

Have I changed my position? NO!!!! Every integrationist is still free to exert all his efforts to persuade others of the correctness of his views, and to try to get them accepted. But if the people cannot be persuaded, they should not be forced at bayonet point, when it is contrary to the law and the Constitution.

An individual is even free to persuade another to take a drink of liquor, but he does not have the right to compel him by force to take the drink.

Now for those who condemn me because I decline to forcibly integrate the public schools, may I suggest that they can best demonstrate their good faith by integrating their own social and religious activities. After they have done this for a reasonable time, they will be better qualified to debate the problem of integration in the public schools.

In conclusion, to you the citizens of Little Rock, I must warn that you will be subjected to a terrific propaganda campaign from now until September 27th. This barrage of slanted, distorted, and even false versions, will emanate—yes, is already emanating—from the same sources as before, both inside and outside the city and the State. I know you, the people will understand.

This issue is now where all public issues belong—in your hands, the hands of the people. The decision is yours to make. Your decision will be my decision, as I am your public servant.

Public sentiment is with you in this struggle to preserve our legal and time-honored rights. If you stand fast, we can win!

J.P. COLEMAN

J.P. Coleman was born on a farm near Ackerman, Mississippi, and began his political career when he was elected circuit judge in 1946. He was appointed to the State Supreme Court in 1950, then resigned to become the state attorney general. He was elected governor in 1956. Coleman served as Mississippi's governor during the early years of the Civil Rights Movement and established clearly that state's course as the conflict developed. During his administration, the Mississippi Sovereignty Commission was formed as a propaganda machine to counter attacks on segregation in the state. Before it was disbanded in 1973, the agency spied on civil rights workers and did all in its power to derail integration in Mississippi.

Coleman's career spanned all three branches of government. While in his last year as governor, he was elected to the Mississippi House from Choctaw county, where he continued to serve until 1965. In that year, President Johnson nominated him to the federal appeals bench where he served as chief judge for two years and as senior judge until he retired in 1984.

Although Coleman clearly defended the side of segregation as this speech shows, he was viewed by many of his contemporaries and by later historians as a racial moderate. He vetoed a bill designed to hamper federal civil rights investigations and rebuffed repeated calls in his state to outlaw the NAACP in Mississippi. In addition, he developed a reputation as a progressive governor for some of his social and economic programs and his efforts to increase industrialization in Mississippi.

Coleman suffered a stroke on December 13, 1990, at his home near Fentress, Mississippi, where he was active in directing his family farming operations. He died in Ackerman at age 77 on September 28, 1991.[10]

SETTING THE RECORD STRAIGHT[11]

Jackson, Mississippi
June 29, 1959

MY FELLOW MISSISSIPPIANS:
I have firmly believed all of my life that if the people could get the facts, they would know what to do with those facts. In recent months, however, we have seen the real facts so warped and distorted every day that I am now faced with the duty of setting the record straight. I believe you will agree that no self-respecting governor can remain forever silent when he knows, and his friends

know, that his efforts and his accomplishments are daily being misrepresented. In any case, a well-informed public is the best hope of good government.

Tonight, I shall state the facts as the facts actually are, not as they have been painted to be. I have suffered in silence for many months, but the time has come to talk.

ACCOMPLISHMENTS

We hear a great deal of general talk to the effect that there are no issues before the people of Mississippi. I respectfully submit that a great deal of this is due to the fact that we have settled these issues during the past four years.

The enactments of the Mississippi Legislature during this Administration comprise 1,892 printed pages. Time will not permit discussion of this volume of work in a thirty-minute speech.

Here are some of the issues we have settled and the things we have accomplished:

A guaranteed nine months school term for the first time in history;

The salaries of our school teachers were raised more in 1958 than ever at any one time in history;

The enactment of the great Port Development Program;

The Tennessee-Tombigbee Compact;

The Pearl River Reservoir Authority;

A new Public Utilities law;

The abolition of marriage mills;

The reorganization of the State Game and Fish Commission;

A 100% increase in our industrial program;

A new Probation and Parole Act;

The regulation and supervision of Small Loan Companies;

An Act outlawing the possession of beer and wine in those Counties where the people have voted against the traffic. . . .

There are many others contained in these 1,892 pages which I do not have time to discuss.

When I became Governor there were hundreds of aged people who could not get old age assistance checks because there was a rule disqualifying them if they had a son or daughter working somewhere, either in or out of the State. At my insistence, this rule was abolished and ten thousand of our senior citizens who needed help have been getting the benefits which otherwise would have been denied them.

I have had one outstanding experience which no other Governor of Mississippi has ever had. It has been my happy privilege to appear on five nation-wide television programs, including two appearances on "Meet the Press" in which I represented Mississippi before the entire Nation. If the taxpayers of Mississippi had bought and paid for this television time, it would have cost them nearly a quarter of a million dollars.

I have had the honor of being unanimously elected Chairman of the Southern Governor's Conference and also a Member of the Executive Committee of the Governor's Conference of the forty-eight states.

On August 1, 1956, in the meeting at Atlanta, I had the honor of being unanimously elected Chairman of the Southern States at the Democratic Convention in Chicago. It was in this Convention that we successfully prevented the endorsement of the 1954 School decision of the Supreme Court of the United States . . .

SEGREGATION

In 1955, I said in my official platform: And I am reading the exact language.

There will be no necessity to abolish public schools, nor will there be any mixing of the races in any of the State operated educational institutions. This is no task for the amateur or the hothead.

I said this again in my inaugural address when I took the oath of office on January 17, 1956.

Tonight, the people of Mississippi know that I have kept this pledge inviolate. They know that we have had absolutely no mixing of the races in our public schools. And they further know that the schools have been in no danger of closing. We have done this with what amounted to almost complete quietness and we have done it without keeping up a daily atmosphere of fighting and tension. If there be those who would have enjoyed an uproar they must remember that four years ago I promised the people that the job would be done in quietness and dignity, and the people elected me on that promise. By their votes in 1955, the people indicated that they did not want to be forever in a stew about the safety of racial separation and the existence of their public schools.

There have been a few individuals running around over Mississippi saying that no one man is entitled to this happy state of affairs. I do not know of any one man who wishes to claim all the credit. I do know that if the cause had been lost and if Mississippi had been integrated, or if we had lost our public school system, these same individuals would be yelling at the top of their well exercised lungs that the Governor was wholly and solely to blame for the entire catastrophe. They would be dancing on my grave with savage glee. The cold truth is that they have been disappointed with my success and they have done a mighty poor job of hiding their disappointment.

When I was sworn in as Governor, many people fearfully but frankly told me in private that they thought I had overspoken myself in promising that there would be no race mixing and that there would be no school closing. They said I had made a promise I could not keep. You see, however, that I have kept that promise to the last letter, and I know I shall go out of office on the 19th day of next January with racial separation still intact in Mississippi. I ask you, the people of Mississippi, could those who attack me in the newspapers have done a better job than your governor has done? Your answer would be that they could not, because the situation has been perfect insofar as we are concerned. And Mississippi is **the only state** which enjoys such conditions.

I am sure everybody within the sound of my voice remembers when Clennon King tried to integrate the University of Mississippi. I am sure they remember that when I came face to face with this dire threat I did not sit scared to death in the governor's office at the State Capitol, nor did I go into a panic, issuing newspaper statements every hour on the hour. I went in person to Oxford, Mississippi, and everybody knows what happened to Clennon King. Where were my critics them? Where were the Monday morning quarterbacks? They offered no suggestions, they provided no remedies, and they rendered no assistance. When the University had been saved from integration, when Clennon King had left the State, and when our educational systems sailed ahead as if nothing had ever happened, the habitual critics did not have the courtesy to offer one word of congratulations or to say one word of approval.

What Mississippi needs is leadership possessed of the experience, the courage, the wisdom, the ability, and resourcefulness to preserve racial separation and at the same time preserve and improve our public schools. Therein lies the only hope for the future of our children.

I am well aware that a little hand-full of my political adversaries have tried to destroy my place in the affections of my fellow Mississippians by claiming that I am a "moderate." Apparently, these people cannot tell a moderate from a successful segregationist. They have made a great sham of this, and everytime they can get a chance they try to stir it up. I ask you to ignore what **they say** and look at what the **record says**. The Bible teaches by their fruits shall ye know them. In other words, the Bible said that true worth is determined by performances and not by promises. I have been a candidate many times. There is an old saying that "a candidate is a magician before the election and hard to find after the election." I stand on a record of performance and I have delivered the goods. I am not entitled to be called a moderate, and I notice that none of my friends have called me that.

Which had you rather have, my friends, the conditions we have enjoyed in Mississippi under my leadership as Governor, or those existing in other Southern States?

The record says that we have had total separation of the races, and I have had to preserve it with one hand while keeping the political pop-guns knocked back with the other hand. You would have thought that these attackers who claim to be such great friends of segregation would have spent their time trying to help me instead of hindering me.

As I said at the outset: when the people get the facts they know what to do.

The people of this State are not gamblers, and they never have been. I know they have no intention of gambling with the future of their own children.

FOLLOWING FAUBUS

The people of Mississippi know that I have never offered the first public criticism of Governor Faubus of Arkansas. Even if I had wanted to criticize, I most certainly would have refrained from it, because it is very unbecoming in the Governor of one state to criticize the official acts of the Governor of another state. What Governor Faubus does in Arkansas is none of my business—it is nobody's business but his own and that of the people of his State. As a matter of fact, Governor Faubus is my personal friend, Mrs. Coleman and Mrs. Faubus are close friends, and I would have no occasion whatever to get into a dispute across the state line with Governor Faubus. He was the first Southern Governor to come out in the newspapers at Lexington supporting me for Chairman of the Southern Governor's Conference, and I appreciate it.

For several months, however, those who do not know the full story or who do not want the people to know the full story, have been attacking Governor Coleman of Mississippi for not following the Governor of Arkansas.

On several points it has been impossible for me to follow Governor Faubus. I do not think he expected me to follow him on considerations which did not apply to Mississippi, and I think it would be impossible for any Governor of Mississippi to follow him.

Let us examine the record. Nobody can argue with the record.

When the schools were integrated at Hoxie, at Van Buren, at Fort Smith, and other places in Arkansas, Governor Faubus made no effort to stop that integration. When race mixing finally got to the State Capitol at Little Rock, he did try to stop it. Do you believe it would be right for me to let the NAACP integrate Lexington, or Greenwood, or Macon without raising my hand to stop it? Do you believe it would be right for me to refuse to fight until it got within the shadow of the State Capitol at Jackson? In my view of things, if I were to follow this policy, I would not be the Governor of Mississippi, I would simply be the Governor of Jackson. I have adopted the rule of stopping integration anywhere it raises its head, regardless of the town, and I have enforced that rule.

Governor Faubus has done nothing about race mixing at the University of Arkansas. I could not follow him in this. When they attempted to mix the races at the University of Mississippi, I stopped it cold.

Many of you have heard Governor Faubus say on nationwide television that his son attended an integrated college. I cannot follow the Governor in sending his son to an integrated college. I have sent my son to the University of Mississippi, where the races are separate. People ordinarily do not send their children to schools that they do not approve of, and I feel that if I were to send my son to a mixed school I would be publicly approving race mixing, and I would be setting an example for the people to follow.

Governor Faubus appointed a Negro to a high party office in Arkansas. If I had followed him on this, Mr. Bidwell Adam, who got beat for re-election as Lieutenant Governor by 44,000 votes twenty-seven years ago, and who introduced Mr. Faubus at Biloxi, would no doubt have had a stroke. However, since Governor Faubus appointed a Negro it was, of course, perfectly all right with Bidwell.

In a speech which he delivered on June 13th at Biloxi, at the Mississippi Bar Association, Governor Faubus said the people ought to be allowed to mix the races in public schools if they wanted to, or that they should be allowed to keep the races separate if they wanted to. That might please both sides, but that is not the public policy of the State of Mississippi. We believe that it is to the best interest of both races that they have their own schools throughout the State and that everybody operate under the same rule. Therefore, I could not follow Governor Faubus in supporting local option on segregation.

According to the Associated Press, Governor Faubus made a speech on May 15th to the Illinois Press Association up at Peoria, Illinois. I did not see the news story in any of the Jackson papers, but it was on the front page of the Tupelo Journal for May 16th. The Governor was directly quoted as follows: "In the state at large, (meaning Arkansas) more public schools have been voluntarily and peaceably integrated than in nine other Southern States combined."

He is further quoted: "All forms of transportation (that means buses and trains) have been integrated and both the Democratic and Republican parties of Arkansas have had Negroes as members of their state central committees."

I cannot follow Governor Faubus on this. I cannot go North of the Mason and Dixon line and claim that Mississippi has more peaceably integrated schools than all the rest of the South put together because we do not have any integrated schools at all, period.

When any man promises to follow Faubus then

1. He is promising that he will not intefere with race mixing until it gets to the State Capital;

2. He is promising not to interfere with race mixing at our Colleges and Universities;

3. He is promising to send his children to a race mixed College;

4. He is promising to permit race mixing where the people want it— although I do not think either the white or responsible Negro people want it in Mississippi.

5. He is promising to go North and brag about the race mixing which he has permitted in Mississippi.

All this is the record and none of it can be disputed.

It seems to me, if I may be allowed to say so, that Mississippi has been safer in following Coleman than Arkansas has been in following Faubus.

Now let me make it crystal clear. I am not quarreling with Governor Faubus; I am simply telling the public why I cannot always follow him on the race mixing question. I repeat, what he does in Arkansas is none of my business and it is nobody's business but his and that of the people of Arkansas. I do think it is high time that these shouters who do not know what they are shouting about should quit jumping on the Governor of Mississippi.

If I were not being continually stomped by the political propagandists for not following Faubus I would not have even mentioned this matter. By their underhanded tactics they have left me no choice and they have forced me to set the record straight. I am sorry they made this recital of the facts necessary. . . .

POPLARVILLE

In conclusion, my friends, it is imperative that I direct your attention to one further fact. That fact is this: The NAACP is too weak, it is too lacking in ability, and it is too short on leadership ever to control Mississippi with its own steam. The only hope for the NAACP is that we, the people of Mississippi, will lose our heads and do something which will give Congress some kind of an excuse to do the job for them. If Congress should do that, the results would be the same and the consequences would be just as fatal as if the NAACP had been able to succeed under its own power.

The realization of this fact prompted me when I heard of the Poplarville lynching to take every step in my power to head off retribution at the hands of the Federal Congress. **It is true** that I invited the FBI into the case because under the Federal Kidnaping Statutes they could have come in, anyway, in twenty-four hours. Had I not invited the FBI, the NAACP would have been pounding on the doors of Congress, claiming that none other than the Governor of the State, who represents the sentiments of all the people, was giving the lynchers a **head start** to conceal the crime, and that he was doing whatever else he could to assist the lynchers. As a matter of fact, weeks before this, State officials had called in the FBI to help clinch the case with scientific proof against the Negro attacker, and had received full assistance from the FBI.

The first result of what I did was that the President of the United States told a nation-wide press conference that Mississippi was conducting itself honorably in the Poplarville matter and that **no further Civil Rights Legislation was needed on account of Poplarville**. In other words, what I did enlisted the badly needed assistance of the most powerful man in the United States. So far as I know, this was the first time in his career that he has publicly defended the people of Mississippi. . . .

The case of the Negro Goldsby who murdered the white lady at Vaiden, and which has been pending in the Courts for nearly four years, came into the Poplarville case. I think the people of Mississippi remember that back in 1951 it took me six months to dispose of Willie McGee after that case had been in the courts for six years. On next January, I will again be a practicing attorney-at-law . . . I am hereby tendering my services to the State of Mississippi free of charge to assist in bringing Goldsby to justice. And I promise you that if given an opportunity we will make short work of the job. In making this offer, I am not criticizing our most able Attorney General, Honorable Joe T. Patterson. He has had to handle this case in the federal courts on the record compiled in the Court below. The delays in the Goldsby case have not been Mr. Patterson's fault. The truth is that if the District Attorney and the Special Prosecutor had asked one simple question, which they did not ask, in open Court at Vaiden and had put it in the record Goldsby would have been executed at least two years ago.

CONCLUSION

My friends, there is no sum of money on earth for which I would exchange the honor of having served as Governor of my native State. If I had the television time I could talk to you for hours about the experiences of the past four years.

So far as I know, this will be the last time I shall have any occasion to make a state-wide television address in an official capacity. This is my swan song. I want to thank all who elected me and all who have so faithfully supported my efforts in these perilous times. I hope you are pleased with what I have done, and that you will miss me when I am gone. I am quite sure that I shall miss my daily association with people from all over Mississippi, the greatest, the finest, and most generous people in the world. Without you I could not have survived the rigors of the Governor's Office.

My experiences as Governor remind me of those famous words of Rudyard Kipling: "If you can keep your head while those all about you are losing theirs and blaming it on you, you will be a man, my son."

And I might quote:

"There is many a man with a gallant air
Goes galloping to the fray
But the valuable man is the man who's there
When the smoke has cleared away."

God bless you, my fellow Mississippians.
Goodnight.

NOTES

1. John Dittmer, *Local People: The Struggle for Civil Rights in Mississippi* (Urbana: University of Illinois Press, 1994), 53–55.

2. James W. Silver, *Mississippi: The Closed Society* (New York: Harcourt, Brace & World, 1963).

3. See biographical sketch in Marjorie Hunter, "James O. Eastland Is Dead at 81; Leading Senate Foe of Integration." *The New York Times*, February 20, 1986; and from *The National Cyclopaedia of American Biography*, vol. I, 1953–59 (New York: James T. White & Company, 1960), 118–19.

4. JoHanna Neuman, "Mississippians Bid Farewell to 'Big Jim'." *Pensacola News Journal*, February 20, 1986, p. 4A.

5. James O. Eastland, "The Supreme Court, Segregation, and the South." Speech presented by Senator Eastland in the Senate of the United States, May 27, 1954 (Washington: U.S. Government Printing Office, 1954). Manuscript located in Special Collections, University of Arkansas Libraries, Fayetteville, Arkansas.

6. *Who Was Who in America*, vol. V (1969–1973) (Chicago: Marquis Who's Who, Inc. 1973), p. 82.

7. Thomas Pickens Brady, "Segregation and the South." Speech presented to Commonwealth Club of California, San Francisco, October 4, 1957. Text reprinted with permission from Ernest J. Wrage and Barnet Baskerville, eds., *Contemporary Forum: American Speeches of Twentieth-Century Issues* (New York: Harper & Brothers, 1962), pp. 333–43.

8. See biographical sketch in Peter Applebome, "Orval Faubus, Segregation's Champion, Dies at 84," *The New York Times*, December 15, 1994, 1, B24; Robert Sobel and John Raimo, eds., *Biographical Directory of the Governors of the United States 1789–1978*, vol. 1 (Westport, CT: Meckler Books, 1978) pp. 94–95; and John D'Emilio, *The Civil Rights Struggle: Leaders in Profile*, (New York: Facts on File, 1979), 56–57.

9. Orval E. Faubus, "Speech on the Little Rock Crisis," September 18, 1958. Typescript text from the Special Collections Department, University of Arkansas Libraries, Fayetteville, Arkansas.

10. This biographical sketch is taken from various obituaries on Coleman in the Jackson, Mississippi, *Clarion-Ledger* (September 29, 1991); the *Washington Post* (September 30, 1991); the *Greenwood Commonwealth* (September 29, 1991); and the Vicksburg, Mississippi, *Evening Post* (September 30, 1991).

11. Presented on state-wide television from Jackson, MS, on Monday, June 29, 1959. Text located in the Mississippi Department of History and Archives, Jackson, Mississippi.

FOR FURTHER READING

James O. Eastland

Eastland, James O. "We've Reached Era of Judicial Tyranny," speech delivered to state convention of Association of Citizens' Councils of Mississippi, Jackson, MS, December 1, 1955. In W. Stuart Towns, *Public Address in the Twentieth-Century South: The Evolution of a Region*, Westport, CT: Praeger, 1999, pp. 125–33.

Rothe, Anna, ed. "James O. Eastland." *Current Biography: Who's News and Why, 1949*. New York: H.W. Wilson Company, 1949, pp. 184–86.

Thomas Pickens Brady

There is little available biographical material on Judge Brady, but a brief sketch appears in James B. Lloyd, ed. *Lives of Mississippi Authors*. Jackson: University Press of Mississippi, 1981, p. 51.

Orval E. Faubus

Cartwright, Colbert S. "The Improbable Demagogue of Little Rock, Ark." *The Reporter* (October 17, 1957), pp. 23–25.

Faubus, Orval E. "Television and Radio Speech on the Little Rock Situation," September 1, 1957. In W. Stuart Towns, *Public Address in the Twentieth-Century South: The Evolution of a Region*. Westport, CT: Praeger, 1999, pp. 134–40.

Wallace, David. "Thirty-sixth Governor, Orval Eugene Faubus." In Timothy P. Donovan and Willard B. Gatewood, Jr., eds. *The Governors of Arkansas: Essays in Political Biography*. Fayetteville: The University of Arkansas Press, 1981), pp. 215–25.

J.P. Coleman

There is little biographical material on Judge Coleman, except for that cited in note 10.

INDEX

About the Author

W. STUART TOWNS is Professor and Chair of the Department of Communication at Appalachian State University.